PUBLIC ARCHAEOLOGY, Vol. 13 Nos 1–3, 2014, 1–2

Foreword

Tim Schadla-Hall and Jamie Larkin

This special three-issue edition of *Public Archaeology* presents the proceedings of a ground-breaking conference, held at the Institute of Archaeology, University College London in September 2012, on the subject of 'Archaeology and Economic Development'.

Increasingly in the last four decades the economic impact and benefit has been stressed in conjunction with developing archaeology, conservation and heritage across the world. In many cases projects were launched in which archaeologists were mere bystanders or bit players — whether developments dealt with promoting or managing the impact of tourism; the processes for reinvigorating urban cores; the consequences of establishing new World Heritage Sites; for solely commercial purposes; or even to justify the value of archaeological work to government and private funders.

Archaeologists need to be involved, and in many cases should lead developments and not stand idly by whilst others develop their work and use, or misuse, their expertise. They need to consider and understand the potential impact of their work and acquire additional skills, to ensure archaeology (and archaeologists) are financially sustainable and seen to be of value by the public. Having enough grant funding for a project has for the last hundred or more years frequently been the closest that archaeologists have come to economics. The picture is, however, much more extensive than this and encompasses a wide area of different and often conflicting forms of economic development.

The conference organizers assembled an international cast of experts with broad practical experience and diverse perspectives on the issues associated with economic development and archaeology, and for the first time in one volume it will be possible for students and practitioners alike to consider and examine the range of views and possibilities for the development of our subject. *Public Archaeology* is proud to publish the papers that we believe form a critical milestone in the development of the discipline.

The papers reflect the diversity of issues that arise when archaeologists engage with economic opportunities. For example, the need to translate the value of archaeology, which seems obvious to practitioners, into terms embraced by public policy-makers and funders is increasingly a matter of concern in an era dominated by constrained public sector spending on archaeology and heritage. Several papers here explore that terrain specifically. The global spread of the studies presented in this volume testifies to the increasingly widespread practice of using archaeological resources to create economic opportunities at the local level. This practice causes archaeologists and other heritage management professionals to engage intimately with the public on new and untested grounds. Not only do significant ethical issues arise, as several papers

DOI 10.1179/1465518714Z.00000000074

here illustrate, but practical questions are manifold: Which approaches should be employed to encourage development work? What obstacles will be encountered in the implementation of community-based economic development projects? How do the answers to these questions vary across the globe? It also prompts questions of a more fundamental nature: How do we define 'community'? When archaeologists seek to utilize archaeological resources to improve economic conditions, there is no engagement of the discipline with the public with more latent potential — and with potential problems.

The papers in this special issue constitute a landmark effort to launch a much-needed discourse about the relationship of archaeology to economic development and the consequences of that engagement. They illustrate successes and failures; they describe political and cultural challenges to success; they explore the problems from theoretical, ethical and intensely practical perspectives. The aspirations of archaeologists to 'Do Good and Do Research', as Ran Boytner's paper puts it, are subjected to intense scrutiny and a considerable dose of reality in many of the contributions.

In their introductory essay, which follows, the conference organizers and guest editors of this volume, Paul Burtenshaw and Peter Gould, provide an overview of the conference and place the various papers in context. From the perspective of *Public Archaeology*, the editors are pleased that this journal, as so often has been the case in the past, is providing the initial platform for what we anticipate will be an increasingly prominent critical dialogue in the years to come.

PUBLIC ARCHAEOLOGY

VOLUME 13   NUMBERS 1–3   2014

CONTENTS

Special issue: Archaeology and Economic Development
Guest Editors: Peter G. Gould and Paul Burtenshaw

PUBLIC ARCHAEOLOGY, Vol. 13 Nos 1–3, 2014, 3–9

GUEST EDITORIAL

Archaeology and Economic Development

PETER G. GOULD

University of Pennsylvania Museum of Archaeology and Anthropology, USA

PAUL BURTENSHAW

Sustainable Preservation Initiative, USA

Introduction

The papers in this special volume of *Public Archaeology* are the outcome of the 2012 'Archaeology and Economic Development' conference held at the Institute of Archaeology, University College London. The use of archaeology and heritage as resources for economic and social development has become increasingly important within the practice of archaeology. Demands for archaeology to contribute to society, economically, culturally, or otherwise, are increasing, prompted by local communities, governments, or archaeologists themselves. While some individuals and organizations have tried to understand archaeology's economic role or have instigated projects to use heritage and archaeological resources to produce public benefits, archaeologists presently lack the theoretical and ethical foundations and the practical understanding necessary to do this work. The aim of the conference and of this volume is to begin to address this deficiency in the field.

The linkage of archaeology with economic development conjures up conflicting visions, and many in the field see a contentious relationship between the two. Typically, archaeology is seen as contending *against* the development of land for economic purposes — whether for the construction of houses, exploitation of minerals, building roads, or any other use of land that threatens the archaeological record. Frequently, the usurpation of heritage for commercial purposes is decried as commodification that destroys authenticity. These issues have been the subject of much debate among practitioners of commercial archaeology, cultural resource management, and heritage preservation.

Much less discussed in the field is the potential positive contribution that archaeology and heritage, when viewed as economic assets, may make to local community livelihoods. This contribution is often, though not always, through tourism, and discussion of tourism and its impact played a large part in this conference. However, viewing archaeology and heritage as economic assets raises many questions — How do we balance economic and cultural values? How do we conceptualize and measure these resources as economic assets? How should projects be managed practically to

                    DOI 10.1179/1465518714Z.00000000075

deliver sustainable economic benefits? What is the role of archaeologists in this effort and what ethical concerns should they have foremost in mind?

The conference aimed to tackle these issues. Speakers were recruited to speak from their different areas of expertise. The goal was to attract participants from a variety of backgrounds and contexts who could offer new perspectives on this subject, and particularly to attempt to bring economists and development experts into the conversation. We had three goals in assembling this distinguished and varied group of speakers. One was to define the 'state of the art' in the theory of archaeology's engagement with economic development. A second was to assemble in one place leading practitioners from governments, NGOs, and the academy, in order to sketch out the theoretical, practical, and ethical issues associated with attempting economic development shaped around archaeological and heritage sites. The goal here was to begin the quest to identify best practices. Finally, we hoped that the conference would, through the interaction of speakers and participants, begin to identify an agenda for future work in this emerging field being created by the convergence of heritage and archaeology, tourism, and economic development.

Economics and the heritage disciplines

The terms of reference for this conversation have been set largely by economists, who have approached the problems posed by the rising economic importance of heritage from the perspective of the market. Economic theories of markets have proven to be robust tools for explaining the behaviour of individual actors in transactions based on actual commodities, and they have been extended with success to address problems arising in circumstances in which markets can be created or market-like behaviour emulated. For example, costs can be attached — through penalties or performance standards — that cause corporations to cease or mitigate polluting behaviour. The tools of economics have not proven so useful in the case of archaeological sites or other heritage resources, however.

An essential problem is that the value of heritage is viewed differently by different users of heritage. For example, indigenous peoples may value their landscapes for customary or religious reasons, while property developers may see only recreational and construction opportunities. Moreover, indigenous peoples and archaeologists may value heritage for future generations in perpetuity, a timeframe that differs starkly from users with more commercial objectives. Finally, proponents of heritage and economists articulate value on different scales. Economists focus on financial metrics. Cultural specialists, on the other hand, refer to the artistic, educational, social, symbolic, spiritual, historical, authenticity, or social values of tangible and intangible heritage — all concepts that cultural scholars generally would support, but none of which is easily reduced to euros or dollars.

However, governments and private funders will and must make choices between investments in heritage and investments in other priorities. The lack of any agreed theoretical foundation for making heritage-preservation decisions (beyond formal designations such as 'scheduling') too often leaves governments, non-governmental organizations, heritage professionals and local communities at odds over policies and practices. Furthermore, efforts to turn heritage into a tourism asset — a primary focus of archaeologists' efforts related to economic development — encounter both challenges relating to demonstrating the economic return on monies spent to valorize a heritage asset and practical and ethical challenges relating to the implementation of projects in communities otherwise ill-prepared to enter the arena of the marketplace. Many papers in this volume illustrate both this clash of values and the real-world issues of implementation at the community level.

The globalization of the world economy compels an effort to address these matters. Three major factors are at play. First, tourism — much of it driven by interest in heritage and archaeological sites — has become a vast global industry and an economic engine for countries in both the developed and developing world. In 2012, for the first time, more than one billion people visited other countries as tourists — and millions more were tourists inside their own countries. Second, the expansion of travel has occurred at a time when global product sourcing has undermined domestic producers of raw materials and finished goods across the globe. Heritage tourism is one of the very few offerings that countries can make to the global economy that cannot be displaced by lower-cost foreign competition. Finally, the need to provide resources for an increasingly urbanized and materially prosperous world has created demands to exploit open land and natural resources, often at the expense of archae-ological sites, indigenous peoples, and sacred landscapes. Economies are going to continue to develop and communities are going to continue to be confronted with change. Heritage and archaeology cannot avoid being at the centre of that process.

Thus, the conversation initiated in this volume is essential. Despite the theoretical gaps and the practical problems, despite the ethical dilemmas that development poses for archaeologists and heritage professionals, and despite the problematic track record of development economists, the competing interests of current and future generations with regard to heritage need to be reconciled. This is not merely, or even primarily, a matter of theory. As the papers in this volume demonstrate, it is emphatically a search by the archaeological community for ways to interact with development imperatives in a manner that is ethically sound, honours the values of heritage, and above all is practically effective.

The organization of this volume

We have sorted the papers in this volume into four sections. The first two papers presented in this volume were the keynote addresses at the conference. By design they are antipodes. Richard Hodges offers a history of the Butrint Foundation's efforts over the past two decades to inaugurate a new exploration of the archaeology of this ancient site and to wrestle with the social and political development challenges to make Butrint National Park in Albania an economic benefit to the surrounding communities. His story touches on virtually every aspect, positive and negative, of the effort by archaeologists to engage with economic development. He concludes by stressing the value of non-governmental organizations as vehicles for creating eco-nomic impact through archaeology. By contrast, Dallen Timothy offers a summary of the current key trends in heritage tourism, the primary means through which archaeology and heritage are seen today to benefit the public economically. His paper underscores the importance of heritage and archaeological sites to the global tourism industry and explains the latest ways in which heritage is being taken up by for-profit and non-profit entities to foster economic development.

These introductions are followed by four papers that examine conceptually how archaeologists should think about the 'economic value' of archaeology and how that value is managed and communicated. Paul Burtenshaw examines the prevailing view in academia that economic and cultural values are in opposition, arguing instead for a professional awakening to the importance of understanding and using economic tools and concepts. Arjo Klamer takes this discussion further by articulating the various measures of value in the field of cultural economics and arguing that archaeologists and heritage organizations need to find methods to quantify, if not monetize, social and cultural values, if only to persuade policy-makers of their significance. However, Alexander Herrera offers a cautionary warning about the adverse consequences of 'commodifying' heritage in pursuit of economic gain with a discussion focused on case studies from Peru. Johannes Linn, in his commentary, offers a methodology for thinking through the linkages demonstrated by the other papers, between cultural values and economic values, and suggests a path forward.

There then follow a number of papers addressing archaeology's interactions with national and international governmental structures, non-governmental organizations, and corporations. Two papers examine the practice of archaeology and heritage management from a regional standpoint. Pedro Paulo Funari links the emergence of democratic governments in Latin America with archaeology's move away from colonial and academic interests to a more socially inclusive stance. Luca Zan describes in detail the massive Chinese investments in heritage and archaeology and positions that effort in a broader theoretical model of heritage management.

Lisa Ackerman brings to the fore the important role of non-governmental organizations through her case studies from the World Monument Fund's projects. She argues that professionals need to look beyond the immediate confines of their projects and consider the wider role economics plays in the conservation process. She suggests that those who are engaged in the conservation field need to ensure that preservation efforts directly contribute to, rather than detract from, local economic resources. Douglas Comer offers a vision of heritage as a 'public good' to support his argument for the need for international guidelines to control what he sees as the *laissez-faire* attitude of the tourism industry. Arlene Fleming outlines in detail the role the World Bank group — the leading funder of development programmes — can play in providing protection and funding for archaeology and heritage preservation. She argues that professionals in the field need to pay greater attention to such processes to ensure they can maximize the outcome of these projects for archaeology. This message for greater professional involvement in the processes of development is echoed by Gerald Wait and Jeffrey Altschul, who describe their commercial archaeology work associated with mining projects in Senegal and Mongolia. Their paper shows that the involvement of professional archaeologists in these projects can mitigate conflict between commercial development and archaeological practice. Like Comer, they call for the development of better international standards to help govern this relationship.

The third group of papers describes the challenges facing archaeologists who seek to promote economic development at the community level. Peter Gould examines small community heritage projects in Ireland and Belize, and presents five key governance principles common to them that have contributed to their sustainability over time. Papers by Terry Little and Gloria Borona, and also by David Morris, discuss the challenges of building tourism upon archaeological resources, in both cases African rock art, to advance community economic development. Dougald O'Reilly addresses the same sort of challenges in his review of Heritage Watch's capacity-building efforts in Cambodia. Richard Leventhal et al. describe a community-focused project relating to the nineteenth-century Caste War in the Yucatan, Mexico, and offer insights into the ways that communities value their heritage. The paper emphasizes the need to enable such communities to define for themselves which heritage matters most to them and to direct how such projects will be implemented. K. Anne Pyburn reviews projects in Belize and Kyrgyzstan in which she has been involved in order to evaluate the role of archaeologists in development. Like Leventhal, she embraces the idea that local communities not only should take the lead in defining their heritage, but that by doing so they may create projects that are both more valuable to the community and more sustainable.

The four final papers in the volume address, from varying perspectives, the challenge of measuring and communicating archaeology's contributions to economic development. Robert Bewley and Gareth Maeer describe how heritage delivers economic benefits to the UK and, importantly, how this benefit is appropriately and effectively communicated to funders and decision-makers. Deborah Gangloff also shows the importance of data and communication in her account of the significant economic impact of the Crow Canyon Archaeological Center, as a resource attracting significant out-of-state revenue, on its immediate environs in Colorado. Ran Boytner puts data to the proposition that archaeological field schools in fact can contribute meaningfully to local economic conditions. Lawrence Coben describes the metrics used in and the early results of the Sustainable Preservation Initiative's projects to underwrite entrepreneurial artisans in archaeology-rich villages in Peru.

Looking forward

Individually, these papers each make valuable contributions to the overall theme, and to addressing questions pertinent to this emerging area of research and practice. Taken together, these papers point the discipline in important directions.

One key lesson is the need for archaeologists to understand better the concepts which underpin the use of archaeology as an economic asset that contributes to society. Economic concepts and commercial incentives drive much of heritage management in practice, as shown by Comer. The concepts laid out in this volume offer a starting point, but to move forward meaningfully archaeologists must engage with economists and development practitioners to bring fresh perspectives into the field. Herrera, like many other of the authors, makes clear that such concepts must be used in ways that are ethical and appropriate to cultural heritage. However, there is an urgent need for archaeologists to master the economics, and then to have the confidence and creativity to develop successful new models.

As Gangloff and Bewley and Maeer show, those new models are vital if archaeology is to successfully communicate the economic, cultural, and social value of archaeology and heritage to policy-makers and stakeholders. This is not just a question of accumulating data. The profession needs to better understand the requirements and agendas of its stakeholder audiences, the conceptual framework in which data must be presented to be meaningful, and the most effective means of communicating that data to different audiences. The failure of archaeologists to interact with development practitioners and economists was often commented upon during the two days of the conference. Archaeology and heritage are not sufficiently recognized as assets that can contribute to social and economic development, yet archaeologists are often reluctant to reach out to economists and those who work in development, as Fleming and Wait and Altschul make clear. Because archaeology needs the support, it is incumbent on archaeologists to make the effort to correct that lapse.

The need for more and better quantitative and statistical data about the impact of archaeology was frequently commented upon during the conference. Conceptual models will help guide us about what to collect and how to present it, but we also simply need more data and more practice at collecting it. Archaeologists need data not only to present to outside stakeholders, but also to improve their own ability to recognize economic benefits and direct them for the good of the public and of archaeology itself. Though many papers presented data on individual projects, methods for measuring impact (whether economic, social, or on the value of archaeology) were demonstrated to be in their infancy and subject to tremendous collection challenges on the ground. Innovative methods and practical experience will be required to determine what data to collect, how to collect it, and how to utilize it to manage and improve projects.

A general thread of discussion concerned the need for heritage practitioners to present their case studies, including both successes and failures, and to discuss candidly their motivations, goals, and outcomes. Projects that are only partially successful tend to be swept under the rug, as do failures. Yet the papers by Hodges, Pyburn, O'Reilly, Little and Borona, and Morris illustrate the important lessons to be learned from projects that face severe challenges or perhaps even fail. While there was general acknowledgement that every project has its own unique context and issues, a vision of best practices will only emerge when there is a far greater body of case study material to draw upon.

Archaeologists need to look inward and clarify the role and aims of the profession in this regard. Wait and Altschul make the most pronounced argument, calling for the creation of a global professional organization to codify and enforce through peer review the emerging standards of the profession. As Pyburn argues, understanding our own motivation is vital. Coben observes that the pool of archaeologists who have the desire and capability to take part in economic development projects is too small. The archaeology profession requires commitment to its public archaeology goals and needs to integrate appropriate skills and knowledge into its training and academic curricula. If engagement with tourism and other forms of economic development is unavoidable, then the profession urgently needs to be defining and training the next generation in the skills they will need to execute these tasks effectively.

Altogether this is an ambitious agenda for a discipline burdened with other challenges. Yet this agenda also defines one route to lift archaeology and heritage into a more socially relevant and economically valued position from which to advance both the intellectual and societal goals of the discipline. The pressure on archaeology to achieve these goals will only grow as archaeologists themselves increasingly wish to make wider use of the materials and knowledge they create. The campaign by UNESCO to have a greater role for culture in the next set of Millennium Development Goals, due to be completed in 2015, places even greater expectations on archaeologists to deliver solutions that advance the human condition even as they also advance our knowledge of the past. Achieving a theoretical and practical intersection of archaeology, heritage, and development is perhaps the most potent way to make archaeology relevant, particularly for disadvantaged communities, in both cultural and economic terms.

★   ★   ★

We wish to close this introduction by acknowledging the financial support for the conference in 2012 that we received from the Institute of Archaeology at University College London, the Sustainable Preservation Initiative, the National Museum of the Royal Navy, the Heritage Lottery Fund, and Maney Publishing. We also received extensive advice and support from George Smith of Florida State University in assembling the speakers. We wish to acknowledge the enormous effort by Jamie Larkin to edit and facilitate the publication of these papers. Finally, we wish to thank the conference participants for the enormous effort they put into preparing for the conference, their active participation at the meetings, and their patience as we husbanded these papers through the publication process.

PUBLIC ARCHAEOLOGY, Vol. 13 Nos 1–3, 2014, 11–29

Escaping Enver Hoxha's Shadow: A Short History of the Butrint Foundation's Project in Albania, 1993–2012

RICHARD HODGES

American University of Rome, Italy

This essay describes the work of the Butrint Foundation between 1993–2012, as it developed a major archaeological research project in post-communist Albania that included creating an archaeological park with its own administrative authority. This history attempts to be reflexive, defining four phases from the initial collaboration to the end of the Foundation's active operations at Butrint. The essay sets the experiences of the Foundation against the backdrop of changing attitudes to cultural heritage practice in Albania as the newly democratic republic became more stable. The conclusion considers how the experience at Butrint might inform future capacity building in archaeology.

KEYWORDS archaeology, conservation, management, post-communism, NGOs

> The person who finds his homeland sweet is still a tender beginner; he to whom every soil is as his native one is already strong; but he is perfect to whom the entire world is as a foreign place. The tender soul has fixed his love on one spot in the world; the strong person has extended his love to all places; the perfect man has extinguished his. (Hugh of St Victor's *Didascalicon*, quoted in Said (1994: 335))

Introduction

Archaeological fieldwork in foreign lands has long bred a strong sense of Boy Scout machismo. 'Going into the field' conveys connotations of undertaking something courageous as well as scientific. You can picture the team photos with the proud-as-punch director centre stage, holding trophy finds. You can picture the jolly camaraderie of the dig dinner, all laid on by cheap local (i.e. native) staff (i.e. servants) in the 'mission's' base, intentionally isolated from any local community. Digging, of

   DOI 10.1179/1465518714Z.00000000051

course, is about the appropriation of something tangible that burnishes one's career back in the academy, where, by contrast, the rhythm of life can be characterized as almost timeless, safe, and verging on the monastic. Notwithstanding globalization, go to one of the big archaeology congresses and in the fifteen-minute presentations these binary attitudes between home and 'Other' (Said, 1994) are the stuff of just about every hour. Traditionally, fieldwork is not concerned with the communities associated with the excavations.

However, in an increasingly reflexive age, such attitudes are changing. More of us, mostly untrained it must be said, are aware that, in today's world, archaeology and cultural heritage has a major role in local, national, and international politics, and in one of the globe's biggest industries, tourism (see Timothy, this volume). Similarly, more of us, untrained of course, consider ourselves to be place-makers,[1] responsible to local communities, above all for site (visitor) presentation and for publications to all audiences to justify our (often) destructive actions. Some of us are even prepared to develop conservation and management strategies that involve capacity building in local communities. Some of us have even worked with local communities in developing such strategies. This said, almost all archaeologists know that if you enter local political spheres, however benignly reflexive you aim to be, these will consume you, leaving no time to practice archaeology. Presently, then, there is a grotesque trade-off between doing archaeology in a more traditional way and venturing to be a place-maker so that these research efforts bring economic benefits to the communities living close to or on the archaeological site being studied.

This paper will consider why there is a trade-off between the needs of the academy and the wider world. I shall attempt to answer this question while describing a case study spanning the past twenty years; a history of the Butrint Foundation's work at Butrint in south-west Albania. This short history, however, only touches tangentially on the large-scale excavations and surveys that are amply described elsewhere (Bowden & Hodges, 2011; Hansen, et al., 2012; Hansen & Hodges, 2007; Hodges, 2006; Hodges, et al., 2004) and a self-appraisal of those field projects (see Bowden & Hodges, 2012).

This short history encompasses four phases of the Butrint Foundation's work, from 1993–2012, which, thanks to support from the Packard Humanities Institute, culminated in a national discussion about the long-term reform of cultural management practice in Albania in the context of asset and economic priorities. This is the kind of discussion that is long overdue in neighbouring Eurozone countries like Greece and Italy where cultural heritage is a significant tourist-driver, but delivered by entrenched central agencies indifferent to advancing the economy of local communities. At issue in Albania is the role of the past as an asset in civil society and of course, how this asset is protected for a global society (see Hodges, 2006: 203–13). This sensitive territory has been identified as a critical issue for environmentalists:

> The environmental challenge is part of a more general problem related to resource allocation involving 'public goods', where the commodity is enjoyed in common rather than separately by one consumer only...We have to consider the possibility of state action and social provisioning, we also have to examine the part that can be played by the development of social values and a sense of responsibility that may reduce the need for forceful state action. (Sen, 1999: 269)

The quest to see 'our' — dare I say, Sen's — social values respected at Butrint, in retrospect, is perhaps the main issue of the short history I am about to describe.

The Butrint Foundation: a short history

In 1992, when Albania held its first democratic elections seven years after the death its communist dictator Enver Hoxha, archaeology and archaeologists were prized. Such was their status that several Albanian archaeologists soon emerged as senior politicians (notably Neritan Ceka, Aleksander Meksi, and Genc Pollo). One of the principal problems faced by Albania during the communist period was the organization of efficient control mechanisms for all human sciences in order to provide the country with a distinctive identity. The task of historians and archaeologists was to construct a systematic and well-documented Albanian past (Bowden & Hodges, 2004: 2012). In order to counter the territorial claims of surrounding powers (notably Greece, Italy, and Yugoslavia), the principal objective was to prove that the Albanians had inhabited their country from the most ancient of times. To this end, the main line of research supported by the authorities was to shape an origin myth about the Illyrians, with particular emphasis on their ethnogenesis and their ethnic and cultural links with the modern Albanian population (Vickers, 1995). Signal importance was attached to their social structures, especially with relation to a Marxist view of historical development. Hoxha himself made this perfectly clear in a speech at Shkodra in 1979:

> We are the descendants of the Illyrian tribes. Into the land of our ancestors have come the Greeks, the Romans, the Normans, the Slavs, the Angevins, the Byzantines, the Venetians, the Ottomans and numerous other invaders, without having been able to destroy the Albanian people, the ancient Illyrian civilization and later the Albanians. (Hoxha, 1985: 40)

His sentiment was soon repeated in 1988 and cast in metal in a sign above the museum at Butrint, a prized tourist destination in communist times. This pronounced: 'Besides the Greek and Roman cultures, another ancient culture developed and prospered here: the Illyrian culture' (Hodges, 2012a: 5).

Hoxha invested in archaeologists throughout the forty-year history of his regime. In the 1950s the first generation was trained in the Soviet Union. These archaeologists introduced new standards in the 1960s and trained a second generation who were shaped to Hoxha's nationalist goals, and at the same time, as in the case of Butrint, they laid the foundations of cultural heritage tourism for communist tourists in order to gain hard currencies. In 1988, while there were bread lines in the capital, the Albanian Institute of Archaeology boasted forty-eight field missions (pers. comm., Ilir Gjipali, Deputy Director, Institute of Archaeology). Of course, this was an archaeology shaped by limited theoretical goals, limited methodological techniques and, above all, by a government that actively restricted local economic growth. The photographs of the Institute of Archaeology's missions in the 1960s reveal the same heady machismo of Western archaeologists venturing into the 'Other' that I described above. The difference, this time, was that the 'Other' was regions of Albania inhabited by poorly educated peasants. Consequently, the collapse of the communist regime in

Albania (1990–92) was hard on this privileged class of archaeologists, and understandably made them extremely reluctant to engage with new, foreign concepts and methods, and even more reluctant to engage with Albania's local communities.

The Butrint Foundation was created in 1993 as a registered British charity by Lords Rothschild and Sainsbury to research, protect, and present Butrint. With a house on Corfu, overlooking Butrint, Lord Rothschild responded to a request by President Berisha of Albania in 1992 to launch this initiative, and involved his friend, Lord Sainsbury, in supporting it. Their shared interest in cultural heritage was well established, but this was their first collaborative venture outside the United Kingdom. Its focus was the World Heritage Site of Butrint, ancient Buthrotum, inscribed by UNESCO in 1999 (see Figure 1). Motivated by a desire to assist Albania as well as to

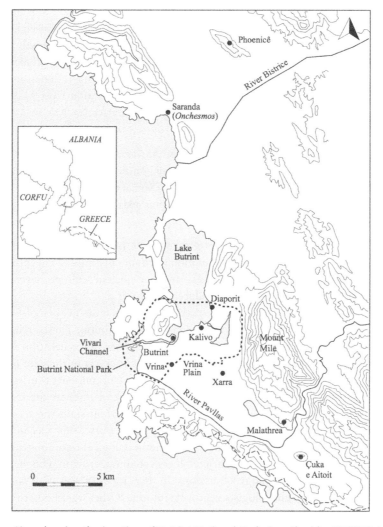

FIGURE 1   Map showing the location of Butrint National Park, inscribed by UNESCO in 1999.

grasp the challenge of investigating a quintessential Mediterranean Graeco-Roman port and its picturesque hinterland, this project was palpably born of 1990s excitement created by the fall of east European communism. With this remarkable support, there was a secure chance to assist Albania in a way, given the NGO status of the Foundation, which was almost as baffling in the 1990s to British archaeologists as it was to the Albanians.

Phase 1: No meeting of minds (1993–97)

The first period of this project can best be described as an often savage confrontation of scientific cultures (cf. Hall, 1999; Vickers & Pettifer, 1997). The opportunity to engage in economic development was extraordinarily limited.

The Butrint Foundation formally signed a memorandum of understanding with the Albanian Prime Minister in July 1994, and under my direction as its Scientific Director the Foundation began active operations in September 1994. A large-scale, interdisciplinary archaeological research project was started immediately, but then permission for the excavations was almost immediately withheld. At the same time the team assessed the prospects for creating an archaeological park to protect the site's beautiful woodland with multi-period ruins as well as its picturesque, lagoonal setting from unplanned tourist development (see Hodges, 2006: xi–xiii). Central to our project was the belief that the Foundation could bring support to this impoverished 'foreign land' that in time might situate Butrint within a Mediterranean tourist arena leading to economic development in south-west Albania. Economic growth, we tacitly surmised, would permit individuals to make choices, improving their quality of life; many predicted it might be 'a showcase for tourism' (see Lewis & Kanji, 2009: 53).

The shadow of Enver Hoxha was everywhere. As the newly elected democratic president of Albania, Sali Berisha bemoaned that Hoxha '[...] was the most tragic figure in our history. You cannot stand anywhere in Albania without seeing bunkers. He buried us in bunkers' (quoted in Sullivan, 1992: 18–19). Much more perplexing than the ideological mania of Albania's 600,000 bunkers were deep scars of isolation and repression. Coming from Britain, it was impossible for the Butrint Foundation team to grasp what Dipesh Chakrabarty (2007: 78–79; cf. Majumdar, 2010: 125) terms 'historical wounds' — wherein a broad segment of society owe their marginalization to a discrimination and oppression suffered, not in this case as a result of a colonial past, but from extreme totalitarianism. These wounds existed somewhere between history and memory. Sympathetic yet protected by our cultural firewalls, we naively sought to introduce modern European archaeological practice to Albanian colleagues who were led to believe, as a result of isolation, that they were the premier archaeologists in the world (Bowden & Hodges, 2004). No less idealistic were our plans for a new museum, drawn up in 1995. Elegantly designed to contemporary first-world standards, it was all too easily dismissed by our puzzled Albanian colleagues.

Hoxha's celebrated claim that Albania was close to paradise on earth was suddenly followed, with the fall of the regime, by 'a utopian and amoral world of unrestricted fulfilment of the individual consumerist's imagination, without any collective, political and ethical dimension' (Mai, 2002: 218). Understandably, our Albanian colleagues, trapped in the alarming instability of this transition between

1993–97, hung on desperately to their nationalist training and resisted any methodology that might challenge it (see Bowden & Hodges, 2004; 2012). Accordingly, they believed that they should be handsomely paid by the Foundation for permitting it to operate in the privileged domain of Butrint: three apartments in Paris and five Mercedes Benz cars were their price. On the other hand, inculcated in Hoxha's ideologically driven cultural heritage strategy, they were doggedly resistant to any kind of conservation strategy and, more significantly, to 'tourist archaeology', as an erstwhile Director of the Institute of Archaeology derisively termed it. Their business was science, not management.

As a result, our approach to the project was forced to change. We consciously altered course and adopted a strategy to pit one Albanian institution against another in order to pursue a strategy to help (i.e. impose) development. Any EU-funded research project would have failed after two years, but, following a high-profile visit by James Wolfensohn, President of the World Bank, the Foundation supported a third season of activities in 1996 in which the first conservation and presentational initiatives accompanied initial archaeological enquiry. These included the erection of the first site information panels in Albania — haughtily dismissed by a British travel writer, Robert Carver[2] — and the production of a simple site brochure to promote Butrint and places in its region, and, most significantly, the reintroduction of woodland management (which had ceased with the end of communism). Alongside this, we embarked upon the first field survey in Albania resulting in the entire team being briefly arrested for espionage!

After the first season in 1994, we lived and worked with local communities, which gave us an important perspective on the internal tensions of this first experience of democracy. Local people had no status at Butrint in the face of the government-supported archaeologists from the capital, Tirana. The Tirana archaeologists, being disdainful of these communities, instead chose to live in isolation on the archaeological site itself. Tellingly, the ancient city of Butrint — contrary to Robert Carver's travelogue (1998: 102) — was not damaged during the bitter uprising of 1997, although some stores were robbed of minor objects. The local community, no longer alienated by this national asset as effectively the property of the state archaeological authorities, actively attempted to protect it.

Before describing Phase 2 of this history let me be clear. The neo-liberal development strategy we deployed was colonialist insofar as we soon treated our disgruntled Albanian colleagues as 'the Other'. As we did not pay them the high fees they demanded, they refrained from embarking upon any genuine scientific collaboration. There was simply no meeting of minds. Nevertheless, we attempted to adhere to the principals of post-colonialism in our broader strategic thinking (cf. Patterson, 2008: 31–32): with some satisfaction I can say that by the end of the third campaign in 1996 we had forged an outline management plan for Butrint and an estimated fifteen out of possibly 100 households in the nearest village, Vrina, had installed bathrooms courtesy of the Foundation's investment.

Phase 2: Making the park (1998–2000)

After the civil uprising in January 1997, the World Bank and the Getty Grant Program encouraged the Foundation to be more aggressive in pursuing our objectives. Support from the Packard Humanities Institute made this practically possible. During the

1990s governments, donor agencies, and corporations all came to see heritage and tradition as reified public goods that could be mobilized for the greater public good (cf. Serageldin, 1999). More than its simple economic instrumentality, heritage might also proffer a seemingly novel vehicle for national pride, spiritual recovery, and reconciliation. Lynn Meskell recently captured this spirit of the 1990s in her vivid description of the Kruger National Park in South Africa: 'capitalizing culture, literally the attempt to transform culture's liquid assets into permanent heritage capital, has proven more challenging than promoting and consuming the modern and global imperatives of nature conservation and biodiversity' (2012: 208).

Phase 2 at Butrint began with a version of a values-based workshop funded by the Getty Grant Program in April 1998, from which we intended to pursue a collaborative research and management strategy. This was not a 'meeting of experts [. . .] best [. . .] seen as a piece of political theatre in which archaeologists (and conservation professionals) played the role of the white-coated specialist on a television commercial for an over-the-counter cold remedy' (Joyce, 2005: 267). On the contrary, the high-level and diverse Albanian participants, perhaps artfully manipulated by the foreigners present, concluded that first and foremost the magical spirit of Butrint needed to be protected as its asset of greatest significance. The gravitational pull of the monuments themselves was resisted (cf. Joyce, 2005: 263 — describing a similar meeting at Copan in Honduras at this time).

From this 1998 workshop there followed the making of a greatly enlarged protected area — a buffer zone encompassing the surrounding wetlands and lagoon — an area that was inscribed by UNESCO (at Fez in 1999), and similarly, thanks to my secondment to Albania's Ministry of Culture, Butrint was inscribed as Albania's first archaeological park (in 2000).

All of this appealed to our patient donors; the virtues of a romantic wilderness were harnessed to the scientific inventory of the archaeological site. Yet behind this apparent moral position lurked a fundamental problem. The local representatives in the 1998 workshop (from the regional town of Saranda, not the villages in the immediate vicinity of the park) openly rejected such romanticism. They charged the new government with selling the place to 'Prince' Rothschild, cunningly appealing to a global audience sensitive to the political incorrectness of neo-colonialism. These local representatives wanted a marina at Butrint as well as golf courses. As local stakeholders, experiencing an impoverishment unimaginable in the Hoxha era, their view was that this was their chance to exploit Albania's premier cultural asset. The Ministry of Culture, aware of Albania's reputation as a rogue state in the aftermath of the 1997 uprising,[3] overruled this, not without difficulty, using its bureaucratic apparatus to authorize a new management concept for the park. Behind this was a set of compromises. Essentially, the foreign Foundation was encouraged to support the shaping of the park, bringing international esteem to the government in its dealings with major agencies and foreign enterprise. At the same time, the national cultural heritage institutions were given an opportunity to participate in the relatively small revenues from the then minimal tourism at Butrint. For all parties it was a pragmatic partnership which helped to release funding and support the international branding of Butrint.

In the wake of the 1997 uprising there was no will on the part of the government to involve local communities in the new Butrint National Park. Many of these villages, at first, were considered to be dangerous, and the educational levels were considered to be low. All the villages suffered from abject poverty, modestly relieved by remittances. As a result there was resistance from the Albanian government to any further attempts to incorporate the values given to the site by all interest groups, ensuring the inclusion of villagers within the park itself (cf. Bluestone, 2000; Demas, 2002: 27). Instead, separately, an Italian NGO, Comitato Internazionale per lo Sviluppo dei Popoli (CISP) from 1999–2004 set out to assist the villages, initiating small development programmes around the park. By 2005, the Foundation recognized it should have collaborated more closely with CISP and, with its closure, it adopted its broad aims. This change of direction by the Foundation followed the appointment of a new government-appointed director of the park, which in turn facilitated the first steps to include the mayors of the villages in subsequent decision-making.

Meanwhile, the government treated the new park as a minor political asset, from which its directors might financially benefit. These discrete compromises appeared at the time to be a small price to pay for discarding the mass tourist development schemes advocated by local stakeholders. It took a further decade to confront these compromises in order to create a park structure free of corruption. At the same time, with hindsight, the Foundation expended only limited resources on capacity building to create a new managerial direction for the Butrint National Park. We focused instead upon safeguarding Butrint as an exceptional place and sustaining a research project to a point where we might publish a new history of it. Our reasoning, with hindsight, reveals how limited our understanding was of the social circumstances in Albania less than a decade after the fall of communism and equally our protectionist determination.

Phase 3: Developing the park infrastructure (2000–06)

The creation of the Butrint National Park in 1999 facilitated major developments at Butrint over the following seven years. A management plan based upon a condition survey of the monuments paved the way for a strategy that included regular conservation, a new museum, new trails though the buffer zone, new information panels, a new website, new guidebooks, wide-ranging capacity building including a guide-training programme, an archaeological and conservation training school and a major research programme including archival studies. Significantly, in 2003 the Foundation also instigated the inscription of Butrint and its region with following the Ramsar convention (for the protection of wetlands), creating an even larger environmentally protected zone encompassing Lake Butrint and its immediate surroundings.

Investment in the archaeological park soon attracted increased year-on-year visitorship, consistent with the original goals of the Butrint Foundation. These achievements, in the circumstances, should not be understated. Along with the research reports, as place-makers, the Foundation significantly altered the way cultural heritage was perceived in post-communist Albania. Indeed, in 2005 UNESCO sponsored a meeting to make at least six other archaeological parks following the Butrint model.

Community projects within the park, as already noted, were introduced by CISP in 1999 and then advanced after its closure by the Butrint Foundation from 2005–10. Three villages are situated within the Butrint National Park are Shën Dëlli, Vrinë, and Xarrë with populations of 383, 1204, and 2362 respectively in 2008. Ksamili, on the northern edge of the park, possesses a fluctuating population of up to 10,000. In Shën Dëlli, poverty levels are some of the highest in Albania, with an average family income (in 2008) of approximately 200 USD a month; in Vrinë it is 500 USD and in Xarrë 800 USD (Gorica & Paloka, 2006; Phelps, 2010: 23). The Foundation's major community engagement projects included an on-site community shop where locals might sell handmade products, school visits to the site, and environmental awareness activities. Additionally, after 2005 the park began to employ upwards of fifty locals on a seasonal basis as workmen, ticket vendors, and tour guides. At the same time local fishermen and farmers received special fishing and agriculture rights to work within the park, demonstrating its interest in supporting local industries. The Foundation also introduced a Schools' Programme, having refurbished Vrinë School itself in 2001. The programme aimed to integrate Butrint into the local schools' curriculum so that teachers could help their students recognize and appreciate the site's vital role in their history and future. A school activity book based on the site's primary monuments was distributed to every child attending school within the area of the park (Phelps, 2010: 11).

These achievements were greatly facilitated by an almost exponential growth in tourism since 2000. Notwithstanding Albania's status from 1997–2002 as a dangerous place to travel, tourists began to venture there. The Foundation from 1999 invested in a consultancy to explore how visitorship to Butrint might be facilitated. Working with tour agents and the Corfu tourism authority, the Foundation encouraged what has become known as actor-networking: 'many people and things interacting as cogs and wheels' (van der Duim, 2007: 971–72). This was actively facilitated by agents building constituent entities, giving credence to the value of visiting an erstwhile pariah state. Since 2003, with the withdrawal of advisories on travel in Albania, initially day-tourism from Corfu, then individual tourism as well as group tours around the country has grown steadily. Butrint is a fixed point on all these itineraries. From this time, too, Albanians, intrigued by the television and media coverage, were drawn in significant numbers too.

But, in reality, did Albania really adapt to a post-Soviet moment in this new essentially capitalist sector, with the adoption of the Butrint model? It did not. On the contrary, the state-controlled management at Butrint effectively meant that Albanian investment in the park remained minimal and eccentric (limited to events such as the Miss Albania beauty contest). In bald terms park revenues were illicitly siphoned off, while the local communities remained marginalized. By 2007, ten years after the civil uprising, the spirit of the place was secure, but only a small amount of the revenues associated with it were supporting specific families in the local communities.

Phase 4: Towards a sustainable future? (2007–12)

By 2008, Albania had ostensibly completed its transition from rogue state to an emerging market-based democracy and on the eve of the global financial crisis beginning that September, the future of the park seemed set. This was the occasion to reflect upon the future of the Butrint Foundation.

Edwards (2008: 47) has observed that 'The rules of the international NGO world seem to stay pretty much the same. Does anyone believe that development NGOs still aim "to work themselves out of a job" [...]?'. The elephant in the room, Edwards has written, is that NGOs favour 'institutional imperatives' such as maximizing income, opportunities and profile over 'developmental imperatives such as handing over the baton, empowering marginalized groups, because donors have demanded this' (2008: 47). Conscious of this critique, the Foundation encouraged the Albanian authorities to take the lead at Butrint, and in 2009 began to signal an exit strategy. Over the following four years the Foundation made the transition from an operating NGO to a grant-giving entity.

The success of the park as a visitor attraction has its brought own impetus. Over 69,000 tourists brought €210,000 to the Butrint National Park in 2011, revenue that was appropriated by central government (Butrint National Park internal document). This is perfectly consistent with the World Tourist Organization's findings on tourist growth. World tourism grew by 4.4% in 2011 to 980 million. Europe had the strongest at 6% growth; this was actually higher in advanced as opposed to emerging economies. Tourism is now responsible for 5% of the world's GDP and 6% of total exports, employing one out of twelve people worldwide. In 2011 central and southern Europe experienced 8% growth (UNWTO, 2012). Albania and Butrint in particular, have benefited from this pattern: sixty to ninety local people are now employed in the activities as a result of this managed tourism at Butrint. As in many similar countries, the tourist revenues in real terms in Albania are a small but significant windfall as foreign remittances plummeted as a result of the global economic crisis. Notwithstanding this success, the government interceded on one issue, manoeuvring with its own resources to contemplate development of the buffer zone protected by the 1999 UNESCO World Heritage inscription (UNESCO, n.d.).

Over the course of the decade after 1998, UNESCO completely altered its approach to Butrint. While the organization encouraged the preparation of a new management plan for the site (and in its initial deliberations sought to involve local stakeholders), ultimately, its new approach has sanctioned the state to pursue its own goals. Here let me simply echo a recent commentary in *The Economist* (2012: 70): 'UNESCO, like most other UN agencies, suffers from a house culture which prefers to deal with governments, and lives happily with the fiction that governments genuinely care about citizens and their heritage'.

In 2010, a new road was driven through the park's olive groves with brutal determination, significantly meeting no resistance from UNESCO (Hodges, 2012b: fig. 17.3). As the road was completed, the wetlands that make up much of the buffer zone were drained, leading to the suspicion that the government might either sell off the area to major political donors for development as seaside conglomerates or less probably, repurpose these lands for intensive agriculture.

Not all the signs are troubling reminders of the situation in 1993–97. A positive new initiative occurred in 2012 as the Albanian American Enterprise Fund, having signed an accord with the Albanian government, began supporting the Butrint National Park on a project-by-project basis, implementing projects identified by the Foundation at first, and then by stages supplanting the Foundation as the principal outside influence on investment in and protection of the site. With the installation of electronic ticket-gates, some 90% of the park's income is now to be kept by the park to spend on the park itself. This act of decentralization by the Ministry of Culture, albeit under pressure from two foreign NGOs, bodes well in the short term, and certainly will help to keep Butrint, as Albanian visitors expect, as little short of paradise on earth.

Discussion

In many respects the Foundation's project at Butrint has been a success. The large excavations and their fulsome publication have established the importance of the place in the southern Adriatic region, giving it a lasting scientific prominence, while Butrint has been visited by almost half a million people since the 1998 workshop. In abstract terms, the archaeological park has certainly brought revenue and created employment in the region. Put simply, the Foundation met the objectives set in 1993 and possibly exceeded them.

Nevertheless, it has also proved an uncomfortable learning experience. Let me now consider three issues pertinent to the creation of the cultural heritage programme at the site.

The international community and the issues of identity

What draws visitors to Butrint? Is it the spirit of the place, as the 1998 workshop concluded, or the monuments, or its history, or a combination of all these? How has the Foundation's research altered the national and international identity of the place?

After a decade of collaboration starting in 1994, and especially after the civil uprising in 1997, Albania's post-communist archaeologists warmed to the idea of archaeology for the public or, as they conceptualized it, 'tourist archaeology'. Making money from archaeology conformed to the new capitalist order. On the other hand they, and the students of this transition era, resisted any challenge to their nationalist history and thus new interpretation of Butrint. These two interpretations, it has to be said, could not be more different. Nevertheless, no interest whatsoever was expressed in the excavated results that show a largely discontinuous history, common to other Adriatic Sea ports between the Archaic Greek and Ottoman eras (Hodges, 2012a: 1–3). On this issue Enver Hoxha's nationalist influence has been sealed in aspic.

A third interpretation of Butrint's history also exists. The UNESCO inscription made in 1992, however, describes an entirely different (pre- and post-communist) history:

> Inhabited since prehistoric times, Butrint has been the site of a Greek colony, a Roman city and a bishopric. Following a period of prosperity under Byzantine administration, then a brief occupation by the Venetians, the city was abandoned in the late Middle Ages after marshes formed in the area. (UNESCO, n.d.)

This inscription stems from an overtly Grecophile interpretation of the place, arising from the brief resurrection in the 1990s of the movement to revive the independence claims made in 1913–14 (following the creation of the republic of Albania) for the republic of Epirus Vetus. Butrint, as such, was the short-lived republic's prized archaeological asset, although its ancient Greek monuments are, in fact, few and hardly impressive. The UNESCO interpretation also promotes a continuous history drawn from the contemporary texts associated with Butrint rather than from the archaeological evidence (cf. Hodder, 2009: 202–03). These texts have been deployed to define it as Greek, Roman, Christian, Byzantine, and briefly Venetian, signally omitting an Ottoman presence altogether. Here, I am reminded of Michael Herzfeld's indignation about the air-brushing out of Ottoman presence from Greece: 'why is it that nation-states so often seem hell-bent on trying to reduce the richness of cultural life to a kind of crass materiality [...]?' (cited in Byrne, 2009: 156).

As noted already, the Butrint Foundation excavations made between 1994–2009 aimed to show a much more episodic history, often shaped by the environmental circumstances of the lagoon. The divergences between these three histories — that of the Epirote independence movement, of Enver Hoxha, and now the Butrint Foundation — serve different universes. Of course, this goes unnoticed by the Albanian public and media who adhere to Hoxha's paradigm, and the neighbouring Greeks who adhere to the UNESCO model, while the Foundation's model is proclaimed in the interpretive panels and the Museum.

Perhaps the most intriguing aspect of this identity crisis at Butrint is that Albanians in their post-communist dilemma are still connected to Hoxha's paradigm (Mai, 2002: 218–19). Albania is in many ways experiencing a huge problem not uncommon in our post-Soviet world: there is a collision between authoritarian-homogeneous conceptual frameworks and democratic-heterogeneous ones that have created fragmentation and competition, hindering the development of a democratic political culture (Mai, 2002: 222). The education of the Albanian elite has taken place under the influence of a homogeneous logic: issues are right/wrong, good/bad, white/black, patriotic/treasonous, while the democratic political institutions have been founded upon a heterogeneous structure (Fuga, 1998: 133). The development of a homogenous cultural heritage, embedded in the erstwhile authoritarian logic of the country, refuses to contemplate the different, 'the Other', the competitor.

So what should the interpretation of this place be? The Butrint Foundation attempted to promote a past that is marked by multiple, historically specific temporalities (using the Foundation's archival research) that preceded modernity and came to be integral to colonialism as we usually think of it (cf. Renton, 2006). This interpretation in the museum, refurbished by an Albanian architect and reopened in 2005, redeployed the old 1988 galleries rather than building new ones (cf. the 1995 plan, mentioned above) (Renton, 2006). The questions raised by divergent colonialisms concern migrations, relations of centre-periphery, and imperial expansion. A key aspect of this approach is that it is multi-vocal and can be challenged: 'A historiographical approach [...] unravels the stories that nations tell of their own pasts, whether as colonizers or as the colonized, and addresses the fictions of empire — from multiple, dialectically related historical standpoints' (Fuchs & Baker, 2004: 339).

As yet, though, twenty years after the fall of the dictatorship, there has been no self-conscious search for a multi-cultural past in Albania congruent with a contemporary reformulation of a nation with many ethnicities (cf. Joyce, 2005: 271). These three histories, for sure, notwithstanding greater freedoms of expression in Albania, will exist in parallel for some time to come.

The local community and the issue of identity

To consider this identity crisis more broadly, we must consider how it affects communities and their opportunity to engineer their national and local economies. The World Heritage List created at the UNESCO general conference of 1972 to safeguard sites of outstanding universal value was an awareness-raising convention, intended to galvanize financial support for the protection of designated sites. It also aimed to establish a fund for this purpose, involving individuals, private and public foundations, and nation-states. The convention was explicitly based upon the United States national parks system. The model was unambiguous: 'economically, the US national parks remain an enormous engine for tourism revenue and tourism-related jobs' (Comer, 2006: 26). The national parks are supported by tax dollars, but these are protected as tangible portions of the national heritage. This model, of course, was alien to the administrators of Albania's patrimony in the transition to democracy. Balancing the interests of preservation, while involving local communities, invokes the skilful role of government. Herein is a fundamental problem, as we have seen, as the ruling elite resisted any relaxation of their grip upon their nationalist history.

This separation between the state and its communities was identified by many of the respondents to Dana Phelps' survey of community engagement with Butrint made in 2010. Nearly all respondents from the park's villages had visited the Butrint museum, and most villagers had had a comprehensive tour of the site. The majority of respondents from Shën Dëlli and Vrinë said that they or the community was making an income from the site. However, this was not the case for Xarrë, a more distant village, where more respondents felt they were not involved in any way. This is not a surprise, however, considering that the majority of the workmen and handicraft producers come from Shën Dëlli. Many villagers expressed resentment towards the park's management for not engaging the community more and helping them to gain from tourism at Butrint (Phelps, 2010: 66). Many from Tirana, as has been noted already, still consider the local people to be too poorly educated to be effective participants in the management and activities of the park.

This widely acknowledged separation puts Western-trained archaeologists in difficult position. We were unprepared for the recidivist nationalism and inflexible, homogeneous approach to the place. Local rights were rejected, and we found it difficult to intervene to realign this. Concurrently, our attempts to serve all audiences within Albania attracted only diffidence in central government. In short, while we aimed to articulate our research and cultural heritage strategy for the widest possible audiences (using television, the press, and digital media), for internal political purposes we were repeatedly charged with being colonialists by those who wanted to appropriate Butrint for their own financial and political ends.

Our experiences confirm Brian Fagan's (2006) view that the teaching of archaeology is far removed from the circumstances we encounter on the ground in places like Albania. Attacking the academic treadmill, Fagan pleads for new standards in archaeology in universities. I would go further than Fagan. As place-makers, there are responsibilities to both the community and the curation of cultural assets themselves, that need to be part of our training in any standard programme encompassing archaeological theory and method. Presently the archaeology of emerging and third world countries and its critique, like much cultural heritage training, are essentially little more than first-world rhetoric, alien to the daily operations of communities like Butrint.

I am not alone in reaching such conclusions. Lynn Meskell has recently struggled with this issue as it affected the making and management of the Kruger national park in South Africa. According to Meskell, 'many academics [do not] effectively convey the relevance of the past to the present'. She continues: 'significantly, it would be historians not archaeologists who would take the lead in the crafting of heritage legislation [. . .] Historians [. . .] filled the vacuum left by a certain unwillingness on the part of archaeologists to engage publicly. Archaeologists are generally reluctant to assume the role of public intellectuals' (Meskell, 2012: 172).

Why has archaeology failed to address such crucial issues? In a nutshell, our Western values in archaeology are not measured in capacity building. Instead, universities discretely measure overheads and boast about publications, and meanwhile, unsurprisingly, the tourism and development industries treat archaeology as a quirky add-on, at worst bemusedly mindful of the gravitational pull of the 'authentic' monument, its art, and its spirit of place. Capacity building involving leadership programmes remain the domain of foundations (such as UNESCO), and outside the academic arena. The meeting of minds across this divide seldom occurs, meaning the notion of 'one world' archaeology is both academic and therefore it is often ineffective at engaging and developing those communities in which it operates. The absence of a meeting of minds may leave deeper scars because, as Douglas Comer anxiously concluded in the case of Petra, this is a pivotal generation in the history of archaeological site management (2012: 175, 186).

The academic community and the issue of identity

We live in a confused era in archaeology. The cultural heritage 'industry' needs extensively excavated sites to draw visitors. These need to be managed to modern standards in terms of conservation and presentation. The 'industry' requires excavations made on the grand scale of archaeology as it was carried out in the 1930s and 1950s, not field-survey or trenching. The grand scale, though, is inconsistent with the present human and financial resources of modern archaeologists in the academy. Finding resources to excavate, publish, conserve, and present archaeological sites is realistically beyond the present university archaeologist (Bowden & Hodges, 2012: 236–37). So what is the answer? There is a place, of course, for small-scale archaeological research managed by and for university departments, but running research excavations and pursuing community engagement, for example, are ostensibly very different operations. This, then, is the context for the NGO, an operation with an explicit purpose that functions in parallel to the present university rhythm (which is itself being scrutinized in a digital, global market).

The Butrint Foundation has unwittingly been a positive experiment in this emerging archaeological arena. I would now like to take a moment to examine its characteristics because these are notably different from a university department.

First, a NGO is subject to strict reviews by its trustees and an annual audit. Such business-like strictures are uncommon in most university operations.

Second, its operations, like those of similar organizations in Albania in myriad social and economic sectors, has promoted an universalistic ethos rather than furthering the interests of its members, occupying its own space within the state (cf. Heins,

2008: 4). As such it has attempted to nest within the interstices of power in order to modify the way in which power is exercised. These operations in practical terms mean dealing directly with government, the media, and with other agencies, all of which, in a transition economy, is extraordinarily time-consuming. As new studies of NGO practice reveal (e.g. Edwards, 2008; Heins, 2008), the entity brings with it a great deal of baggage. In many ways it is akin to development politics and the binary opposite of the archaeological mission in its dig house resistant to engaging with 'the Other'.

In the case of the Butrint Foundation, our work led us to develop and promote, to quote Volker Heins, 'liberal and social democratic values against the rule of increasingly anonymous and unaccountable forms of global governance' (2008: 5). On reflection, we might go further: NGOs like the Butrint Foundation are: '[. . .] actors involved in struggles over recognition against basic forms of abuse [. . .]What observable NGO activities [. . .] have in common is their shared opposition to elementary forms of abuse, disrespect and misrecognition' (Heins, 2008: 10–11). In this respect, the NGO can act as a quintessential 'agent of global connectedness' (Kaldor, 2003: 2; cf. Lipschutz, 1992: 389–420).

Like other NGOs operating in post-communist Albania, the Foundation assembled good researchers, many of whom might be described as guilty of wishful thinking on behalf of disempowered local constituents. They put themselves in the shoes of distant strangers, but their empathy was often laced with well-intentioned cultural misunderstandings. They spoke on behalf of others without being able to represent them. Their conspicuous goodness sometimes played into the hands of those with self-serving strategic interests.

Nevertheless, being small and flexible, the Foundation managed like other small NGOs to mobilize non-political opinions. It also expropriated the moral concerns of the wider public by confining the arena of debate to media campaigns and professional lobbying, while simply promoting the case for the efficient delivery of services.

There is no doubt that NGOs like the Foundation 'are bulwarks against public cynicism and the excesses of governments and corporations. But if they want to realize their better intentions, they will always have to tap into the power of forces bigger than themselves' (Heins, 2008: 14). It is scarcely surprising, then, that like other NGOs, the Foundation has been seen by way of its moral intervention as the frontline force of imperial invention (Ferguson, 2004: 11; Hardt & Negri, 2000: 36). The most conspicuous illustration of this was the jibe in several Albanian newspapers that 'Prince' Rothschild had bought Butrint in 1998 when the concept of the park was adopted by Prime Minister Nano. Similarly, as the Foundation confronted corruption in the park in 2003, leading to a debate in the Albanian parliament, the counter-attack involved criticizing the Foundation as colonialist.

Lastly, there is the issue of the Foundation's exit strategy. Having negotiated an Albanian future for the Butrint park, in the context of often overt political corruption, there is concern amongst those Albanians trained by the Foundation. Many are anxious for the future of the park and its principles. These Albanians cannot envisage any organization that might replace it. With this vacuum, only the worst imaginable will happen to the archaeological park as the Albanian authorities appear only respond to exogenous forces. We shall see.

This experience has taught me a simple and perhaps obvious lesson: there are two very different rhythms — one for research practice that can be enacted through a university department, and one for developing the political structures that are fundamental to development and economic activity, wherein the NGO, as a free-standing agency, is an effective instrument. Melding the two together is a new challenge for the field of archaeology. This involves political and entrepreneurial skills, not entirely different from administration in the modern university arena, but different from the machismo of field archaeology. To meet industry needs as well as contemporary standards in archaeological practice, as in most professional fields in highly ranked universities, university archaeology departments need to embrace the NGO concept in order to create the institutional context to train its students in real world contexts as opposed to just theoretical issues.

Conclusion

I can take two lessons from this twenty-year experience with the Butrint Foundation, conscious of the often dispiriting trade-off between managing research and managing the political relationships with the different communities engaged in this project. First, I wholeheartedly echo John Barrett's sentiments:

> Cultural policy is increasingly driven by the demands for preservation and conservation, but the routine emphasis upon the preservation of a material record for future generations must not over-look the need to encourage the sense of enquiry, urgency and skill with which the contemporary world desires to know the past. (Barrett, 2006: 208)

At Butrint, we have proudly advanced a revised and updated Mediterranean history for the place (cf. Hodges, 2012a). Against the odds, and with the privilege of having great operating freedoms, we undertook major new archaeological research. But beyond our trenches, given our neo-liberal aims in 1993, how successful was this project? Did we substantively improve the quality of life for the diverse communities engaged directly or indirectly with the World Heritage Site?

Some alumni of the capacity building programmes are employed in archaeology and cultural heritage throughout Albania. But, on the whole, the capacity building in management that we had hoped for has not happened (cf. Comer, 2012: 13–14). As for the local communities who might have benefited from tourism to Butrint, the trickle-down effects are limited to certain families living in the nearest villages: perhaps as many as fifty families have found employment as a result of the project and its enduring tourist-focused model. Without the adoption of effective governance to challenge the residual institutions and attitudes from the communist system, instilling local as well as 'national social values' — as Sen calls them (1999: 269) — the Foundation was unable to ensure the implementation of essential structural reforms, and create local economic growth (cf. Lewis & Kanji, 2009: 53).

In sum, while we successfully brought an actor-network approach to bear upon delivering tourists to Butrint (cf. van der Duim, 2007), we failed at grassroots level to encourage the cultural heritage community to assert greater control over the stubbornly reactionary environment in which they worked. With this failure of empowerment it is hard to believe that the Butrint project will prove sustainable. This, then, makes these reflective recollections, our publications and archives all the more important because it is easy to imagine that in the near future the homogeneous intellectual and political opposition we faced in Albania will be breached by local communities, cognizant of their economic agency within an irreversible globalization. But will these communities prize assets like Butrint or turn them into an uninformed pastiche that devalues their economic value? This distinctly uncomfortable conclusion begs a question that UNESCO urgently needs to confront: can the past be managed effectively in a country when Sen's 'social values and a sense of responsibility' (1999: 269) are absent?

As a pivotal generation in the history of cultural heritage management, as the 'authentic' assets we have helped to curate becoming increasingly more valuable, paradoxically our legacy is far from secure and questions like these need to be confronted. This said, Albanians love Butrint. They see it as theirs to cherish as opposed to a neo-liberal import. But their voices are muted. Dark paladins in the form of government-supported private developers eager to profit from construction projects will remain a constant threat until Albania has finally cast off the shadow of Enver Hoxha. Perhaps the biggest tribute to the Foundation's achievements and its record is that we can ask such questions. Archaeology and local communities will only prosper if this conflict of interests is openly confronted, and on the world stage.

Acknowledgements

I am grateful for the encouragement of Peter Gould to write this essay, and for the comments of Diana Ndrenika, Jacob Rothschild, and Danny Renton on its contents. Thanks, too, to Dana Phelps, who provided me with a copy of her thesis about the community survey in 2010. As ever, my greatest debt is to the Butrint Foundation and Packard Humanities Institute who supported this research.

Notes

[1] Archaeologists help to define and brand places by their excavations and research, hence I have described their role here (and elsewhere) as place-makers (see Hodges, 2012b).

[2] Carver noted: 'I was sorry to see that British archaeologists had been allowed in to do their usual level best to destroy the delicate atmosphere by erecting large, ugly and quite unnecessary signboards at every point, token of the vanity of the archaeologists, which merely obscured the stones and statues about which they purported to inform' (1998: 101).

[3] In January–February 1997 a failed pyramid scheme led to an uprising, principally in southern Albania, against the government of President Sali Berisha. Nearly two thousand people died before, through intervention by the European Union, Mr Berisha agreed to new elections.

Bibliography

Barrett, J. C. 2006. Archaeology as the Investigation of the Contexts of Humanity. In: D. Papaconstantinou, ed. *Deconstructing Context. A Critical Approach to Archaeological Practice*. Oxford: Oxbow Books, pp. 194–211.

Bluestone, D. 2000. Challenges for Heritage Conservation and the Role of Research on Values. In: E. Avrami, R. Mason, & M. De la Torre, eds. *Values and Heritage Conservation: A Research Report Organized by the Getty Conservation*. Los Angeles: Getty Conservation Institute, pp. 65–67.

Bowden, W. & Hodges, R. 2004. Balkan Ghosts? Nationalism and the Question of Rural Continuity in Albania. In: N. Christie, ed. *Landscapes of Change: Rural Evolutions in Late Antiquity and the Early Middle Ages*. Aldershot: Ashgate, pp. 195–222.

Bowden, W. & Hodges, R. 2011. *Butrint 3: Excavations at the Triconch Palace*. Oxford: Oxbow Books.

Bowden, W. & Hodges, R. 2012. An 'Ice Age settling on the Roman Empire': Post-Roman Butrint Between Strategy and Serendipity. In: N. Christie and A. Augenti, eds. *Urbes Extinctae: Archaeologies of Abandoned Classical Sites*. Aldershot: Scolar Press, pp. 207–41.

Byrne, D. 2009. Archaeological Heritage and Cultural Intimacy: An Interview with Michael Herzfeld. *Journal of Social Anthropology*, 11(2): 144–57.

Carver, R. 1998. *The Accursed Mountains: Journeys in Albania*. London: John Murray.

Chakrabarty, D. 2007. History and the Politics of Recognition. In: K. Jenkins, S. Morgan, and A. Munslow, eds. *Manifestoes for History*. London: Routledge, pp. 77–86.

Comer, D. C. 2006. Ideology, Economics, and Site Management. In: N. Agnew and J. Bridgland, eds. *Of the Past, for the Future: Integrating Archaeology and Conservation*. Los Angeles: Getty Conservation Institute, pp. 23–26.

Comer, D. C. 2012. *Tourism and Archaeological Heritage Management at Petra. Driver to Development or Destruction?* New York: Springer.

Demas, M. 2002. Planning for Conservation and Management of Archaeological Sites: A Values-Based Approach. In: J. M. Teutonico and G. Palumbo, eds. *Management Planning for Archaeological Sites: An International Workshop Organized by the Getty Conservation*. Los Angeles: Getty Conservation Institute, pp. 27–56.

The Economist. 2012. The Heritage Debate: Living Treasure [accessed 2 April 2014]. Available at: <http://www.economist.com/node/21558560>.

Edwards, M. 2008. *Just Another Emperor? The Myths and Realities of Philanthrocapitalism*, London: Demos.

Fagan, B. 2006. Looking Forward, Not Backward: Archaeology and the Future of the Past. In: N. Agnew and J. Bridgland, eds. *Of the Past, for the Future: Integrating Archaeology and Conservation*. Los Angeles: Getty Conservation Institute, pp. 7–12.

Ferguson, N. 2004. *Colossus: The Price of America's Empire*. New York: Penguin.

Fuchs, B. & Baker, D. J. 2004. The Postcolonial Past. *Modern Language Quarterly*, 65(3): 329–40.

Fuga, A. 1998. *L'Albanie entre la pensée totalitaire et la raison fragmentaire*. Paris: L'Harmattan.

Gorica, K. & Paloka, F. 2006. Community-Based Tourism: The Case of the Butrint National Park, South Albania. *Economic Interferences*, 19: 1–8.

Hall, D. R. 1999. Albania: Representations of Place. *The Geographical Journal*, 162(2): 161–72.

Hansen, I. & Hodges, R. 2007. eds. *Roman Butrint Reassessed*. Oxford: Oxbow Books.

Hansen, I., Hodges, R., & Leppard, S. 2012. eds. *Butrint 4: The Archaeology and Histories of an Ionian Town*. Oxford: Oxbow Books.

Hardt, M. & Negri, A. 2000. *Empire*. Cambridge: Cambridge University Press.

Heins, V. 2008. *Nongovernmental Organizations in International Society. Struggles over Recognition*. Basingstoke: Palgrave Macmillan.

Hodder, I. 2009. Mavili's Voice. In: L. Meskell, ed. *Cosmopolitan Archaeologies*. Durham, NC: Duke University Press, pp. 184–204.

Hodges, R., Bowden, W., & Lako, K. 2004. eds. *Byzantine Butrint*. Oxford: Oxbow Books.

Hodges, R. 2006. *Eternal Butrint*. London: Penne publishing.

Hodges, R. 2012a. Excavating Away the 'poison': The Topographic History of Butrint, Ancient Buthrotum. In: I. Hansen, R. Hodges, & S. Leppard, eds. *Butrint 4: The Archaeology and Histories of an Ionian Town*. Oxford: Oxbow Books, pp. 1–21.

Hodges, R. 2012b. Archaeologists as Placemakers: Making the Butrint Natuonal Park. In: I. Hansen, R. Hodges, & S. Leppard, eds. *Butrint 4: The Archaeology and Histories of an Ionian Town*. Oxford: Oxbow Books, pp. 309–22.

Hoxha, E. 1985. Enver Hoxha mbi arkeologjinë historinë e lashtë të Shqipërisë. *Iliria*, 15(1): 29–47.

Joyce, R. 2005. Solid Histories for Fragile Nations: Archaeology as Cultural Patrimony. In: L. Meskell and P. Pels, eds. *Embedding Ethics*. Oxford: Berg, pp. 253–73.

Kaldor, M. 2003. *Global Civil Society: An Answer to War*. Cambridge: Polity.

Lewis, D. & Kanji, N. 2009. *Non-Governmental Organizations and Development*. London: Routledge.

Lipschutz, R. D. 1992. Reconstructing World Politics: The Emergence of Global Civil Society. *Millennium: Journal of International Studies*, 21(3): 389–420.

Mai, N. 2002. Youth NGOs in Albania. In: S. Schwanders-Sieves and B. J. Fischer, eds. *Albanian Identities. Myth and History*. Bloomington: Indiana University Press, pp. 215–25.

Majumdar, R. 2010. *Writing Postcolonial History*. London: Bloomsbury Academic.

Meskell, L. 2012. *Nature of Heritage: The New South Africa*. Malden, MA: Wiley-Blackwell.

Patterson, T. 2008. A Brief History of Postcolonial Theory and Implications for Archaeology. In: M. Liebmann and U. Z. Rizvi, eds. *Archaeology and the Postcolonial Critique*. Lanham: Altamira Press, pp. 21–34.

Pettifer, J. & Vickers, M. 1997. *Albania: From Anarchy to Balkan Identity*. London: Hurst and Company.

Phelps, D. 2010. An Evaluation of Community Development at Butrint National Park, Southern Albania. Unpublished MA thesis, University College London.

Renton, D. 2006. The Butrint Museum: A Long Road Travelled. *Minerva*, 17(2): 23–24.

Said, E. 1994. *Culture and Imperialism*. New York: Vintage Books.

Sen, A. 1999. *Development as Freedom*. New York: Anchor Books.

Serageldin, I. 1999. *Very Special Places. The Architecture and Economics of Intervening in Historic Cities*. Washington, DC: The World Bank.

Sullivan, S. 1992. Special Report: Starting from Below Zero. *Newsweek*. 18 May: 18–19.

United Nations Educational Scientific and Cultural Organization (UNESCO) n.d. Butrint [accessed 2 April 2014]. Available at: <http://whc.UNESCO.org/en/list/570>.

United Nations World Tourism Organization (UNWTO). 2012 [accessed 4 April 2014]. Available at: <http://media.unwto.org/en/press-release/2012-09-12/international-tourism-track-hit-one-billion-end-2012>.

Van der Duim, R. 2007. Tourismscapes. An Actor-Network Perspective. *Annals of Tourism Research*, 34: 961–76.

Vickers, M. 1995. *The Albanians. A Modern History*. London: I. B. Tauris.

Vickers, M. & Pettifer, J. 1997. *From Anarchy to Balkan Identity*. London: I. B. Tauris.

Notes on contributor

Richard Hodges served as Scientific Director of the Butrint Foundation, 1993–2012. He has excavated in Britain, Italy, and Turkey as well as Albania. He has been Director of the British School at Rome, Director of the Prince of Wales's Institute of Architecture, Director of the Institute of World Archaeology, Williams Director of the University of Pennsylvania Museum, and is currently President of the American University of Rome.

Correspondence to: Richard Hodges, American University of Rome, Via Pietro Roselli 4, Rome 00153, Italy. Email: r.hodges@aur.edu

PUBLIC ARCHAEOLOGY, Vol. 13 Nos 1–3, 2014, 30–47

Contemporary Cultural Heritage and Tourism: Development Issues and Emerging Trends

DALLEN J. TIMOTHY

Arizona State University, USA

Cultural heritage is one of the most important and ubiquitous tourism resources in the world, and heritage tourism is one of the most salient forms of tourism today. Many places look to the built environment or other forms of heritage for their socio-economic development through tourism. The development implications of heritage tourism are well established in the research literature. This paper describes the role of cultural heritage in social and economic development and examines several emerging trends in the field of heritage tourism that have salient bearings on destination development. These include the heritage tourism market, heritagization of the everyday past, the value of authenticity, branding heritage places, the spread of cultural routes, intersections between heritage and other forms of tourism, and the heritagization of non-traditional heritage spaces.

KEYWORDS heritagization, economic development, social development, trends, vernacular heritage

Introduction

Every place on the globe has heritage, and many regions have utilized the cultural past as a tool for economic development through tourism. Heritage tourism is one of the most ubiquitous forms of tourism in the world today, and according to some estimates, between 50 and 80 per cent of all domestic and international travel involves some element of culture such as visiting museums and historic sites, enjoying music and arts, or being immersed in the living culture of a destination (Timothy, 2011).

Realizing the enormous economic potential of cultural heritage, countless locations in all parts of the world have rallied to develop and support cultural tourism as an important part of their service economies. Many changes and notable patterns have emerged in recent years in response to the increased attention on cultural heritage. This paper briefly examines heritage tourism as a development tool. It then describes several emerging trends that relate to the socio-economic development role of cultural heritage.

    DOI 10.1179/1465518714Z.00000000052

Heritage tourism and development

Many definitions of heritage have been proposed from a multitude of disciplinary perspectives, but what all definitions agree upon is that heritage is what humankind inherits from the past and utilizes in the present (Graham, et al., 2000; Hall & McArthur, 1998). There are two prominent misunderstandings, however, regarding the meaning of heritage. The first is that something must be old to be heritage. This viewpoint illustrates a lack of understanding about the past as a cultural resource. Wall (1989) reminds us that ruins and ancient monuments were not always old. At some time in the past they were new, but they have gained heritage value by virtue of their age and in some cases their dereliction. There are strong geographical variations in what is old or new, and the concept is relative to history. For example, built heritage in the United States is relatively recent compared to that of Europe, Africa, or South-east Asia. For Americans, eighteenth-century colonial homes in the eastern United States are very old, while the Native American ruins of the south-west are ancient, yet many of these are recent relative to sites in other world regions. Similarly, there is a tendency to favour the ancient past over the modern past for conservation and tourism promotion. For instance, a traditional Navajo dwelling (a hogan) abandoned in the 1970s is usually deemed far less important in socio-economic terms than a native dwelling abandoned four centuries ago (Timothy & Boyd, 2003). Scholars today are beginning to realize that something does not have to be 'old' to be important, for heritage can even be produced from the recent past.

The second common misunderstanding suggests that heritage must be tangible. This, too, is a faulty assumption. Traditions of cultural heritage among the leisure classes of the nineteenth and twentieth centuries focused overwhelmingly on the built environment and elements of material culture (Veblen, 1965), as did some of the Medieval and Early Modern forerunners to modern-day cultural tourism, such as the Grand Tour and Holy Land pilgrimages. However, such a limited view of heritage is no longer acceptable within academic circles or among cultural industry practitioners. Built heritage depicts only one element of the past that is used for tourism and other purposes in the modern day. Intangible heritage, such as music, language, dance, religion, folklore, art forms, traditional knowledge, gastronomical traditions, social relations, rituals, hunting methods, and ceremonies, is now rightfully recognized as being worthy of conservation and tourism promotion (Smith & Akagawa, 2009; Stefano, et al., 2012; Vaz da Silva, 2008). In some places, such as Australia and many Pacific islands, few, if any, tangible remains of the indigenous past exist, leaving intangible culture the most prominent form of heritage. UNESCO's recent recognition of this and its development of an intangible heritage list has led to an increasing awareness of the need to protect immaterial elements of the cultural past (UNESCO, 2013a). While music, dance, and other forms of intangible patrimony have long been consumed by tourists and marketed in tourist destinations, only recently have scholars and industry observers begun to recognize it as an important part of the conservable heritage product (Smith & Akagawa, 2009; Stefano, et al., 2012).

Development

There are many different ways of thinking about 'development'. From a global quality of life viewpoint it includes health care, education, access to clean water, and other indicators. From a tourism perspective, the concept varies from place to place. In less affluent countries, development is usually seen only in direct economic terms, so that places earning a great deal of money from tourism are considered more 'developed' than those that do not. In these situations, personal and regional incomes often determine the level of development. From a heritage perspective, it is difficult to encourage residents, politicians, and other stakeholders to look beyond the fiscal potential to appreciate heritage for its intrinsic values. It is, in effect, very hard to require heritage conservation beyond tourism for its aesthetic, scientific, or educative value when people's basic survival is in jeopardy. Conservation for the sake of conservation is unheard of and nearly always requires an economic rationale (Timothy & Nyaupane, 2009).

Developed, Western societies tend to be more open to alternative definitions of development. Quality of life, which includes economic stability but also things like free time, human rights, freedom of travel, freedom of speech, education, and health care, entails much more than simply putting food on the table. In many Western societies, quality of life is valued very highly, sometimes more than monetary wealth (Budruk & Phillips, 2011).

Regardless of where tourism grows, it is often seen as an economic panacea for communities and regions, and most places in the world have a fervent desire to utilize it as a development tool. Since all places have heritage, some with sites of international acclaim and potential for widespread appeal, heritage tourism is a natural focus for many places in their development efforts. Even destinations that have traditionally eschewed cultural heritage tourism (e.g. most Caribbean islands) in favour of a 'sun, sea and sand' product, have recently begun emphasizing their living culture and built heritage as a viable new resource (Cameron & Gatewood, 2008; Jordan & Jolliffe, 2013). Some destinations, which lack other opportunities, rely almost solely on cultural heritage for their tourism industries. Countries such as Georgia and Armenia, while endowed with remarkable natural environments, rely a great deal on their religious built heritage and other cultural resources for tourism (Metreveli & Timothy, 2010). Likewise, Egypt and Israel have long focused nearly all tourism promotional efforts on their ancient built heritages.

From both socio-political and economic development perspectives, cultural heritage-based tourism is commonly targeted as a leading development tool. Tourism is labour-intensive, brings in foreign exchange earnings, and raises tax revenues. Heritage tourism in particular plays an important role in justifying the relevance of archaeological digs, museums, interpretive centres and other cultural establishments. Despite its noteworthy negative socio-cultural and ecological impacts (Timothy & Nyaupane, 2009; Wall & Mathieson, 2006), heritage tourism can play an important role in conserving the human heritage of places by funding conservation efforts and providing a rationale for establishing parks and other protected heritage areas.

In many cases, long-time heritage destinations have been the mainstay of tourism's focus. Historic cities such as Rome, Paris, Beijing, Boston, and London are good examples. These well-established destinations have benefited from their notoriety. Despite the importance of traditional historic sites as heritage destinations, tides are changing as more and more places without world famous heritages desire to become involved in tourism as a medium for socio-economic development. In addition, tourists' tastes are changing (Novelli, 2005; Poon, 1994). People are becoming more sophisticated in their interests and are less accepting of the heretofore 'McDonald-ized', or standardized and predictable experiences afforded by most traditional tour-istic encounters (Ritzer, 2002; Smart, 1999). As consumers become more educated and discerning in their choices of leisure pursuits, they are demanding more realistic and accurate portrayals of the past, different heritage products to what was offered before, and more experience-oriented outcomes. More accurate portrayals of the past are illustrated in the United States by the increasing visibility of slaves in the heritage narrative of the southern states. Whereas the interpretation and presentation of historic sites, including plantations, were once dominated by white people's stories, they are becoming more balanced and truthful in their depictions of the lives and sufferings of the slave populations (Alderman & Campbell, 2008; Butler, 2001; Buzinde & Santos, 2009).

Industry stakeholders and academic researchers have begun to accept these changes and are identifying forms of heritage and trends in tourism that are broadening the appeal of this cultural subsector (Bartlett, 2001). All forms of heritage can be seen as resources for tourism and have potential socio-economic implications for destination communities that can contribute significantly to their economic, social, political, and psychological empowerment (Scheyvens, 2002).

Trends in cultural heritage-based tourism development

While there are many new and emerging trends in the realm of heritage/cultural tour-ism, the remainder of this paper highlights and describes only a few of the more prominent ones, including heritage demand as a niche market, heritagization of the ordinary past, the marketability of authenticity, heritage branding, cultural trails, heritage and other types of tourism, and non-traditional heritage spaces. Each of these has an important place in the socio-economic development of heritage destinations, and each one is examined briefly in the sections that follow.

Heritage tourists as a niche market

In the 1980s, researchers began examining the demographic characteristics, motives, and experiences of people who visit historic sites and museums and found some common patterns (Herbert, et al., 1989). These patterns include higher education levels, and higher incomes than the general traveling population. They also have a propensity to stay in the destination longer than non-heritage tourists and are slightly older in average age (Prentice, 1989a). Some observers have suggested that different nationalities seek different heritage experiences, with Europeans tending to be more perspicacious about World Heritage Sites than other travelling nationalities, and Chinese tending to desire cultural experiences at the growing number of 'ethnic theme parks' in China (Di Giovine, 2009; Li, 2011). Contemporary researchers have moved beyond these more normative and descriptive accounts of heritage demand to include more experiential depth and outcomes of visiting. Yet, heritage consumers as a niche tourism market have yet to be explored by their motivations and experiences.

One useful way of understanding the general demand for cultural heritage is the level of interest of visitors and how that translates into their motives for visiting.

Stebbins (1996) outlined two extremes of interest among cultural heritage consumers: serious and casual. On one end of the spectrum, serious heritage visitors are enthusiastic about visiting cultural sites, events, and regions. For many, learning about the past is an important hobby. They intend to learn something new, and they seek opportunities to visit historic places whenever possible. On the other end of the spectrum are casual heritage consumers who do not necessarily seek heritage experiences before their visit, but might take advantage of cultural attractions once they arrive at their destination. Many of their heritage experiences are happenstance, and seeing local cultures and sites may simply be a way of using up extra time. According to Stebbins, there are many different levels of devotion to heritage between these two ends of the continuum. Each of these groups has its own impacts in historic locations; serious heritage tourists are more willing to spend more money on entrance fees (Prentice, 1989b), and the general assumption is that they respect the built environment more than casual visitors do. As a result, they are typically thought to effect fewer negative impacts since learning is their primary goal, which according to Tilden (1977), ought to result in more respect for the places they visit.

Another way of viewing the market for cultural heritage is scale of the resource being visited in terms of connection to the visitor and the level of demand (Timothy, 1997). At the highest scale are attractions of truly global proportions. Many of these can be found on UNESCO's World Heritage List, although some have not been designated. Nonetheless, they are world-renowned 'anchor' attractions that draw large masses of people every year from the local vicinity and from all over the globe. Stonehenge, the Egyptian Pyramids, the Eiffel Tower, Beijing's Forbidden City, and Hadrian's Wall are a few examples of global attractions. On a lesser scale, but very important for tourism, are national-level heritage attractions. These might also catch international tourist attention, but their primary market is domestic tourists who visit for nationalistic or related heritage reasons. Such attractions are typically associated with civil wars, founding pioneers, national development, national cemeteries, and other such places that exude a patriotic appeal and which people have learned about since their days at school. For many domestic tourists, visits to these sites take on a quasi-spiritual nature, resulting in what some experts have termed 'secular pilgrimages' (Digance, 2006; Hyde & Harman, 2011).

The next level down is local heritage, which may or may not appeal to domestic tourists or international travellers, but the primary market for this patrimony are local residents and regional visitors who visit on day trips or stop by in conjunction with outings to other attractions, such as amusement parks, sporting events, or national heritage sites. Local heritage typically includes parks, monuments, museums, churches, schools, and other marked attractions that have helped define a place's historical identity.

The lowest scale of heritage, personal heritage, is the hardest to measure in terms of its economic implications and tourism reach and the least understood by scholars. Personal heritage tourism involves travel to experience sites, locations, people and events associated with one's own personal or familial past. Ancestral homelands are important destinations for these tourists. Common activities include doing genealogical research, visiting cemeteries and churches, meeting distant relatives, attending clan gatherings, and eating local foods. Most people who travel to their ancestral homelands are searching for something within themselves; the places they visit and the activities they undertake help them feel rooted in their own places (Basu, 2005; Lowenthal, 1996; Meethan, 2004), but they also help connect with their forebears. Some people describe these experiences as highly spiritual and extremely meaningful (Timothy, 2008).

The 'heritagization' of the everyday past

For centuries, the focus of conservation, interpretation, and tourism commercialization of cultural resources has been the lavish and stately features of the built environment that have national and global appeal. Castles, palaces, cathedrals, government edifices, fortresses, ancient monuments, and other imposing elements of the built environment have long been the mainstay of heritage tourism. Since the ancient days of human mobility, people have desired to see the wonders of the world. In the modern era, the Great Wall of China, Machu Picchu, the Egyptian Pyramids, the cathedrals and castles of Europe, and centres of government are high on many people's lists of 'things to see before they die'. Heritage destinations have long relied on the iconic images of such internationally renowned sites to entice tourists, but there are signs of change from the market, causing the supply of heritage presentation of heritage attractions to evolve as well.

As travelling consumers become more sophisticated, better educated, and more dissatisfied with traditional attractions on the beaten tourist path, the heritage product is expanding to include features that were not heretofore considered attractive to mass tourists. This includes elements such as farm buildings, rural cemeteries, fisheries, and derelict industrial landscapes. Thus, we are seeing an evolution wherein travellers still desire to see the grandiose built heritage, but they also want to consume more balanced, accurate, inclusive, and less sanitized versions of the past that reveal how ordinary people managed to survive, not just how the aristocracy lived (Timothy, 2011; Timothy & Boyd, 2006). In short, they want a more accurate portrayal of the past, 'warts and all' (Hardy, 1988; Hewison, 1987). While there are only a few empirical studies that examine this phenomenon of the 'heritage of the ordinary' or the 'heritagization of the vernacular past', there are a number of trends and studies that point in this direction.

One manifestation of democratized vernacular heritage is the increasing prominence of certain elements of 'dark' attractions. Dark heritage places (e.g. battlefields, disaster sites, prisons, slave quarters, and concentration camps) have long been attractions but only recently recognized as key tools in depicting the past of minorities and the imprisoned (Ashworth & Hartmann, 2005; Lennon & Foley, 2000). The increased emphasis on the 'marginalized' peoples of the past, such as indigenous groups in colonial societies, or slaves in the North American context, is one manifestation of this changing heritage landscape and narrative. Cemeteries are seen as places of death and commemoration but also places of peace and solitude. They are replete with stories of individuals who experienced a wide range of deaths, both peaceful and violent. With the exception of a few famous graveyards, cemeteries have until now been almost ignored by tourists as heritage attractions, despite their abundance of historical information and ability to contextualize the past.

Rural landscapes, villages, and the 'peasant' past are now well established as important attractions for tourism. These settings allow visitors to learn about and appreciate what life was like for peasants and commoners — a much different per-spective to the bygone emphasis on the patrimony of the social elites. In this regard, the mundane environment is no longer seen as boring. Barns, fences and fields, rural schools and churches, dwellings, and agricultural patterns and practices are part of a larger narrative that provides a more comprehensive glimpse into the human past (Carr, 2008; Timothy, 2011).

Similar trends of the ordinary heritage include agritourism, where people learn about and participate in traditional farming practices and processes (Sznajder, et al., 2009). As well, the material and non-material culture of native peoples is an increas-ingly important part of the heritage product, including indigenous knowledge, music, family relations, religious beliefs, folklore, and hunting practices (Butler & Hinch, 2007). Cuisine and 'foodways' are also heritage because they reflect cultural values and practices, historic recipes, eating habits, human struggles with nature, and realities of geography. Cultural identities are intimately intertwined with regional cuisines that help formulate pride, build nationalism, and maintain ethnic identities (Holtzman, 2006; Pilcher, 1996; Tellström, et al., 2006; Timothy & Ron, 2013). Cuisine, particularly that associated with ethnic foods in tourist destinations, is becoming an ever more important part of the cultural heritage experience. These and many other vernacular cultural resources reflect a shift toward more balanced views of heritage and a heritagization of the ordinary cultural landscape.

Authenticity sells

The notion of 'authenticity' in cultural tourism experiences has received considerable attention since the 1960s, with MacCannell (1973) arguing that tourists seek authen-tic experiences and places but are usually fooled into consuming experiences that are contrived or staged, unbeknownst to the traveller. Thus, owing to their inexperience, they participate in fake events and see simulated places without knowing the differ-ence. As early as 1961, Boorstin argued that people travel to enjoy themselves, whether or not their experiences with the past are authentic. Tourists are, in Boorstin's think-ing, unable to differentiate between genuine events, artefacts, or places, and are quite content visiting prefabricated places and contrived experiences. The later writings of Urry (1995) propose that 'post-tourists' are in fact able to distinguish between fake and real experiences, but they care little about the distinction. Many people pursue encounters with pretend, staged places, such as Las Vegas or Disneyland, because their sole desire is to enjoy themselves rather than learn or soak in the true identity of any locale. In Urry's view, travellers have a choice, and while many elect to visit a place for its meaningful heritage, others select their destinations for their entertainment value.

The conceptual debate has in recent years gone in a different direction. Of princi-pal concern is the meaning of authenticity and how different people perceive it in their experiences. Many scholars have examined a wide range of authenticity issues as regards places and visitor experiences (e.g. Chhabra, 2007; Chhabra, et al., 2003; Cohen, 1979). Reisinger and Steiner (2006) point out three ways of viewing the authenticity of heritage settings: objectivism/realism, constructivism, and postmod-ernism. Objective authenticity suggests that places, events, artefacts, and sites can be verified genuine and that authenticity can be measured impartially and verified empirically. There has been a great deal of work in recent years to deconstruct the intrinsic attributes of material culture and intangible heritage in an effort to evaluate their genuineness against established measures of reality, such as traditional building materials, absolute location, indigenous crafters, original colours, accurate time-frames, and 'official' certifications of authenticity (e.g. Littrell, et al., 1993).

The constructionist perspective intimates that authenticity is not objective; rather, it is subjective and idiosyncratic. According to this line of thinking, the past and its relics mean different things to different people, and authenticity is negotiable. Thus, authenticity is not inherent in heritage. It is constructed by each individual user based on his or her own life experiences or personal relationship to the site being visited (Jamal & Hill, 2004; Timothy, 2011). This perspective also suggests that multiple authenticities can exist, with whatever the current site management or political regime desires to be identified as 'real' until the next administrator re-orients the story to suit the needs of those in power. Timothy and Boyd (2003) hinted at this perspective in suggesting that bona fide heritage may be distorted through the 'sanitization' or idealization of the past, cultural imposters, authentic relativism, and unknown facts of history. As well, new heritages are often created to look or feel original, creating objectively inauthentic, subjectively authentic spaces that appeal to cultural tourists and others.

Postmodernist outlooks suggest, as Urry (1995) and Ritzer and Liska (1997) do, that most visitors care little about whether or not a place, event, or work of art is authentic. To these post-tourists (Urry, 1995) authenticity is always suspect, irrelevant to having fun, and unnecessary for a satisfying experience.

Regardless of whether authenticity at a heritage attraction can be substantiated objectively, or seen by visitors as authentic in a more existential way, authenticity has become a buzzword of the twenty-first century. In the spirit of marketing, authenticity sells. Chhabra (2010) found that authenticity is important in how people enjoy and are satisfied by their heritage visits. Genuine, authentic, original, and other related words are often used in promoting heritage objects and places. Countless online ads and brochures promote 'authentic places', and 'genuine experiences', reflecting people's desires, as MacCannell (1976) argues, to seek out real heritage experiences in time and place. From a material culture perspective, many souvenir vendors today sell products that are marked as authentic — one of Littrell et al.'s (1993) markers of objective authenticity — with the use of authenticity certificates and photos of the artisan attached to the artwork. These are important indications of authenticity, which adds value to the crafts and renders them more sellable. An anecdotal experience helps to illustrate this concept well. On a recent stop at a Navajo trading post in Arizona, USA, the author observed a basketful of rugs made with South-western Native designs. Hanging above the rugs, a small hand-written sign read: 'authentic Indian rugs, only $10'. Upon closer inspection, however, the tag revealed that the inexpensive rugs were 'Made in India'. Most certainly these were 'authentic Indian rugs' sold by American Natives with stereotypical South-western designs. The perceived added value of authenticity was clear in this commercial setting.

Heritage branding

At the time of writing, there were 759 cultural sites and twenty-nine mixed natural and cultural sites on UNESCO's World Heritage List (UNESCO, 2013b). Several countries have listed numerous sites (e.g. China, Mexico, Italy, and France), with many more on the tentative list. There is a common perception, particularly in the developing world, that World Heritage List inscription will naturally result in tourism growth. There is even limited evidence to suggest that in some cases it does (Yang, et al., 2009), although, as Frey and Steiner (2011) clarify, the most notable increases after UNESCO listing occur at less-established and lesser-known heritage sites. For well-established locations that were already significant tourist attractions, there tends to be no notable increase in visitors after World Heritage List inscription (Buckley, 2004; Cellini, 2010). Thus, popular attractions remain popular, while lesser-known sites may or may not receive a boost in tourists after World Heritage List inscription, depending on whether or not they were previously known or physically accessible to increasing demand. Contrary to popular belief, a number of scholars have argued that being registered on the World Heritage List does not, in fact, by default increase tourist arrivals (Buckley, 2004; Cellini, 2010; Hall & Piggin, 2001; 2003), and according to van der Aa, et al. (2004), an increase in visitation might not even be desirable in some locations where tourist crowds already overburden the local environment.

Regardless of the debate and research findings for or against the effects of the World Heritage List on tourism, the potential for increased tourism (in conjunction with conservation) causes many countries to create lengthy inventories of cultural and natural sites for consideration by the International Council On Monuments and Sites (ICOMOS) and UNESCO. The reason for this is the increasingly visible brand associated with UNESCO (Dewar, et al., 2012; Hall & Piggin, 2003; Leask & Fyall, 2006; Poria, et al., 2011). To be 'branded' by this organization deems a country's patrimony universally valuable and important enough to be recognized as a pre-eminent example of human heritage. It thus adds status, sanctity, and appeal to particular sites — all characteristics that have potential economic value.

Similar examples exist at the national level. In the United States, for instance, there are more than 80,000 cultural properties on the National Register of Historic Places — a list maintained by the US National Park Service (NPS) of historic buildings, sites, and objects that comprise important elements of America's historic resources. The National Historic Landmarks Program is similar in that it is operated by the NPS and designates nearly 2500 historic places as National Historic Landmarks (NHLs). These are defined as nationally significant places of 'exceptional value or quality in illustrating or interpreting the heritage of the United States' (NPS, 2012).

Like the UNESCO example above, these two designations in the United States are meant to assist communities in the preservation or conservation of their heritage. However, they also have brand value for tourism (Page & Mason, 2004). Almost every county in the United States has at least one property on the National Register, and many communities are petitioning the NPS to include their cultural assets in the NHL Program. The importance of these brands was illustrated in 2004 in Tombstone, Arizona, when the NPS threatened to revoke the community's NHL status owing to inauthentic representations, such as non-period building materials, inaccurate dates on buildings, and over-commercialization (Martens & Timothy, 2006). According to the NPS, many buildings not only depicted inaccurate construction dates but were repaired or altered with plans and materials 'that didn't have any basis in history'

(Pollack, 2005). Tombstone was unique in that most of the approximately ninety 'threatened' NHLs are considered threatened 'because of deterioration, not decoration' (Pollack, 2005). With the looming threat of negative press in the US and abroad and decreased tourism as a result, community leaders and business owners began the 're-authentification' process. As a result, the town was upgraded from threatened to 'watch' status in 2006. Tombstone and its building owners had until 2007 to comply with NPS requirements to invest in restoration efforts to make the buildings more authentic of the period it aimed to represent. As of 2012, restoration efforts have effectively returned many buildings and streetscapes to those appropriate for the period of historic significance (1880–1931). However, Tombstone remains under the 'watchful eye' of the NPS and Arizona state preservation agencies to ensure that progress continues (NPS, 2012).

Heritage trails and cultural routes

Wall (1997) proposed a threefold spatial typology of forms of tourist attractions (points, areas, and lines) that help in understanding a site's physical characteristics and developing the commercial aspects of heritage sites. Points are characterized by high concentrations of people in a small space, who come to enjoy a single resource or collection of resources. Examples include museums, churches, monuments, and waterfalls. Small towns, historic city centres, and national parks are examples of area attractions, which are often comprised of several point attractions that become nodes in a broader attraction area. The final spatial arrangement is lines, or linear resources and corridors. These include attractions with linear properties, such as rivers and coastlines, but also include sets of nodes and points that are connected along themed corridors, such as trails or transportation routes.

Academic research has revealed a lot about the characteristics of points and areas and the ways in which tourism impacts these types of locations. Thousands of studies have been done on individual heritage attractions (points) and even heritage areas, such as Angkor Wat, Machu Picchu, and various museums (e.g. Larson & Poudyal, 2012; Prentice, et al., 1998; Wager, 1995), but we know little about the supply and demand dynamics of heritage trails, cultural routes, and scenic corridors, which have properties unique from other types of attractions. They link individual sites together to promote a common heritage theme, and they provide a connected critical mass of similar cultural sites, rather than each point functioning in isolation of others. From a management perspective, they help spread the benefits of tourism (e.g. jobs, taxes, regional income) to a wider range of communities or businesses (depending on scale) and can help alleviate tourism pressures on individual sites (Timothy & Boyd, 2015).

From a supply perspective, there are many types of heritage trails and routes, depending on the nature of the resource and the type of experience being sought by their users. Scale is critical in this context as well, for trails range from small walks in city parks or archaeological sites to citywide trails (e.g. the Boston Trail), national trails (e.g. Hadrian's Wall Path), and multi-nation, long-distance routes (e.g. the Silk Road and the Way of St James). These trails are a critical part of the tourism product in destinations and regions and are often marketed as such: Hadrian's Wall Path was designated a national trail in England with important tourism implications

(National Trails, 2013), and Spain's official tourism promotional website emphasizes that the Way of St James is 'a thrilling route through northern Spain', where visitors can 'discover a wealth of monuments, charming towns and villages, spectacular natural attractions' (Turespaña, 2013).

Besides their linear forms, what these all have in common is their focus on many divergent aspects of cultural heritage, including religion and spirituality, immigrant societies, slavery, mining and manufacturing, art, transportation innovations, explorers, wine and agriculture, architectural styles, and many more. Some cultural routes originated and developed organically as an historic corridor, such as explorer routes or pilgrim trails. Trails of a more recent vintage are purposely devised to link comparable attractions together into themed routes that appeal to people interested in a specific historic topic. Literary trails, such as the Catherine Cookson Trail in Northeast England, link locales associated with the lives of famous authors and the places depicted in their writings. Similarly, food trails, whiskey or ale trails, and wine routes connect producers, processors, and sellers of cuisine, viticultural, or agricultural heritage, just as industrial routes create networks between sites of industrial archaeology and resource extraction (e.g. Otago Goldfields Heritage Trail, New Zealand, and the Iron Road in Central Europe) (EICR, 2013; Frost, 2005).

As destinations begin to look for alternatives to traditional mass tourism, themed routes have become a more commonplace focus for promotion and marketing. Perhaps the most salient appeal of heritage trails, besides their dispersion of benefits and costs, is their ability to link individual sites together into marketable and manageable destinations that promote knowledge about specific people, places, objects and events in history (Timothy & Boyd, 2015).

The intersection of heritage with other forms of tourism

Categorizing tourism into discernible types is an important exercise both for practitioners and academics, as it makes marketing and researching tourism more precise. Researchers define forms of tourism from supply and demand perspectives, based upon the type of attraction or resource being visited and people's motives for visiting. As a result, many different types of tourism have been identified, including volunteer tourism, sport tourism, shopping tourism, religious tourism, agritourism, and many others. One issue that is not well understood is the relationship between heritage and other types of tourism. While we know that there is a great deal of overlap between these types, the intricacies of heritage from a sport, volunteer, religious, shopping, or agricultural perspective have yet to be the focus of much study.

Nevertheless, we are beginning to see that shopping relates closely to heritage, the relationships ranging from people purchasing heritage while on holiday (i.e. artefacts and antiques) to empirical evidence that heritage tourists tend to be more enthusiastic spenders than other types of visitors (Timothy, 2011). Sport tourists may also be considered heritage tourists in that they participate in or follow sports and games, which are intangible heritage, and visit historic stadiums (Ramshaw & Gammon, 2010). Some volunteer travel is heavily involved in heritage, such as that associated with work in museums, national parks, and archaeological digs. The farming heritage of an area forms the very foundation of agritourism; picking pineapples in Hawaii, visiting a kiwi farm in New Zealand, or touring a tea plantation in Sri Lanka are all heritage activities based upon those regions' agricultural past. Likewise, religious tourism is based upon pilgrims' desires to visit holy places, venerate deity, or seek forgiveness and healing. The faith traditions they espouse, the sacrosanct sites they visit, and the rituals they undertake are all part of intangible and tangible spiritual heritage.

Non-traditional heritage spaces

As already noted, heritage is everywhere, which has been a problem in some places, such as India, Israel, and Greece, where cultural sites and artefacts are so plentiful there are not enough public funds or human resources to protect and promote them all. In these cases, decision-makers must select which heritage elements will be marketed and which will be ignored. Cities are best known for historic buildings, industrial archaeology, museums, and parks, which lend considerable tourist appeal to the urban milieu. The countryside is commonly enjoyed for its rural landscapes, archaeological sites, historic villages, and farmsteads. There are, however, other spatial contexts that have rarely been considered by heritage scholars because they are interstitial spaces that lie 'in between' normative locations where heritage has always been rooted and identities connected with concrete place-bound histories. Two of the best examples of interstitial spaces, or non-places, which have been largely ignored by tourism scholars are international borders and transportation hubs (e.g. airports, railway stations, bus depots) (Adey, 2006; Wood, 2003). Both are points of transit and therefore not an origin or destination, rendering them essentially deterritorialized spaces with little heritage appeal or cultural identity of their own. These placeless loci of transit are thus ephemeral in nature, and people's experiences with them are fleeting and forgettable (Timothy, 2001).

These interstitial spaces are starting to be recognized as venues for sharing heritage, even if it is displaced from elsewhere. A good example of this is the establishment of museums inside of airport transit spaces and at train and bus stations in the United States. The *Legacy of a Dream* exhibit, complete with artefacts and stories, at Hartsfield-Jackson Atlanta International Airport commemorates the legacy of Martin Luther King, Jr, and the Civil Rights Movement in the US. Sky Harbor International Airport, in Phoenix, Arizona, is home to the Phoenix Airport Museum, which displays and interprets art and wildlife of the desert, as well as Native American material culture. Similarly, films portraying the natural and cultural heritage of Iceland are available in sound theatres at the country's Keflavik International Airport transit area. Such exhibitions are useful marketing tools for the surrounding region, and they provide an educational and entertaining pastime for transit passengers. Even the light rail stops in Phoenix are adorned with sculptures by local artisans and historic photo displays with interpretive media to focus the attention of urban rail passengers.

Like airports, the placelessness of borders is often overlooked by tourists and tourism scholars. Nonetheless, borderlands are in many cases significant tourist destinations for drinking, gambling, shopping and prostitution, or because they are themselves interesting anomalies in the cultural landscape (Timothy, 2001). These elements, together, comprise the 'heritage of tourism' in many border communities. In addition, how borders were formed, be it through war, accession, or accretion, is an important part of the history of border regions, and many borderlines and their demarcations have become historic markers as well (Jones, 1988; Pelkmans, 2012). Frontier regions and border towns in Europe and North America now realize the potential of tourism to help boost their local economies. This has resulted in the establishment of growing numbers of border and border-related museums and historic sites, including the Grænselandsmuseet in Denmark, only a few metres from the border with Germany, more than twenty Grenzmuseums near the former East–West Germany divide, the Chamizal National Memorial (US–Mexico), and the tiny Douane-Controlehuis Museum, just inside the Netherlands at Vaals.

Conclusion

With the development potential of cultural heritage through tourism, communities and their stakeholders are becoming more accepting of tourism as a means to an end. Even heritage curators, religious organizations, and others who have heretofore at least minimally loathed the idea of tourism at their sacrosanct sites, are now becoming more open to the potential of tourism to assist in community development efforts. As well, many of these same heritage stewards, including museum managers and archaeologists, realize that tourism provides an increasingly important justification for their discovery and conservation endeavours. These changing attitudes, together with shifts in the market in terms of people's expectations and desires have led to a number of interesting trends in how heritage tourism is developing.

Scholars and industry professionals now realize that the market for cultural heritage is not a homogenous group of indistinguishable consumers. While segmenting tourist markets has been a long-time exercise on the business side of tourism studies, it has only recently become the norm in examining demand for cultural heritage. As well, simplistic ways of segmenting the market psychographically (e.g. travel motives and behaviours), geographically, or demographically are inadequate for understanding the depth and breadth of experiences at cultural attractions. Other factors must necessarily come into play, including scale of resource and individual desires and level of determination to visit heritage places. By understanding heritage consumers as a unique market, tourist destinations and cultural properties can more effectively provide educational and impactful experiences. These can translate not only into satisfied customers who may return, but also from an economic development perspective, can increase visitors' likelihood of supporting conservation efforts and making a fiscal impact in the host community. Understanding the market can also help with social development wherein people's cultural or national identities are strengthened and community solidarity is fortified as visitors experience elements of a common past and collective values. This is evident among immigrant or diaspora communities (Basu, 2007; Meethan, 2004), but is likely to be found in many market contexts. Social development also entails visitors becoming more mindful of the past and appreciating heritages beyond their own.

With people's shifting interests in the cultural past, they are now demanding more historically accurate and inclusive interpretations of the past and have a widened desire to see more vernacular of everyday life, rather than principally an aristocratic patrimony. This means that more destinations will be able to capitalize on their heritage. Small towns that have long boasted a historic jail, an interesting barn and silo architectural style, or a small motel where a famous celebrity slept are now seeing nascent potential for economic growth. While most small historic sites alone are not enough to draw large crowds of visitors, in collaboration with other similar communities or larger anchor attractions linked together in cultural routes or tourist trails, the benefits of tourism can reach towns and villages that have long been ignored by most tourist itineraries.

Branding is an important concept in selling tourist destinations. This can be done by being listed consistently in travel guidebooks, such as *Frommer's* or *Lonely Planet*, and in myriad other ways. Tourist destinations and individual service providers (e.g. hotels, restaurants, attractions, and taxi companies) vie for exposure and 'branding' in these famous guides. Countries and regions that are home to cultural heritage look at their resources in much the same way. UNESCO is the most salient worldwide brand for heritage places and is being tapped competitively by the majority of countries to help them 'brand' their heritage, so that it will receive broader international recognition and hopefully tourism. UNESCO's World Heritage List and other national registers are commonly sought by heritage site managers and national governments, not only for the potential benefit for conservation but also as a mechanism to help them meet their economic development goals.

Authenticity is another branding mechanism. Tourist destinations and attractions often label, or brand, their products 'authentic' or 'genuine' to lend credence to their claims of originality, to attract attention, and increase sales. Many tourists are becoming more concerned about value for money, and growing numbers of tourists are willing to pay more for what they consider to be more authentic experiences. Thus we may talk of the importance of 'perceived authenticity'. For some people, authenticity is irrelevant to their experience, while for others it is the core of their experience. As such, site managers, crafters, and destination leaders realize that authenticity has potential to bring in additional foreign exchange and even create additional jobs for indigenous crafters who understand the heritage behind the arts, interpreters who can provide more realistic portrayals of the past, and curators who can verify more accurately that events and places are realistic and legitimate.

Heritage pervades many other forms of tourism. Destinations are able to capitalize on this overlap to suggest that many other types of tourism can also be considered forms of heritage tourism given the heritage value of the resources being used. While this is an unusual way of viewing sport tourism, volunteer tourism, agritourism, ecotourism, and others, co-branding these as forms of heritage tourism can broaden their appeal to wider market segments.

Finally, spaces that have long been seen as non-places, or in-between places, are now more commonly used as locales of heritage. Interstitial spaces such as airports and borders not only have unique heritages of their own, local tourism promoters now actively use these spaces for educating and inducing captive audiences who utilize transit spaces during their travels. There is little doubt that these kinds of efforts will continue into the future and become even more prominent for purposes of marketing, authenticating, preserving, and educating passers-by who might not consider an airport stopover or a border crossing as actually having been somewhere. Museums and cultural displays can help make these deterritorialized spaces into real places for tourism.

Heritage tourism is clearly an important mechanism for boosting the economies of many tourist destinations throughout the world. It is in no way, however, a panacea for all development-related problems. Traditional forms of mass tourism are no longer adequate for sustainable economic development. As the trends and issues highlighted throughout this paper illustrate, alternative forms of tourism, such as heritage tourism, are vitally important in allowing places to diversify their products, expand their tourism supply, and tap into markets that are driven to appreciate the human past in tourist destinations.

Bibliography

Adey, P. 2006. Airports and Air-Mindedness: Spacing, Timing and Using the Liverpool Airport, 1929–1939. *Social and Cultural Geography*, 7(3): 343–63.

Alderman, D. H. & Campbell, R. M. 2008. Symbolic Excavation and the Artifact Politics of Remembering Slavery in the American South: Observations from Walterboro, South Carolina. *Southeastern Geographer*, 48(3): 338–55.

Ashworth, G. J. & Hartmann, R. 2005. *Horror and Human Tragedy Revisited: The Management of Sites of Atrocities for Tourism*. New York: Cognizant.

Bartlett, T. 2001. Virginia Develops African-American Tourism Sites. *Travel Weekly*, 4 June: 16.

Basu, P. 2005. Pilgrims to the Far Country: North American 'roots-tourists' in the Scottish Highlands and Islands. In: C. Ray, ed. *Transatlantic Scots*. Tuscaloosa, AL: University of Alabama Press, pp. 286–317.

Basu, P. 2007. *Highland Homecomings: Genealogy and Heritage Tourism in the Scottish Diaspora*. Abingdon, UK: Routledge.

Boorstin, D. 1961. *The Image: A Guide to Pseudo-Events in America*. New York: Harper and Row.

Buckley, R. 2004. The Effects of World Heritage Listing on Tourism to Australian National Parks. *Journal of Sustainable Tourism*, 12(1): 70–84.

Budruk, M. & Phillips, R. eds. 2011. *Quality-of-Life Community Indicators for Parks, Recreation and Tourism Management*. London: Springer.

Butler, D. L. 2001. Whitewashing Plantations: The Commodification of a Slave-Free Antebellum South. *International Journal of Hospitality and Tourism Administration*, 2(3/4): 163–75.

Butler, R. W. & Hinch, T. 2007. *Tourism and Indigenous Peoples: Issues and Implications*. Oxford: Butterworth Heinemann.

Buzinde, C. N. & Santos, C. A. 2009. Interpreting Slavery Tourism. *Annals of Tourism Research*, 36(3): 439–58.

Cameron, C. M. & Gatewood, J. B. 2008. Beyond Sun, Sand and Sea: The Emergent Tourism Programme in the Turks and Caicos Islands. *Journal of Heritage Tourism*, 3(1): 55–73.

Carr, A. 2008. Cultural Landscape Values as a Heritage Tourism Resource. In: B. Prideaux, D. J. Timothy, and K. S. Chon, eds. *Cultural and Heritage Tourism in Asia and the Pacific*. London: Routledge, pp. 35–48.

Cellini, R. 2010. Is UNESCO Recognition Effective in Fostering Tourism? A Comment on Yang, Lin and Han. *Tourism Management*, 32: 452–54.

Chhabra, D. 2007. Exploring Market Influences on Curator Perceptions of Authenticity. *Journal of Heritage Tourism*, 2(2): 110–19.

Chhabra, D. 2010. Branding Authenticity. *Tourism Analysis*, 15(6): 735–40.

Chhabra, D., Healy, R., & Sills, E. 2003. Staged Authenticity in Heritage Tourism. *Annals of Tourism Research*, 35: 427–47.

Cohen, E. 1979. Rethinking the Sociology of Tourism. *Annals of Tourism Research*, 6: 18–35.

Dewar, K., du Cros, H., & Li, W. 2012. The Search for World Heritage Brand Awareness Beyond The Iconic Heritage: A Case Study of the Historic Centre of Macao. *Journal of Heritage Tourism*, 7(4): 323–39.

Digance, J. 2006. Religious and Secular Pilgrimage: Journeys Redolent with Meaning. In: D. J. Timothy and D. H. Olsen, eds. *Tourism, Religion and Spiritual Journeys*. London: Routledge, pp. 36–48.

Di Giovine, M. A. 2009. *The Heritage-Scape: UNESCO, World Heritage and Tourism*. Lanham, MD: Lexington Books.

European Institute of Cultural Routes (EICR). 2013. European Routes of the Industrial Heritage [accessed 3 May 2013]. Available at: <http://www.culture-routes.lu/php/fo_index.php?lng=en&dest=bd_pa_det&id=00000170>.

Frey, B. S. & Steiner, L. 2011. World Heritage List: Does it Make Sense? *International Journal of Cultural Policy*, 17(5): 555–73.

Frost, W. 2005. Making an Edgier Interpretation of the Gold Rushes: Contrasting Perspectives from Australia and New Zealand. *International Journal of Heritage Studies*, 11(3): 235–50.

Graham, B., Ashworth, G. J., & Tunbridge, J. E. 2000. *A Geography of Heritage: Power, Culture and Economy*. London: Arnold.

Hall, C. M. & McArthur, S. 1998. *Integrated Heritage Management: Principles and Practice*. London: The Stationary Office.

Hall, C. M. & Piggin, R. 2001. Tourism and World Heritage in OECD Countries. *Tourism Recreation Research*, 26(1): 103–05.

Hall, C. M. & Piggin, R. 2003. World Heritage Sites: Managing the Brand. In: A. Fyall, B. Garrod, and A. Leask, eds. *Managing Visitor Attractions: New Directions*. Oxford: Butterworth Heinemann, pp. 203–20.

Hardy, D. 1988. Historical Geography and Heritage Studies. *Area*, 20(4): 333–38.

Herbert, D. T., Prentice, R. C., & Thomas, C. J. eds. 1989. *Heritage Sites: Strategies for Marketing and Development*. Aldershot, UK: Ashgate.

Hewison, R. 1987. *The Heritage Industry: Britain in a Climate of Decline*. London: Methuen.

Holtzman, J. D. 2006. Food and Memory. *Annual Review of Anthropology*, 35: 361–78.

Hyde, K. F. & Harman, S. 2011. Motives for a Secular Pilgrimage to the Gallipoli Battlefields. *Tourism Management*, 32(6): 1343–51.

Jamal, T. & Hill, S. 2004. Developing a Framework for Indicators of Authenticity: The Place and Spaces of Cultural and Heritage Tourism. *Asia Pacific Journal of Tourism Research*, 9: 353–71.

Jones, J. B. 1988. An Analysis of National Register Listings and Roadside Historic Markers in Tennessee: A Study of Two Public History Programs. *The Public Historian*, 10(3): 19–30.

Jordan, L. & Jolliffe, L. 2013. Heritage Tourism in the Caribbean: Current Themes and Challenges. *Journal of Heritage Tourism*, 8(1): 1–8.

Larson, L. R. & Poudyal, N. C. 2012. Developing Sustainable Tourism through Adaptive Resource Management: A Case Study of Machu Picchu, Peru. *Journal of Sustainable Tourism*, 20(7): 917–38.

Leask, A. & Fyall, A. eds. 2006. *Managing World Heritage Sites*. Oxford: Butterworth Heinemann.

Lennon, J. & Foley, M. 2000. *Dark Tourism: The Attraction of Death and Disaster*. London: Thomson.

Li, Y. 2011. Ethnic Tourism and Cultural Representation. *Annals of Tourism Research*, 38(2): 561–85.

Littrell, M. A., Anderson, L., & Brown, P. J. 1993. What Makes a Craft Souvenir Authentic? *Annals of Tourism Research*, 26: 589–612.

Lowenthal, D. 1996. *Possessed by the Past: The Heritage Crusade and the Spoils of History*. New York: Free Press.

MacCannell, D. 1973. Staged Authenticity: Arrangements of Social Space in Tourist Settings. *American Journal of Sociology*, 79: 589–603.

MacCannell, D. 1976. *The Tourist: A New Theory of the Leisure Class*. New York: Schocken.

Martens, T. & Timothy, D. J. 2006. Burying Tombstone: Fading Authenticity in a Wild West Tourist Destination. Paper presented at the Association of American Geographers Annual Conference, Chicago, Illinois, 7–10 March.

Meethan, K. 2004. 'To stand in the shoes of my ancestors': Tourism and Genealogy. In: T. Coles and D. J. Timothy, eds. *Tourism, Diasporas and Space*. London: Routledge, pp. 139–50.

Metreveli, M. & Timothy, D. J. 2010. Religious Heritage and Emerging Tourism in the Republic of Georgia. *Journal of Heritage Tourism*, 5(3): 237–44.

National Park Service (NPS). 2012. National Historic Landmarks Program [accessed 30 November 2012]. Available at: <http://www.nps.gov/nhl/?\>.

National Trails. 2013. Hadrian's Wall Path National Trail [accessed 25 September 2013]. Available at: <http://www.nationaltrail.co.uk/hadrianswall/>.

Novelli, M. 2005. *Niche Tourism: Contemporary Issues, Trends and Cases*. Oxford: Butterworth Heinemann.

Page, M. & Mason, R. eds. 2004. *Giving Preservation a History: Histories of Historic Preservation in the United States*. New York: Routledge.

Pelkmans, M. 2012. Chaos and Order along the (Former) Iron Curtain. In: T. M. Wilson and H. Donnan, eds. *A Companion to Border Studies*. Oxford: Blackwell, pp. 269–82.

Pilcher, J. M. 1996. Tamales or Timbales: Cuisine and the Formation of Mexican National Identity, 1821–1911. *The Americas*, 53(2): 193–216.

Pollack, A. 2005. Wyatt Earp Fought Here, but the Corral isn't O.K. *New York Times* [online] 8 August [accessed 30 November 2012]. Available at: <http://www.nytimes.com/2005/08/08/national/08tombstone.html?page wanted=all&_r=0>.

Poon, A. 1994. The 'new tourism' Revolution. *Tourism Management*, 15(2): 91–92.

Poria, Y., Reichel, A., & Cohen, R. 2011. World Heritage Site: Is it an Effective Brand Name? A Case Study of a Religious Heritage Site. *Journal of Travel Research*, 50(5): 482–95.

Prentice, R. C. 1989a. Visitors to Heritage Sites: A Market Segmentation by Visitor Characteristics. In: D. T. Herbert, R. C. Prentice, and C. J. Thomas, eds. *Heritage Sites: Strategies for Marketing and Development*. Aldershot, UK: Avebury, pp. 1–61.

Prentice, R. C. 1989b. Pricing Policy at Heritage Sites: How Much Should Visitors Pay? In: D. T. Herbert, R. C. Prentice, and C. J. Thomas, eds. *Heritage Sites: Strategies for Marketing and Development*. Aldershot, UK: Avebury, pp. 231–71.

Prentice, R., Guerin, S., & McGugan, S. 1998. Visitor Learning at a Heritage Attraction: A Case Study of *Discovery* as a Media Product. *Tourism Management*, 19(1): 5–23.

Ramshaw, G. & Gammon, S. 2010. On Home Ground? Twickenham Stadium Tours and the Construction of Sport Heritage. *Journal of Heritage Tourism*, 5(2): 87–102.

Reisinger, Y. & Steiner, C. J. 2006. Reconceptualizing Object Authenticity. *Annals of Tourism Research*, 33: 65–86.

Ritzer, G. ed. 2002. *McDonaldization: The Reader*. Thousand Oaks, CA: Sage.

Ritzer, G. & Liska, A. 1997. 'McDisneyization' and Post-Tourism: Complementary Perspectives on Contemporary Tourism. In: C. Rojek and J. Urry, eds. *Touring Cultures: Transformations of Travel and Theory*. London: Routledge, pp. 96–110.

Scheyvens, R. 2002. *Tourism for Development: Empowering Communities*. Harlow, UK: Prentice Hall.

Smart, B. 1999. *Resisting McDonaldization*. Thousand Oaks, CA: Sage.

Smith, L. & Akagawa, N. 2009. *Intangible Heritage*. London: Routledge.

Stebbins, R. A. 1996. Cultural Tourism as Serious Leisure. *Annals of Tourism Research*, 23: 945–48.

Stefano, M. L., Davis, P., & Corsane, G. 2012. *Safeguarding Intangible Cultural Heritage*. Woodbridge, UK: Boydell.

Sznajder, M., Przezbórska, L., & Scrimgeour, F. 2009. *Agritourism*. Wallingford, UK: CAB International.

Tellström, R., Gustafsson, I. B., & Mossberg, L. 2006. Consuming Heritage: The Use of Local Food Culture in Branding. *Place Branding*, 2(2): 130–43.

Tilden, F. 1977. *Interpreting Our Heritage*. Chapel Hill, NC: University of North Carolina Press.

Timothy, D. J. 1997. Tourism and the Personal Heritage Experience. *Annals of Tourism Research*, 34(3): 751–54.

Timothy, D. J. 2001. *Tourism and Political Boundaries*. London: Routledge.

Timothy, D. J. 2008. Genealogical Mobility: Tourism and the Search for a Personal Past. In: D. J. Timothy and J. Kay Guelke, eds. *Geography and Genealogy: Locating Personal Pasts*. Aldershot, UK: Ashgate, pp. 115–35.

Timothy, D. J. 2011. *Cultural Heritage and Tourism: An Introduction*. Bristol, UK: Channel View Publications.

Timothy, D. J. & Boyd, S. W. 2003. *Heritage Tourism*. London: Prentice Hall.

Timothy, D. J. & Boyd, S. W. 2006. Heritage Tourism in the 21st Century: Valued Traditions and New Perspectives. *Journal of Heritage Tourism*, 1(1): 1–17.

Timothy, D. J. & Boyd, S. W. 2015. *Tourism and Trails: Cultural, Ecological, and Management Issues*. Bristol, UK: Channel View.

Timothy, D. J. & Nyaupane, G. P. 2009. *Cultural Heritage and Tourism in the Developing World: A Regional Perspective*. London: Routledge.

Timothy, D. J. & Ron, A. S. 2013. Heritage Cuisines, Regional Identity and Sustainable Tourism. In: C. M. Hall and S. Gössling, eds. *Sustainable Culinary Systems: Local Foods, Innovation, and Tourism & Hospitality*. London: Routledge, pp. 275–90.

Turespaña. 2013. The Way of Saint James [accessed 20 September 2013]. Available at: <http://www.spain.info/en_US/que-quieres/rutas/grandes-rutas/camino-santiago/>.

United Nations Educational, Scientific, and Cultural Organization (UNESCO). 2013a. UNESCO Culture Sector — Intangible Heritage [accessed 25 September 2013]. Available at: <http://www.unesco.org/culture/ich/index.php?lg=en&pg=00001>.

United Nations Educational, Scientific, and Cultural Organization (UNESCO). 2013b. World Heritage List. [accessed 25 September 2013]. Available at: <http://whc.unesco.org/en/list/>.

Urry, J. 1995. *Consuming Places*. London: Routledge.

van der Aa, B. J. M., Groote, P. D., & Huigen, P. P. P. 2004. World Heritage as NIMBY? The Case of the Dutch Part of the Wadden Sea. *Current Issues in Tourism*, 7(4/5): 291–302.

Vaz da Silva, F. 2008. *Archeology of Intangible Heritage*. New York: Peter Lang.

Veblen, T. 1965. *The Theory of the Leisure Class*. New York: A. M. Kelley.

Wall, G. 1989. An International Perspective on Historic Sites, Recreation, and Tourism. *Recreation Research Review*, 14(4): 10–14.

Wall, G. 1997. Tourism Attractions: Points, Lines, and Areas. *Annals of Tourism Research*, 24(1): 240–43.

Wall, G. & Mathieson, A. 2006. *Tourism: Changes, Impacts and Opportunities*. Harlow, UK: Prentice Hall.

Wager, J. 1995. Developing a Strategy for the Angkor World Heritage Site. *Tourism Management*, 16(7): 515–23.

Wood, A. 2003. A Rhetoric of Ubiquity: Terminal Space as Omnitopia. *Communication Theory*, 13(3): 324–44.

Yang, C.-H., Lin, H.-L., & Han, C.-C. 2009. Analysis of International Tourist Arrivals in China: The Role of World Heritage Sites. *Tourism Management*, 31: 827–37.

Notes on contributor

Dallen J. Timothy is Professor of Community Resources and Development and Senior Sustainability Scientist at Arizona State University (ASU). Professor Timothy is the Director of the Tourism Development and Management Program at ASU and visiting professor at the Universiti Teknologi MARA in Malaysia, Indiana University, USA, and formerly the University of Sunderland, England. He is editor-in-chief of the *Journal of Heritage Tourism* and serves on the editorial boards of thirteen social science journals. His research interests in heritage include the politics of the past, conservation, political heritage, religious tourism, vernacular cultural landscapes, and heritage branding for tourism.

Correspondence to: Dallen J. Timothy, Arizona State University, School of Community Resources and Development, 411 N. Central Ave, Suite 550, Phoenix, AZ, 85004, USA. Email: dtimothy@asu.edu

PUBLIC ARCHAEOLOGY, Vol. 13 Nos 1–3, 2014, 48–58

Mind the Gap: Cultural and Economic Values in Archaeology

Paul Burtenshaw

Sustainable Preservation Initiative, USA

The use of archaeology for economic development represents a non-traditional use of resources normally valued for their cultural aspects. Economic benefits and uses are often presented in opposition to cultural ones in much of heritage management theory and practice. This divide has lead to a lack of data and an inadequate consideration of the economic value of archaeology and its place in economic development. Based on research in Scotland and in Jordan, this paper presents concepts to help bridge the gap between these values and provide a more holistic view of archaeological resources which considers the relationships between cultural and economic values.

KEYWORDS capital, economic value, cultural economics, economic development, value of archaeology

Introduction

The use of archaeological sites, materials, and knowledge for economic development may sit uncomfortably with many in the discipline of archaeology. It is an explicit use of the economic value (in the sense of its ability to generate revenues, jobs, and investment) of a resource traditionally appreciated for its cultural worth. Archaeology and cultural heritage are commonly valued for their impact on society and culture — for the formation of identity, for curiosity, for education, and for inspiration, among other things. The use of such material and knowledge for clear economic aims seems for many at odds to these more accustomed goals. Perhaps Graham et al. encapsulate this mood best when they state:

> [...] there is a strongly felt, and frequently articulated, view that any attempt to attach economic values to heritage, and to other cultural products and performances, is at best a pointless irrelevance and at worst an unacceptable soiling of the aesthetically sublime with the commercially mundane. (Graham, et al., 2000: 129)

This feeling appears to stem from a view that economic and cultural values are opposed: two different philosophies which cannot possibly be reconciled. There is a

   DOI 10.1179/1465518714Z.00000000053

view that economists are only interested in profit and look little beyond balance sheets, while economists may view those who work with culture, including archaeologists, as not existing in the 'real world' and not understanding how it works. Klamer (2004; see also Klamer, this volume) describes the opposing groups as 'economists' and 'culturalists'.

This paper explores the gap between the economic and cultural in archaeology and its management. It suggests that the gap should be bridged and an informed, fresh approach taken to the economic values of archaeological material and knowledge. Archaeology currently lacks the concepts and data crucial to managing the economic aspect of the resource, an aspect which is becoming increasingly important to the management of cultural heritage. The paper suggests some ideas which might help to bridge this divide and allow both the economic and cultural elements of archaeology to support each other.

The gap

Economists have attempted to close this gap and persuade 'culturalists' that their intentions towards cultural resources are not limited to profit. The field of Cultural Economics aims to maximize the welfare (in the widest sense) that cultural resources can provide current and future society (Hutter & Rizzo, 1997; Klamer & Zuidhof, 1999; Peacock, 1998; Towse, 2011). The basic argument is that as the market does not set the value of heritage 'goods', other measurement mechanisms should be employed to produce data which can inform heritage policy. Cultural economics has suggested a variety of methodologies designed to capture the value that a population may feel for any particular cultural resource and produce a quantitative measure of that value, such as Contingent Valuation and Choice Modelling.[1] 'Value' in these methodologies is often expressed in monetary measures as this is the 'language' of decision-making and so offers the opportunity to be directly compared to the value of other goods and opportunities (Mason, 2008; O'Brien, 2010). It is important to stress that this does not mean that only financial benefits are considered, rather the methodologies are an attempt to articulate and communicate all the values of a cultural resource in a common language.

A decade ago, Mazzanti envisaged that 'such economic valuation techniques, might quickly form part of the new lexicon of the cultural industry and a useful component of the cultural analyst's tool kit' (2003: 550) and a 'promising new frontier [...] within the cultural heritage arena' (2003: 566). However, despite this optimism, archaeologists have not typically embraced the methods and theories of cultural economics. Application of the valuation methodologies to cultural heritage and archaeology has been marginal (Kinghorn & Willis, 2008; Noonan, 2003; 2004). While these methods and concepts certainly have their limitations and difficulties (McLoughlin, et al., 2006), an underlying reason for this lack of uptake seems to be perceptual. What is notable are the continued efforts of economists to combat negative views of their intentions, rather than facing more practical questions on the approaches they suggest. Bakshi et al., discussing cultural resources in general, note that:

'Good' economics — the rigorous application of cultural economics — can thus reverse a traditional but obstructive line-up which pits economists, cast as architects of instrumentalism and all things philistine, against arts leaders, cast as beleaguered defendants of intrinsic value and all things aesthetic. (2009: 2–3)

Mason presents the merits, as well as the dangers, of economic approaches but acknowledges the continuing presence of a divide: 'Yet from the perspective of heritage professionals, economics is regarded as an alien, threatening discourse' (2008: 304).

There seems to be a persistent distrust of economics and a feeling that it is somehow outside archaeology. However, that is not to say that the economic aspects of archaeology are not acknowledged and considered within the discipline. The economic contribution of archaeological sites to tourism, regeneration and branding is well documented. Lipe (1984; 2009) considers them part of the benefits of heritage in his value schemes while English Heritage (2005; 2010) include it in their material on what heritage offers society. However, in other schemes the economic aspect is deemphasized or excluded, particularly in the Burra Charter (Australia ICOMOS, 2000; Lafrenz Samuels, 2008). Darvill (1995; 2005) is influenced heavily by cultural economics in his theories of the value of archaeology, while such ideas do have a historic precedent, as has been noted in the works of nineteenth-century art historian Alois Reigl (Svoboda, 2011). Carman (2005) argues for the influence that economic thinking has on our view of heritage in the new millennium but also acknowledges that:

There is sometimes a tendency among archaeologists to be scornful of the 'dismal science' of economics, based upon the misconception that all that economists care about is money. This is not necessarily true, as economists take a sophisticated approach to question of value, grounded in the recognition of the environment as a scarce (that is, finite) resource. (2005: 49)

Carman (2002) develops his own model for why people value archaeology, combining three conceptual schemes that consider transformations of materials and people to different states. Carman asserts that something being declared as 'heritage' is a promotion from the private to the public, from the economic to the social and cultural, and equates the economic with the 'tawdry everyday rather than the higher appreciation of things of taste' (2002: 174). While the definitions of heritage and archaeology may be distinct, Carman's perspective does represent a wish to separate material from the past from economic considerations which seem to be distasteful. In Carver's scheme (1996) archaeological value is a 'human' value, in contrast to the market and community values which compete for the use of land, emphasizing that its worth lays in the information that archaeology contains.

While economic concepts and approaches have impacted theoretical thinking on the value of archaeology and heritage, practical research into the economic aspects of archaeology remains relatively thin. Several recent volumes on Public Archaeology have attempted overviews of archaeology's relationship with the public (Okamura & Matsuda, 2011; Rockman & Flatman, 2012; Skeates, et al., 2012). However, despite the broad range of topics covered between them, the potential of archaeology to contribute to people's lives economically receives little dedicated attention beyond issues around the antiquities market and the commercial archaeology sector. This is despite one editor, in his conclusion to the volume, pronouncing that one of the main reasons that archaeology is valued is for its economic benefit:

> Why is archaeology relevant now? Because it does all of the above. Because it shapes places and people and makes money — and because if Britain for one stopped doing it, then that country would be both culturally as well as pure and simply fiscally poorer. That is why archaeology is relevant now. (Flatman, 2012: 294)

The lack of a focus on the economic aspects of archaeology means that data in this area can be patchy. While economic impact studies have been carried out by government bodies, few studies have been generated by academic archaeologists, and enthusiasm to do so seems slim. In the UK and Europe, the commercial archaeological sector has received attention recently (Schlanger & Aitchison, 2010). Primarily in response to the economic crisis, UK organizations, with the Heritage Lottery Fund leading the way, have produced reports on the economic value of the historic environment (e.g. Ecotec, 2008; Eftec, 2012; HLF, 2010). These are often the first reports of this kind, with no longitudinal data for comparison, and often comment on the lack of basic data with which to build these calculations. Rypkema et al.'s report (2011) on measuring the economic impacts of historic preservation highlights large data gaps and the need for dedicated research by all stakeholders in the sector. Similarly, the lack of data to assess the effectiveness of projects around heritage sites to distribute tourism benefits equitably has been highlighted by Adams (2010). While archaeologists have implemented many local initiatives to use sites to create economic and other benefits, data about the results and effectiveness of these can often be lacking (e.g. Hastorf, 2006; Moser, et al., 2002). A skills gap amongst archaeologists in using sites as an economic asset has been commented upon, with many attempts by academic archaeologists to provide benefits to local populations well meaning, but ad hoc (Coben, 2006; Pyburn, 2009; see also Pyburn, this volume).

Lafrenz Samuels (2008) has explored the concepts of value and significance in archaeology, examining specifically the role of the World Bank. She concludes that the economic context of heritage has been largely concealed and must be brought out for debate as other agents are influencing the concept of the significance of heritage (such as the World Bank's aims of poverty reduction). She argues that:

> It is our responsibility to start thinking critically again about significance, to offer some alternatives, and when using material heritage for economic development to try and incorporate economic considerations into significance without letting them run the show. (2008: 90)

This is the current challenge to archaeologists: to be able to better understand and think about the economic aspects of archaeology so that they are in control of it rather than leaving it to others. Having said that, the concerns that archaeologists have about economics are real and not trivial. Economic (in the financial sense) impacts and benefits are often much easier to demonstrate than other social or cultural impacts and so economic impact data can 'swamp' other aspects of archaeology. The pursuit of revenue from archaeological resources can, for instance, damage the physical condition as well as other values of cultural heritage through unsustainable tourism and commodification. In addition, the timeframe of traditional economic thinking can be short term compared to archaeology's traditionally longer-term perspective (Ingram in Minnis, 2006: 18–19). Given these potential issues, why should archaeologists understand, and have the skills to manage, the economic aspects of archaeology? There are several main reasons why it is crucial to develop this area. The first, outlined by Lafrenz Samuels above, is that if archaeologists do not then other interested parties will. Further, and perhaps a more practical consideration, is that for some groups and stakeholders economic reasons are why they are interested in investing in and preserving archaeology. As Mason suggests:

> Why? Economic motives and values are among the reasons that societies are willing and even eager to undertake heritage conservation — the cultural values of heritage are key for conservation advocates, but are *not* the most important ones for everybody. (2008: 309, emphasis original)

Mason stresses that archaeologists must be conversant in the language and data of economics to be able to communicate effectively with these groups. He goes on to say:

> This is not simply a case of deciding whether cultural or economic value is more important — it's not a zero-sum game. Economic and cultural values of heritage sites are intimately linked. (2008: 309)

This is perhaps the more important reason — the interconnection between economic and cultural values. The economic activities, performance and values of archaeology do not exist independently from other social or cultural values: understanding one requires understanding of the others.

The capital of archaeology

To explore these reasons we need an appropriate vocabulary. The term 'value' presents difficulties when discussing economic aspects as it can have both financial (economic) and moral (cultural) meanings (see Miller, 2008). The term itself can therefore express philosophies on both sides of the divide. Instead, the concept of 'capital' may offer a useful perspective on this issue. This term is common within economics to designate stocks which generate flows of services and other goods. Traditional forms of capital include physical capital, human capital, and natural capital. Throsby (2001; 2002) defines 'Cultural Capital' as an asset that gives rise to a flow of goods and services that have cultural value. The use of the term highlights the need for investment and sustainable management of this stock to maintain the flows and goods it might produce, mirroring ideas about natural capital.

Klamer (2002; 2004; see also this volume) has used 'capital' to try and expand the scope of economics to include the social and cultural aspects of life. He defines capital as an 'ability' — that a certain good has the power or capacity to satisfy wants, and so a collection of goods has the capacity to generate values. Klamer (2002: 465–67) outlines three types of capital that goods may have:

- Economic: the capacity to generate economic income or economic values
- Social: the capacity to generate social values like friendship, collegiality, trust, respect, and responsibility
- Cultural: the capacity to inspire and be inspired

Archaeology in terms of sites, materials, and knowledge can be thought of as a good that contains all these capitals — it has the capacity or power to generate money, social cohesion (including group identity), or inspiration amongst other things. These categories here might not be all the 'capitals' which archaeology contains and the exact definitions may be debated, but they do serve to encapsulate the variety of capacity within archaeology and cultural heritage. Of course, different archaeological resources will have different quantities of different capitals. Major 'world heritage' sites draw large crowds of tourists, are part of national identities, and may be artistic icons. However, any archaeological remain, down to a humble pottery sherd, contributes to the knowledge that, for instance, motivates people to visit somewhere, or is relevant to the family history of someone.

Capital produces flows, however, these can be better described as 'impacts' as this highlights the recipient of those flows. Impacts can be positive or negative. In this way the concept of 'capital' differs from some value schemes in that what the public receives is emphasized, rather than the characteristics of the archaeological resource itself. An archaeological site may have historic value, or be unique, but this does not necessarily mean that it has the potential to inspire someone, create a job, or contribute to the formation of an identity. This depends on such things as the context of the audience, their needs, and the ability of archaeologists to convert that potential into real impacts. 'Value' here can be thought of in terms of importance — that it matters to someone or a group — and the magnitude of this value for archaeology relates to its impacts. It might be difficult for someone to pinpoint exactly why they feel an archaeological resource is valuable to them; it might be only a feeling that it 'should' exist as part of a world view. However, these feelings are still real and connected to a certain resources' ability to (i.e. its capital) 'do' something for them, however intangible that may be.

Different capitals and impacts will matter to different individuals and groups, producing different sets of reasons for importance. As Mason (2008) points out above, for some, a particular site might be important because it gives them a job, for others it is connected to their history, or it is a beautiful place to walk their dog, or it represents the heritage of their country, even if they never visit it. No reason — economic, social, cultural — should be considered more important, or more worthy, than any other.

Economic capital is often mobilized as one way to make a resource more valuable to certain stakeholders. The relationship between economic development and conservation, which is explored in some of the other papers in this volume (see particularly Ackerman Coben; Gangloff; Gould; O'Reilly), relies on this link — that economic capital produces impacts for certain groups, increasing their value for archaeology and their willingness to invest time, money and effort to protect it.

Different sorts of capital also do not exist in isolation. Although the concept of capital has many points to discuss, for the purposes of this paper the most important is the inter-relationship between the different sorts of capital and impacts of archaeology. These relationships have been overlooked, particularly with regard to economic capital, and should be key to any view of archaeology. Archaeology's social, cultural, and economic capitals are dependent on each other and changes in one can increase and decrease the others. Making decisions which increase the capital and impacts in one area (say, economic) may increase or decrease the ability of archaeology to offer positive impacts in other areas.

Some of these relationships are well known. The promotion of tourism at a site to increase economic capital may diminish cultural meanings and access for some populations, reducing cultural and social capital. Physical degradation of sites can harm these capitals too, and in the long term reduce economic capital itself (Drdácký & Drdácký, 2006). However increasing economic capital may increase other capitals. Tourism and identity (at local, regional, and national levels) can go hand in hand (Díaz-Andreu, 2013). While iconic images from sites can define areas, the economic wealth that sites generate can also be part of that image and a source of pride for people. Tourism may be a catalyst to bring certain groups together and elicit cooperation between groups that might otherwise be estranged (or exacerbate differences as discussed below). The emphasis on certain messages and stories of archaeological material can increase social and cultural capital for some interest groups, but decrease it for others (Silverman, 2002). For example, archaeology may be used to support political agendas which enhance the position of some groups and cut out others. Archaeological materials can be the source of artistic inspiration, create images and art which may form the symbols for co-operative social agendas, or form the basis of souvenirs to be sold to tourists for economic gain (Medina, 2003).

Kilmartin Glen, Scotland

Research into economic values carried out by the author has highlighted these connections (Burtenshaw, 2008). An economic impact assessment was conducted at Kilmartin House Museum, a small local museum in Scotland, and the archaeology of the surrounding area, Kilmartin Glen. The Museum wanted data to aid in the protection of the archaeology of the area which was previously damaged by mining, and to better understand their economic contribution to the area. The area has archaeological remains ranging from the Neolithic to the Medieval period, and is one of the most significant archaeological areas of Scotland (RCAHMS, 1999). While the study produced figures for the economic activity of both the museum and the archaeology, what was perhaps more interesting was the interaction of the museum's economic activities with its other local roles. While the museum was established with a variety of aims including education and the return of local artefacts, its economic role is important locally as the only significant way in which revenue is gained from the freely accessible archaeology. A policy of local employment and procurement means that much of the revenue generated from tourism can be retained in the area. The other cultural activities, research, and courses which the museum runs proved a major boon to other local tourism services, as these were often out-of-season, providing vital business in a highly seasonal tourism market. The economic tools of the museum — its shop and restaurant — are primarily there to generate money to support the museum's operational costs, education, and research services. However, local residents commented that these economic assets were highly valued as social spaces for the local village community, where such places can be difficult to maintain independently.

Wadi Feynan, Jordan

The author's PhD research into the economic capital of the archaeology of Wadi Feynan, Southern Jordan, also indicates an interesting interaction of capitals (Burtenshaw, 2013: 205–303). Wadi Feynan (Faynan is used in naming archaeological sites of the area) lies between the Wadi Arabah and the central plateau, a short way north of Petra. The archaeology of the area includes significant Neolithic remains, Iron Age and Roman remains centred on the area's copper deposits, and Byzantine churches and cemeteries, which relate to pilgrimages to the area due to the Christian slaves used in the copper mines by the Romans (Finlayson & Mithen, 2007; Levy, et al., 2002a; 2002b). Archaeological excavations have been carried out in the area by a variety of international and Jordanian teams over the past twenty-five years. A modest level of tourism comes through the area; the majority of visitors coming for walking, wildlife, and to experience an eco-lodge established in the area on the edge of the adjacent Dana Biosphere Reserve. Very few tourists had heard of the archaeological remains of the area, and fewer come for them directly. Several tribes live in the local area, with different tribes benefiting differently from different forms of tourism.

In interviews carried out with a wide variety of local people, over 90 per cent agreed that the archaeological remains were 'important' to them (Burtenshaw, 2013: 283–85). Two-thirds of these respondents said this was due to the economic contribution from the archaeology through tourism (despite the tourists themselves suggesting this was not why they visited), and through employment in archaeological projects. There seemed to be very little personal or community connection to the archaeology in the sense of any ancestral or historic belonging. However, the fact that their area contained these important remains and that international archaeologists and tourists (in their eyes) wished to come to see it, was a source of pride for many local people. Some hoped the name 'Feynan' would be known internationally, on a par with other popular areas of Jordan, such as Petra and Wadi Rum. On the negative side, disputes about how to organize tourism as well as access to economic opportunities offered by archaeological projects caused significant tension between tribes, and between tribes and national organizations in the area. It seems that the economic and social capital and impacts of the archaeology are very closely intertwined, producing both positive and negative interactions.

Conclusion

As archaeologists, one of our aims is to maximize the value of the archaeological resource, its sites, materials, and knowledge, to the public. This requires archaeologists to be able to mobilize archaeology's capitals to produce public benefits and to use the resource sustainably so that all its capitals will be available for future generations. To do this requires the understanding of all archaeology's capitals and the relationships between them. Social or cultural benefits from archaeology require an understanding of the economic impacts, and, importantly, vice versa. The perspective of the term 'capital' helps demonstrate that archaeology's economic capital is intimately tied in with the other potential benefits and issues which archaeology presents. While they can be opposed, they can also be mutually beneficial, and the dangers of the unsustainable promotion of economic capital are no more or less than with any other capital. Any understanding of archaeology's relationship with the public requires an understanding of the social, cultural, and economic dimensions of it. As Lafrenz Samuels challenges, when we consider the use of archaeology for economic development, we must bear these links in mind and use economic capital positively without damaging other aspects of the archaeological resource.

The distrust of the 'economic' and its perceived opposition to the cultural must be tempered within archaeology so that research of it can be furthered, skills related to it developed within archaeology, and discussions about its management and use carried out. While there are potential negatives of economic approaches and the use of the economic capital of archaeology, these are best overcome by increased research and understanding.

Acknowledgements

Thank you to Amara Thornton for commenting on this paper, the Arts and Humanities Research Council (AHRC) and UCL for financial support, and Tom Levy (UCSD) and Bill Finlayson (CBRL) in Jordan, and Sharon Webb in Kilmartin.

Note

[1] Both of these methodologies are 'stated-preference' techniques. Contingent valuation methodologies create a hypothetical scenario of change to a resource and ask respondents to state financial amounts they would pay or receive to allow, or prevent, such a change. Choice Modelling creates similar scenarios but asks respondents to choose from a variety of options to model which aspects are more valuable (Nijkamp, 2012).

Bibliography

Adams, J. L. 2010. Interrogating the Equity Principle: The Rhetoric and Reality of Management Planning for Sustainable Archaeological Tourism. *Journal of Heritage Tourism*, 5(2): 103–23.

Australia ICOMOS (International Council on Monuments and Sites). 2000. *The Burra Charter. Revised* [acessed 23 January 2014]. Available at: <http://australia.icomos.org/wp-content/uploads/BURRA_CHARTER.pdf>.

Bakhsi, H., Freemand, A., & Hitchen, G. 2009. *Measuring Intrinsic Value: How to Stop Worrying and Love Economics*. MPRA (Munich Personal RePEc Archive) Paper No. 14902.

Burtenshaw, P. 2008. Archaeology, Economic and Tourism: The Economic Use-Value of Archaeology with the Case Study of Kilmartin Glen and Kilmartin House Museum (unpublished MA dissertation, University College London).

Burtenshaw, P. 2013. The Economic Capital of Archaeology: Measurement and Management (unpublished PhD dissertation, University College London).

Carman, J. 2002. *Archaeology and Heritage: An Introduction*. London: Continuum.

Carman, J. 2005. Good Citizens and Sound Economics: The Trajectory of Archaeology in Britain from 'Heritage' to 'Resource' In: C. Mathers, T. Darvill, and B. Little, eds. *Heritage of Value, Archaeology of Renown: Reshaping Archaeological Assessment and Significance*. Gainsville, Florida: University Press of Florida, pp. 43–57.

Carver, M. 1996. On Archaeological Value. *Antiquity*, 70: 45–56.

Coben, L. 2006. The Museums' Object(ive)s. In: H. Silverman and E. Shackel, eds. *Archaeological Site Museums in Latin America*. Gainsville, Florida: University Press of Florida, pp. 249–55.

Darvill, T. 1995. Value Systems in Archaeology. In: M. A. Cooper, A. Firth, J. Carman, and D. Wheatley, eds. *Managing Archaeology*. New York: Routledge, pp. 40–50.

Darvill, T. 2005. 'Sorted for ease and whiz'?: Approaching Value and Importance in Archaeological Resource Management. In: C. Mathers, T. Darvill, and B. Little, eds. *Heritage of Value, Archaeology of Renown: Reshaping Archaeological Assessment and Significance*. Gainsville, Florida: University Press of Florida, pp. 21–42.

Díaz-Andreu, D. 2013. Ethics and Archaeological Tourism in Latin America. *International Journal of Historical Archaeology*, 17: 225–44.

Drdácký, M. & Drdácký, T. 2006. Impact of Tourism on Historic Materials, Structures and the Environment: A Critical Overview. In: R. Fort, M. Alvarez de Buergo, M. Gomez-Heras, and C. Vazquez-Calvo, eds. *Heritage, Weathering and Conservation*. London: Taylor and Francis, pp. 805–25.

Ecotec, 2008. *Economic Impact of the Historic Environment in Scotland: A Final Report by ECOTEC for the Historic Environment Advisory Council for Scotland*. Birmingham: ECOTEC [accessed 4 September 2012]. Available at: <http://www.heacs.org.uk/documents.htm>.

Eftec, 2012. Study of the Economic Value of Northern Ireland's Historic Environment. London: Eftec [accessed 3 September 2012]. Available at: <http://www.doeni.gov.uk/niea/built-home/information/study_of_the_economic_value_of_ni_historic_environment.htm>.

English Heritage, 2005. *Heritage Works: The Use of Historic Buildings in Regeneration*. Swindon, UK: English Heritage.

English Heritage, 2010. *Heritage Counts 2010 England*. London: English Heritage.

Finlayson, F. & Mithen, S. 2007. The Early Prehistory of Wadi Faynan, Southern Jordan: Excavations at the Pre-Pottery Neolithic A Site of WF16 and Archaeological Survey of Wadis Faynan, Ghuwayr and Al Bustan. *Wadi Faynan Series 1, Levant Supplementary Series 4*. Oxford: Oxbow Books.

Flatman, J. 2012. Conclusion: The Contemporary Relevance of Archaeology — Archaeology and the Real World? In: M. Rockman and J. Flatman, eds. *Archaeology in Society: Its Relevance in the Modern World*. London: Springer, pp. 291–303.

Graham, B. Ashworth, G. J., & Tunbridge, J. E. 2000. *A Geography of Heritage: Power, Culture and Economy*. London: Arnold.

Hastorf, C. A. 2006. Building the Community Museum at Chiripa, Bolivia. In: H. Silverman and E. Shackel, eds. *Archaeological Site Museums in Latin America*. Gainsville, Florida: University Press of Florida, pp. 85–99.

Heritage Lottery Fund (HLF). 2010. *Investing in Success: Heritage and the UK Tourism Economy*. London: Heritage Lottery Fund.

Hutter, M. & Rizzo, I. eds. 1997. *Economic Perspectives on Cultural Heritage*. Basingstoke: Macmillan.

Kinghorn, N. & Willis, K. 2008. Valuing the Components of an Archaeological Site: An Application of Choice Experiment to Vindolanda, Hadrian's Wall. *Journal of Cultural Heritage*, 9: 117–24.

Klamer, A. 2002. Accounting for Social and Cultural Values. *De Economist*, 150(4): 453–73.

Klamer, A., 2004. Cultural Goods are Good for More than their Economic Value. In: V. Rao and M. Walton, eds. *Culture and Public Action*. Stanford: Stanford University Press.

Klamer, A. & Zuidhof, P. 1999. The Values of Cultural Heritage: Merging Economic and Cultural Appraisals. In: R. Mason, ed. *Economics and Heritage Conservation: A Meeting Organised by the Getty Conservation Institute. December 1998. Getty Center, Los Angeles*. Los Angeles, California: The Getty Conservation Institute, pp. 23–61.

Lafrenz Samuels, K. 2008. Value and Significance in Archaeology. *Archaeological Dialogues*, 15(1): 71–97.

Levy, T. E., Adams, R. B., Anderson, J. D., Najjar, N., Smith, N., Arbel, Y., Soderbaum, L., & Muniz, M. 2002a. An Iron Age Landscape in the Edomite Lowlands: Archaeological Surveys Along the Wadi Al-Guwayb and Wadi Al-Jariyeh, Jabal Hamrat Fidan, Jordan. *Annual of the Department of Antiquities*, 47: 247–77.

Levy, T. E., Adams, R. B., Hauptmann, A., Prange, M., Schmitt-Stecker, S., & Najjar, M. 2002b. Early Bronze Age Metallurgy: A Newly Discovered Copper Manufactuary in Southern Jordan. *Antiquity*, 76: 425–37.

Lipe, W. 1984. Value and Meaning in Cultural Resources. In: H. Cleere, ed. *Approaches to the Archaeological Heritage*. New York: Cambridge University Press.

Lipe, W. 2009. Archeological Values and Resource Management. In: L. Sebastian and W. Lipe, eds. *Archaeology & Cultural Resource Management: Visions for the Future*. Sante Fe, New Mexico: SAR Press, pp. 41–63.

Mason, R. 2008. Be Interested and Beware: Joining Economic Valuation and Heritage Conservation. *International Journal of Heritage Studies*, 14(4): 303–18.

Mazzanti, M. 2003. Valuing Cultural Heritage in a Multi-Attribute Framework Microeconomic Perspectives and Policy Implications. *Journal of Socio-Economics*, 32: 549–69.

McLoughlin, J., Sodagar, B., & Kaminski, J. 2006. Economic Valuation Methodologies and their Application to Cultural Heritage. In: J. McLoughlin, J. Kaminski, and B. Sodagar, eds. *Heritage Impact 2005: Proceedings of the First International Symposium on the Socio-Economic Impact of Cultural Heritage*. Budapest: EPOCH Publication, pp. 8–27.

Medina, L. K. 2003. Commoditizing Culture: Tourism and Maya Identity. *Annals of Tourism Research*, 30(2): 353–68.

Miller, D. 2008. The Uses of Value. *Geoforum*, 39: 1122–32.

Minnis, P. E. 2006. Answering the Skeptic's Question. *The SAA Archaeological Record*, November: 17–20.

Moser, S., Glazier, D., Phillips, J. E., Nemr, L. N. el, Mousa, M. S., Aiesh, R. N., Richardson, S., Conner, A., & Seymour, M. 2002. Transforming Archaeology through Practice: Strategies for Collaborative Archaeology and the Community Archaeology Project at Quseir, Egypt. *World Archaeology*, 34(2): 220–48.

Nijkamp, P. 2012. Economic Valuation of Cultural Heritage. In: G. Licciardi and R. Amirtahmasebi, eds. *The Economics of Uniqueness: Investing in Historic City Cores and Cultural Heritage Assets for Sustainable Development*. Washington, DC: The World Bank, pp. 75–106.

Noonan, D. S. 2003. Contingent Valuation and Cultural Resources: A Meta-Analytic Review of the Literature. *Journal of Cultural Economics*, 27: 159–76.

Noonan, D. S. 2004. Valuing Arts and Culture: A Research Agenda for Contingent Valuation. *The Journal of Arts Management, Law, and Society*, 34(3): 205–21.

O'Brien, D. 2010. *Measuring the Value of Culture: A Report to the Department for Culture Media and Sport*. London: DCMS [accessed 20 July 2013]. Available at: <https://www.gov.uk/government/uploads/system/uploads/attachment_data/file/77933/measuring-the-value-culture-report.pdf>.

Okamura, K. & Matsuda, A. eds. 2011. *New Perspectives in Global Public Archaeology*. London: Springer.

Peacock, A. ed. 1998. *Does the Past Have a Future? The Political Economy of Heritage*. London: The Institute of Economic Affairs.

Pyburn, K. A. 2009. Practising Archaeology as if it Really Matters. *Public Archaeology*, 8(2–3): 161–75.

The Royal Commission on the Ancient and Historical Monuments of Scotland (RCAHMS). 1999. *Kilmartin Prehistoric & Early Historic Monuments: An Inventory of the Monuments Extracted from Agryll. Volume 6*. Edinburgh: The Royal Commission on the Ancient and Historical Monuments of Scotland.

Rockman, M. & Flatman, J. eds. 2012. *Archaeology in Society: Its Relevance in the Modern World*. London: Springer.

Rypkema, D., Cheong, C., & Mason, R. 2011. *Measuring Economic Impacts of Historic Preservation: A Report to the Advisory Council on Historic Preservation* [accessed 3 September 2012]. Available at: <http://www.achp.gov/docs/economic-impacts-of-historic-preservation-study.pdf>.

Skeates, R., McDavid, C., & Carman, J. 2012. *The Oxford Handbook of Public Archaeology*. Oxford: Oxford University Press.

Schlanger, N. & Aitchison, K. 2010. *Archaeology and the Global Economic Crisis: Multiple Impacts, Possible Solutions*. Belgium: Culture Lab Editions.

Silverman, H. 2002. Touring Ancient Times: The Present and Presented Past in Contemporary Peru. *American Anthropologist*, 104(3): 881–902.

Svoboda, F. 2011. In Search of Value: Vienna School of Art History, Austrian Value Theory and the Others. *The Journal of Socio-Economics*, 40: 428–25.

Throsby, D. 2001. *Economics and Culture*. Cambridge: Cambridge University Press.

Throsby, D. 2002. Cultural Capital and Sustainability Concepts in the Economics of Cultural Heritage. In: M. de la Torre, ed. *Assessing the Values of Cultural Heritage*. Los Angeles, California: The Getty Conservation Institute, pp. 101–17.

Towse, R. ed. 2011. *A Handbook of Cultural Economics*, 2nd edn. Cheltenham: Edward Elgar.

Notes on contributor

Paul Burtenshaw received his PhD from the Institute of Archaeology, UCL. His research advances conceptual and practical approaches to the economic value of archaeology, examines the role of economic impacts in mobilizing support for heritage conservation, and develops practical tools to measure and manage economic value as part of sustainable archaeological management. He has carried out economic impact and value assessments in Scotland and Jordan, and was a Research Fellow at the Council of British Research in the Levant, Amman, Jordan. He is now Director, Projects at the Sustainable Preservation Initiative.

Correspondence to: Paul Burtenshaw, c/o Sustainable Preservation Initiative, 40 W. 22nd St, Suite 11, New York, NY 10010, USA. Email: paul.burtenshaw@gmail.com

PUBLIC ARCHAEOLOGY, Vol. 13 Nos 1–3, 2014, 59–70

The Values of Archaeological and Heritage Sites

Arjo Klamer

Erasmus University, The Netherlands

For an evaluation of the values of archaeological and heritage sites, we need to look beyond economic notions such as price and consider the relevant artistic, historical, and social values that such sites generate. The realization of values requires awareness of them and the making real of them. Such realization requires the involvement of the relevant stakeholders. Archaeological sites, therefore, need to be realized as shared goods, rather than as public or market goods.

KEYWORDS values, cultural economics, archaeology, cultural heritage, shared goods

Introduction

The care of old stuff is expensive. When the city of Amsterdam decides to construct a new metro line, a major expense is for archaeological work. Whenever the digging hits a piece of old wood, the work has to stop for the archaeologists to do their work. 'Who cares?' the workers may ask. The Dutch government apparently does, as it has a policy that requires builders to engage archaeologists to salvage the valuable old stuff (Monumentenwet, 1988).

In the meantime, builders and farmers all over the world dig and plough without any consideration of the old stuff in the ground. Who cares?

Does the Dutch community care? Would taxpayers be willing to pay for archaeological work when that means giving up something else, like a visit to the pub, or an extra day of vacation?

While cultural professionals care about things and practices with a cultural or artistic significance, economists are trained to ask: who pays, and who benefits? When the latter note that those who pay for culture are not those who benefit and are sometimes not those who care, they scratch their heads. Economists like markets so much because market transactions guarantee that those who pay are the same people (or organizations) who benefit. When I buy an expensive Etruscan vase you can be sure that I do so because I benefit from the purchase. But when an organization acquires the vase with a grant or subsidy from a foundation or government agency,

   DOI 10.1179/1465518714Z.00000000054

those who pay (the funders of the foundation or the taxpayers) are not those who benefit; the beneficiary is the buyer. The people of that organization care, of course, but it is not their own money with which they express their care and concern. That makes an economist nervous.

These questions point to a dilemma for cultural heritage in general and archaeology in particular. Every community has plenty of stuff (their tangible heritage), but also customs and rituals (their intangible heritage), to preserve or not. Historians, art historians, archaeologists, and relevant organizations are prone to stress the historic and artistic values of all that heritage. I would call them the 'culturalists'. Economists will quickly point out the costs of preservation, including the benefits that communities forsake when they hold on to things and habits, when modernity calls for new material things and new cultural habits. Conservation is costly, but when the culturalists retort that heritage that is destroyed will be lost forever, economists will want to know who is going to pay to preserve it? Who pays? Who benefits? Culturalists would like to see one government or another foot the bill. Economists would like to know why all taxpayers should pay for something that limited groups of people care about. Cultural economists will try to mediate between these two, as I hope to show.

The following will be an exercise in the application of a particular economic way of thinking about the issue of cultural heritage. It may not provide all the answers to the questions raised but offers a framework in which answers can come about in a way that does justice to both the 'culturalist' and the 'economist' points of view. Whether we are dealing with tangible or intangible heritage does not really matter for the exercise. I want to show that the conventional economic way of thinking is not quite satisfactory when it comes to the dilemma of conserving and preserving, or not. The cultural economic perspective that I am presenting here compels us to look beyond the pricing of cultural heritage, including archaeological artefacts, and to consider the variety of values at stake, as culturalists are wont to do.[1]

We begin with the economic or financial valuation, as that is where economists usually start. Gradually we will see how the cultural perspective will do justice to the valuation of the culturalists. In the end we will see how important the determination of property is, where property is conceived as a moral one or a social ownership, rather that the legal one.

Ways of realizing economic or financial values

Trust economists to point out that virtually everything has economic value, expressed in terms of money. In this section I will use the term financial value in order to accentuate the monetary aspect. I will later consider other ways of expressing values that are in a sense economic as well.

Take a landscape like the flat land in the north of the Netherlands where I was born. Most people would just see a beautiful landscape and fail to perceive its prospective financial value. That is not so strange as it has no price tag: there is no direct market with this visual landscape as its product, with buyers and sellers vying to settle its ownership for a certain price. The absence of a direct market is a problem, at least for economists who are interested in its financial value. If there had been a market, they could have used the price the market generates as a measure of its economic value, but, as such a market does not exist, they attempt to derive its financial value in an indirect way, for example, by calculating what people are willing to pay in order to visit the landscape, or to live in the midst of it. Furthermore, they will investigate whether the beautiful landscape attracts business activities such as hotels and restaurants, and they will see in that activity a manifestation of the economic value of the landscape. When filmmakers use the scenery as a setting for a movie, they will observe that this will persuade even more people to view the landscape with their own eyes. Many of those visitors will spend money in local restaurants and hotels. Economists would conclude that the movie has added financial value to the landscape.

Because of the similar absence of markets for goods such as monuments, archaeological sites, and rituals, economists also have to be inventive in order to determine their financial value.

To the economist, both the landscape and archaeology and heritage resources represent economic capital as they have the potential to realize financial values, that is, a form of income. Policymakers will want to know how great that economic capital really is, especially when they are asked to pay the bill for preserving it. The next question that economists want to see answered is how to realize the financial values.

Accordingly, the economic approach involves a weighing of the costs of maintaining and conserving something and the financial values that may be realized with it. Economic impact studies and contingent valuation studies serve the purpose of assessing the financial values that can be generated with a museum, an archaeological site, a folk tradition, a landscape, or any other heritage item. Economic impact studies try to determine the financial values that are realized due to the presence of the item. They follow more or less the approach that I outlined above, that is, they assess the monetary return of economic activities that the item generates, or may generate. Contingent valuation studies focus on the willingness of people to pay for the item. They may go further than impact studies as they include certain values that are hard to estimate such as option, existence, bequest, and educational values. These four values are defined below:[2]

> Option value is the value placed on the option to visit or to enjoy something: people may be willing to contribute taxes to support archaeological or heritage sites even if they do not plan to visit any time soon because they want to have the option of doing so and that option is worth something for them. This value should be included in a contingent valuation study, as it is about the willingness to pay not only for using a cultural heritage site but also for the option of using it. The same is true for the values that follow.

> Existence value is the value that people attach to the existence of, say, the Great Wall of China or the Easter Island statues, even if they never intend to visit such heritage sites. When someone tells them that these things are at risk, they may donate money to support the rescue campaign. This is exactly what happened when the Taliban threatened to blow up the Bamiyan Buddha statues in Afghanistan; even people, including myself, who did not know those statues existed prior to the threat of demolition, could not stand the idea

that they would be lost for posterity. If asked, I might have paid some amount of money if I had the hope that the funds would have persuaded the Taliban not to engage in their iconoclasm. Now they are demolished, people from all over the world would like to see them restored, partly because of 'bequest value', listed below.

Bequest value is the value that a heritage item has for later generations. People now may care about generations that are following and wish them well, including the enjoyment of things of the past. Such compassion with posterity can further induce the willingness to pay.

Educational value refers to the importance that the heritage site has for the historical and artistic instruction of school children and students; museums especially represent important educational value. Such value may also influence the willingness to pay (although many will readily shift the responsibility to the government).

When advocates of cultural heritage try to persuade charitable foundations, government agencies, or benefactors to subsidize the preservation of cultural heritage, the use of terms such as option, existence, bequest, and educational values may add weight to their arguments, especially when policymakers are eager to quantify the generation of financial values. These values are usually pertinent to cultural goods; the problem is that they cannot be realized by means of the logic of the market, that is, by selling tickets or gaining sponsors. People appreciate that the cultural good is there to be enjoyed and admired, but they simply do not show up to pay the price. The point here is basically that heritage is economic capital that can generate financial value if only people figure out how to realize such values. 'Your funds will really help us doing just that', so the suggestion will be, with the implication that the funding does not only help to preserve precious heritage but also the economy.

A sceptic, however, is going to wonder who the beneficiaries are of all the economic or financial value that may be generated. The same question can be asked when an economic impact study shows significant impact. For example, if restaurants and hotels stand to gain significantly from the preservation of cultural heritage, why should they not foot the bill? It might be in their interest to help finance the conservation project. Ideally, those who pay are also those who benefit. So even though economic impact studies continue to appear to have an impact in policy discussions on what to preserve and how to pay, they miss an important dimension of the actual discussion.

Both economic impact studies and contingent valuation studies suffer from economic myopia, as they focus too strictly on financial values, are too preoccupied with the moment of transaction, or the imagined moment of transaction ('if you have to pay, what would you be willing to pay?') and presume the conventional economic assumptions that the preferences of people are a given. Especially the latter presumption does not do justice to the contribution of the culturalists.

As culturalists know all too well, people need to understand the particular historical, symbolic, or artistic values that a cultural heritage site represents. As a matter of fact, it is their job to point out how special those Buddha statues in Afghanistan were, the historical significance of windmills, and why a particular painting is actually very precious. Culturalists work to realize values in the sense of making themselves and others aware of them. A critical part of any heritage programme is clarifying to and persuading others, which values would be lost if such a cultural heritage disappeared. In the nineteenth century the Venetians needed the writings of John Ruskin to become aware of the treasure that they inhabited and the necessity of conserving it. Ruskin (2003), in his *The Stones of Venice* (written between 1851 and 1853), drew attention to the characteristic architecture of the city as well as its artistic richness and historical significance. In general, Italians were compelled by pressure from British historians and art lovers to recognize the great cultural wealth they were harbouring in their country. Likewise, the Dutch only became aware how valuable their possession of paintings was when in the nineteenth century Americans and Russians offered large sums for Dutch art (Stott, 1998). Archaeologists report that they sometimes have to go to great lengths to persuade a local community of the value of their ruins or of whatever is buried in their soil. If the preferences of all these people were respected, preservation or archaeological excavation may not be allowed to begin. The point is that people change their minds and can begin to value a thing that they did not even notice before, or that they even wanted to get rid of. The UNESCO World Heritage List, or, for that matter, any listing of heritage has that very purpose: to make people aware of the values of certain heritage items (Mignosa, 2005).

Social, societal, personal, and cultural values

To address the realizing of values in the sense of becoming aware of them, the cultural economic perspective highlights the variety of values at stake. We could call this also the valorization of values — that is, the enhancement or strengthening of certain values. In the case of cultural heritage the valorization of various values dominates. I distinguish cultural, societal, social, and personal values, as Figure 1 summarizes.

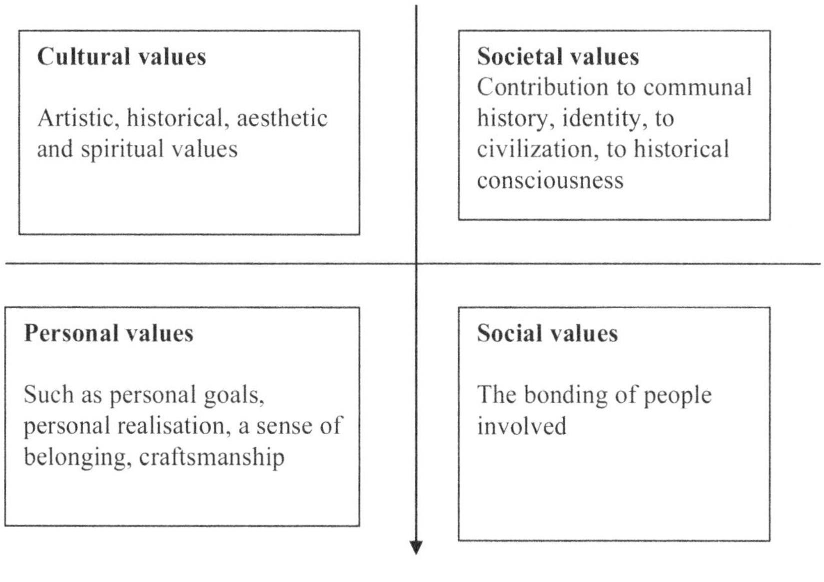

Cultural values Artistic, historical, aesthetic and spiritual values	**Societal values** Contribution to communal history, identity, to civilization, to historical consciousness
Personal values Such as personal goals, personal realisation, a sense of belonging, craftsmanship	**Social values** The bonding of people involved

FIGURE 1   Four types of values.

Cultural values of an archaeological artefact comprise its artistic, historical, aesthetic, and/or spiritual values. A burial place may not so much be admired for its artistic value as for its historical value. The landscape I referred to earlier has mainly aesthetic value, as well as some historical value (because of the old churches with their rare organs, the remnants of some old monasteries, a few old towns, and the dykes that have kept out the water for centuries). A cave painting has artistic value, and an old temple artistic, historical, as well as spiritual value. It is the job of culturalists to be able to characterize these values and to assess how significant they are. Some Roman forts are, of course, only mildly interesting, whereas the Roman Forum is a persistent favourite for tourists.

Societal values concern society at large. Cultural heritage may, for example, contribute to the historical consciousness of community and thus foster a common identity. People of new nations often seek an icon, a remnant of something of the past that can symbolize a shared story, to strengthen that common identity. Historical buildings such as cathedrals, pyramids, and temples are relics of past civilizations; by highlighting their significance and clarifying the meanings they stand for, they contribute to a sense of civilization and its emergence and growth. A museum tells the story of the past and brings it alive in the present. As such it may be a resource for the education of young and aspiring citizens. Another important societal goal of cultural heritage is the attraction of tourists. Each country tries to market its cultural heritage to entice tourists to visit as it contributes to the reputation of a city, a region or a country. It is a point that culturalists will make whenever they get a chance, to enlarge the meanings of the cultural heritage they champion.

Social values are the values of relationships among people, such as status and identity. Heritage preservation may strengthen ties among professionals who have a stake in heritage, such as archaeologists, art historians, and historians. A heritage site may inspire people to get involved by organizing support groups and clubs, by volunteering, by writing or talking about the site or by donating money as with the case of the British Museum. When you tell me how much you *want* to see the Northern Dutch landscape and understand my fondness for it, that may do our relationship some good. People may go on a tour to the pyramids, the Great Wall of China, the Roman Forum, or the historic centre of Amsterdam (a UNESCO world heritage site) and experience all these sights together, thus forging social values in the form of conversations and maybe even relationships.

Personal values are the values that involvement with or experiencing of a cultural heritage item can have for a person. People may cherish iconic places or particular sites for reasons that are strictly personal. People may need to be aware of traditions in order to experience a sense of belonging. They may be inspired by a ritual or have a subliminal experience standing in the Greek temple of Segesta in Sicily. (Culturalists may have more of such experiences, and therefore may care more about cultural heritage for such personal reasons than economists do, but then again, we cannot be sure of this.)

These four values are goal values, that is, values that point at ulterior motives to preserve a cultural heritage item. Some may be inclined to call them the intrinsic values, but that terminology may be misleading as others may easily detect other values that these point to, rendering the first instrumental. The importance of distinguishing these goal values is to distinguish them clearly from instrumental values, such as the amounts of money and attention that a cultural heritage item generates, or the number of visitors a site draws. They all may be critical for its sustenance, but that does not make them a purpose, its raison d'être.

Stressing these four sets of values is a way to address the culturalists' concerns. The economists have a legitimate concern with the means and with the instruments that are needed to realize the cultural, societal, social, and personal values. They will therefore stress the importance of realizing the financial values of cultural heritage. The relevant stakeholders need to become aware of the financial values of a heritage site before they can figure out ways to actualize that value. Mount Rushmore in South Dakota is a great sight to enjoy from a great distance. Its financial value is not immediately obvious till you get close. The US National Park Service figured out that people are willing to pay a substantial fee for parking and for entrance to the visitor centre with information on the presidents whose heads are sculpted on the mountain and about the process that produced this amazing sight, of course with a gift shop and a restaurant. The willingness to pay for all that is an indication of the economic value of the site.

With regard to these values the cultural economic perspective points towards several important features:

a) The **realization of values** has two aspects. Cultural, societal, social, personal, and also financial values need to be realized in two ways. First the decision-makers need to become aware of these values. Once the cultural heritage is preserved, the values need to be actualized in the sense that they are generally recognized and shared. As to the awareness part, culturalists may be sufficiently aware of the historical and artistic value of the Greek temple of Segesta in Sicily, but how many other people know? Tourists still flock to the Parthenon in Athens, whereas the temple of Segesta may be as impressive. You might say that the authorities that preserve the Segesta temple still have work to do to actualize the value of their temple and to make it more widely known and recognized. In both cases people have to change their minds to recognize these values, and so we can speak in both cases of a process of valorization.

b) The valorization usually involves **persuasion**. Directors of museums and heritage sites have to be skilled in articulating the social, societal, and especially cultural values of their institutions in order to persuade governments, foundations, and donors to direct their money to them. And then they need to persuade the public to visit. That is why they will issue educational folders, publicize their institution, and set up an accessible website with all kinds of information.

c) Values may vary among **stakeholders**. Children tend to have an interest in archaeology and heritage that may be quite different from adults. Education matters. So the question has to be which people, which stakeholders need to be persuaded, or are worth spending effort on? Some stakeholders may be more willing to pay or contribute than others. Swarms of visiting kids may be a great sight, but will they contribute somehow? Opera lovers obviously will be willing to pay more for an opera than those who would rather pay to attend a soccer game.

d) Economic or financial values can **crowd out** cultural values (Frey, 1998). This happens when the cultural appreciation for a site goes down because of its commercial success. Sometimes the increase in commercial value may bring about an increase in cultural appreciation; that is called **crowding in** (Frey, 1998). The great advantage of the site of Segesta is its quietness. With only few fellow travellers to admire the temple and the theatre nearby, the visitor experiences the serenity and the sacredness of the place. Yet, when inventive authorities succeed in actualizing its values, and tour operators unload their buses right there, the serenity will be gone. In that case the financial valorization crowds out cultural values. As soon as the British allowed the commercial venues around Stonehenge, the place lost some of its special quality. Mount Rushmore is a great sight from a distance, but when you trample at its foot over busloads of tourists, it changes from a great view into a tourist trap. It is also possible that when a heritage gets priced high, as when interest in a painting is awakened by a high price, culturalists start to pay attention with a greater cultural valuation as result. In that case, economic valorization crowds in cultural value. When the Dutch central bank paid around 34 million euros for the *Boogie Woogie* (Coppes, n.d.), an unfinished painting/collage of Piet Mondrian, newspapers wrote extensively about Mondrian, and visitors lined up to see the painting. If it is that expensive, it must be something.

e) **The mode of financing matters**. The values for which a cultural heritage item is preserved may be affected by the way it is financed. When the owner of a temple decides to organize a theme park next to it in order to generate the funds necessary for the upkeep of the temple, the cultural value of that temple may be crowded out. The government as financier has many advantages, and is for that reason the most common source, but it has the disadvantage that there is little incentive to actualize the values of the site by making it known, by figuring out how to attract people.

The last point requires elaboration. After all, even if culturalists will stress the values of cultural heritage, economists are right to point out that without financial means there is in general no chance to preserve the cultural heritage. The cultural perspective makes clear that the mode of financing matters for the realization of the relevant values.

Items of cultural heritage, including archaeological artefacts and archaeological sites, are above all social and cultural goods

Carman (2005: 36–101), in his important book on cultural property, distinguishes four types of property. I summarize his list here to point out that something crucial is missing:

a) **Private property** is property to which individuals or organizations are legally entitled. Any good that can be bought and sold on a market is such property. Intellectual property rights are intended to extend private property to include intangibles such as ideas and practices. Archaeological artefacts can be privately owned; when they are, they can be traded.

b) **State property** is any good or object owned by the collective, i.e. a state. Economists would speak of collective or public goods. According to the definition, a good is public when 1) nobody can be excluded from its consumption and

2) there is no rivalry among consumers — so if I consume it, this is not at the expense of your consumption of it. In case of monuments, landscapes, folk songs, etc., a lot can be said for their public character in this sense.

c) **Common property** is property that is shared by a group of people. Others are excluded from use of the property. For example, a native Indian community can enjoy common ownership of their land and can control access to it.

d) **Open access (non-property)** such as non-territorial waters or non-designated areas.

In discussions on the value of cultural heritage and archaeological sites, the public good aspect is usually stressed, as that particular characteristic may warrant government financing. But the purity of this property type's non-exclusion clause can often be called into question. A museum may be so crowded that people are refused entrance, or the ticket price may be prohibitive for some. Exclusion also occurs when people lack the appropriate cultural capital to be able to make sense of what a museum shows. And Stonehenge can be so crowded that it gets almost impossible to enjoy it. In that sense, there is also some rivalry. More importantly, by calling cultural heritage a public good we risk missing an important dimension to the detriment of its valuation.

For what reason would people care for a public good? How will they engage or, even better, contribute to its sustenance when nobody can be excluded from its enjoyment anyway? Free riding will be too tempting. Yet, that is not what we observe. People become members of museums and contribute generously to their upkeep and enrichment. People form clubs and associations to preserve battlefields, graveyards, and archaeological sites.

To make sense of these actions I have introduced the notion of the 'social good' (Klamer, 2004).[3] Such a good is different from any of the goods Carman (2005) refers to as its ownership is not a legal matter. A social good is a good that people own together, without legal implications and also without the possibility of transactions. A social good is valuable to people, and will be costly to procure. A typical example is friendship. A friendship has all kinds of values for both friends and it is costly to get started and to maintain, in the sense that both friends have to sacrifice time and also money for the sake of the friendship. Friendship is not a private good as it is not for sale and an individual cannot claim private property right of the friendship. It is, so I suggest, a social good. A social good has several important characteristics:

a) The ownership of a social good is shared.

b) The ownership is usually a social or moral construction rather than a legal one (friends do not draw up contracts).

c) A social good is usually not appropriated by means of the logic of the market (that is, you can not purchase it) or the logic of governance (governments can not arrange friendships).

d) The degree of ownership usually depends on the quality of the contributions someone makes. Contribution is the key notion here. By contributing to a friendship, the value of the friendship may deepen.

e) All those who do not contribute to a social good are excluded from its benefits. A social good excludes. It requires a contribution of some kind — money, a visit, a donation, attention, knowledge — in order to gain its possession.

f) Contrary to a public good, a social good does not permit free riding, as the free rider risks losing possession of the social good. An artistic community is a social good for everyone who contributes. Membership of such an informal community is determined by the quality of the contributions someone makes. Free riders may be able to hold on for a while, but at one point they will be seen as just that, free riders.

Interesting examples of social goods are internet sites such as Wikipedia and Facebook (they are also called creative commons). People contribute to the site to make it their own, to make it their site. They will draw satisfaction from being recognized and will contribute even more. Similarly, a public square can grow into a social good when locals take possession of it, contribute to its atmosphere by showing up every late afternoon, by playing chess, by organizing meetings. In such a way the public square becomes 'my' or 'our' square.

I told this story to archaeologists who were working on a dig in a small Mexican village. They were worried about the suspicion of the locals and wondered whether they could continue their work. My advice was that they had to figure out how to realize their dig as a social good in such a way that the locals would feel that it is their site too. The strategy is then to think of how the locals can get involved and contribute to the dig.

The risk of government programmes for the subsiding of cultural heritage is that too little attention is given to the development of cultural heritage as a good to be shared among the relevant stakeholders. From my experience, they usually do too little to involve them, and especially lack any strategy to enable them to contribute, for example, by way of donations As a consequence, too many cultural heritage items remain public possession and fail to become social goods.

The mode of financing matters

In order to realize the values of their resource or site, managers or owners may need to heed their source of financing. In order to realize social, societal, and cultural values owners or managers may want to promote the social character of the good that they manage. The question that they want to ask themselves is how to get stakeholders involved.

When they rely on one major source of income, such as a government funding or a foundation, they risk ignoring other potential stakeholders. Financed by a grant, archaeologists trek to their site and set to work. It is nice when the locals come and watch, but the archaeologists do not need their attention. That attitude has to change when they are also dependent on the resources of the locals. The archaeologists may need local labour, or other resources such as food and tools. Being forced to persuade the locals to partake in the project, the archaeologists may actually create a sense of co-ownership. And that is what they want if it is their mission that the site has to be valuable somehow to the locals.

A sense of co-ownership is furthered when stakeholders are encouraged to contribute financially. If executed properly, a fundraising campaign may do the project a great deal of good as the campaign gets people to pay attention, gets them to realize the special values of the project, and when they give for the good cause they may develop a sense of ownership. Fundraising is hard work, but it is part of the work that is needed to realize the values of cultural heritage. Persuading government or foundation officials does not suffice; efforts may be rather directed at the relevant stakeholders.

Conclusion

When we are dealing in social, societal, and cultural values we have the disadvantage compared to those who are dealing in economic pricing that it is hard to produce solid data. We can say that a few million euro is a lot of money, but how will we ever be able to say that the cultural value of a cathedral is worth a million? The lack of clear indicators makes the assessment of the impact of investments in cultural heritage difficult. When can we tell whether the important social, cultural and societal values have been realized? And how many have been realized?

In order to address this shortcoming in our knowledge, I am working on a cultural monitor that not only registers how people experience cultural heritage on the social, societal and cultural levels, but also what their values are (the base for this approach can be found in Klamer, 1996). Such a monitor should give an indication of the efficacy of the policies of those managing or controlling cultural heritage. It may show that the heritage is well managed and preserved but when it fails to raise interest among stakeholders the project could still be called a failure. The cultural monitor can also register shifts in values. When the investment in a cultural heritage has as an objective to raise the historical consciousness of local people, the cultural monitor can show whether it has been a success, or not. Contrary to contingent valuation studies, the cultural monitor accounts for the value changes that culturalists tend to seek.

In that sense, the cultural economic perspective does justice to the culturalist position with its emphasis on cultural values, while acknowledging the importance of the economic dimension. The realization of economic values is an art just as the realization of social, societal, and cultural values is.

Notes

This paper was originally presented at the Archaeology and Economic Development conference held at University College London in September 2012. A version of the paper was subsequently included as a chapter in I. Rizzo & A. Mignosa, eds. *Handbook on the Economics of Cultural Heritage*, published by Edward Elgar in September 2013. This paper is presented here with the permission of Edward Elgar and the Editors.

[1] For an elaboration for this perspective, see Klamer (2004: 200); Hutter & Throsby (2008); Throsby (2001).

[2] For a useful survey of all the techniques that economists have developed, see Snowball (2008).

[3] At first I called social good a common good but, as common good tends to have a more general meaning in the sense of doing things for the common good, I have adopted at the suggestion of Bruno Frey the notion of a social good. Incidentally, a social good is what may be realized in what Ostrom and others have called the commons (see Ostrom, 1990).

Bibliography

Carman, J. 2005. *Cultural Property: Archaeology, Heritage, and Ownership*. London: Duckworth.

Coppes, W. n.d. *Victory Boogie Woogie: meesterwerk* [Victory Boogie Woogie: Masterpiece] [accessed 31 February 2014]. Available at: <http://www.mondriaan.nl/artikel/victory_boogie_woogie_meesterwerk>.

Frey, B. 1998. *Not Just for the Money*. Boston, Massachusetts: Beacon Press.

Hutter, M. & Throsby, D. 2008. *Beyond Price*. Cambridge: Cambridge University Press.

Klamer, A. 1996. *Value of Culture*. Amsterdam: Amsterdam University Press.

Klamer, A. 2004. *Art as a Common Good* [accessed 19 January 2014]. Available at: <http://www.klamer.nl/index. php/subjects/art-culture/185-art-as-a-common-good-presented-at-the-bi-annual-conference-of-the-association-of-cultural-economics-at-chicago-june-3-5-2004>.

Mignosa, A. 2005. *To Preserve or Not to Preserve? Economic Dilemmas in the Cases of Sicilian and Scottish Cultural Heritage*. Rotterdam: Erasmus University.

Monumentenwet (monument law). 1988. Article 53 [accessed 19 January 2014]. Available at: <http://wetten. overheid.nl/BWBR0004471/geldigheidsdatum_04-11-2013#HoofdstukV_7>.

Ostrom, E. 1990. *Governing the Commons*. Cambridge: Cambridge University Press.

Ruskin, J. 2003 (1851–53). *The Stones of Venice*. Cambridge, Massachusetts: Da capo Press.

Snowball, J. 2008. *Measuring the Value of Culture: Methods and Examples in Cultural Economics*. Berlin: Springer.

Stott, A. 1998. *Holland Mania: The Unknown Dutch Period in American Art & Culture*. New York: Overlook Press.

Throsby, D. 2001. *Economics and Culture*. Cambridge: Cambridge University Press.

Notes on contributor

Arjo Klamer is Professor of Cultural Economics at the Erasmus University and Professor of Social Innovation at Fontys in Tilburg. Prior to that and after acquiring his PhD at Duke University, he taught for many years at several universities in the US, including Wellesley College and George Washington University. His research focuses on the relationship between culture (including the arts) and the economy. He is developing a cultural monitor to provide an evaluation of the artistic and social impacts of artistic organizations. With former students he is running the Atelier in Creativity and Cultural Entrepreneurship. The objective of this organization is to assist cultural organizations in their adaptation to new circumstances. Furthermore, he conducts workshops on his value-based approach to cultural economics all over the world.

Correspondence to: Prof. Arjo Klamer, Erasmus University Rotterdam, Erasmus School of History, Culture and Communication t.a.v. Arjo Klamer, Postbus 1738, 3000 DR Rotterdam, The Netherlands. Email: Klamer@eshcc.eur.nl

PUBLIC ARCHAEOLOGY, Vol. 13 Nos 1–3, 2014, 71–84

Commodifying the Indigenous in the Name of Development: The Hybridity of Heritage in the Twenty-First-Century Andes

ALEXANDER HERRERA

Commission for Archaeology of Non-European Cultures, Germany

To ask how prioritizing the commodifiable aspects of heritage transforms the relationships that define it, this paper begins by tracing the historical development of mercantile perspectives on archaeological objects, sites, and landscapes in the central Andes. From colonial looting and the mining of treasure to the illustrated emphasis on testimonial value which gave rise to modern national archaeologies in the early twentieth century, contingent encounters define processes of mercantilization, including current drives to deploy archaeology to produce commodities for the tourism industry. After scrutinizing the roles of heritage legislation, local government, entrepreneurs, local communities, and archaeologists in this process, the differing intentions, mechanisms, and effects of commoditization are highlighted. The production of essentialized identities and the invisibilization of meaningful relations between people about things and places are exclusions emanating from the marriage of archaeology and development. These are showcased in the budding cultural tourism context of the Cordillera Blanca, Peru, as an attempt to chart the ethical minefield of emergent hybrid indigeneity.

KEYWORDS heritage, indigeneity, commoditization, tourism, Peru

> A maior desgraça de uma nação pobre
> é que em vez de produzir riqueza, produz ricos.
> Mas ricos sem riqueza
> Mia Couto[1]

Introduction

In the aftermath of the neo-liberal turn that swept across Latin America during the final decade of last century, the commodification of heritage is increasingly

    DOI 10.1179/1465518714Z.00000000055

encouraged as a means to foster economic development. Its value as historical testimony, whence archaeology came into being and was consolidated during the twentieth century, has taken second place in development policy. Attempts to reduce heritage to its materiality and foreground its marketable aspects signal an epistemic shift that has brought about three major, inter-related challenges for archaeology: commodification, trivialization, and enforced trusteeship. These are issues at the heart of heritage as a development process, not least because the transformation of indigenous land, objects, and people into commodities has a long history of producing poverty.

Archaeology helps establish testimonial value and warrants the authenticity of material singularity in located historical trajectories, but commoditization — the process of making commodities out of objects, places, or landscapes (*sensu* Appadurai, 1986) — can impact negatively upon historical accuracy.[2] The narratives best supported by archaeological evidence and, as such, the most plausible interpretations, can no longer take political support for granted when the emancipatory Kantian ethos of the Enlightenment (*sapere aude*) is replaced by economic neo-liberalism. Stories that sell well, and thus help in the production of destinations, raise the additional challenge of trivialization. Esoteric or mystic tourism, an expanding specialist branch of the tourism industry (Pérez, 2011), provides a poignant example.

Trivialization is not only a distorting simplification of discourse; it can affect the physical integrity of architecture. There are many ways to rearrange the stones at an archaeological site to enhance visitors' experience, ranging from rubble clearance and path demarcation, to area excavations, large scale restoration and outright recreation. In Chucuito, Peru, for example, the interests of local restaurant owners, tour operators, New Age gurus and culture authorities gave rise to the creation of a 'Temple of fertility' in line with Eurocentric preconceptions (Kummer, 2006). Turned into a consumable commodity, the little-known Colla site of Inka Uyo helped position a small highland town by Lake Titicaca as a major international destination for New Age tourists in less than one decade. While local children peddle tours explaining the 'ancient fertility cult' to site visitors, economic benefits have concentrated in the hands of operators, hoteliers, guides, and gurus who seem to have agreed that 'Lake Titicaca must be the first port of call for the pioneers of the New Age pilgrims of light' (Cedeño, 2001: 20, author's translation).

It may not surprise that groundless interpretations of cultural heritage can count on the support of state-funded cultural institutions, if they are profitable. State-funded archaeology in Peru has been increasingly geared towards the creation of economic value and is working hard to turn a growing number of selected sites into destinations while upholding the national historical narrative. Economic exploitation of archaeological sites by the tourism industry, however, has tended to widen and deepen the existing gaps between rich and poor as there is a structural tendency to disproportionately favour the interests of entrepreneurs, operators, and traders (e.g. Ruiz Rubio, 2010). Local communities, in contrast, face the risk of physical displacement, the imposition of essentialized identities through exoticizing representations (Herrera, 2013b) and remain most exposed to the volatile cycles of the industry (Trivelli & Hernández, 2009).

Archaeology has proved its willingness to act as an accomplice in enabling and furthering economic development across the Andes — in mining, road construction, and other major works of infrastructure and the extractive industries (Haber, 2013) and archaeologists may be at odds about more or less orthodox restorations and be tempted to turn a blind eye to over-zealous restorations for the benefit of the local economy. These commonplace practices of heritagization (*patrimonialización*), however, are coupled to the disempowerment of local communities at many levels, not least by alienating places and objects from local practices and discourse. In Peru, its practitioners have additionally shown that they are (again) willing to treat sites, landscapes, and identities as newly discovered treasure troves that have long lain buried (Rostworowski, 2002). In doing so, I argue, they recast the colonial negation of the indigenous (*sensu* de la Cadena, 2006; cf. Lumbreras, 2000). Contemporary heritage *relations*, however, pertain to a third phase of heritage, a hybrid construct that aims to balance earlier mercantile and testimonial valuations with the challenges raised by resurgent indigeneity. In following, I briefly show how the history of commoditization came about in Peru and exemplify the present conjunctures that replicate colonial exclusion, before focusing upon the roles of archaeology and archaeologists in a budding tourist hotspot.

The development of heritage relations

The relationships between people, objects, images, and techniques are historically imbedded in genealogies of practice that structure how societies remember (Connerton, 1989; cf. Van Dyke & Alcock, 2003). Under the liberal paradigm these tend to be classed together as property (Hann, 1998) and, since the roots of current notions of heritage in Latin America can be traced to the impact of enlightened despotism during the late colonial and early republican periods (see below), archaeological study of remembrance has proved doubly elusive (e.g. Lau, 2013; Moore, 2010).

Mortuary archaeology and studies of architecture, iconography, and techniques in general have provided important glimpses. Bundles containing ancestral remains, usually kept in special structures, were venerated across the Andes, often over centuries, indicating that deep memory was embedded in mortuary practice (e.g. de Leonardis & Lau, 2004; Isbell, 1997). The location and accoutrement of tombs may inform about claims and rights of access, including the allocation of water rights and the communal organization of labour (Herrera, 2007), but dating usage and the duration of circulation of specific artefacts can prove challenging in contexts repeatedly looted by Christianizing priests and treasure-hunters (e.g. Gerdau & Herrera, 2010). Religious imagery making explicit reference to earlier images is usually referred to as archaism (Cordy Collins, 1992; Menzel, 1960; Patterson, 2004; Rowe, 1971) and has been argued to show long culture-historical continuities or recurring structural conjunctures in religious beliefs. How such memory tied into notions of relatedness akin to collective/individual, inclusive/exclusive ownership, however, has only recently begun to be explored in studies of alterity (Lau, 2013).

Techniques and practices also inform upon long trajectories of knowledge transmission and are often seen in an economic light today (e.g. Kendall & Rodriguez, 2010), thus giving room to the argument that they constitute an ancient form of heritage. Yet, while there is no doubt that systematic knowledge was consciously transmitted, little is known about how it was passed on and it is unclear whether certain techniques or practices were regarded as 'ancient' or 'from the past' at all. There is little indication of indigenous forms of relatedness that might parallel contemporary usage of heritage, and it seems likely that the templates for intention that become manifest in objects would have tended to be seen as less valuable or important than the situated performance of social memory itself.

It is under colonial rule that objects and places become entangled in mercantile relations that linger into the present, marked by systematic destruction, violent appropriation, and selective collection. Looting tombs to extract valuable (metal) objects is first recorded in AD 1534, shortly after the arrival of Conquistadors (Rost-worowski, 2002), and commercial looting thrived throughout the colonial period, in spite of the occasional threat of excommunication (Zevallos Quiñones, 1994). By the late eighteenth century the search for treasure had become a regulated form of min-ing; a duly taxed extractive industry in which *criollos* (those of European descent), *mestizos* (those of mixed race), and indigenous leaders, workers, and slaves partici-pated (Zevallos Quiñones, 1994), albeit for different reasons (Rostworowski, 2002). A combination of need, greed, and religious persecution, coupled to forced resettle-ment, gradually helped transform monuments and cemeteries into heaps of rubble and reshape people's relations to them. The first recorded instances of 'heritage', in the narrower sense of valuable objects that were meant to be inherited, are little-known collections of indigenous objects from early colonial Trujillo mentioned in the testaments studied by the late Jorge Zevallos Quiñones (1994).

With the enlightenment turn of the eighteenth century, intellectuals such as Bishop Baltasar Martínez de Compañón began challenging reductionist materialism and highlighting the aesthetic and evidential value of ancient objects and tombs (Alcina, 1995; Pillsbury & Trever, 2008; cf. Wylie, 2005). Crates containing hundreds of objects were to be shown to the king of Spain, along with his richly illustrated manuscript, so that the Prince of Asturias would 'become acquainted to the study and knowledge of the arts, civility and culture of the Indians of Peru' (quoted in Alcina, 1995: 187).

While the most blatant forms of commercial looting are slowly receding, the trade in antiquities for art collectors continues, both locally and internationally. A combi-nation of resource depletion and more effective policing (Valencia, 2008a) is affecting all forms of looting, but sporadic searches for objects to create, expand, or embellish study collections continue at some rural schools in Peru. Like many urban collectors, the teachers driving rural collectionism tend to rise up as enlightened custodians of the local heritage, arguing testimonial value before commercial worth.

Colonial practices of commodification notably included the dismantling of build-ings and the quarrying of stones, such as the commonplace construction of Christian temples on or near earlier sacred locales. This tradition of re-using ancient building materials and places, at odds with the exclusionary 'glass-box' approach deployed to enforce the protection of archaeological heritage (see below), continues. Destruction of spectacular proportions is regularly reported by the media, often accompanied by archaeologists' objections to the loss of the touristic potential excavations might have raised. Lamenting the lost chance for archaeology's remedial interventions, however, does little to challenge commoditization as a driver of the destruction of historical testimony and the transformation of places important in local identity formation.

The new readings of the past required since the advent of Peruvian independence in the early 1820s have tended to shift around one central theme: the restoration of the glorious past of the Inca. The multiple publications of *Antigüedades Peruanas* by Mariano Eduardo de Rivero y Ustariz and Johann Jakob von Tschudi during the mid-nineteenth century mark the rise of *criollo*'s preoccupation with archaeological objects as an alternative source for studying the past (Coloma, 1994): '[Colonial] historians do not transmit anything positive about the government, laws, traditions and customs before the establishment of the empire of Manco Cápac' (de Rivero, 1994 [1827]: 8, author's translation). The enlightenment thinking of Martínez de Compañón, Antonio de Ulloa, Jorge Juan, Pedro Franco Dávila (Alcina, 1995), and Mariano Eduardo de Rivero provided the seed for the idea of testimonial value that would give rise to the transition between the mercantile perception predominating under colonial rule and the testimonial valuation underlying Peruvian National Heritage.

Archaeology, development, and the protection of heritage

In most of Latin America the value of historical testimony of places and objects is part of the ideological foundations upon which archaeology consolidated as a discipline in the early twentieth century. If the foundation of testimonial value during the Borbonic age was in 'extracting the knowledge of the increases and decreases of these lands in remote times' (after Solano, 1979: cxlviii, as cited in Alcina, 1995: 80), then their importance under the Republic rests on the foundational myth that declares the Nation as sole legitimate heir of the sovereignty and liberty of the indigenous people and, by extension, of all their past (Hernández, 2013; Herrera, 2011b; 2013). The responsibility of guarding the 'incalculable value' of the remains of the past was institutionalized in heritage legislation as academic archaeology consolidated during the second half of the past century (Macera, 2000; Ravines, 2000; Ubilluz, 2000).

Today, frictions between local populations and national cultural institutions in Peru typically revolve around the protection of heritage sites and objects. A handful of sites around cities and some outstanding destinations receive strict custody, but there are so many transgressions to the declared intangibility of the vast majority of sites that it is impossible for statutory protection to be effective in practice. Tremendous efforts have been made over the last century to stem looting, to inventory the national heritage, protect the intrinsic fragility of the archaeological resource, and develop innovative approaches to heritage education. And yet, effecting protection through exclusion has proved ineffective, not because the vast majority of an estimated 50,000 sites in Peru are neither declared nor fenced, but because of the weak trust underlying an enforced relation of trusteeship (Wylie, 2005). Additionally, most of the material legacy of the past — as we shall transitorily define heritage here — is hard to circumscribe in terms of sites.

The development process whereby places are turned into sites, and sites declared heritage, is an administrative process that rests upon effective territorial control and laid out in detail in current legislation (Ley, 28296: see Valencia, 2008b). Commodification, in turn, is a second, more loosely regulated step, which local level state authorities as well as private entrepreneurs and sectors of the Catholic Church have explored in different ways and to varying degrees.

Despite criticism, current legislation appears to have been generally effective in enabling the state to take measures to protect archaeological sites, especially in or near urban centres. However, the emphasis on sites in the legislation is a focus inherited from the regional archaeology — in vogue until the 1980s (Foley, 1981) — that marginalizes the extensive transformations of the Andean landscape, as Lumbreras (2000) has commented. This includes about one million hectares of terraces and half a million hectares of raised and sunken fields, as well as hundreds of kilometres of relic canals and innumerable reservoirs and artificial wetlands (Herrera, 2011a), all of them 'archaeological'. These are not only unprotected, as Rostworowski (2000) and others have vocally criticized, it is hard to imagine ways of effectively applying an exclusionary approach to their conservation. A major international project has begun addressing the long-neglected landscapes associated with the Inka road system, assessing and ascribing values to them. And yet, although the living human populations that inhabit these landscapes are recognized as partners of the project, their active participation in the definition and protection of heritage has been as negligible, as the development of mechanisms to ensure inclusiveness and participation in economic development (Korstanje & Garcia, 2007).

National policy in Peru has recognized the potential of archaeology in the production of attractions for the global tourism industry and has set its sights on expanding this market through the transformation of a selected handful of archaeological sites into destinations at an unprecedented scale. In order to protect the national heritage, legislation has taken a glass-box approach towards the conservation of sites through exclusion, followed by research and conservation. It seems timely therefore, to ask more precisely who, in the name of economic development, is being kept out or brought into what kinds of places at what times, and how this situation developed? It may seem ironic that forms of heritage management that foreground economic development should place such emphasis on avoiding physical alterations. Doctrines of development are usually a reaction to the negative impacts brought about by modern development processes (Cowen & Shenton, 1996). Informed by archaeology, however, the administration and conservation of heritage often leaves the old buildings as new.

Heritage and the indigenous

Recent history compounds the colonial split between people and landscape brought about through Christianization and forced resettlement. Current politics of indigeneity are marked by ongoing strategic shifts of identifiers and the identified, where purified and static indigeneity tends to be rejected in favour of the contested hybridity of the mestizo (de la Cadena 2000; 2006). In part, this is due to the enlightened twentieth-century paternalist indigenism in which Julio César Tello, founding father of Peruvian archaeology, played a prominent role (Burger, 2009). Thus, while expressions of indigeneity are publically celebrated in the rural calendar of catholic festivities and highland holders of municipal office actively seek to appropriate elements of local traditions to bolster political discourse, traditional indigenous authorities tend to be disregarded, not only in matters regarding archaeological sites.

The existence of a large indigenous population in the highlands of Peru is broadly acknowledged internationally, but it is rarely regarded openly as Indian from within.

Quechua- and Aymara-speaking rural populations are typically acknowledged, but most often describe themselves as *campesino* farmers. Mestizaje, the complex processes of transformations that have re-shaped people and traditions (de la Cadena, 2000; 2006), are glossed over as a 'distinctly Peruvian blend' of indigenous and European traditions in tourist brochures. In this they echo dominant state discourse, and silence the lasting impacts on economic development of the colonial restructuring of the landscape (e.g. Gade, 1992).

The colonialization of heritage is inescapable when discussing the conceptual linkages between archaeology and economic development. Both are invariably linked to the legislations that give States the power to appropriate material objects and places, over and above their private or collective property and customary or traditional rights of use. *Patrimonio*, as heritage is usually translated into Spanish, derives from the Latin *patrimonĭum*: 'that which is to be inherited'. For there to be an estate, however, there must be a deceased. The application of the principle of patrilineal inheritance to enforce trusteeship is especially problematic in Andean regions with large indigenous populations and descendant communities (Herrera, 2011a; 2011b), particularly in contexts where indigeneity is resurgent.

Sumaq Kawsay / Buen Vivir / Vivir Bien, the central document or Manifesto of the Andean Coordination of Indigenous Organisations CAOI (Huanacuni, 2010), clearly lays out the role of land as a central element of the 'historic debt' with the indigenous populations of the Andes. In Peru, the strategies of resistance deployed in this debate have been shaped by the extraction of natural resources, mining especially. The occupation of ancestral places by indigenous groups in Ecuador and Colombia, and their increasing appropriation for (re)invented rituals in Peru, draws standard notions of 'the indigenous' and 'archaeological site' into questions, challenging the role of archaeology in different processes of appropriation, not only of land, but of time (Haber, 2013).

Andean calendars of subsistence farming integrate people from dispersed settlements across ecological gradients into communities through cyclic gatherings for work and ritual, segmenting linear time into livable, cultured parts that express historically sedimented relations of power (Gell, 1992). Current strategies to promote heritage tourism take elements of tradition out of context, by displacing, resignifying, and rescheduling dance performances to fit the calendars of the tourism industry, for example. Deployed to give a sense of authenticity, such fragments are often major components of reinvented traditions performed at archaeological sites. Self-exoticizing exercises in commodification, however, tend to display little regard for the demands of the inter-annually shifting agricultural and religious calendars.

Archaeology and economic development in the Callejón de Huaylas today

From the perspective of the State, the protection of heritage can be understood as a contemporary form of a cult to the indigenous ancestors, a practice which contributes to the construction of legitimacy by founding authority in officially sanctioned history. In this light, the study and protection of monumental remains and complex artefacts are privileged because they support the foundational thesis of the myth of the 'ancient Peruvians' as civilized people that attained liberty and sovereignty

FIGURE 1   Anointment 'ritual' and beauty contest at Tumshuqaiku sponsored by the local municipality as part of Tourist Week. Note traditional authorities in background.
Photograph courtesy of Oficina de Imagen Institucional, Municipalidad Provincial de Huaylas

independently (Herrera, 2011b; 2013a; 2013b). In a parallel vein to the discourse on underdevelopment and poverty (Escobar, 1995; 1997; Sachs, 1991; cf. Alloo, et al., 2007), the doctrine of development in which national archaeological practice is currently inserted is predicated on the construction of a ghost. It is not poverty but 'lack of identity', sometimes even 'lack of patriotism'. A prominent Peruvian archaeologist has even gone as far as to suggest that only archaeologists' disciplinary practice is capable of producing the active ingredient in the antidote to the supposed illness: authentic historic value (Shady, 1999). In the Callejón de Huaylas, a region better known for its snow-capped mountain landscape than for its archaeology, the national state, provincial governments, sectors of the church, and NGOs have all deployed a range of strategies to increase tourism revenues by focusing on archaeological heritage. Ongoing efforts showcase a diversity of publically and privately funded approaches to heritagization which have not led to a successful production of destinations. Unresolved tensions have instead given rise to a dysfunctional hybrid.

Despite standing within the urban perimeter of the provincial capital, the local government first turned its attention to Tumshuqaiku (also known as Tunshucaico) in the late 1990s. After centuries of quarrying the site had been stripped like an onion, tunnelled and bulldozed for treasure, and squatted for generations. The municipality funded two seasons of archaeological endeavours, which succeeded in exposing the south-west front of a monumental structure (Bueno, 2008). Despite a propaganda campaign highlighting the antiquity of the cleared walls, tourists failed to flock to the site. The threat of torrential rains instead forced the construction of a protective cover which has since collapsed, causing damage to the exposed façade. Tumshukai-ko's fortunes changed briefly when a 'ceremony of anointment' became the symbolic focal point of Huaylas Tourist Week in 2008. This idiosyncratic beauty contest — overseen by an all-male panel of notables, animated by hired dance troupes, and with traditional authorities in compulsory attendance — was framed as an election in honour of Quispe Sise (Inés) Huaylas Yupanqui, daughter of Francisco Pizarro, who became a prominent mestiza (Rostworowski, 2003).

The performance, at which the chosen Ñusta — a title that alludes to high-status Incan maids — receives a pseudo-traditional costume worn to promote tourism when accompanying the Mayor on official business, has been annually repeated, but the archaeological setting has been dropped in favour of the modern sports coliseum. Its original intention to revaluate local history (G. Huamaní, pers. comm., July 2008) has shifted towards a folkloristic branding of the region intended for tourists. Excavation results remain unpublished, initiatives to resettle on-site residents have failed, and the site's heritage status remains in limbo. Under these circumstances it is hard to envisage effective legal protection as a basis for inclusive development strategies. The symbolic legitimacy afforded by the archaeological location, moreover, is no longer wished or required. Unlike in neighbouring Yungay, trivializing exoticization of indigenous traditions by urban mestizo elites appears to be a viable driver of economic development.

The setting for reinventing tradition and promoting tourism chosen by the provincial government of Yungay is dramatically situated between the glaciers of Huascarán and Huandoy. The high plain of Keushu straddles the intakes of two major irrigation systems and architectural remains are spread over 100 hectares. Unlike Tumshuqaiku it is far removed from the urban centre at the valley bottom and colonial destruction and looting at Keushu gave way to herding well into the 1970s, when the lands were collectively adjudicated to a farming community (Comunidad Campesina Unidos Venceremos). Huarca, a staunchly independent local community faction, claims Keushu as part of its territory but intra-community disputes about access and control are frequent. Additionally, the higher reaches of the site fall within Huascarán National Park, a UNESCO World Heritage since 1985. Notwithstanding, Keushu received few visitors until 2004 when private entrepreneurs began promoting it as a tourist destination.

The Raimi Killa, an Inca re-enactment 'festival', was twice promoted by the head of a nearby museum. Ignoring the lack of evidence for Inca settlement and bypassing community leadership, dancers were hired in the regional capital for an afternoon of music, dance, sports, and beer. The number of tourists appears not to have made it worth the while to continue the enterprise, but several local artists have since used the lake as a setting for music videos. Shortly after, construction of a luxury mountaineering lodge nearby prompted a rush by cultural authorities to delimit and declare the site as a means of legal protection. The running of a private business on collective property also raised tensions between different sectors of the community (Herrera,

2013b). To compound matters, the provincial municipality recently (2010) used heavy machinery on site and within the national park to remodel the ancient irrigation system. Efforts to effect economic development by recourse to the archaeological resources in Keushu have, in sum, given rise to legal challenges which touch upon sensitive issues of community birth right, land-use and superimposed jurisdiction which will take the courts years to resolve. Unregulated business ventures have exacerbated tensions between the state institutions entrusted with conservation, private and community actors pushing the tourism agenda and local campesino farmers. In a telling twist of the hybridity tale, the most recent public performance at Keushu had a more overtly political edge: the provincial Mayor came to commemorate Dia del Campesino or peasant's day (formerly Día del Indio). After a public offering to the Pachamama (Earth Mother), a re-enactment ceremony by local school children was held for the local community and a modest number of tourists (Huaraz Noticias, 2012). The legend of Huascar and Wandy, a popular neo-indigenist story taken up by a succession of regional mestizo writers, is a reinvented tradition which sees ancestral tutelary deities turn into mountains as they escape an impossible love. Like the Caraz' beauty contest, its public deployment in an archaeological setting places social memory at odds with what happened in history.

Facing the hybridity of heritage

The emergence of hybrid heritage epistemologies raises multifaceted challenges, many of which stem from overlaps in regimes of value giving rise to conflicts. The deployment of archaeology as a driver of economic development in the Andes still hinges heavily on the special relationship between the State and archaeologists which foregrounds the historical, testimonial and scientific value entrusted to professional custodians — the 'patrimonial pact' established in the early decades of the twentieth century (Hernández, 2013). Since the neoliberal turn of the 1990s, archaeologists have increasingly come to be charged with developing economic potential. Since heritage is deployed as a pre-set category predicated on this pact, colonial exclusions are inevitably replicated in the process of heritagization itself. With state funding and legitimized through archaeology, ancient farmland, settlements, and places of gathering are delimited as territories and transformed into intangible sites, often curtailing customary rights of use and transit. Additionally, heritagization tends to alienate officials, usually urban mestizos, and rural populations — often indigenous farmers — reifying long-seated divisions which promote an unfavourable climate for the development of consensual approaches. Entrepreneurs who develop and sell products to outsiders on the back of such appropriations, usually outsiders themselves, tend to bear the brunt of the emerging grudges, although field archaeologists often feel them as well.

Intentions to effect economic development have long been built on the ideas of a handful of decision-makers, but as the framing of the indigenous established during the heyday of paternalist indigenism and nationalist archaeology crumbles, the role of things, places, and landscapes in the construction of local identity has come to the fore. Archaeologists have traditionally operated in the context of state policy, putting into practice development doctrines rooted in nation-building, and many continue to benefit from direct investment in research and restoration, geared to the production of destinations. Growing numbers are engaged in impact assessment for the private sector or drawing up itineraries for the tourism industry, but the successful production of destinations has proved elusive, and research and heritage outcomes from salvage archaeology remain rare. In the Ancash highlands re-enactments at archaeological sites, often the outcome of opportunistic alliances driven by powerful local or regional actors, have been moderately successful in attracting visitors. While openly acknowledging indigeneity and the role of places, invented rituals provide a weak basis for building a more consensual approach to heritage.

To think about *patrimonio* more openly the different development intentions and goals pertaining to regimes of value grounded in economics, science, and identity need to be distinguished. What is there, locally, that all concerned have inherited — why and in which ways? On-site discussions towards consensual and contextual definitions of heritage seem a promising first step that may provide a measure of effective protection for the material remains and surrounding ecosystems, as well as bolstering local community organization and provide a more solid base to discuss yearned-after possibilities for long- term benefits. As I have pointed out, however, the calendar of tourism often comes into conflict with calendars of festivities meaningfully grounded in traditional agricultural practice. Synching thus seems an important avenue for archaeologists and heritage practitioners to explore.

Finally, and beyond fostering, timing, and siting inter-cultural dialogues on heritage, archaeologists can point to the ways in which people in the past interacted and negotiated the uses of landscapes, locales, and objects in ways that inform local debates surrounding development ideals, intentions, practices, and consequences. Once heritage is consensually defined in context, stakeholders may participate in shared visions of development that engage invariably painful histories and address ongoing processes of exclusion, as well as producing material benefits. Producing wealth, rather than riches, will undoubtedly require archaeologists to develop deeper understandings of the local meanings of things, places, and landscapes.

Acknowledgements

I am grateful to Paul Burtenshaw and Peter Gould for the invitation to attend the London conference and submit the present article. Their editorial assistance and the comments received from them, Jamie Larkin, and anonymous reviewers were most helpful. My participation and subsequent work was made possible by the Gerda Henkel Foundation through an M4Human Marie Curie Fellowship.

Notes

[1] 'The tallest disgrace for a poor country is that instead of producing wealth it produces rich people. Rich people without wealth [. . .]' (Couto, 2005: 23, author's translation).

[2] In this paper, commoditization and commodification are used interchangeably when reference is made to the process whereby things become commodities — in the sense of Appadurai (1986), whereas commodification is reserved to highlight the reductivist transition of mercantile regimes of value.

Bibliography

Alcina Franch, J. 1995. *Arqueólogos o Anticuarios. Historia antigua de la Arqueología en la América Española*. Madrid: Ediciones del Serbal.

Alloo, F., Antrobus, P., Berg, R. J., Emmerij, I., Escobar, A., Esteva, G., Horn, J., Kerr, J., Kothari, S., Mahfouz, A., Moseley, S. F., Mumtaz, K., Mwapachu, J., Okello, D., Raghuram, S., Rice, A. E., Sachs, Sadik, W., & Van Gennip, J. 2007. Reflections on 50 Years of Development. *Development*, 50(1): 4–32.

Appadurai, A. 1986. Commodities and the Politics of Value. In: A. Appadurai, ed. *The Social Life of Things: Commodities in Cultural Perspective*. Cambridge: Cambridge University Press, pp. 3–63.

Bueno, A. 2008. *Tunshukaiko*. Caraz: El Inca.

Burger, R. 2009. *The Life and Writings of Julio C. Tello: America's First Indigenous Archaeologist*. Iowa City: Iowa University Press.

Cedeño, R. 2001. *La magia de los Andes*. Lima: Grupo metafísico de Lima.

Coloma, C. 1994. *Los inicios de la arqueología en el Perú o 'Antigüedades Peruanas' de Mariano Eduardo de Rivero*. Lima: Instituto Latinoamericano de Cultura y Desarrollo.

Connerton, P. 1989. *How Societies Remember*. Cambridge: Cambridge University Press.

Cordy Collins, A. 1992. Archaism or Tradition? The Decapitation Theme in Cupisnique and Moche Iconography. *Latin American Antiquity*, 3(3): 206–20.

Couto, Mia. 2005. *Pensatempos: textos de opinião*. Lisbon: Editorial Ndjira.

Cowen, M. P. & Shenton, R. W. 1996. *Doctrines of Development*. London: Routledge.

De la Cadena, M. 2000. *Indigenous mestizos: The Politics of Race and Culture in Cuzco, Peru, 1919–1991*. Durham, North Carolina: Duke University Press.

De la Cadena, M. 2006. ¿Son los mestizos híbridos? Las políticas conceptuales de las identidades andinas. *Universitas Humanística*, 61: 51–84.

De Leonardis, L. & Lau, G. 2004. Life, Death and Ancestors. In: H. Silverman, ed. *Andean Archaeology*. Oxford: Blackwell Publishing, pp. 77–115.

De Rivero, M. 1994 [1827]. Antigüedades peruanas. In: C. Coloma, ed. *Los inicios de la arqueología en el Perú: o 'Antigüedades peruanas' de Mariano Eduardo de Rivero*. Lima: Instituto Latinoamericano de Cultura y Desarrollo, pp. 86–147.

Escobar, A. 1995. *La invención del Tercer Mundo: construcción y deconstrucción del desarrollo*. Barcelona: Norma.

Escobar, A. 1997. Antropología y desarrollo. *Revista Internacional de Ciencias Sociales*, 154: 497–515.

Foley, R. 1981. Off-site Archaeology: An Alternative Approach for the Short-Sited. In: I. Hodder, G. Isaac, and N. Hammond, eds. *Pattern of the Past: Studies in Honour of David Clarke*. Cambridge: Cambridge University Press, pp. 157–83.

Gade, D. 1992. Landscape, System and Identity in the Post-Conquest Andes. *Annals of the Association of American Geographers*, 82: 460–77.

Gell, A. 1992. *The Anthropology of Time*. Oxford: Berg.

Gerdau, K. & Herrera, A. 2010. Why Dig Looted Tombs? Two Examples and Some Answers from Keushu (Ancash Highlands, Peru). *Bulletins et Mémoires de la Société d'Anthropologie de Paris*, 22: 1–11.

Haber, A. 2013. Arqueología y desarrollo: anatomía de la complicidad. In: A. Herrera, ed. *Arqueología y desarrollo en América del Sur. De la práctica a la teoría*. Bogotá and Lima: Universidad de los Andes and IEP, pp. 13–17.

Hann, C. M. 1998. Introduction: The Embeddedness of Property. In: C. M. Hann, ed. *Property Relations: Renewing the Anthropological Tradition*. Cambridge: Cambridge University Press, pp. 1–47.

Hernández, R. 2013. ¿De qué hablamos cuando hablamos de participación comunitaria en la gestión del patrimonio cultural? *Revista Argumentos*, 7(3) [accessed 19 August 2014]. Available at: <http://revistargumentos.org.pe/participacion_patrimonio.html>.

Herrera, A. 2007. Social Landscapes and Community Identity: The Social Organisation of Space in the North-Central Andes. In: S. Kohring and S. Wynne-Jones, eds. *Defining Social Complexity: Approaches to Power and Interaction in the Archaeological Record*. Malden, UK: Oxbow Books, pp. 161–85.

Herrera, A. 2011a. *La recuperación de tecnologías indígenas: arqueología, tecnologías y desarrollo*. Bogotá and Lima: Universidad de los Andes, Instituto de Estudios Peruanos and Consejo Latinoamericano de Ciencias Sociales.

Herrera, A. 2011b. Indigenous Archaeology . . . in Peru? In: C. Gnecco and P. Ayala, eds. *Indigenous People and Archaeology in Latin America*. Walnut Creek, Califorinia: Left Coast Press, pp. 67–87.

Herrera, A. 2013a. Arqueología y desarrollo en el Perú. In: A. Herrera, ed. *Arqueología y desarrollo en América del Sur. De la práctica a la teoría*. Bogotá and Lima: Universidad de los Andes and IEP, pp. 75–95.

Herrera, A. 2013b. Heritage Tourism, Identity and Development in Peru. In: *International Journal of Historical Archaeology*, 17: 275–95.

Huanacuni, F. 2010. *Buen Vivir / Vivir Bien. Filosofía, políticas, estrategias y experiencias regionales andinas*. Lima: Coordinadora Andina de Organizaciones Indígenas — CAOI.

Huaraz Noticias. 2012. Yungay rindió homenaje a los campesinos y la tierra. Huaraz Noticias [accessed 27 June 2013]. Available at: <http://www.huaraznoticias.com/reportajes/yungay-rindio-homenaje-a-los-campesinos-y-la-tierra>.

Isbell, W. 1997. *Mummies and Mortuary Monuments: A Postprocessual Prehistory of Central Andean Social Organization*. Austin, Texas: University of Texas Press, Austin.

Kendall, A. & Rodriguez A. 2010. *Desarrollo y perspectivas de los sistemas andenería en los Andes Centrales del Perú*. Lima and Cusco: Instituto Francés de Estudios Andinos and Centro Bartolomé de las Casas.

Korstanje, M. A. & García, J. 2007. The Qhapaq Ñan Project: A Critical View. *Archaeologies*, 3(2): 116–31.

Kummer, L. J. 2006. How Real is that Ruin? *New York Times* [online], 21 March [accessed 19 January 2014]. Available at: <http://www.nytimes.com/2006/03/21/arts/design/21inca.html?pagewanted=all and_r=0>.

Lau, G. 2013. *Ancient Alterity in the Andes*. New York: Routledge.

Lumbreras, L. G. 2000. Comentario. In: W. Alva, F. de Trazegnies and L. G. Lumbreras, eds. *El Patrimonio Cultural del Perú, vol. 1*. Lima: Editorial del Congreso de la República, pp. 79–93.

Macera, P. 2000. Patrimonio cultural: historia del debate. In: W. Alva, F. de Trazegnies, and L. G. Lumbreras, eds. *El Patrimonio Cultural del Perú, vol. 1*. Lima: Editorial del Congreso de la República, pp. 61–78.

Menzel, D. 1960. Archaism and Revival on the South Coast of Peru. In: F. C. Wallace, ed. *Men and Cultures. Selected Papers of the Fifth International Congress of Ethnological and Anthropological Sciences, Philadelphia 1–9 September 1956*. Philadelphia: University of Pennsylvania Press, pp. 596–600.

Moore, J. 2010. Making a huaca. Memory and Praxis in Prehispanic Far Northern Peru. *Journal of Social Archaeology*, 10(3): 398–422.

Patterson, T. 2004. Class Conflict, State Formation and Archaism. Some Instances from Ancient Peru. *Journal of Social Archaeology*, 4(3): 288–306.

Pérez, B. 2011. Nuevas y viejas narrativas turísticas sobre la cultura indígena en los Andes. In: Ll. Prats & A. Santana, eds. *Turismo y patrimonio, entramados narrativos*. El Sauzal: Asociación Canaria de Antropología, pp. 27–48.

Pillsbury, J. & Trever, L. 2008. The King, the Bishop, and the Creation of an American Antiquity. *Ñawpa Pacha*, 29: 1–29.

Ravines, R. 2000. Los bienes culturales y su pertenencia. In: W. Alva, F. de Trazegnies, and L. G. Lumbreras, eds. *El Patrimonio Cultural del Perú, vol. 1*. Lima: Editorial del Congreso de la República, pp. 562–63.

Rostworowski, M. 2000. Patrimonio Cultural: crisis y futuro. In: W. Alva, F. de Trazegnies, and L. G. Lumbreras, eds. *El Patrimonio Cultural del Perú, vol. 1*. Lima: Editorial del Congreso de la República, pp. 115–17.

Rostworowski, M. 2002. Los infinitos tesoros del antiguo Perú. In: M. Guerra, O. Holguín, and C. Gutiérrez, eds. *Sobre el Perú: Homenaje a José de la Puente Candamo*. Lima: PUCP, pp. 1140–50.

Rostworowski, M. 2003. *Francisca Pizarro, una ilustre mestiza 1534–1598*. Lima: IEP.

Rowe, J. H. 1971. The Influence of Chavín Art on Later Styles. In: E. P. Benson, ed. *Dumbarton Oaks Conference on Chavín*. Washington: Dumbarton Oaks research Library and Collection, pp. 101–24.

Ruiz Rubio, R. 2010. Neoliberalismo y su impacto sobre las políticas públicas de turismo en Perú. In: R. Fernandez Miranda and R. Ruiz Rubio, eds. *Políticas públicas, beneficios privados: mecanismos, políticas y actuaciones públicas para la globalización del turismo*. Madrid: Foro de Turismo Responsable and AECI, pp. 201–27.

Sachs, W. ed. 1991. *The Development Dictionary: A Guide to Knowledge as Power*. London and New Jersey: Zed Books.

Shady, R. 1999. El patrimonio arqueológico y su contribución al desarrollo nacional. In: M. Burga, ed. *Cultura y desarrollo: educación, patrimonio cultural y proyectos de desarrollo. Primer ciclo de conferencias, vol. 1*. Lima: Instituto Nacional de Cultura and Asociación de Amigos del Libro, pp. 87–105.

Solano, Francisco de. 1979. *Antonio de Ulloa y la Nueva Espanña*. México: UNAM.

Trivelli, C. & Hernández, R. 2009. Apostando por el Desarrollo Territorial Rural con Identidad Cultural: La Puesta en Valor del Patrimonio Prehispánico de la Costa Norte de Perú. In: C. Ranaboldo and A. Schejtman, eds. *El valor del patrimonio cultural. Territorios rurales, experiencias y proyecciones latinoamericanas*, pp. 201–36.

Ubilluz, J. 2000. La legislación sobre el patrimonio cultural: una visión en el tiempo. In: W. Alva, F. de Trazegnies, and L. G. Lumbreras, eds. *Patrimonio cultural del Perú, vol. 2*. Lima: Fondo Editorial del Congreso del Perú, pp. 515–27.

Valencia, F. 2008a. *El tráfico ilícito de bienes culturales en el Perú* [online] [accessed 13 October 2012]. Available at: <http://blog.pucp.edu.pe/item/24634/el-trafico-ilicito-de-bienes-culturales-en-el-peru>.

Valencia, F. 2008b. *Modifican la Ley General del Patrimonio Cultural de la Nación — Ley N° 28296* [online] [accessed 13 October 2012]. Available at: <http://blog.pucp.edu.pe/item/24636/modifican-la-ley-general-del-patrimonio-cultural-de-la-nacion-ley-n-28296>.

Van Dyke, R. M. & Alcock, S. E. eds. 2003. *Archaeologies of Memory*. Malden, UK: Blackwell.

Wylie, A. 2005. The Promise and Perils of an Ethics of Stewardship. In: L. Meskell and P. Pels, eds. *Embedding Ethics*. Oxford and New York: Berg, pp. 47–68.

Zevallos Quiñones, J. 1994. *Huacas y huaqueros en Trujillo durante el Virreinato*. Instituto Nacional de Cultura, Trujillo, pp. 1535–1835.

Notes on contributor

Building on regional research into the ecological and economic aspects of settlement strategies in the central Conchucos region, Alexander Herrera turned to the study of mortuary and ceremonial landscapes across the Ancash highlands. His focus on identity and territory as colonial tools of archaeological discourse led him to address the role of archaeologists and the appropriation of archaeological knowledge in rural development projects and in heritage tourism. Currently he conducts research into symbolic and technical aspects of water management. He has lectured at Universidad de los Andes, Colombia, since 2006 and is currently a Fellow of the Commission for Archaeology of Non-European Cultures at the German Archaeological Institute. Recent books include: *La recuperación de tecnologías indígenas: arqueología, tecnología y desarrollo en los Andes*, and *Arqueología y desarrollo en América del Sur: de la práctica a la teoría*.

Correspondence to: Alexander Herrera. Email: alherrer@uniandes.edu.co

PUBLIC ARCHAEOLOGY, Vol. 13 Nos 1–3, 2014, 85–90

Comment: Concepts in Archaeology and Economic Development

Johannes F. Linn

Emerging Markets Forum, & the Brookings Institution, USA

This note is a comment on the papers and presentations by Paul Burten-shaw, Alexander Herrera, and Arjo Klamer. It aims to provide a simple conceptual framework to help bridge the gap between cultural and economic values in archaeology, by considering the meaning of and circular interaction between the key concepts of cultural assets, values, stakeholders and conservation. It further explores the notion of sustainability and scaling up as significant elements of an effective and high impact approach to conservation.

KEYWORDS cultural assets, values, stakeholders, conservation, scaling up

Introduction

The 2012 Archaeology and Economic Development conference was about closing 'the gap [between] cultural and economic values in archeology' (Burtenshaw). In the first session of the conference authors were asked to explore whether and how concepts commonly used within these two disciplines can be interpreted or clarified to help close this gap. I believe their presentations contributed the building blocks for a bridge across the divide between the perspectives of archaeology and of economics. The following commentary is intended to help put these building blocks together.

A simple graph may help. Figure 1 highlights the key concepts used by the presenters. Five separate boxes and ovals are shown in an interactive cycle: 'cultural assets' generate 'values' for 'stakeholders' who need to 'conserve' the 'cultural assets'. A number of facilitating factors ('information', 'results', 'persuasion', etc.) support the interactions in this cycle. Let us look at each of these five key components in some greater detail and then also consider the important concepts of sustainability and scalability, which were discussed repeatedly during the conference.

Cultural assets

The presenters used different concepts to represent the stock of cultural assets: Burtenshaw preferred the term 'capital' and Hererra discussed 'patrimony', while

 DOI 10.1179/1465518714Z.00000000056

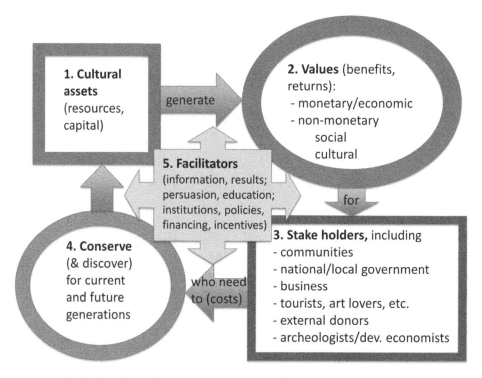

FIGURE 1   A simple picture of common concepts and their interactions.

economists and archaeologists have used both these terms as well as 'resource' and 'asset'. Each term is anchored in a different strand of analysis, and hence carries different connotations and intellectual baggage. The term 'capital' is central to economic analysis; 'assets' are usually associated with financial markets; 'resources' is a term used in environmental analysis; and 'patrimony' reflects a sense of historic significance linked to national or ethnic legacy and identity (as used by Herrera, based on the Spanish term *patrimonio*).

My feeling is that the term 'asset' may be the least freighted with connotational baggage and most readily accepted across the intellectual divide between archaeologists and economists. But, more importantly, while not disputing the possible differences in connotations, I believe that all four terms are in fact interchangeable. Rather than dwelling on the possible differences, it is useful to focus on the commonality that they all share: the cultural asset (or capital, resource, etc.) generates a return or benefit (i.e. something of value), to certain stakeholders. This brings us to our second set of concepts.

Values

The presenters were concerned with values (or, alternatively, returns and benefits) generated by cultural assets. Klamer went to some lengths to lay out various concepts of value developed by economists (option, existence, bequest) that could be relevant to cultural assets. But, like Burtenshaw, I think for our current purposes it suffices to distinguish between economic, social, and cultural values, with economic values taking mostly a monetary form, while the other two are largely non-monetary. The presenters noted that there may be trade-offs between different types of values, for example, maximizing the economic value of a cultural asset may reduce its cultural and social value, as reflected in Herrera's concern about the 'McDonaldization' of cultural assets. At the same time, it is worth noting that there can also be strong complementarities between the different types of values. Most obviously, privately owned cultural objects have become a major form of financial investment while their collectors also treasure them for their cultural value. And, as Klamer noted, many stakeholders who treasure (and are willing to pay for) cultural assets because of the cultural values they convey find that by joining forces in preserving cultural assets they also generate social value among themselves.

Stakeholders

Each of the presenters considered various stakeholders who are concerned with cultural assets (i.e. who derive some form of value from them).[1] Stakeholders include communities where the assets are located,[2] government (national and local), business, tourists, art lovers, donors and philanthropists, and — not to be forgotten — archaeologists and development economists. Each of these stakeholders has a potential interest in the cultural asset, and more specifically in a particular combination of values generated by the asset.[3] Because of the differences in interests, and because interests may be competing with each other, there may be tensions among different stakeholders over what type of value (or combination of values) is to be maximized for a particular cultural asset. Such tensions may arise between and within commonly identified groups of stakeholders, as in the case of opposing groups within a community, or the not uncommon competition between different government ministries. But besides tensions, there is also the potential for coalitions to be formed among stakeholders. The case of Butrint, Albania, which Richard Hodges describes in this volume, represents an example of conflicting government and business interests on the one hand, and the external donor and archaeologists' community on the other.

Conservation

Ultimately, the various stakeholders have to cooperate in some fashion to discover and conserve the cultural assets for current and future generations. In this context they will incur certain costs — financial and non-financial — to preserve the asset.[4] How the asset is preserved will affect both the values derived by different stakeholders and the costs each stakeholder incurs. For each stakeholder a key question is then how the values or benefit she or he derives from the asset stack up against the costs incurred in preserving it in a particular form. The degree of support or opposition for a particular form of conservation by a particular stakeholder will depend on this balance between costs and benefits.

Facilitators[5]

A number of factors facilitate (or obstruct) this circular process of cultural heritage conservation. One key factor stressed by the presenters was *information* about the various aspects of the cycle: about the cultural assets and the values generated, about the stakeholders and their interests, and about the costs and benefits (and their distribution across stakeholders) of maintaining cultural assets. Another way to look at information is to try and determine and measure what are the *results* of actions taken by different actors or stakeholders in this circular process, a question increasingly asked by donors and governments engaged in supporting cultural heritage preservation.[6]

The presenters also stressed the need of *persuasion* and *education*, presumably based on factual information and measured results as a way to ensure that there is a convincing *narrative* which leads to greater understanding and increased valuation (sometimes referred to as 'valorization') of cultural heritage assets by the stakeholders.[7]

Finally, there is a set of overarching organizational factors including:

(a) the setting up and strengthening of *institutions* and *policies* in support of the cycle of conservation;

(b) the establishment of *financing* mechanisms, which are designed to ensure that the financial costs are sustainably covered by financial contributions from various stakeholders (an aspect stressed by Klamer);

(c) exploring the *incentives* for various stakeholders to support the process of conservation of cultural heritage assets.[8]

Sustainability and scalability

Finally, two key concepts — sustainability and scalability — surfaced repeatedly during the conference and directly relate to the cycle of conservation of cultural assets reflected in Figure 1:

> 'Sustainability' means ensuring that the conservation cycle in Figure 1 can be maintained over time. This requires that the key stakeholders have a sustained incentive to invest in maintaining the cultural asset, that the results of their efforts are adequately captured by information and measurement and that the financing mechanisms are sustainable.

> 'Scalability' means that a conservation process can be expanded for greater impact on a specific site or that it can be replicated across sites nationally or internationally.[9] Figure 2 shows this scaling up process schematically: over time one moves from one asset (site) to the next, replicating the circular process of conservation and adapting it as needed to the specific circumstances of the additional assets. As one does so, the beneficial impact in terms of additional value created expands (or is scaled up).

Scalability is more demanding than sustainability, in terms of the number of stakeholders that need to be considered, number and quality of institutions that have to be created or strengthened, the enabling policies that have to be put in place, and the financing that has to be mobilized. At the same time, as Dallan Timothy pointed out

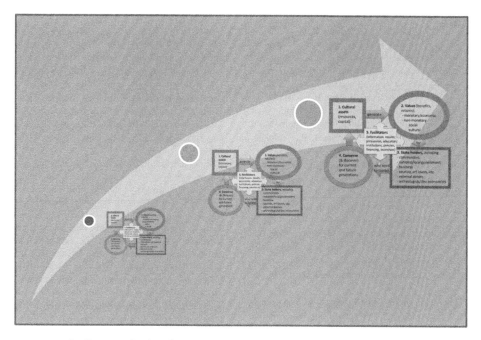

FIGURE 2   Scaling up of cultural asset conservation processes.

in this volume, the systematic development of multiple cultural sites along 'trails and routes' can much enhance the economic impact of cultural asset development. In any case, if the great challenge of preservation of the world's cultural heritage is to be met, and if cultural heritage conservation is to contribute significantly to address the global development needs, scaling up of effective and sustainable conservation process will be essential.

Conclusion

I believe the gap between archaeologists and development economists can be bridged by:

- A more consistent and widely shared language of common concepts;
- A clearer understanding of the dynamic linkage of key aspects of the process of cultural asset preservation;
- The recognition among archaeologists that the economic and financial dimensions of their projects are critical for the sustainability and scalability of their efforts;
- The recognition among development economists that non-economic values play an important role and that the conservation of cultural assets sustainably and at scale will make a real contribution to human welfare.

Notes

[1] This value (net of costs; see more on costs below) may be negative for some stakeholders, as in the case of communities displaced from access to traditional objects of worship or land by the public or commercial development of a cultural asset.

[2] This is the most common understanding of 'community' in the context of community-based development initiatives (see Coben, this volume); but at times broader concepts of community are also employed, referring in effect to the community of all stakeholders concerned with a particular cultural asset.

[3] As Leventhal (this volume) points out, some presumptive stakeholders may not even define an asset as 'cultural' (or at least not as relevant to their culture), even if others do. Leventhal's example is the lack of interest by contemporary Mayan communities in ancient Maya sites located nearby in the Yucatan Peninsula.

[4] These costs may be simply the costs of archaeological excavation and conservation, but they can also be costs of opportunities foregone (or 'opportunity costs', as the economist would say such as a community's opportunity to earn a living on now protected land or its ability to maintain its traditional way of life (as stressed by Herrera).

[5] This somewhat clumsy term is not used by the authors. However, I introduce it here, not as a technical concept, but as a term that helps describe the role of various factors mentioned by the authors as contributing to the preservation of cultural assets.

[6] While this preoccupation with results and their measurement is not reflected in the essays dealt with here, it is a topic discussed in other papers in this volume.

[7] The importance of archaeologists developing convincing narratives for the cultural assets with which they work is stressed by Boytner (this volume).

[8] Gould (this volume) rightly stresses the role of institutions and incentives. In terms of the concepts used here, incentives arise for individual stakeholders from the balance of benefits (or values broadly defined above) and costs (again broadly defined). The greater the positive net benefit for the stakeholder, the stronger the incentive to support conservation; or the more negative the net benefit (i.e. costs greater than benefits) the greater is the disincentive for stakeholders to do so.

[9] The papers in this volume that particularly point to the importance of scale are Timothy and Coben. For a general review of experience with scaling up in the development literature and practice, see Hartmann and Linn (2008).

Bibliography

Hartmann, A. & Linn, J. 2008. Scaling Up: A Framework and Lessons for Development Effectiveness from Literature and Practice. *Wolfensohn Center for Development Working Paper No. 4* [accessed 21 January 2014]. Available at: <http://www.brookings.edu/research/papers/2008/10/scaling-up-aid-linn>.

Notes on contributor

Dr Johannes F. Linn is Senior Resident Scholar at the Emerging Markets Forum and Non-resident Senior Fellow of the Global Economy and Development program at the Brookings Institution. He holds a PhD in economics from Cornell University and subsequently worked at the World Bank for thirty years, including as Vice President for Europe and Central Asia. He served on the Board of Directors of the Global Heritage Fund from 2004–10.

Correspondence to: Dr Johannes F. Linn, 2869 N. Beechwood Circle, Arlington, VA 22207, USA. Email: jlinn@brookings.edu

PUBLIC ARCHAEOLOGY, Vol. 13 Nos 1–3, 2014, 91–98

A Regional Perspective on Government, Archaeology, and Economic Development: The Americas

Pedro Paulo A. Funari

University of Campinas, Brazil

This paper considers archaeology, economic development, and government through a critical approach. It discusses the role of democracy, the rule of law, and the relationship between economic development and public policies aimed at improving the lives of ordinary people. It is argued that diminishing social inequalities are a shared concern and public policies are set up by democratic states to cope with this goal. The paper then turns to archaeology as a practice resulting from economic development and public policies. For the first century and a half, the discipline has been scholarly, elitist, and often colonialist. More recently, archaeology has been increasingly considered as a socially relevant endeavour in the Americas. Economic development, democracy, and the rule of law have been related in the last few decades. The paper concludes by stressing the role of public archaeology for a progressive role for archaeology in economic development in the future.

KEYWORDS economic development, rule of law, democracy, cultural resource management, the Americas

Introduction

The subject of this volume — archaeology and economic development — is a most important one, especially for the discipline of archaeology, if not for economics. And yet it is a neglected subject, seldom addressed in the archaeological literature and less so in development studies. This is even more amazing, considering that archaeology has been particularly affected by economic development in the last few decades. Whilst archaeology has been a scholarly (and imperialist) discipline since its inception in the nineteenth century, it is now mostly a practice linked to economic development. Worldwide, practical archaeology is mostly a field activity paid for by economic developers, be they private or of the state, usually thanks to mandatory environmental and heritage legislation. It is probably only too natural that economists were not

 DOI 10.1179/1465518714Z.00000000057

interested in considering the role of archaeology and development, but it is even more amazing that archaeologists took so long to pay any notice to the subject. In this paper, I will try to address these issues, paying especial attention to the context of the Americas. The paper will initially explore economic development, before turning to the role of archaeology in the Americas not only, nor mainly, in fostering economic development, but as way of contributing to less unequal social relations in the Americas and the world.

Development economics, government, and a critical approach

Development is a modern concept. It was, for example, never considered in antiquity. Classical Greek authors were concerned about love (*eros*), war (*polemos*), citizenship (*politeia*), even frankness (*parrhesia*), arrogance (*hybris*), and fate (*moira* or *tykhé*), but not something growing from inside out — this is the ultimate meaning of development (in plain English, development means 'unfolding', (cf. Fattal, 2011: 38)). It definitely is a modern concept. It is not ethical, nor personal, even less erotic. It is indeed modern, as it refers to the realm of the practical world, to the reproduction of economic capital: *Entwicklung*, as Karl Marx would say. For contemporary economists, there is no mystery, as Lucas notes, 'By the problem of economic development I mean simply the problem of accounting for the observed pattern, across countries and across time, in levels and rates of growth of per capita income' (1988: 3).

Still, economic development is much more complex than that. Great Britain was the first modern nation to significantly develop its economy as it emerged as a world power in the nineteenth century: the Empire with no sunset. Karl Marx was mesmerized by Britain, no doubt. Then, the United States got the prize and still keeps it, being challenged by Japan and Germany (since the 1980s) and more recently the emerging economies of China, India, and Brazil. However, whatever our stand on the relevance of economic development — as opposed to human development or happiness — it is beyond dispute that it matters a great deal to governments all over the world. This leads us to our second subject: government and policies (including archaeology).

Governments are increasingly concerned with the wellbeing of their citizens and there is a growing recognition that public policies are central to the implementation of effective and socially relevant strategies (Isin & Turner, 2002). Since Theodore Lowi's (1964) simple inversion of a political banality — that politics determines policies — political scientists continue to discuss whether and how 'policy determines politics' (cf. Rodrigues, 2010: 44; see also Mooney, 1995: 599). This discussion is particularly relevant in the context of the Americas, considering the long-standing democratic tradition in the United States and Canada and the late twentieth-century democratic trend throughout most of the Americas. However, democracy is not necessarily prone to social justice and '[...] democracies are not necessarily more efficient economically than other forms of government' (Schmitter & Karl, 1991: 227).

In any case, democracy and the rule of law are huge social achievements and they enable people to fight for their rights, not a mean feature, at least from my own Latin American standpoint, considering the heavy weight of dictatorial rule suffered in the region for so long and considering, furthermore, the secular authoritarian and patriarchal Iberian background (DaMatta, 1987; 1990; cf. Funari, 2006). Democracy is not enough to wipe out inequalities (Singer, 1986: 7), but still it is probably a *sine qua non* for diminishing them without suppressing freedom. Democracy also entails fairer public policies, taking them as 'government wide institutional rules and routines' (Barzelay, et al., 2003: 20), always subjected though to political, rather than narrow technical imperatives (Pelletier, 2005: 893; cf. the classic study by Lasswell, 1936). Public policies in democracies are taken here as no neutral endeavour, but as potentially challenging attitudes, as was pointed out recently (Goodin, et al., 2008: 7).

The job of the policy analyst is to 'speak truth to power' (Wildavsky, 1979), where the truths involved embrace not only the hard facts of positivist science but also the reflexive self-understandings of the community both writ large (the polity) and writ small (the policy community, the community of analysts) (Goodin, et al., 2008: 7).

To 'speak truth to power' is an expression with Biblical connotations (cf. Acts, 3: 3–4) and consequently associated with human and civil rights movements (Cuomo, 2003). Public policy scholars have been stressing the importance of a critical approach, as Dryzek (2008: 195) recently noted, 'The impetus of critique is also toward evaluation and improvement, not just description and explication'. There is thus a need to put government decisions and public policies in the due historical and political context, so that we can propose not only a critical assessment, but also the avenues open for action in the direction of more just and fair social relations. This approach is often associated with the left and social reformers, and rightly so. However, the concerns regarding social inequalities are equally at the heart of conservative thinking (Ferguson, 2012). As British novelist and Prime Minister Benjamin Disraeli observed in his novel of 1845, *Sybil of the two Nations*: 'Two nations; between whom there is intercourse and no sympathy [. . .] the rich and the poor' (Disraeli, 1998: 66).

Even if we do not agree with the conservative diagnosis or remedies (cf. Murray, 2012), the larger point is that social inequalities are seen as a problem to be addressed by any government. All this leads us to archaeology, for it is now mostly part of the public policies enacted by governments and the state apparatus, comprising legislative requirements. Economic development is a key strategy in developing countries such as Brazil to diminish social inequalities. This move inevitably involves the destruction of the natural environment and cultural heritage. In a democratic context, as we shall see, this implies involving rescue, salvage, and public archaeology strategies. We must then tackle the main challenges of these issues.

Archaeology as a practice resulting from economic development and public policies

Archaeology has, from its beginnings as a disciplinary practice, been linked to economic development, particularly through the institutional powers, as attested by the archaeological schools at Athens and Rome, and the prestigious chairs of archaeology in the most distinguished universities, such as Cambridge, Oxford, or Harvard (Alcock & Osborne, 2007; Dyson, 1998). From the 1960s onwards, archaeology departments in universities and museum sprouted, first in developed countries and later spreading to peripheral ones, including notably Latin America (Funari, et al., 2009). Scholarly archaeology has always been part of economic development, for it was a phenomenon of nationalist, capitalist, and imperialist moves (Hamilakis & Duke, 2007). Even the apparently most abstruse subjects, such as Maya civilization expansion, acme, and decline, were closely linked to American economic interests in modern Central America. Academic research has traditionally been driven by scientific issues, such as understanding the settlement of North America since the last glacial age (Adovasio & Page, 2002), or the dynamics of Mayan civilization (Brumfiel, 2009), but the academic archaeologists studying them were mostly Americans who depended indirectly on the economic development of their universities and grants from the United States government to set up projects to carry out fieldwork in remote and almost inaccessible sites, as was the case with the Maya heartland (Hendon & Joyce, 2004).

However, all this changed substantially in the last few decades, thanks to Cultural Resource Management (CRM), understood as archaeological heritage management practice resulting from systems of laws and regulations designed to minimize conflicts between the goals of economic development, on the one hand, and cultural heritage preservation and use by society at large on the other (Green, 2008: 389), particularly in the Americas. Thanks to the growing recognition of the importance of cultural heritage, CRM is now a main force in the Americas, being the organizing mechanism used for most of the archaeological field and lab work in several countries, from the United States (Patterson, 1999) to Brazil (Funari & Robrahn-González, 2007). Even in countries with no private archaeological enterprises, as is the case in Cuba, most of the archaeological work is paid for by tourism and is thus directly related to market forces (Curet, et al., 2005).

Of course, this says nothing about interpretation, for the source of funds coming from CRM or tourism does not impose a sole interpretive framework: quite the contrary. Strands of Marxist approaches flourish in Cuba (Domínguez, 2005) and the United States (Orser, 1996), but cultural history, processual and post- processual tenets are even more widespread, and interact in conflicting ways.

CRM, tourism, and other economic development trends in the Americas, in detriment to traditional research, scholarly archaeology, has not been entirely negative, considering the role archaeology traditionally played in defending the status quo and reactionary social practices (Funari, et al., 2011). As the Peruvian archaeologist Luis Lumbreras said in the 1960s, archaeology had been for a long time an 'arma de oppression' ('force for oppression'; author's translation) (Lumbreras, 1981: 6), concerned with the elite, as American historical archaeologist Charles E. Orser has also stressed (2011a; 2011b). The concern with heritage, even if mandatory and thanks to environmental legal constraints, has thus contributed to a change of focus from the colonizers to the colonized, from males to females, from rich to poor, from homogeneity to heterogeneity. Not necessarily, though, as Orser cautions himself:

> Given that so much American archaeology is now conducted within the cultural resource management environment, archaeologists may have difficulty making a case that a given site associated with 'the poor' is significant within federally mandated guidelines. (Orser, 2011: 152)

Mandated guidelines depend on power relations and public policies and thus on how economic development is, or is not, considered as related to justice, fairness, and the respect for diversity of behaviour and standpoints. Archaeology for justice depends thus on both a commitment by archaeologists and on society at large (Funari, 2009; Little, 2009). It is also true that 'A growing number of archaeological projects around the world have engaged in the process of community involvement' (Steen, et al., 2010: 174).

Community involvement is directly related to the understanding that any scholarly activity must be relevant to society at large and not only to fellow professionals. Again, this is the result of public policies resulting from economic development law and legal requirements, particularly in the Americas. To paraphrase Madonna, 'we're living in a material world', and materiality, by virtue of its very ability to exceed and subvert narratives, intentions, and signification, can help us to produce alternative histories of the past that surprise, displace, and critically interrogate conventional imaginations and explanations of social relations in the past and present (Richard, 2011: 172). It is noteworthy that subjects like the poor have benefited from CRM, considering that archaeological evidence may be a subject due to heritage concerns with ordinary people, even if in their relation with the wealthy, as Chris Matthews notes, 'in modern world archaeology, an essential starting point is to look at how poverty and wealth mutually construct persons and places in the modern landscapes that make up a project' (2011: 42).

This is clear in several initiatives, such as the Ludlow Colorado Coalfield War Archaeological Project — a university-based initiative (McGuire, et al., 2003), and the Canudos rebel community in late nineteenth-century Brazil. Canudos was a rebel community destroyed by the military in a few short years. Most rebels were killed, others were jailed, and the site itself was flooded. A century later, in a context of democratic rule and deploying CRM, Paulo Zanettini (2002) carried out fieldwork there revealing the life ways of both rebels and assailants. Tourism has also been responsible for the sponsoring of creative and critical archaeological initiatives in the United States and particularly in Latin America, where 'Tourism has increasingly become an important source of income and an important part of the development strategies in Latin American countries' (Baud & Ypeij, 2009: 5).

This process is fraught with contradictions and mixed results. For examples, Maya communities sometimes benefit but are sometimes opposed to tourist archaeology (Magnoni, et al., 2007: 374–75; see also Leventhal, this volume). Anglos and descendants of Pueblo inhabitants are not necessarily in agreement over heritage use (Atherton & Rotschild, 2008: 261), but this is no surprise, for, quoting Shanks (2009: 547): 'archaeologists work on the remains of the past. It is now widely accepted that archaeology is as much about our contemporary interests and active attentions to the past as it is a passive discovery of past ways of life'.

Conclusion

In this paper I stressed that economic development is a recent issue, stretching back to the industrial revolution at most, and foreign to other historical and social contexts. There is nothing natural or inevitable about it; it is a modern obsession. From this obsession comes several drivers, including archaeology as a nationalist, imperialist endeavour. In the last few decades, democracy, social inclusion, and the valorization of diversity have led to several moves aimed at countering earlier oppressive uses of the discipline. For example, in Brazil, democratization since the late 1979s has led to a greater spread of CRM practices, which has always been in conjunction with economic development concerns

There is no archaeological knowledge or practice without context and history (Shepherd, 2008: 207). However, archaeological interpretation has come a long way from earlier eras of un-nuanced positivism and full confidence in the objectivity of specialized scholarship (Silberman, 2007: 179) and economic development issues and resulting public policies played a role in this process. Public archaeology has a special role in forging this path (Schadla-Hall, 2006). In the Americas, this process has been particularly acute and comprehensive, considering the role economic development has been playing in developed and developing countries alike. In the last few decades, democratic trends led to generalized concern with social inclusion and the setting up of public policies aiming at reducing inequality.

Archaeology has come a long way from being a pursuit defending the status quo to one contributing, at least potentially, to more humane social relations.

Acknowledgements

My first thanks go to University College London and the organizers of the Archaeology and Economic Development Conference, particularly Tim Schadla-Hall, who was responsible for my coming to London. I also owe thanks to Louise Alfonso, Aline Vieira de Carvalho, Shannon Lee Dawdy, Michel Fattal, Yannis Hamilakis, Sandra Kishi, Gabino La Rosa, Barbara Little, Erika Robrahn-González, Fabiana Manzato, Chris Matthews, Randal McGuire, Charles E. Orser, Jr, Thomas Patterson, Michael Shanks, Nick Shepherd, Neil Silberman, Inês Virgínia Prado Soares, Emily Stovel, Paulo Eduardo Zanettini, Andrés Zarankin. I am also grateful for the support of Campinas University, the Brazilian National Science Foundation, São Paulo Science Foundation, and University College London. I am solely responsible for the ideas in the paper.

Bibliography

Adovasio, L. & Page, J. 2002. *The First Americans: In Pursuit of Archaeology's Great Mystery*. New York: Random House.

Alcock, S. E. & Osborne, R. 2007. *Classical Archaeology*. Oxford: Blackwell.

Atherton, H. & Rotshild, N. A. 2008. Colonialism, Past and Present. *Archaeologies*, 4(2): 250–63.

Barzelay, M., Gaetani, F., Cortazar Verlarde, J. C. & Cejudo, G. 2003. Research on Public Management Policy Change in Latin American Region: Conceptual Framework, Methodological Guide and Exemplars. *International Public Management Review*, 4(1): 20–42.

Baud, M. & Ypeij, A. 2009. *Cultural Tourism in Latin America*. Leiden: Brill.

Brumfiel, E. M. 2009. Mesoamerica. In: B. Cunliffe, C. Gosden, and R. A. Joyce, eds. *The Oxford Handbook of Archaeology*. Oxford: Oxford University Press, pp. 611–46.

Cuomo, K. K. 2003. *Speak Truth to Power. Human Rights Defenders who are Changing our World*. New York: Umbrage.

Curet, L. A., Dawdy, S. L., & La Rosa, G. 2005. *Dialogues in Cuban Archaeology*. Tuscaloosa: University of Alabama Press.

DaMatta, R. 1987. A questão da cidadania num universo relacional. In: *A casa e a rua*, Rio de Janeiro: Guanabara, pp. 71–104.

DaMatta, R. 1990. 'Você sabe com quem está falando?' Um ensaio sore a distinção entre indivíduo e pessoa no Brasil. In: *Carnavais, malandros e heróis: para uma Sociologia do dilema brasileiro*. Rio de Janeiro: Guanabara, pp. 146–204.

Disraeli, B. 1998 [1845]. *Sybil, Or the Two Nations*. Oxford: Oxford University Press.

Domínguez, L. 2005. Necklaces used in the *santería* of Cuba. *Beads: Journal of the Society of Bead Makers*, 17.

Dryzek, J. S. 2008. Policy Analysis as Critique. In: M. Moran, M. Rein, and R. E. Goodin, eds. *The Oxford Handbook of Public Policy*. Oxford: Oxford University Press, pp. 190–206.

Dyson, S. 1998. *Ancient Marbles to American Shores: Classical Archaeology in the United States*. Philadelphia: University of Pennsylvania Press.

Fattal, M. 2011. *Paroles et actes chez Héraclite. Sur les fondements théoriques de l'action morale*. Paris: L'Hamarttan.

Ferguson, N. 2012. Rich America, Poor America. *Newsweek*, 23 January, pp. 32–37.

Funari, P. P. A., Manzato, F., & Alfonso, L. P. 2011. Turismo e Arqueologia — uma abordagem pós-moderna em dois estudos de caso. In: S. Cureau, S. A. S. Kishi, I. V. P Soares, and C. M. F. Lage, eds. *Olhar interdisciplinar sobre a efetividade da proteção do patrimônio cultural*, 1st ed. Belo Horizonte: Fórum, vol. 1, pp. 431–67.

Funari, P. P. A. 2006. Conquistadors, Plantations, and *quilombo*: Latin America in Historical Archaeology Context. In: M. Hall and S. Silliman, eds. *Historical Archaeology*. Oxford: Blackwell.

Funari, P. P. A. & Robrahn-González, E. 2007. Ethics, Capitalism and Public Archaeology in Brazil. In: Y. Hamilakis and P. Duke, eds. *Archaeology and Capitalism*. Walnut Creek: Left Coast Press, pp. 137–49.

Funari, P. P. A. 2009. Historical Archaeology and Global Justice. *Historical Archaeology*, 43(4): 20–122.

Funari, P. P. A., Zarankin, A., & Stovel, E. 2009. South American Archaeology. In: B. Cunliffe, C. Gosden, and R. A. Joyce, eds. *The Oxford Handbook of Archaeology*. Oxford: Oxford University Press, pp. 958–97.

Goodin, R., Rein, M., & Moran, M. 2008. The Public and its Policies. In: M. Moran, M. Rein, and R. E. Goodin, eds. *The Oxford Handbook of Public Policy*. Oxford: Oxford University Press, pp. 3–35.

Green, T. J. 2008. Cultural Resource Management. In: R. Alexander Bendley, H. D. G. Maschner, and C. Chippindale, eds. *Handbook of Archaeological Theories*. Lanham, MD: Altamira, pp. 375–94.

Hamilakis, Y. & Duke, P. 2007. *Archaeology and Capitalism, from Ethics to Politics*. Walnut Creek: Left Coast Press.

Hendon, J. A. & Joyce, R. 2004. *Mesoamerican Archaeology: Theory and Practice*. Oxford: Blackwell.

Isin, E. F. & Turner, B. S. 2002. Citizenship Studies: An Introduction. *Handbook of Citizenship Studies*. London: Sage, pp. 1–10.

Lasswell, H. D. 1936. *Politics: Who Gets What, When, How*. Cleveland, OH: Meridian.

Little, B. 2009. What can Archaeology do for Justice, Peace, Community, and the Earth? *Historical Archaeology*, 43(4): 115–20.

Lowi, T. 1964. American Business, Public Policy, Case-Studies, and Political Theory. *World Politics*, 16(4): 677–715.

Lucas, R. E. 1988. On the Mechanics of Economic Development. *Journal of Monetary Economics*, 22: 3–42.

Lumbreras, L. 1981. *Arqueología como ciencia social*. Lima: Huastar.

Magnoni, A., Ardren, T., & Hutson, S. 2007. Tourism in the Mundo Maya: Inventions and (Mis)Representations of Maya Identities and Heritage. *Archaeologies*, 3(2): 353–83.

Matthews, C. N. 2011. Lonely Islands: Culture, Community, and Poverty in Archaeological Perspective. *Historical Archaeology*, 45(3): 41–54.

McGuire, R. H. & Reckner, P. E. 2003. Building a Working-Class Archaeology: The Colorado Coal Field War Project. *Industrial Archaeology Review*, 25(2): 83–95.

Mooney, C. Z. 1995. Legislating Morality in the American States: The Case of Pre-Roe Abortion Regulation Reform. *American Journal of Political Science*, 39(3): 599–627.

Murray, C. 2012. *Coming Apart: The State of White America 1960–2010*. New York: Crown.

Orser, C. E. 1996. *Historical Archaeology of the Modern World*. New York: Plennum.

Orser, C. E. 2011a. Beneath the Surface of Tenement Life: The Dialectics of Race and Poverty during America's Gilded Age. *Historical Archaeology*, 45(3): 151–65.

Orser, C. E. 2011b. The Archaeology of Poverty and the Poverty of Archaeology. *International Journal of Historical Archaeology*, 15(4): 533–43.

Patterson, T. 1999. The Political Economy of Archaeology in the United States. *Annual Review of Anthropology*, 28: 155–74.

Pelletier, D. L. 2005. The Science and Politics of Targeting: Who Gets What, When, and How. *The Journal of Nutrition*, 135(4): 890–93.

Richard, F. G. 2011. Materializing Poverty: Archaeological Reflections from the Postcolony. *Historical Archaeology*, 45(3): 166–82.

Rodrigues, M. M. A. 2010. *Políticas Públicas*. São Paulo: Publifolha.

Rowan, Y. M. & Baram, U. 2004. *Marketing Heritage, Archaeology and the Consumption of the Past*. Walnut Creek, CA: AltaMira.

Schadla-Hall, T. 2006. Public Archaeology. In: R. Layton, S. Shennan, and P. Stone, eds. *A Future for Archaeology*. London: University College London Press, pp. 77–82.

Schmitter, P. C. & Karl, T. L. 1991. What Democracy is . . . and is not. *Journal of Democracy*, 2(3): 75–88.

Shanks, M. 2009. Engagement: Archaeological Design and Engineering. *Archaeologies*, 5(3): 546–56.

Shepherd, N. 2008. Archaeology and the Weight of History. *Archaeologies*, 4(2): 205–07.

Silberman, N. 2007. 'Sustainable' Heritage? Public Archaeological Interpretation and the Marketed Past. In: Y. Hamilakis and P. Duke, eds. *Archaeology and Capitalism, from Ethics to Politics*. Walnut Creek, CA: Left Coast Press, pp. 179–93.

Singer, P. 1986. *Repartição da Renda. Pobres e ricos sob regime militar*. Rio de Janeiro: Jorge Zahar Editora.

Steen, D., Jacobs, J., Porter, B., & Routledge, B. 2010. Exploring Heritage Discourses in Central Jordan. In: R. Boytner, L. S. Dodd, and B. J. Parker, eds. *Controlling the Past, Owning the Future*. Arizona: University of Arizona Press, pp. 159–77.

Wildavsky, A. 1979. *Speaking Truth to Power: The Art and Craft of Policy Analysis*. Boston: Little, Brown.

Zanettini, P. E. 2002. *Arqueologia e reconstituição monumental do Parque Estadual de Canudos: etapa 1: o Parque Estadual de Canudos; etapa 2: o salvamento arqueológico emergencial do arraial de Canudos*. Salvador: UNEB.

Notes on contributor

Pedro Paulo A. Funari is Professor in the Department of History, University of Campinas, Brazil. He is a former World Archaeological Congress secretary, and research associate at the Illinois State University (USA) and Barcelona University (Spain). He is editor of several volumes, notably *Memories from Darkness* (2009), *New Perspectives on the Ancient World* (2008), *Global Archaeological Theory* (2005), *Historical Archaeology, Back from the Edge* (1999), and author of several papers published in such periodicals as *Antiquity*, *Current Anthropology*, *International Journal of Historical Archaeology*, *Journal of Social Archaeology*, *Historical Archaeology*, and *Révue Archéologique*. Professor Funari is committed to socially engaged scholarly activity.

Correspondence to: Pedro Paulo A. Funari, Instituto de Filosofia e Ciências Humanas Rua Cora Coralina, 100 CEP 13083-896, Cidade Universitária Zeferino Vaz, B. Geraldo, Campinas, São Paulo, Brasil. Email: ppfunari@uol.com.br

PUBLIC ARCHAEOLOGY, Vol. 13 Nos 1–3, 2014, 99–112

Cultural Heritage in China: Between Policies, Development, Professional Discourse, and the Issue of Managing

Luca Zan

University of Bologna, Italy

China is one of the richest countries in terms of cultural heritage. However, the unprecedented economic development of the last three decades has posed serious challenges to its survival. The growing importance of salvage excavation raises serious tensions between the textual-historical tradition and archaeological finds, with controversial impacts in terms of conservation and research, due to administrative mechanisms. To understand these phenomena it is necessary to reconstruct the role played by the complex process of reform, following the open-door policy and its impacts on the 'Heritage Chain' in terms of preservation, archaeological excavation, conservation, research, and museum and site access.

KEYWORDS heritage management, China, heritage chain, conservation, public management

Introduction

As in any paper, elements of specificity can be viewed on two different levels: the ontological and the perspectival. The former relates to what is actually happening in China in the field of cultural heritage: more than focusing on archaeology per se as a distinct area of research, the focus is on the broader area of heritage. The latter relates to the perspectives adopted by the researcher and the specific perspectives that are used. In this introduction, I attempt to make explicit some of the basic elements of my approach, to help the reader understand the overall positioning of my research and my ultimate research goals.

First, drawing on critical management studies, I am interested in issues of organizing (and managing) entities (or organizations), whatever their contents and tasks are. While sometimes professionals tend to associate the notion of 'management' with commercial and profit-seeking activities, I am concerned with looking at issues of 'managing/organizing' (Czarniawska, 2008) in any potential activity within a heritage

   DOI 10.1179/1465518714Z.00000000058

organization (excavation itself is a complex activity that is, in one way or another, 'managed').

Second, I am particularly interested in practices more than abstract ways of looking at management as a set of principles, procedures, and normative statements strictly determined by experts or by law and regulations. In that sense I am more concerned with actual behaviours — what is actually done and how — rather than what should be done.

Third, I am interested in contextualist approaches to management (see March, 1978; Pettigrew, 1987). Management tends to be shaped by 'local' contexts and conditions, more than being defined by any 'one best way'. In the case of China, the context plays a role that is even more crucial than in other countries. It would be impossible to understand what is happening in the heritage field without understanding some basic contextual features of the country at different levels: the overall political situation, the economic development, some general elements affecting professional discourse, and some aspects in cultural policies. These elements tend to have a strong interaction between themselves, and an impact on ways in which organizations are run.

Finally, my epistemological preferences are towards non-positivistic explanations. In general that means the weakening of cause-and-effect relationships, calling for more dialectical and uncertain interactions by various elements in a given context. This also applies to decision-making, looking at the decisional context in non-linear ways, leaving room for 'unanticipated consequences in human action' (Merton, 1936), or 'unintentional consequences' (see Hayek, 1952; Popper, 1959). More specifically, in Organizational Theory, this has led to an extremely rich debate on decision-making processes, drawing on the original notion of 'bounded rationality' to the development of a series of contributions about the complex, uncertain, ambiguous, fragile status of decisions within organizations (for example, the work of Herbert Simon, Michael Cohen, James March, Andrew Pettigrew, Richard Normann, Henry Mintzberg, etc.). Far from being something specific to the arts and heritage field, this applies also to profit-seeking organizations, if not in general to organizational settings as such (see the work by Allison, 1972, on the Cuban missile crisis).

In this view, the potential interaction between multiple levels of the context (the political, economic, professional, and cultural policy) is likely to take place within a situation of partial awareness, partial consistency, leaving substantial room for unanticipated consequences in many respects. Moreover, while the interdisciplinary attitude toward the interplay between government, archaeology, and economic development is welcome, there is an additional set of elements that are likely to play an important — and often overlooked — role: the administrative realm. Administration indeed matters. If one wants to compare the changes that occurred in the last few years in, say, Machu Picchu, Pompeii, and the Qin Mausoleum, it is clear that a good part of these changes are explained by the evolution of professional discourse at the global level, including the increasing role played by international agencies (UNESCO, ICOMOS, etc.). Surely, the general politics and the condition of economic development in the three contexts play a huge role. Nonetheless, a good part of the differences is explained by internal dynamics of public sector in Peru, Italy, and China.

The context: a fast-developing country, a 'revolutionary' process of gradual multidimensional change

China has experienced an exceptional process of transformation in the last thirty years, at all levels. Some of the most important changes are detailed below to underline their potential impacts on all activities that can be found in the cultural heritage field.

The general political change

The history of China in the twentieth century is one of tremendous waves of radical change: the collapse of the last dynasty; the early experiment of democracy; the Japanese invasion; the Second World War; the establishment of the republic; the complicated history of Maoism, from the initial alliance with the USSR to the great leap forward and later the cultural revolution; the new wind of the post-Mao 'gradual revolution' (Wang, 1994), and the last thirty years, since the Open Door Policy (the re-establishment of trade and political cooperation with the West set up by Deng Xiaoping in 1978).

The Open Door Policy tends to be investigated particularly in terms of the creation of the 'socialist market' economy, arising from a process of privatizing a number of activities that were directly run by the state in the planned economy. But the state still persists, and activities still under the public domain — what can be now referred to as the Chinese 'public sector' — are not irrelevant (especially for the heritage field). A very important process in the reform of the state/public sector has taken place in the last thirty years, parallel to the creation of market economy, though less visible from both Western and Chinese points of view.

Administrative reforms

The general climate at the political level has crucial impacts on the design and working of the state administration in many ways. For the sake of simplicity, focusing only on the Open Door era, from the initial situation of a totally planned economy huge reforms were introduced at various levels, changing ways in which public administration is run (Zan & Xue, 2011). This regards the decentralization of central apparatus (Burns, 1989; Caulfield, 2006; Chan, 1996; Lin, et al., 2005; Straussman & Zhang, 2001); fiscal reforms over time (Bahl & Martinez-Vazquez, 2003; Jin & Zou, 2000; Ma & Norregaard, 1998; Wong & Bird, 2007); the transformation of *shiye danwei* (referred to as Public Sector Units, PSUs, in English) (OECD, 2005; World Bank, 2005); and changes in the national budget system (Chan, 1996; Lou, 2002).

At a general level, China has become one of the most decentralized countries in the world: most of the expenditures in public sector are taking place at the Province or lower level, though the fiscal system presents a relatively centralized collection of revenues. This causes deficit at the periphery and surplus at the centre (Wong & Bird, 2007). In such a situation reallocation and transfer of resources becomes critical. This explains the importance of national budget reform in the recent decades, and the role that public sector accounting plays in this picture.

Within this context a radical process of decentralization also characterizes the heritage sector. Indeed, 90 per cent of the expenditures for culture are taken below the Province level; in terms of employees, out of the 77,000 people working in the sector only a few hundred work in the central offices in Beijing (OECD, 2005). The importance of the public sector in the running of cultural heritage in China is not that different from what happens in many non Anglo-Saxon countries (such as Italy, France, and many countries under the influence of the Roman code tradition). What is specific to China is the radical decentralization affecting institutions and funding. Very few entities are run at the central level — there are few 'national' institutions. Rather, activities are structured, funded, and run at town level, with an intermediate role in terms of developments projects played by higher levels (although funding incentives are utilized more than direct power).

Professionalism

An interesting element in this history is the relationship between central power and professionalism, and the ways in which idiosyncratic, specific professional knowledge is institutionalized, ruled, and, in this case, controlled. To make a long story short, what matters here is that a similar pattern is shared by several professional fields in cultural heritage over the last century. While China experienced interesting processes of development under the Western influence during the 1920s–30s, these processes were in a sense frozen by the dramatic events of the Japanese invasion in 1937 and the Second World War. To some extent reactivated with the establishment of the People's Republic (1949), they were suspended during the Cultural Revolution era (1966), and eventually reopened and developed in the new era of the Open Door policy (1978).

The genesis of Chinese archaeology is conventionally dated to 1928, with the first excavation by Chinese archaeologists in Anyang (see Guo, et al., 2008). Then, after 1937, archaeological excavations were suspended in the country until the 1950s, with alternate fortunes during the Cultural Revolution. Similarly, the China National Institute for Cultural Heritage (CNICP) was established in 1935, but then substantially suspended until the 1970s due to the Second World War and later Cultural Revolution. The development of museums too seems to be dramatically reoriented in terms of meanings in relation to the general political climate (Mitter, 2000), from the development of museums of the revolution, and only recently the rediscovery of the value of the long history of China, overcoming the usual lack of interest towards heritage by the traditional Chinese Marxist view of it as feudal remains.

In particular, a common element in the Open Door era is the rediscovery of professionalism, compared to the previous situation during the Cultural Revolution (cf. the situation of the medical profession described by the movie 'To live' by Zhang Yimou). An important shift from a principle of belonging (what was crucial was to be 'a good comrade') to a principle of performing (what matters is to do the right job in the right way) can be pointed out at different levels, as for instance in the 10th Five Years plan or 'Relics', or for accounting regulation (see Xue & Zan, 2012).

Economic development

It is well known that the rate of development of China in the last decades has been huge, a unique phenomenon in contemporary history. The reduction of poverty has affected 500 million people, according to the World Bank (2009: iii), also involving an unprecedented process of urbanization.

Serious implications of the fast-developing context have an impact on the heritage sector, both in positive and negative terms. First, the rate of growth of urban areas, infrastructure building, and the like has posed serious threats to the physical preservation of heritage (Chan & Ma, 2004). Second, in a general context of crisis and issues of deficit reduction at the worldwide level, China represents the exception to the rule. Though some serious concerns could be levelled in terms of the sustainability of the 'Keynesian' patterns, where governmental expenditures are still supported as part of the growth of the economy, public funding seems to be more abundant than anywhere else in this current period. Finally, the aggregate process of growth has also had an impact on the distribution of income, with the establishment of a new financial elite and the development of internal consumption. More particularly, tourism has become and continues to develop as a business on its own (du Cros & Lee, 2007; McKann, 2001; Nyíri, 2006; Sofield & Fung, 1998). Domestic flows present huge numbers, with mass tourism also investing the upper segment of cultural tourism.

Cultural policy

Despite decentralization, cultural policies present interesting dynamics in terms of centre/periphery relationships. At a general level — similar to health policies, education, and so on — the centre has to play a role in the coordination, development, diffusion of efforts and initiatives, aiming at preserving levels of harmonization and equity across the country. However, unlike health care and other public services, there is a softer aspect related to 'cultural' policies that has to deal with the construction of national identity if not nationalism. Of course, the situation of healthcare is likely to have an impact on the consensus among the country about the ruling class and institutions: but defining how one can/should celebrate the past (from the Xia dynasty to the Cultural Revolution) is much more delicate an issue (which makes this type of research even more interesting).

From this point of view, interesting contradicting elements seem to shape cultural policies in the country. At the central level a tentative effort is made by professional institutions to rule, shape, and coordinate the ways in which heritage is dealt with at the periphery (see the role played by central institutions in terms of archaeology, museology, conservation, and research in defining professional standards, providing funding for ad hoc projects, and setting priorities). At the same time, at the central level, a more 'political' (propaganda) use of the heritage is done as an element to enhance the identity of China and the idea of Chinese-ness. The Beijing Olympics gave a very clear representation of this. Anyone who has visited a Chinese museum may be impressed by the reference to the oldest culture, the longest history of a language, and the nationalist tone under which the issue of 'Chinese civilization' is dealt with. At the periphery level sometimes, these (potentially antithetical) pressures tend to be resisted, where an attitude of commercial exploitation or economic development is preferred — the over-commoditization of Lijiang represents an astonishing example in this regard (see Zan & Wang, forthcoming).

The Chinese Heritage Chain: some preliminary comments

In this section, I provide a qualitative representation of major issues that characterize the Heritage Chain in China, based on field research by our team at the University of Bologna in the last decade.

The 'Heritage Chain' (for an extensive illustration see Zan & Bonini Baraldi, 2012) derives from the notion of the supply chain that was developed in the field of industrial organization. It aims at reconstructing the set of activities that takes place — from the production or discovery of heritage (the equivalent of 'raw material') to possible uses of it by visitors (the 'final product'), including actors within the chain. Macroactivities can be aggregated and generally defined — from preservation, to archaeological excavation, conservation, research, and museum presentation (see Figure 1). However, the internal structure and meaning of each individual macroactivity and the relations between them can vary in different contexts. Understanding the specificity in the qualification of the heritage chain in a given context — how the professional discourse sets up the individual categories within each macroactivity — is our way to study the sector.

This notion can be used at different levels. On the one hand, it can be used at the level of individual discovery/excavation, as a way to reconstruct the evolution of the discovery and its impact in following links of the chain over time: this is what has been done at the Horse and Chariot excavation/museum in Luoyang (Zan & Bonini Baraldi, 2012). On the other hand, it can be used at the aggregate level, as a tool to describe, characterize, and compare the different national heritage systems: how the structure/conduct/performance within the chain differs from one country to another. With a huge activity of data gathering and analysis, this is what has been done with reference to Turkey (Bonini Baraldi, et al., 2012).

In the case of China, I will not systematically reconstruct the 'Heritage Chain' in its quantitative terms here (the way in which data are organized and presented is not particularly meaningful, with categories such as 'administrative organizations, other relics' organizations, museums, scientific research organizations, relics shop', as expressed by Chinese statistics: see Table 1). However, some qualitative preliminary notes can be provided (Figure 2 provides a synopsis of the analysis).

Preservation

Many efforts have been taken in the recent years to improve the protection of heritage in China, in terms of legislation (e.g. with the Law of the People's Republic of China on Protection of Cultural Relics, No. 76, 28 October 2002). Generous budgets were

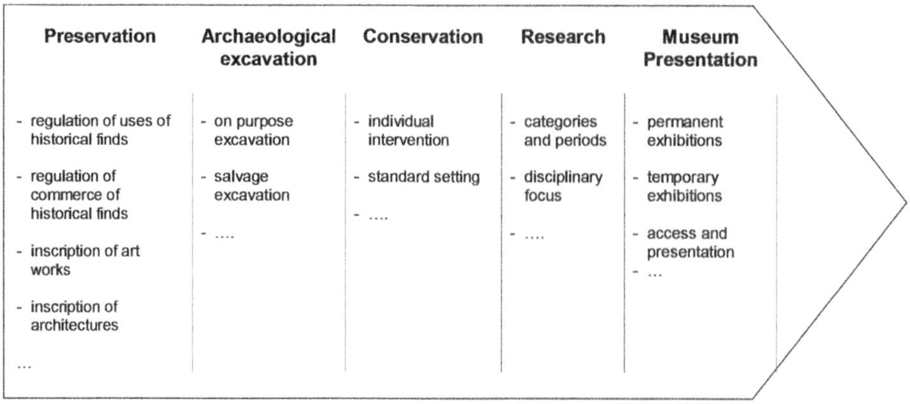

FIGURE 1   The 'Heritage Chain'.

TABLE 1

CULTURAL RELICS INSTITUTIONS AND ADMINISTRATIVE LEVELS, 2004 (see Guo, et al., 2008: 18)

	Central level		Provincial level		City level		County level		Total	
	number of entities	employees	number of entities	employees	number of entities	employees	number of entities	employees	number of entities	employees
Administrative organizations			19	609	396	12,167	1,736	15,352	2,151	28,128
Other relics organizations	5	412	27	437	21	1,502	26	1,515	79	3,866
Museums	4	2,356	99	8,502	479	14,087	966	14,321	1,548	39,266
Scientific research organizations	1	96	35	2,279	37	934	8	54	81	3,363
Relics shops			32	1,302	65	1,032	9	144	106	2,478
Total	10	2,864	212	13,129	998	29,722	2,745	31,386	3,965	77,101

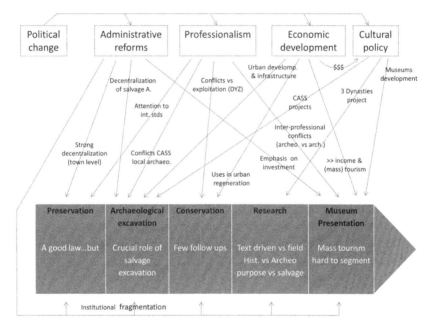

FIGURE 2   The Chinese 'Heritage Chain'.

provided for enhancement projects by the State Administration for Cultural Heritage (SACH), with growing international collaborations with the international community (Agnew, et al., 2005). However, it is one thing to have a law; it is another for it to impact behaviours and outcomes. In addition to the relatively late establishment of the law compared to the booming development of the 1990s, several issues have been acknowledged, for instance the lack of any idea of an historical town centre in the Chinese tradition. Many heritage sites have been anyhow destroyed in the last decades, because of the pressure of major projects (see Gruber, 2007, for the Three Gorges Dam), or more diffusedly because of the law itself was disregarded (He, 2000). In a word, the empowerment of a relatively 'good' protection law seems to be still a major problem in the country, similar to other sectors.

One of the major problems in this regard is actually the high degree of decentralization characterizing the heritage field, a consequence of the general process of administrative and political decentralization seen above. At the local level (prefecture, municipality, town) there is often a Cultural Relics Bureau (CRB), which reports directly to the cultural department (which reports to the mayor), with mere professional relationships with higher levels of the same functional department. For instance, the CRB of Luoyang reports directly to the municipality, while the relationship with higher levels of the professional body — the CRB at the Province level, and the SACH — are involved only in case of special projects, extraordinary events, or in a mere supervisory role.

This institutional design is largely responsible for heritage destruction related to building and infrastructure construction in the booming economy. Suppose the local administration is aware of economic development initiatives that have negative impact on heritage preservation: in this case, the professionals in charge of heritage protection have very little ability to resist such projects. They can try to stop them — through discussion and persuasion. In the end, though, the power of decision is in the hands of the mayor, as well as the career development and the assessment of their professional contribution. The same situation would be different in Italy: the Superintendents — representatives of the Ministry of Culture at the local level — could easily express their negative opinion to the Ministry in ways that are less subject to local dynamics and the pressure of vested interests at the local level. Although the term 'centralization' tends to be seen as outdated, one of the serious problems in China's preservation of heritage is indeed the excess of de-centralization, or the lack of adequate levels/mechanisms of centralization.

Archaeological excavation

The general context of the transformation of the country has other impacts on approaches to heritage management in China in two important ways. On the one hand, huge projects of archaeological excavation have been implemented with the aim of better defining imperial dynasties, with particular reference to the early period (the Xia-Shang-Zhou Chronology Project, for example: for a reconstruction, see Lee, 2002: 16–17): archaeology has received funding and support in the last decade in ways that are difficult to find elsewhere.

On the other hand, however, the extraordinary rates of economic growth and the associated rate of urbanization imply unprecedented levels of building and construction all over the country, and, consequently, there are extraordinary levels of new archaeological finds in more diffuse ways. These huge archaeological activities, however, are once again related to administrative issues, with the explosion of salvage archaeology activities, which are responsible for most of the finds in recent years. According to the 2002 Law of the People's Republic of China on the Protection of Cultural Heritage (articles 30–32), before any construction can start a preliminary archaeological inspection has to be undertaken by the local administration (by the excavation team of the CRB at the local level). If a sign emerges of archaeological finds, more extensive archaeological excavation is then run and funded — and this is the relevant peculiarity — by the construction company. Should the finds be of high value, the building activity would be halted. This administrative mechanism could be seen as a very positive solution for China's archaeology: the 'business model' is that building and development activities 'pay' for archaeological excavations (which mean huge amounts of money in a booming economy). Unfortunately, there are several shortcomings in such situations (Guo, et al., 2008): in the lack of clear definition of principal and related activities, the archaeological teams at the local levels have strong incentive mechanism for 'digging': no budgets are devoted to research or to conservation of the finds. Indeed, the archaeological teams in archaeology-rich areas — such as Luoyang, for instance — are unusually wealthy departments.

Another aspect of the Chinese public administration — institutional fragmentation which does not address the collaboration between different entities — worsens the situation. For instance, in Luoyang there are two archaeological teams from the local CRB doing almost exclusively salvage excavation. They have little if any coordination with the four archaeological teams of the Institute of Archaeology of the China Academy of Social Science whose excavation stations are in the area, including Erlitou, a crucial excavation for the debate on early dynasties. Here again actual behaviours matter more than norms: even when laws define norms, norms are not always followed. For instance, extensive reports on excavation should be presented within three years; finds should be transferred to the local museum's depot after this period. Actually, the lack of excavation reports is a serious problem undermining the possibility of knowledge diffusion; excavation teams sometimes are accused of not transferring the finds to museums.

Conservation

Conservation in China has been the locus of an incredibly rich activity of international collaboration during the 1990s (with national central institutions from Italy, Germany, Australia, and later, with private entities such as the Getty Research Institute). The issue of local traditions and different approaches to conservation is surely a major controversy in East/West comparison, with various implications for different kinds of heritage (see, for example, the Nara debate on authenticity: ICOMOS, 1994; see also Kono, 2013; Micheli & Zhan, 2006).

However, there also are additional aspects that tend to be overlooked, such as administrative and institutional features. The fragmentation of excavation, conservation, and research in salvage excavations has been already mentioned: this is an aspect that is likely to increase costs and decrease effectiveness and knowledge sharing amongst the many local initiatives. The lack of incentives for conservation intervention within salvage excavation is also a serious issue. The duplication at different provincial levels of conservation institutes seems to be more related to local politics than clear issues of organizational design.

Research

Starting from the unusual effort in archaeological excavation, two different impacts can be traced back, one related to deliberate excavation and the other to salvage excavation. By its own nature, deliberate excavation tends to have a significant research impact. Indeed, the whole Xia-Shang-Zhou Chronology Project achieved relevant outcomes in terms of publication (Lee, 2002; Li, 2002; Liu, 2004). However, doubts and controversies have not been solved, despite this being the goal of the proponents of this national research project. On the contrary, according to critics, this will be the definitive demonstration that the first dynasty never existed (Lee, 2002; Liu & Xu, 2007). This controversy is perhaps the best example of the dialectic between different forms of archaeology, where research archaeology was explicitly aimed at giving evidence to the five thousand years of Chinese history within a nationalist framework (Lee, 2002: 16–17). Archaeologists have addressed these aspects in their substantive elements (sometimes Western archaeologists: Bagley, 1999; von Falkenhausen, 1993; sometimes Chinese archaeologists outside China: Lee, 2002; Liu & Xu, 2007). Here the administrative foundations of this revolution can be addressed.

Salvage excavation has many more difficulties in creating meaningful research: particularly in the context of the perverse incentive mechanism of the law, where local archaeologists have an interest in digging as a money-making, if not 'profit maximizing', behaviour. The weakness of the law in addressing their time in either conservation or research (and in any case the actual lack of application of the law itself in terms of research reports) represents a great problem and risk in the whole chain. Just a small portion of potential knowledge generated by the huge amount of salvage excavation is made available to the professional community (even inside China). However, there are also positive aspects related to the explosion of salvage archaeology, that is its intrinsic anarchist nature in pluralizing the past (the impossibility to plan and direct it in any systematic way). From this point of view, salvage excavation appears as a strong antidote to ideological uses of heritage from any central (and centralist) views. The variety of empirical evidence that has characterized Chinese archaeology in the last few decades, largely based on salvage archaeology, has questioned traditional views of linear developments in China over millennia, with the emergence of a very interesting — and unusual elsewhere — conflict between archaeology and historiography, between empirical evidence and text-driven explanations.

Access: museums and archaeological sites

The general administrative transformation of the country also has direct implications for the ways in which museums are run, in terms of both design and development. From a formal point of view, museums (the same applies for archaeological sites) are defined as *shiye danwei*, as public sector units (PSU), as this term is usually translated in English (Pilichowski, 2005). They are, in a sense, 'entities' established as operative arms of the respective governmental level, with their own collections and often building, financial statements, personnel, and, in a word, their administrative identity.

There are very few national museums (directly reporting to the SACH); some important ones are Provincial museums (they report to the Cultural Relics Bureau at the Province level); most are district, municipal, or town museums. In any case, the process of decentralization is to be intended as devolution more than anything similar to the Anglo-American mechanism of the arm's-length principle. The transfer of power is from the central government to the provincial level, and for the most part at lower levels, more than from each governmental level to autonomous operating entities. In other words, at each governmental level there is strict control over the museums reporting to this level, and there is not an issue of autonomy of the entity in itself.

In any case, in day-to-day life museums have to use administrative rules that are common to other (almost one million) *shiye danwei* in the country. This is raising serious problems for activities that are so crucial for museums (e.g. conservation, maintenance), but for which it is even impossible to find a specific item inside the national table of accounts that museums have to use. Indeed, maintenance and conservation are some of the most problematic issues for Chinese museums (Li, 2005), as it has been explicitly acknowledged even in formal documents (see, for instance, the eleventh Five Year plan).

In terms of developments at the central level, there is a strong policy to build new archaeological sites (about a hundred, in the eleventh Five Year Plan) and museums. According to the new twelfth Five Year Plan for Cultural Heritage there should be one museum in each of the 333 prefectural levels, with a goal of passing from 3020 to 3500 museums in the five years. This is partly explained by the tourism increase in recent years, but it is also linked to the politics of national identity building, if not nationalism (a well-known issue in the international debate: see Denton, 2005; Vickers, 2007). For this developmental programme, the centre had already defined a sort of plan during the previous Five Year Plan horizon, offering a huge amount of money to gain the consensus at lower governmental levels. For instance, for the archaeological parks the initial assumption — later further expanded — was about 36 billion Yuan for 2006–10 (where 53 per cent was provided by central government: see the draft of the eleventh Five Year Plan on Heritage). However, running costs were not identified nor budgeted, and so funded fewer items. This is likely to pose serious problems in the future, once the investment phase for new museums and parks is over, the issue of 'running costs' will emerge. Maybe some of the new entities will be self-funding; for the rest, serious problems of sustainability will take place. Also the decision taken by the centre to extend free entrance to museums (but not to sites or archaeological parks) has already begun, with only a few exceptions since 2008. As always, the issue of sustainability only appears to be a problem in the later stages, if it has not been addressed earlier. This happens very often in the arts and heritage sector: what is peculiar to the Chinese situation is the scale of the phenomenon.

It is more difficult to foresee how the dialectic between centralization and decentralization will have an impact in terms of museums and archaeological parks. On the one hand a tension between different policy preferences emerges: the central government pushes a policy of national identity building and free entrance, while often the periphery would be more seduced by profit-maximizing museums projects, related to tourism development. The over-commoditization of Lijiang is the best example of this (McKann, 2001; Sofield & Fung, 1998). Heritage professionals (archaeologists, museologists, and historians) and their values sometime find themselves in conflict with both extremes of this kind of policy. On the other hand, the administrative mechanism makes the overall result of such tensions more uncertain than usual. The separation between investment and running conditions — a recurrent problem in the heritage field — is here associated with a separation between governmental levels in funding extraordinary projects and their running costs at a later stage.

Conclusion

Administration matters. Both longer term administrative traditions and recent transformations have an impact on the ways in which heritage is managed in China, from excavation, to research, to museum opening. Curiously enough — and quite counter-intuitively if one does not know the Chinese administration — the excess of decentralization explains to some extent the destruction of heritage often referred to (professionals in charge of protection are 'hostages' to the local administration; incentive mechanisms toward digging activities; institutional fragmentation and jealously; lack of respect of norms).

Compared to other countries the heritage chain is here concentrated on the early stages, on excavation and new finds, which has tended to completely revisit the traditional view of Chinese history, with very interesting controversies between archaeology and text historiography (Bagley, 1999; von Falkenhausen, 1993) though with unbalanced outcomes in terms of conservation, research, and access.

The need to draw a more detailed (and quantified) picture of these developments emerges. While the (re)writing of institutional histories of the various disciplines involved in the field is important, the reconstruction of the actual impacts of recent policies is also crucial (in particular the impact of development projects established by the eleventh Five Year plan, both in terms of museums and big sites).

Despite similarities in the language used, things in China seem to be rather unique compared to general discussions of heritage management at a worldwide level. The power conflicts between administrative levels seem to be the major issues, with superficial assonance in terms of what is normally referred to as autonomy, accountability, transparency, and with substantive losses of coordination from the centre on professional issues. Understanding the general administrative structure under which heritage operations take place is needed to avoid uncritical extensions of the heritage jargon.

Bibliography

Agnew, N., Demas, M., Sullivan, S., & Altenburg, K. 2005. The Begetting of Charters: Genesis of the China Principles. *Historic Environment*, 1: 40–46.

Allison, G. T. 1972. *Essence of Decision*. Boston: Little Brown.

Bagley, R. 1999. Shang Archaeology. In: M. Loewe and E. L. Shaughnessy, eds. *The Cambridge History of Ancient China. From the Origins of Civilization to 221 BC*. Cambridge: Cambridge University Press, pp. 124–231.

Bahl, R. W. & Martinez-Vazquez, J. 2003. Fiscal Federalism and Economic Reform in China. *International Studies Program*, Andrew Young School of Policy Studies, Georgia State University, paper 0313.

Bonini Baraldi, S., Shoup, D., & Zan, L. 2013. Understanding Cultural Heritage in Turkey: Institutional Context and Organizational Issues. *International Journal of Heritage Studies*, 19(7): 728–48.

Burns, J. P. 1989. Chinese Civil Service Reform: The 13th Party Congress Proposals. *The China Quarterly*, 120: 739–70.

Caulfield, J. L. 2006. Local Government Reform in China: A Rational Actor Perspective. *International Review of Administrative Sciences*, 72(2): 253–67.

Chan, J. 1996. Budget Accounting in China: Continuity and Change. *Research in Governmental and Nonprofit Accounting*, 9: 1–19.

Chan, W. Y. & Ma, S. Y. 2004. Heritage Preservation and Sustainability of China's Development. *Sustainable Development*, 1: 15–31.

Czarniawska, B. 2008. *A Theory of Organizing*. Cheltenham, UK: Edward Elgar Publishing.

Denton, K. A. 2005. Museums, Memorial Sites and Exhibitionary Culture in the People's Republic of China. *The China Quarterly*, 183: 565–86.

Du Cros, H. & Lee, Y. S. F. 2007. *Cultural Heritage Management in China: Preserving the Cities of the Pearl River Delta*. London: Routledge.

von Falkenhausen, L. 1993. On the Historiographical Orientation of Chinese Archaeology. *Antiquity*, 67: 839–49.

Gruber, S. 2007. Protecting China's Cultural Heritage Sites in Times of Rapid Change: Current Developments, Practice and Law. *Asia Pacific Journal of Environmental Law*, 10: 253–301.

Guo, Y., Zan, L., & Liu, S. 2008. *The Management of Cultural Heritage in China. General Trends and Micro Focus on Luoyang Municipality*. Milan: Egea.

Hayek, F. 1952. *The Counter-revolution of Science: Studies on the Abuse of Reason*. Glencoe, IL: Free Press.

He, S. 2000. The Mainland's Environment and the Protection of China's Cultural Heritage: A Chinese Cultural Heritage Lawyer's Perspective. *Art Antiquity and Law*, 5: 19–35.

International Council on Monuments and Sites (ICOMOS). 1994. Nara Document on Authenticity [accessed 8 December 2012]. Available at: <http://www.icomos.org/charters/nara-e.pdf>.

Jin, J. & Zou, H-F. 2000. Fiscal Decentralization and Economic Growth in China. *Economic Development and Cultural Change*, 49(1): 1–21.

Kono, T. 2013. ed. Special Issue: Reflections on Authenticity and Heritage Values: Toward the 20th Anniversary of the Nara Document and Beyond. *Heritage & Society*, 6(2).

Lee, Y. K. 2002. Building the Chronology of Early Chinese History. *Asian Perspectives*, 41: 15–42.

Li, X. 2002. The Xia Shang Zhou Chronology Project, Methodology and Results. *Journal of East Asian Archaeology*, 14: 321–33.

Li, X. 2005. China Exclusive: Why are Chinese Museums on Edge of Survival? *China Daily* [online], 19 May [accessed 11 May 2014]. Available at: <http://news.xinhuanet.com/english/2005-05/19/content_2977857.htm>.

Lin, J. Y., Ran, T., & Mingxing, L. 2005. Decentralization and Local Governance in the Context of China's Transition. *Perspectives*, 6(2): 25–36.

Liu, L. 2004. Settlement Patterns and Development of Social Complexity in the Yiluo Region, North China. *Journal of Field Archaeology*, 29: 75–100.

Liu, L. & Xu, H. 2007. Rethinking Erlitou: Legend, History and Chinese Archaeology. *Antiquity*, 81: 886–901.

Lou, J. 2002. Government Budgeting and Accounting Reform in China. *OECD Journal on Budgeting*, 2(1): 51–80.

Ma, J. & Norregaard, J. 1998. China's Fiscal Decentralization. Report prepared for the International Monetary Fund. [accessed 11 May 2014]. Available at: <https://www.imf.org/external/pubs/ft/seminar/2000/idn/china.pdf>.

March, J. G. 1978. Bounded Rationality, Ambiguity, and the Engineering of Choice. *The Bell Journal of Economics*, 9: 587–608.

McKann, C. F. 2001. The Good, the Bad and the Ugly: Observations and Reflections on Tourism Development in Lijiang, China. In: C. B. Tan, C. H. Cheung, and H. Yang, eds. *Tourism, Anthology and China*. Bangkok: White Lotus Press, pp. 147–65.

Merton, R. 1936. The Unanticipated Consequences of Purposive Social Action. *American Sociological Review*, 1: 894–904.

Micheli, M. & Zhan, C. eds. 2006. *La conservazione del patrimonio culturale in Cina. Storia di un progetto di cooperazione*. Rome: Istituto Italiano per l'Africa e l'Oriente.

Mitter, R. 2000. Behind the Scenes at the Museum, Nationalism, History and Memory in the Beijing War of Resistance Museum, 1987–1997. *The China Quarterly*, 161: 279–93.

Nyíri, P. 2006. *Scenic Spots: Chinese Tourism, the State and Cultural Authority*. Seattle, WA: University of Washington Press.

Organisation for Economic Cooperation and Development (OECD). 2005. *Governance in China*. Paris: OECD Publishing.

Pettigrew, A. M. 1987. Context and Action in the Transformation of the Firm. *Journal of Management Studies*, 24: 649–70.

Pilichowski, E. 2005. *The Reform of Public Service Units: Challenges and Perspectives*. OECD, Directorate for Public Governance and Territorial Development, JT00176426.

Popper, K. 1959. Prediction and Prophecy in the Social Sciences. In: P. K. Gardiner, ed. *Theories of History*. New York: The Free Press, pp. 276–85.

Sofield, T. & Fung, M. L. 1998. Tourism Development and Cultural Policies in China. *Annals of Tourism Research*, 25(2): 362–92.

Straussman, J. D. & Zhang, M. 2001. Chinese Administrative Reforms in International Perspective. *The International Journal of Public Sector Management*, 14: 411–22.

Vickers, E. 2007. Museums and Nationalism in Contemporary China. *Compare*, 37: 365–82.

Wang, H. 1994. *The Gradual Revolution: China's Economic Reform Movement*. New Brunswick and London: Transaction Publishers.

World Bank. 2005. *China. Deepening Public Service Unit Reform to Improve Service Delivery*. Report no. 32341-CHA. Washington, DC: World Bank.

World Bank. 2009. From Poor Areas to Poor People: China's Evolving Poverty Reduction Agenda. An Assessment of Poverty and Inequality [accessed 11 May 2014]. Available at: <http://documents.worldbank.org/curated/en/2009/03/10427760/china-poor-areas-poor-people-chinas-evolving-poverty-reduction-agenda-assessment-poverty-inequality>.

Wong, C. P. W. & Bird, R. M. 2007. China's Fiscal System: A Work in Progress. In: L. Brandt and T. Rawski, eds. *China's Great Transformation: Origins, Mechanism, and Consequences of the Post-Reform Economic Boom*. Cambridge: Cambridge University Press, pp. 429–66.

Xue, Q. & Zan, L. 2012. Opening the Door to Accounting Change. Transformations in Chinese Public Sector Accounting. *Accounting History Review*, 22(3): 269–99.

Zan, L. & Bonini Baraldi, S. 2012. Managing Cultural Heritage in China. A View from the Outside. *China Quarterly*, 210: 456–81.

Zan, L. & Wang, T. forthcoming. Conservation & Exploitation. Governance and Sustainability Issues in Lijiang Cases. In: J. Hosagrahar, ed. *Urban China 2030*.

Zan, L. & Xue, Q. 2011. Budgeting China, Macro Policies and Micro Practices in Public Sector Changes. *Accounting, Auditing and Accountability Journal*, 24: 38–62.

Notes on contributor

Luca Zan is Professor of Management at the University of Bologna, and EIASM's Professor, Brussels. He is Director of the GIOCA (Graduate degree in Innovation and Organization of Cultural and the Arts) at the University of Bologna, where he teaches 'Critical studies and arts management', and 'Heritage, history and the issue of organizing'. Zan is adjunct faculty at the Heinz College, Carnegie Mellon University, where he teaches 'Managing Cultural Heritage: Identity and Sustainability' within the Master of Arts Management Program. His research interests deal with: management and accounting history; strategic change processes; and the management of heritage and arts organizations, with a focus on international comparison base on field research. He has published extensively in international journals (e.g. concerning the management of the British Museum, Machu Picchu, change processes at Heritage Malta, and changes in the Heritage sector in Turkey and China).

Correspondence to: Luca Zan, Department of Management, University of Bologna, Via Capo di Lucca 34, Bologna, Italy. Email: Luca.zan@unibo.it

PUBLIC ARCHAEOLOGY, Vol. 13 Nos 1–3, 2014, 113–22

The Evolution of Heritage Management: Thinking Beyond Site Boundaries and Buffer Zones

LISA ACKERMAN

World Monuments Fund, USA

Heritage and economics are increasingly intertwined as the cultural sector strives to prove the relevancy of its work to broader social issues and more researchers seek to quantify the economic impact of heritage tourism. Heritage and economics intersect in funding proposals, regional development plans, tourism management strategies, and in myriad other ways. Yet there is often a sense that conservation projects and related economic initiatives evolve on parallel tracks rather than in an integrated way from the conception of the programme. Thus when the success of conservation projects is described, there is much to say about technical achievements but little about the social impact in an equally scientific manner. The dilemma for many in the field is how to move from anecdotal storytelling to scientific data.

KEYWORDS heritage tourism, heritage management, heritage conservation, Lalibela, rock-hewn churches

Introduction

From humanity's earliest records on this planet, we know places have been treasured, destroyed, rebuilt, visited, and appropriated for new purposes. As heritage sites move through processes of creation, neglect, rediscovery, preservation, interpretation, and public presentation, economic development is frequently presented as a foe to conservation. Yet increasingly, as evidenced by this special issue, the heritage dialogue frames sites as valuable educational and community resources, bringing jobs, tourists, and economic investment. Tourism is not a new phenomenon and neither is heritage management. Yet many working in the heritage sector sense strongly that the dialogue is shifting to arenas beyond discussions of artistic merits and cultural values to arguments that are more nuanced. We struggle to find sustainable solutions to balance community needs, visitor satisfaction, and to prove that there is both cultural and economic value in safeguarding the world's history, significant structures,

© Taylor & Francis 2014   DOI 10.1179/1465518714Z.00000000059

cultural landscapes, and natural sites that enrich our lives. The work of World Monuments Fund (WMF) at Lalibela, Ethiopia, provides a striking example of the challenges and opportunities in the field as well as the evolving dialogue about the ways in which the heritage community and those concerned with socio-economic improvement seek common cause.

The launch of WMF's first international collaboration

International Fund for Monuments (IFM) — the original name of the World Monuments Fund[1] — launched a project in 1966 to conserve the historic rock-hewn churches of Lalibela, Ethiopia. By May 1968, IFM had completed the majority of the condition surveys and conservation work envisioned at the outset. In 1967, IFM published *Lalibela Phase I*, which notes:

> Our program has so far been supported by contributions from individuals in sympathy with the aims of the organization. We also use, where possible, locally-held funds generated by the sale of U.S. agricultural surpluses, in a seeding process which preserves the monument for posterity, and at the same time stimulates the flow of tourist dollars into the economy of the host country. The project in Lalibela is a splendid example of this arrangement. It is a joint effort involving close collaboration with the Imperial Ethiopian Government on a fund-matching basis. The International Fund engaged and paid the technical staff and provided the hard currency for the purchase of machinery and equipment. The Ethiopian Government, utilizing Counterpart Funds, paid the local workers and supplied the local currency for the purchase of materials and supplies. (IFM, 1967: 5–6)

When these words were written, IFM could not have guessed that this principle of participatory, collaborative funding would become the hallmark of WMF's Robert W. Wilson Challenge to Conserve Our Heritage[2] — a programme that aims to leverage non-US matching funding contributions and has financed more than 200 conservation projects in nearly fifty countries to date (see Taboroff, et al., 2011: 5). Nor might the leadership imagine that, more than thirty years after the end of the initial conservation project, WMF and UNESCO would return to Lalibela in partnership with Ethiopian heritage authorities to tackle issues of advocacy, conservation, training, and community benefit. The sentiment expressed in the above-cited IFM report in 1967 dispels the notion that the economics of preservation were not being thought about in tandem within the scope of work as it was being developed. Tourism, too, although only beginning to be a significant source of the world's economy with the expansion of international air travel, was clearly cited as a benefit of preservation activities.

In the 1960s and 1970s, the rock-hewn churches of Lalibela were already recognized as an important heritage site, and were listed on UNESCO's World Heritage List in 1978. The churches are still a major religious pilgrimage destination and the seat of the Ethiopian Orthodox Church. As early as 1959, there were published proceedings of the International Conference of Ethiopian Studies, an academic summit convened regularly over more than a fifty-year period: the 18th International Conference of Ethiopian Studies was held in Dire Dawa, Ethiopia, in 2012. Thus it is not surprising that a newly formed heritage organization might well have focused on this site, but it is noteworthy that, against considerable odds, IFM — a fledgling group founded by a retired US Army Colonel — managed to find the resources to implement the project. Then, as today, the conservation challenges may be the easiest to address, but financing projects requires a different level of expertise and creative thinking.

The IFM report went on to describe the art, architecture, history, and cultural importance of the site, but it is telling that the opening statements addressed the financing of the programme and the need to undertake such work with a clear expression of local engagement. It is also critical to understand that the philosophy of IFM was to be an organization supporting the work and principles of UNESCO. Thus the conservation work by design was meant to adhere to the generally accepted principles and standards set through UNESCO's framework that guides much heritage conservation activity in the field.

Conservation and tourism

Tourism has grown and continues to grow worldwide, even in remote locations. According to the United Nations World Tourism Organization's report, tourism in 2010 accounted for the movement of 940 million people worldwide; Africa's market share is 5.2 per cent and growing at an annual rate of just over 6 per cent (UNWTO, 2011: 4). In Ethiopia, tourism statistics have been tracked steadily since the 1960s and much travel is associated with the capital, Addis Ababa, as a result of business interests. For those adventurous travellers who reach Ethiopia, major destinations include the rock-hewn churches of Lalibela, Gondar, Axum, and Hadar, the site of the discovery in the 1970s of the famed skeleton known as Lucy. Not surprisingly, many of the sites visited by international tourists are World Heritage Sites: the World Heritage Centre's website reveals that, at the time of writing, nine of the 962 heritage sites inscribed are found in Ethiopia.

Yet, while there is great media attention paid to heritage traditions and heritage tourism, many worries remain about training enough people (particularly from local communities) to care for heritage sites, about securing enough funding, and convincing those outside the field that the work is essential to our collective wellbeing. As an example, UNESCO's recently stated concerns for reducing risk of disaster at World Heritage Sites notes lack of resources and trained professionals as a contributing factor on the landing page for this section of the website (see UNESCO, n.d.).

IFM's project in the 1960s and 1970s at Lalibela acknowledged the valuable role of tourism by virtue of bringing Ethiopian Airlines into the project as a partner, and the report cited above makes clear the local and regional economic value of the sites. Ethiopian Airlines undoubtedly saw a clear connection between investment in heritage and eventual tourism revenue. Yet, when regional development plans unfold, cultural heritage can often seem marginal rather than essential, and as a result becomes a footnote rather than a central element. For example, when *plaNYC: A Greener, Greater New York* (CoNY, 2011) and *plaNYC: A Stronger, More Resilient New York* (CoNY, 2013) were issued, it was a disappointment that such comprehensive, visionary statements about the future of New York City ignored the many historic assets that give shape and character to the streetscape and vibrant neighbourhoods in all five boroughs. There was no section that addressed how preservation of historic structures could contribute to that more resilient and green city to which New York City might aspire.

Indeed, there are extremely generous foundations and individuals that support the field with great passion. WMF's work at Lalibela demonstrates in many ways this very issue of great attention to conservation, research, and training, but the data that would connect it to larger social issues is not necessarily part of the project planning. This paper demonstrates what has been accomplished at Lalibela, but also shows that the socio-economic information relating to conservation projects can be best described as anecdotal rather than scientific.

Conservation of the churches of Lalibela, Ethiopia

These churches, carved into live rock, first appear on the landscape in the thirteenth century CE. By the time IFM's conservators arrived in the 1960s, numerous changes had occurred over the centuries. While not apparent to the naked eye, a variety of studies commissioned by UNESCO and WMF from 2004 to 2010 confirm that the volcanic stone continued to evolve and was impacted by environmental changes. In keeping with the site's inscription on the World Heritage List, nomination documents and reports on the cultural importance and integrity of the site (ICOMOS, 1978) and periodic State of Conservation reports were produced and presented at World Heritage Meetings. In 1996, at the 20th session of the World Heritage Committee, the State of Conservation report provides details of the conservation issues at the site and references the IFM work supervised in the 1960s. It also importantly addresses some of the mounting urban concerns in the community

> The site of Lalibela has been the object of several restoration campaigns [...] Three successive campaigns were carried out: in 1920, in 1954 and in 1966–68 under the direction of Sandro Angelini [...] the first restorations of 1920 and 1954, which were undertaken in haste, without scientific precautions and with recourse to cement, aggravated the situation. At the present time, several churches are protected by zinc roofing mounted on wooden scaffolding [...] Although they fulfill their purpose, these roofs and scaffolding considerably disfigure the monuments and must be considered as temporary stopgap measures [...] The situation in Lalibela is extremely delicate. (UNESCO, 1996: 14–15)

This report and others subsequently submitted to the World Heritage Committee demonstrate decades of attempted assistance to recurring conservation issues and site management struggles. In the 1990s, five structures at Lalibela (Biet Medhane Alem, Biet Maryam, Biet Masqal, Biet Emanuel, and Biet Abba Libanos) had protective shelters erected and roof improvements completed to address deterioration and water infiltration damage. By the early 2000s it was clear to many that these measures were insufficient, and wind and water erosion continued to plague the structures (Margottini, 2004: 2). All of this came to a head when a plan was formulated to create more substantial shelters for the churches; concerns were raised about the aesthetic impact of the shelters and whether they were addressing the conservation issues. There were also concerns about the potential for the shelters to increase problems by adding additional weight to the area around the structures. All of these are very normal concerns when there is an intervention of this magnitude at a heritage site. To frame this discussion, it is instructive to look at Figure 1, which shows the integration of the churches of Lalibela with the landscape.

FIGURE 1   Biet Amanuel (House of Emmanuel) seen from ground-level during conservation work, c. 1970.
© World Monuments Fund

WMF returned to Lalibela in 2004 as part of a collaborative project with UNESCO and the Ethiopian Authority for Research and Conservation of Cultural Heritage in response to concerns about the introduction of new shelters at Lalibela. These concerns echoed decades of worry about the lack of full understanding of the underlying causes of the problems onsite and the need to engage more fully the local community in the conservation programmes undertaken at Lalibela. As a result, from 2007 to 2011, WMF and the World Heritage Centre commissioned numerous geo-technical surveys, conducted archival research, and completed several years of monitoring at the site. This joint collaboration with the Ethiopian government resulted in new efforts to think strategically about the values of the site: its religious significance, its importance as a tourist destination and as a generator of revenue for the local community. An important goal of the new effort was to assure that Ethiopians participated in the programme of documentation and conservation.

Thus, after an absence of nearly forty years from the site, WMF found itself in many ways beginning the process of collaborative conservation from scratch. The several years of study gave rise to some statements that now frame the conservation programme that is currently underway. The structures are free-standing and it is important that they be experienced as places connected to the landscape. The conservation problems of the churches arise from the materials from which they are carved and the evolution of the rock over time. The volcanic rock is prone to fissures, which leads to water infiltration. Water damage was evident in the mid-2000s when the European Commission announced funding to build shelters over the churches of Lalibela to protect them from further water damage. Regrettably, much water infiltration was from below, not above, and the heavy weight of some of the shelters creates other threats to the stability of the monuments. Shelters were erected over some of the churches, but in some cases they created obstacles to circulation and to the proper use of the spaces for religious functions. The decision to create the new shelters was not without logic, or precedent. As noted previously, in the late 1980s and early 1990s, a temporary roof was placed over Biet Mariam and Biet Emmanuel. The 2007 European Commission project erected four shelters over five churches: Biet Mariam, Biet Maskal, Biet Medhane Alem, Biet Emmanuel, and Biet Abba Libanos. Figure 2 clearly demonstrates why there was concern about the visual impact of the shelters on the wellbeing of the site.

FIGURE 2   Protective shelter over Biet Medhani Alem (House of the Savior of the World), 2011.
© *World Monuments Fund*

New programmes at Lalibela

In 2012, a major milestone was achieved through expanding the collaboration to include training in conservation to ensure local participation in the full breadth of work to be undertaken in the coming years. WMF's goal at Lalibela is to preserve the churches in the least invasive manner possible, using sympathetic materials when replacement or additions are required, and employing craft techniques rooted in local traditions. WMF's aim is to ensure that Lalibela endures, without subtracting from its essential character. In consultation with local authorities and UNESCO, WMF launched its conservation project at one of the churches in most urgent need of repair, Biet Gabriel Rafael. The church was recently closed due to safety fears; structural cracks threaten the building's stability and, during periods of heavy rain, water pours inside.

Training and local engagement is crucial for the success of the conservation programme. WMF's introductory training course with twenty participants began in May 2012. All participants have a background in traditional construction or conservation. Of the twenty trainees, four are women; two are heritage professionals from the Authority for Research and Conservation of Cultural Heritage; two are heritage conservation students from Mekelle University; and twelve are responsible for local management of churches in Lalibela. The training programme includes classroom sessions and field activities. Practical activities in the field include condition surveys, masonry work, and mortar mixing. Classroom discussion addresses conservation theory, understanding the range of methodologies employed at sites, and how safeguarding heritage sites is affected by local, national, and international conservation statutes and standards. The importance of local engagement in the site is multifaceted as it provides employment opportunities so that communities can become less dependent on foreign experts for caring for historic structures. Equally important is that fact that these sites have local, living meaning beyond their historic value and, as such, it is appropriate that local scholars, skilled heritage professionals, and site stewards should be empowered to take control of the long-term wellbeing of the sites.

In the spring of 2012, trainees participated in site visits to understand causes of decay and how rock structures deteriorate (see Figure 3). The group visited Biet Gabriel Rafael and carried out condition assessments of its roof, floor, walls, and surroundings landscape. They reviewed past conservation actions and the effects they had on the structure. The churches of Lalibela were an open-air laboratory for the students and they were encouraged to examine the conditions of other structures to become familiar with the problems common to all the churches. Studies were conducted at Biet Mariam, Biet Medhane Alem, Biet Golgotha, and Biet Giorghis. The group identified materials used to build and repair the churches and discussed the approaches employed, their effectiveness, and reviewed the challenges that remain to be addressed. They examined visitor impact on the churches as well as the effects of nature, such as exposure to the elements and animal populations at the site. Common problems presented included water infiltration, biological growth, and cracks.

The long-term goal is to establish a permanent team at the site to undertake repairs and monitor changes in the structures. Lalibela is the most important place of pilgrimage for Ethiopia's Orthodox Christians. The churches are owned by the

FIGURE 3 Training course participants clear the soil burden at the rock slab over the entrance of Biet Gabriel Raphael (House of Gabriel Raphael), 2012.
© *World Monuments Fund*

Orthodox Church, and thus it was essential that church personnel participate in the training programme. The twelve participants employed by the Church could eventually form the nucleus of a permanent conservation and site management team. The participants are now beginning on site conservation work at Biet Gabriel Rafael, adding hands-on experience to their theoretical knowledge. The success of the first training programme demonstrated viable solutions for Lalibela. There are eleven churches at the site, and all are vulnerable in some way. Four of the most iconic structures are covered by shelters, which do not adequately address the most significant conservation challenges. Preservation across the entire site is now urgently required to ensure Lalibela endures for the benefit of future generations. WMF's partnerships with the World Heritage Centre, the Ethiopian Authority for Research and Conservation of Cultural Heritage, the Orthodox Church, and the training programme are creating a strong foundation for research, analysis, conservation, and long-term stewardship for the Churches of Lalibela. There are many individuals who deserve praise for their vision for the ongoing work at Lalibela: the students in the training programme, the trainers, the Ethiopian authorities, the Church leadership, the World Heritage Centre, and WMF's staff and trusted consultants who have contributed significantly to the development and implementation of the project.

Discussion and conclusion

Lalibela's conservation challenges from the 1960s to today show the evolution of the field, but at the same time show that the best solutions always share certain elements: passion, adequate funding, local engagement, and a vision for stewardship. Fixing problems, as was evidenced from decades of good intentions throughout the twentieth century, can turn out to resolve only short-term issues or superficial problems. The collaborative engagement model, if successful, stands a much greater chance of adding lasting value to the site. Economics plays a key role in these solutions. To protect our shared cultural heritage, we must develop effective methods to show clearly that heritage sites are not a drain on economic resources. Lalibela illustrates that an investment in the site can bring great rewards. While we are trained to speak effectively about the technical conservation work and the cultural significance of sites, we must learn to tell the parallel story of the educational and economic benefits of sustainable conservation solutions that assure these sites contribute effectively to the larger regional and national development plans.

Notes

[1] International Fund for Monuments changed its name to World Monuments Fund in 1984. IFM's initial conception and remit was as follows:

> The International Fund For Monuments, Inc. is a private organization whose program is based upon the concept that the world's great artistic, historic and archaeological monuments are part of the cultural heritage of all mankind, and that the preservation of these treasures is an international responsibility. The International Fund was formed on March 15, 1965 by a group of individuals

who recognized the need, long expressed by UNESCO, for an organization to assist in the costs of preserving monuments in those countries which lack the financial means of doing so alone. Our program has so far been supported by contributions from individuals in sympathy with the aims of the organization. (IFM, 1969: 5–6).

[2] Further information on the Robert W. Wilson Challenge to Conserve Our Heritage can be found here: <http://www.wmf.org/about-us/partner/robert-w-wilson-challenge-conserve-our-heritage>.

Bibliography

City of New York (CoNY). 2011. *plaNYC: A Greener, Greater New York* [accessed 26 March 2014]. Available at: <http://nytelecom.vo.llnwd.net/o15/agencies/planyc2030/pdf/planyc_2011_planyc_full_report.pdf>.

City of New York (CoNY). 2013. *plaNYC: A Stronger, More Resilient New York* [accessed 26 March 2014]. Available at: <http://www.nyc.gov/html/sirr/downloads/pdf/final_report/001SIRR_cover_for_DoITT.pdf>.

International Council of Monuments and Sites (ICOMOS). 1978. Letter to Mr Firouz Bagerzadeh. 7 June [accessed 17 April 2014]. Available at: <http://whc.unesco.org/archive/advisory_body_evaluation/018.pdf>.

International Fund for Monuments (IFM). 1967. *Lalibela Phase I: Adventures in Restoration* [accessed 24 May 2014]. Available at: <http://www.wmf.org/sites/default/files/wmf_publication/pubs_IFMLalibelaPhaseI1967.pdf>.

International Fund for Monuments (IFM). 1969. *Newsletter*. New York: International Fund for Monuments.

Margottini, C. 2004. Report on the UNESCO mission to Lalibela, Ethiopia: Engineering Geology aspects related to the EU feasibility project for rehabilitation of rock hewn churches of Lalibela [accessed 15 April 2014]. Available at: <http://whc.unesco.org/temp/AFR/lalibela/Margottini-Lalibela%20geology%20report%202004.pdf>.

Taboroff, J., Phares, J., Avrami, E., & Avramides, I. 2011. *The Robert W. Wilson Challenge to Conserve Our Heritage: Evaluation Report*. New York: World Monuments Fund.

United Nations Educational Scientific and Cultural Organization (UNESCO). 1996. World Heritage Committee — *20th Session Reports on the State of Conservation of Properties Inscribed on the World Heritage List*. Paris: UNESCO.

United Nations Educational Scientific and Cultural Organization (UNESCO). n.d. Reducing Disaster Risks at World Heritage Properties [accessed 26 March 2014]. Available at: <http://whc.unesco.org/en/disaster-risk-reduction>.

United Nations World Tourism Organization (UNWTO). 2011. *Tourism Highlights* [accessed 26 March 2014]. Available at: <http://mkt.unwto.org/sites/all/files/docpdf/unwtohighlights11enhr.pdf>.

Notes on contributor

Lisa Ackerman serves as Executive Vice President of World Monuments Fund and holds an appointment as Visiting Assistant Professor at Pratt Institute. Previously Ms Ackerman served as Executive Vice President of the Samuel H. Kress Foundation. Ms Ackerman holds an MS degree in Historic Preservation from Pratt Institute, an MBA from New York University, and a BA from Middlebury College. She serves on the boards of Historic House Trust of New York City, New York Preservation Archive Project, and US/ICOMOS. She previously served on the boards of St Ann Center for Restoration and the Arts, Partners for Sacred Places, and the Neighborhood Preservation Center. In 2007 she received Historic District Council's Landmarks Lion award. In 2008, Ms Ackerman was named the first recipient of US/ICOMOS's Ann Webster Smith Award for International Heritage Achievement.

Correspondence to: Lisa Ackerman, World Monuments Fund, 350 Fifth Avenue Suite 2412, New York, NY 10118, USA. Email: lackerman@wmf.org

PUBLIC ARCHAEOLOGY, Vol. 13 Nos 1–3, 2014, 123–34

Threats to the Archaeological Heritage in the *Laissez-Faire* World of Tourism: The Need for Global Standards as a Global Public Good

DOUGLAS C. COMER

Cultural Site Research and Management and ICOMOS International Scientific Committee on Archaeological Heritage Management, USA

Archaeological materials are finite, non-renewable, and irreplaceable. Preserving what they might contribute to human knowledge requires that we safeguard not only archaeological materials themselves, but also the contexts in which they occur. Unfortunately, the archaeological record is threatened by the acceleration of many natural processes (e.g. sea level rise and desertification) and human activities. Among the latter is tourism, now a major global and still burgeoning industry that has acted as a catalyst for rapid development within and around archaeological sites. Global tourism operates in what is essentially a *laissez-faire* environment. Mechanisms that might prevent or limit negative externalities associated with tourism development are present only at the level of the nation-state. I argue here that guidance for sustainable tourism can be found in the concept of global public goods. By committing to the production of global public goods, tourism will at the same time generate sustainable economic and social benefit at the local level.

KEYWORDS global public goods, scientific history, tourism and economic development, archaeological heritage management, cultural resource management

Introduction

Archaeological materials are stores of data. Humans collect data in many different ways, through experience, by word of mouth, and by use of technologies. Information is something different — it is what humans make from data. Information is data structured by theories, habits of thought, preconceived notions, the formulation and testing of hypotheses, and by other means. Information is relevant or irrelevant, useful or misleading, depending upon how data are selected and structured. Histories are

© Taylor & Francis 2014 DOI 10.1179/1465518714Z.00000000060

prime examples of how data are coalesced into information. Here I look at histories in the contemporary marketplace, with particular attention to a 'scientific history'. This term is attributed to the Greek philosopher Thucydides (460–395 BCE), and refers to a history that does not admit of divine intervention and does not privilege oral or written accounts over material evidence.

Donald Kagan, in his book, *Thucydides: The Reinvention of History* (2009: 5–6) notes that:

> Thucydides was not the first to write history. The Greeks believed that Homer's epic poems, the *Iliad* and *Odyssey*, though composed in poetic meter and filled with divine and mythological characters, nevertheless reported real events and people of the distant past [...] In the sixth century, however, a new way of thinking arose among the Greek cities of Ionia on the western coast of Asia Minor and especially Miletus. It is not too much to say that the new approach substituted rational, even scientific, thought for myth as a means of understanding and explaining the world and universe.

Myth and the systems of belief that give rise to myth continue to exert a strong influence on perceptions of the human past. A Gallup poll conducted in May 2012 found that 46 per cent of Americans believe that God created humans all at once, just as they are today, and within the last 10,000 years. The percentage of Americans holding this creationist belief was the same when Gallup first polled on this question thirty years ago. Further, approximately one-third of Americans believe that humans evolved, but that God guided the process. Only 15 per cent of Americans think that humans evolved without the guidance of God (see Newport, 2012). Clearly, scientific history does not hold popular sway, even today.

For those who seek to understand the world through empirical evidence and critical thought, the archaeological record can be used to challenge not only myth but also standard historical accounts (for example, Conkey & Gero, 1991; Kohl & Fawcett, 1995; Leone, 2005; 2010). It can also provide data that can be used to model the interaction of human groups, and the interaction between humans and the environment (for example, Simmons, 1996; Stahl, 1996). As importantly, it can challenge or corroborate such models formulated within other academic disciplines. Some of these, such as economics and political science, have had a profound influence on political and social policy. To rob posterity of the archaeological record is to remove for all time this avenue for reinterpreting the past in ways that might be useful to future generations.

The archaeological record as public good

With this in mind, I suggest that the archaeological record constitutes a certain type of public good: a global public good. The Nobel Prize-winning economist Paul Samuelson (1954: 387) described public goods (or, as he initially termed them, 'collective consumption goods') as '[goods] which all enjoy in common in the sense that each individual's consumption of such a good leads to no subtractions from any other individual's consumption of that good [...]'.

Table 1 has long been standard fare in most microeconomic textbooks (for example, Brown & Jackson, 1978; Gravelle & Rees, 1992; Varien, 1992). Goods are

TABLE 1

TYPES OF GOODS

	Excludable	Non-excludable
Rivalrous	Personal Goods: food, clothing, cars, personal electronics	Common Property Goods: fish stocks, timber, coal
Non-Rivalrous	Club Goods: cinemas, private parks, satellite TV	Public Goods: free-to-air TV, air, national defense, GPS

organized here according to 'rivalry' and 'excludability'. A good is 'rivalrous' if the consumption of a good by one party reduces another party's opportunity to consume it, and 'non-rivalrous' if one party's consumption does not affect another's. A good is excludable if consumption of it can be limited to certain defined parties and non-excludable if consumption of the good cannot be so limited. Table 1 positions public goods, which are non-rivalrous and non-excludable, and therefore are both available to all and undiminished by consumption, among other types of goods. Owners of personal goods (such as clothing one might purchase for one's own wear) can prevent access to them by others, so they are excludable. Further, the stock of clothing is finite. By the purchase of a medium-sized blue shirt manufactured by a certain company, one reduces the opportunity for others to obtain this good; therefore, private goods are rivalrous. Club goods are like private goods in that they are accessible only by a certain community of consumers, such as the members of a country club. Since only those in the club can consume them, they are excludable, but consumption of these goods by members of the club does not lessen the opportunity for consumption of them by anyone else in the club, so they are non-rivalrous. No one can be denied consumption of common property goods, such as books in a public library. They are therefore non-excludable, but consumption of them lessens the opportunity consume them by others, and so they are rivalrous.

Commenting on Samuelson's work, Nordhaus (2005: 1) noted, 'In two and one-half pages, he reshaped the way economists and political philosophers think about the distinction between private goods and public goods'. Nordhaus (2005: 3–4) goes on to make other points very pertinent to the archaeological record:

> Most of economic life involves voluntary exchange of private goods, like bread or blue jeans. These are commodities consumed by one person and which directly benefit no one else. However, many activities involve spillovers among producers or consumers. A polar case of an externality is a public good. Public goods are commodities for which the cost of extending the service to an additional person is zero and for which it is impossible or expensive to exclude individuals from enjoying.

The 'externalities' Nordhaus mentions are spill-over effects of one economic activity onto another. The production of public goods can have positive or negative externalities. For instance, global positioning system (GPS) technologies can be used by anyone with a GPS receiver. GPS is used to guide aircraft, by hikers and sailors, by those who travel by car, by golfers, and many others, none of whom directly pay for the use of the GPS system. They are, in economic terms, free riders. This is a positive externality. The incentive for developing and implementing GPS technology was not provided by the 'invisible hand' of the free-market system; it can be traced to the need for the collective action inherent in national defence. GPS was developed by the United States military, which depends upon funding from the government, and therefore taxation, to operate. As Samuelson (1954) notes, private markets do not promote efficient production of such public goods. Thus, without collective action they would not exist or they would be in short supply.

Negative externalities also affect public goods. While air is often considered a public good because of universal access, some industries pollute the air. As pollution limits the use of air by others, these industries render clean air rivalrous, especially in the immediate locale. Along similar lines, national defence is only non-excludable to citizens of a specific nation that has created a defence system. On a local level, then, goods are most often rivalrous or excludable. Stiglitz (1982: 3–4) goes further, arguing there are no truly public goods on the local level:

> I am concerned here [...] with a class of public goods, which I shall refer to as *local* public goods, the benefits of which accrue only to those who belong to a particular group (which I shall call the community), and not to those who belong to other groups (communities) within the society. There is thus an element of 'privateness' in local public groups; while *within* the community the good is a pure public good, 'between' communities it acts like a private good. Those outside the community receive no benefit.

Following the logic of the table above, Stiglitz essentially argues that what appears to be a 'public' good at the local level may be viewed as a 'club' good by those outside the community. Stiglitz postulated that real public goods are few and exist only at the global level (1998: 118).

Also operating largely on a local level, once goods become rivalrous, are goods that also are non-excludable (and therefore common property goods). Common property goods predictably fall prey to what the ecologist Garret Hardin (1968) terms 'the tragedy of the commons'. Hardin's now classic argument is that individual, rational actors will pursue their own interests at the ultimate expense of others who might benefit from a finite resource accessible to all (and which is therefore non-excludable). Fish stocks in the ocean provide an example. Were only one actor involved, that actor might regulate fishing when it became clear that stocks were diminishing, and would almost surely do so if it seemed that stocks might never recover if overfishing continued. In contrast, individual actors competing in the marketplace will continue fishing as long as fishing is profitable, even if this eventually leads to the destruction of all fishing stocks. Where exclusion proves impossible and use is rivalrous, local, independent actors competing in the marketplace, the argument goes, cause resources that should be managed as a public goods to deteriorate — the tragedy of the commons — through excessive use or misuse.

This discussion of public goods and common goods is pertinent to archaeology. The finite stock of archaeological materials that could provide knowledge about the ways in which humans have organized themselves and the dynamic relationships among human societies and the environment, suffers from the tragedy of the commons. The archaeological record is being regularly undermined worldwide by economic activity — tourism, urban development, mining, and so on — and there are ample and growing economic incentives for local communities to engage in activities that enable private actors to compete with archaeologists to utilize the archaeological record. As a result, archaeology is increasingly becoming an unmanaged commons, which hastens a potential tragedy.

As argued above, the primary product of archaeology is knowledge. The world cannot depend upon the private sector to produce public goods, among them knowledge, efficiently. Knowledge is a good that provides great economic benefit. For example, high-tech industries proliferate near Stanford University, California, and people travel from all parts of the word for medical treatment at institutions near Johns Hopkins University, Baltimore. Those who benefit economically from local public goods are in a sense also free-riders, and for other regions to replicate such benefits would require collective action. Stiglitz (1998: 118) includes knowledge in his list of international public goods:

> Peace, international economic stability and overall international economic management, the global environment and knowledge (especially basic knowledge) are among the more important international public goods. There are many interrelations among these various international public goods [...]

Knowledge, like air, can be polluted: it can be repackaged as ersatz knowledge. This can be seen quite clearly in advertising, but is much more pervasive than that. In a *Foreign Policy* article, entitled 'The Disinformation Age', David J. Rothkopf (1999: 82) begins by saying: 'Trust no one. In today's volatile global markets, deception, misrepresentation, and outright dishonesty are among the few constants. So are incomplete information, inadequate reporting, and biased or otherwise egregiously faulty analyses'. As this pertains to the archaeological record, ersatz knowledge about the past is frequently used to serve local political purposes, many of which involve rationalizing claims for territory or privilege. The 'tragedy' of unbridled tourism threatens the ability of archaeology to offer a global public good and the use of 'scientific history' to counter the pollution of knowledge.

Unbridled tourism

In an article in the 1936 issue of the *Journal of Criminal Law and Criminology*, Don J. Finney describes the duties of the first police officer to arrive at the scene of a crime. If the perpetrator is not arrested or observed, the officer must:

> Preserve Evidence. Protect the crime scene against any intrusion or molestation, Give definite instructions that nothing is to be touched until the uniformed investigator arrives and takes charge. As to the duties of the uniformed investigator: 'The *primary function* of the uniformed investigator is to search for *physical evidence*. Having found such evidence it is his duty to take any steps necessary to preserve it, reproducing it by photographic and casting methods, labeling and preserving it in its proper sequence, and also to interpret its relation to the crime'. (Finney, 1936: 241–42)

The reason for this should be self-evident: one cannot reconstruct and understand past events through examination of material evidence unless that evidence remains uncontaminated and in its original context. As it is at a crime scene, so it is with the archaeological record.

For this reason, allowing great numbers of people into places where archaeological materials of special import are to be found is problematic. In the *laissez-faire* world of tourism, this, unfortunately, is the rule rather than the exception. My experience over thirty years of planning and consulting at archaeological sites in five continents indicates that the capacity to direct visitor flow away from areas that are easily damaged by the presence of humans is rare. Managing visitor flow is challenging in countries where per capita GDP is high. Where per capita GDP is relatively low, priorities are very understandably given to investments in infrastructure, education, and health care, and site management is only one of many emerging fields (see Ackerman, this volume). In the absence of zoning that identifies locations where archaeological materials are very vulnerable, the capacity for monitoring visitor activities and deterioration of archaeological materials, and a large, well-trained, and well-equipped staff, visitors degrade resources in myriad ways. These are outlined in a later section of this paper.

In the section above, Nordhaus notes that a distinguishing feature of public goods is that they are 'stock externalities'. By this he means that the adverse effects of the externality accumulate over time and can affect the entire stock of the public good. He notes that these external forces can be irreversible, as when the stock of a species has disappeared. When these external forces act slowly, it is difficult to ascertain the connection between market forces and the depletion of public goods. Under these conditions, Nordhaus (2005: 6) argues that private markets alone will not properly allocate the public good across generational lines. This logic can also be applied to the local management of archaeology.

Each archaeological site is finite

Archaeological sites that attract tourists are especially notable. They might be a splendid example of architecture or engineering, or associated with an important historical event, trend, or person, or iconic to a group ranging from a clan through a nation-state to the world to create a collective identity. Whatever the case, the material at the site holds the potential to tell us more than can be gleaned from oral or written sources, to add to our understanding of its importance. We can extract dates and sequences of events, and often much more: diet and settlement patterns and seasonality of occupation, evidence that corroborates or is at variance with written and oral histories. Material remains offer a way to critically review arguments and agendas that have been advanced with reference to the site. When the finite supply of evidence is gone, this is no longer possible.

Archaeological material is non-renewable

In this lies the difference between conservation and preservation. Much of conservation thinking has developed around research and management of natural resources. These are renewable. Damage to a species or an ecosystem can be irreversible, but there are limits of acceptable change that can be determined and then can be used as the basis for monitoring the condition of natural resources. If change exceeds that limit, steps can be taken to arrest degradation and allow the ecosystem to recover. That is not the case with archaeological materials. There are no limits of acceptable change, and any degradation of archaeological materials is simply unacceptable because they cannot be renewed.

Archaeological materials are irreplaceable

Damage to monuments can be repaired in ways that are undetectable or, if done in accordance with accepted international guidelines, are detectable, but do not much impair the appearance and aesthetic value of the monuments. All of this is well and good, but material lost is potential knowledge forever lost. Inscriptions, dates, or mason's marks erased by abrasion before they are recorded are simply information expunged permanently. Ravines caused by flash floods because of development and resulting impervious surfaces of areas upslope from archaeological sites can be filled in to ensure access for tourists, but materials washed away are lost.

Thus, absent special care, essential archaeological materials are likely to be destroyed by market forces as well as natural processes despite the fact that the knowledge to be generated by the site is arguably a public good that should be managed across generations for the benefit of all.[1]

While the heritage industry might, or might not, designate more sites as being worthy of preservation, all archaeological materials are not of equal importance. Think, if you will, of the Rosetta Stone. The stock of those artefacts or sites that contain data that might provide information about events and cultures for which we have little, dubious, or no written records is most evidently dwindling rapidly and is finite, non-renewable, and irreplaceable. The material remains associated with human activity are everywhere, true enough, but material remains that can clarify the sequence and exact dates of construction of tombs and monuments at Petra, to use that archaeological site as an example, have yet to be found, and are in locations that are in imminent danger of being disturbed in ways that will prevent our ever determining that sequence or the exact dates of construction.

Case study

In 2012, ICAHM published *Tourism at Petra: Driver to Development or Destruction?* (Comer, 2012). This was the first of four publications produced by ICAHM that will examine the effects of tourism at premier archaeological World Heritage Sites.

Damage done to archaeological materials by tourism can occur in two ways. The first of these occurs when large numbers of people are brought into physical contact, or even into near proximity, with materials at an archaeological site. Abrasion alone can produce substantial damage. Ancient walls can be toppled by vehicles or simply by people leaning or sitting on them. Humidity and temperature changes in closed environments are destructive over the long term. A certain percentage of visitors will practice vandalism, and others will provide a market for looted antiquities. Often, however, damage is caused in a second way: environmental change produced by development around and in the archaeological site, causes the worst damage. At Petra, the construction of impervious surfaces (roads, car parks, buildings, etc.) increases the volume and velocity of water that reaches the tombs and ruins there. Water carries with it salts and other chemicals that damage stone from which tombs are carved and standing structures built. It finds its way into cracks on the surfaces of tombs, gradually wearing away the softer stone beneath the exterior shell of the façade. Eventually, great sheets of rock fall away, taking with it decorative carvings. Alternately, water freezes in these cracks during cold desert nights and thaws during warm days, eventually causing rock to spall away (Comer, 2012).

It should be clear that deterioration of this type is an externality associated with transactions in the tourism industry, an industry that develops and markets goods, services, and experiences to tourists. Just as paper mills use and pollute water and the fishing industry depletes, and ultimately threatens, stocks of fish, the tourism industry has transformed a resource that was once a largely public good into a common good. As with paper mills and the fishing industry, this proceeded apace with advances in technology and engineering, and with societal change. There are many historical precedents for this: for example, buffalo once covered the plains of North America, constituting a public good as long as relatively small numbers of humans hunted them from horseback using bows and arrows. The influx of larger numbers of humans who imposed private property regimens and hunted with firearms rendered the herds of buffalo a common good, which then suffered the tragedy of the commons.

The role of global public goods

Tourism is a *laissez-faire* industry today because it relies on a capacity for sustainable development that exists only in the most affluent of countries. The implications of this to the preservation of archaeological resources are especially alarming because each archaeological site is irreplaceable, and some sites are uniquely informative about issues that are of great contemporary interest (e.g. climate change, political and economic hegemony, the role of material culture in cross-cultural trade of goods and ideas, etc.). Moreover, some of the most important archaeological sites are located in developing countries, and there is a laudable movement to acknowledge these sites on the world stage.

Tourism's industrial 'community', to use Stiglitz's terminology, operates all over the world. The local level is that of the nation-state. While environmental assessments or environmental impact statements might be a legal requirement in many countries, the lack of capacity to execute such planning regimens is clearly in evidence (see Wait & Altschul, this volume). Industrial communities utilize sophisticated technologies and draw upon a global organizational network that overwhelms planning and administrative capacities in all but very affluent countries, and sometimes even in these countries. This being so, I argue here that it is necessary to take a more global perspective, one that brings to the fore such international incentives as there might be for safeguarding public goods.

Of particular note is the comment that Stiglitz makes, cited above, about 'basic knowledge'. Whereas there are multiple accounts of history at the local level that one might expect to have been constructed in accord with local ideologies and agendas set by local social and political leaders, I argue here that a 'scientific history', which as noted above does not admit of supernatural influences on human events and that does not privilege oral or written histories over material evidence, is most likely to provide 'basic knowledge', or the knowledge pertinent to worldwide social and environmental concerns. Stiglitz (1999: 321) notes, 'The efficient production and equitable use of global knowledge requires collective action. The challenge facing the international community is whether we can make our current system of voluntary, cooperative governance work in the collective interest of all'. Stiglitz (2006: 152–53) ultimately argued that global standards would be necessary to generate global public goods, and identified global standards themselves as a global public good:

Global standards are also global public goods. Establishing a set of standards enhances the efficiency with which market economies can function. Standards mean uniform practices and common ways of doing things. Furthermore, huge advantages are associated with the establishment of industry standards.

Global standards and best practices for archaeological heritage management

ICAHM proposes to contribute to the development of industry standards for tourism by the development of best practices for archaeological heritage management. As argued above, archaeological resources provide material evidence that contribute to the 'basic knowledge' provided by a 'scientific history'. Furthermore, programmes built around the preservation of archaeological sites can also serve to alert management to a general deterioration of authenticity and integrity at protected areas. Archaeological resources can be a linchpin in monitoring programmes, where they can be thought of as 'the canary in the coal mine'. That is, when archaeological materials are compromised, it is often a strong indication that the natural and social environment of the protected area is being altered in generally undesirable ways.

To be effective, standards must be embraced by the tourism industry. ICAHM seeks to engage the tourism industry by requiring that the capacity to effectively manage an archaeological site be a prerequisite for inscription on the World Heritage List. The Menorca Statement on the Development and Use of Best Practices in the Management of Archaeological World Heritage Sites was developed from discussions held at and subsequent to the First International Conference on Best Practices in World Heritage: Archaeology, held between the 9–13 April 2012 on the Island of Menorca, Spain. It was organized by the Complutense University of Madrid, sponsored by the Council of Menorca Island (Balearic Islands, Spain), and planned in coordination with ICAHM. The conference was the largest ever assembled for the express purpose of enhancing the calibre of archaeological heritage management.

The Menorca Statement makes public the intent by ICAHM to develop best practices for the management of archaeological heritage. ICAHM invites broad participation in the development of these best practices by all ICOMOS scientific committees, in particular the ICOMOS International Cultural Tourism Committee (ICTC) and the ICOMOS International Committee on Risk Preparedness (ICORP), as well as by recognized professional associations of archaeologists around the world. It will be the position of ICAHM that nominations to the World Heritage List should describe how the nominated site would adhere to these best practices upon their completion and dissemination.

The Menorca Statement does not address policy or establish guidelines, as might Conventions and Resolutions; instead, it is a concise position statement that is based upon the findings and discussions that emerged from an intensive, short-term evaluation of the issue of best practices in heritage management by a group of experienced professionals. This document will provide important guidance as well as a focus for ICAHM activities during this time of unprecedented threats to our archaeological heritage, which remains the only lens through which the human past can be viewed that is not yet distorted to some degree by prejudice or preconceived notion.

The Menorca Statement

The non-renewable archaeological patrimony at many sites inscribed on the World Heritage List is being destroyed at an alarming rate. The cause for this destruction includes but is not limited to: economic development, excessive tourism pressure, agricultural or urban expansion, and climate change. These problems are aggravated by inadequate management of archaeological sites, including lack of financial resources and sufficient numbers of adequately trained personnel.

The economic drive for tourism at World Heritage Sites emerged as the most obvious threat. These fascinating sites are now seen as primarily economic assets instead of repositories of information about the human past.

Moreover, we observed increasing national zeal around the world to inscribe archaeological sites on the World Heritage List. This push is too often happening before the capacity to manage and preserve those resources is in place.

In light of this multi-faceted situation, the following actions are proposed:

❖   *Experts will work together to develop Best Practices for the Management of Archaeological World Heritage Sites.*

❖   *Nomination of archaeological sites to the World Heritage List should expressly address these practices as follows:*

- *Nomination dossiers must establish beyond a doubt that best practices can be adhered to at the time of inscription; alternately*
- *Nomination dossiers will include a detailed plan that will describe the means by which capacity to adhere to best practices will be developed.*
  - ➤ *The plan will include timeframes and cost.*
  - ➤ *If the plan is approved, the inscription of the site will be provisional on establishing capacity according to time frames.*
  - ➤ *The plan also will identify sources of funding required to establish capacity according to time frames.*

❖   *If the nominating States Party is unable to identify sources of funding, the World Heritage Committee should do so.*

Conclusion: managing tourism to generate local benefits and global public goods

Local economic benefit can be increased if tourism is well managed. This is not only because a well managed tourism would be a sustainable tourism — one that would not destroy archaeological materials, or degrade the experience of visiting a site — but because it would minimize the time spent at the archaeological site itself, and maximize the time spent in communities and other locations away from the site where places of consumption could be located. Places of consumption are those that realize economic benefit. These places should provide the comfort that visitors desire after an outing, which is among the experiences that an archaeological site provides. With proper planning, they could be constructed and maintained in ways that are environmentally sound.

Introducing and utilizing best practices should be seen not just as a step away from *laissez-faire*, but a step toward economic productivity as well as effective archaeological heritage management. In economic terms, best practices will be a first step in introducing standards that will acknowledge the threat posed by stock externalities. In the absence of such standards, the transformation of the archaeological record from a global public good into a common good will proceed, with the ultimate outcome of denying that good to future generations. The global public goods of knowledge and global standards are not at variance with the production and marketing of local goods; on the contrary, the production of global public goods renders the production of local goods sustainable.

Note

[1] I take note here of some of the more relativistic approaches to archaeological remains, such as by Holtorf (2001: 289) who notes that '[...] in the future more and more of our lifeworld will be recorded as some sort of historical (or natural) site worthy of preservation'. This approach suggests both that archaeological materials are valued in alternate ways in differing cultural contexts, and that not all archaeological data adds to our common knowledge, therefore some destruction, for example, through tourism, should be permissible. This is an interesting academic argument premised on cultural relativism, but one that is not relevant to the scientific materialist argument advanced by this paper.

Bibliography

Brown, C. V. & Jackson, P. 1978. *Public Sector Economics*. Oxford: Blackwell.

Comer, D. C. ed. 2012. *Tourism at Petra: Driver to Development or Destruction?* New York: Springer Press.

Conkey, M. W. & Gero, J. M. 1991. *Engendering Archaeology: Women and Prehistory*. Oxford: Blackwell.

Finney, D. J. 1936. Police Duties at Crime Scenes. *The Journal of Criminal Law & Criminology*, 27(2): 231–48.

Gravelle. H. & Rees, R. 1992. *Microeconomics*. London: Longman.

Hardin, G. 1968. The Tragedy of the Commons. *Science*. New Series, 162(3859): 1243–48.

Holtorf, C. J. 2001. Is the Past a Non-Renewable Resource? In: R. Layton, P. G. Stone, and J. Thomas, eds. *Destruction and Conservation of Cultural Property*. London: Routledge.

Kagan, D. 2009. *Thucydides: The Reinvention of History*. New York: Viking Press.

Kohl, P. L. & Fawcett, C. P. 1995. *Nationalism, Politics, and the Practice of Archaeology*. Cambridge: Cambridge University Press.

Leone, M. P. 2005. *The Archaeology of Liberty in an American Capital: Excavations in Annapolis*. Berkeley, CA: University of California Press.

Leone, M. P. 2010. *Critical Historical Archaeology*. Walnut Creek, CA: Left Coast Press.

Newport, F. 2012. In U.S., 46% Hold Creationist View of Human Origins. *Gallup Politics* [accessed 25 January 2014]. Available at: <http://www.gallup.com/poll/155003/hold-creationist-view-human-origins.aspx>.

Nordhaus, W. D. 2005. Paul Samuelson and Global Public Goods. A commemorative essay for Paul Samuelson [accessed 11 May 2014]. Available at: <http://www.econ.yale.edu/~nordhaus/homepage/PASandGPG.pdf>.

Rothkopf, D. J. 1999. The Disinformation Age. *Foreign Policy*, 114: 82–96.

Samuelson, P. A. 1954. The Pure Theory of Public Expenditure. *The Review of Economics and Statistics*, 36(4): 387–89.

Simmons, I. G. 1996. *The Environmental Impact of Later Mesolithic Cultures*. Edinburgh: Edinburgh University Press.

Stahl, P. W. 1996. Holocene Biodiversity: An Archaeological Perspective from the Americas. *Annual Review of Anthropology*, 25: 105–26.

Stiglitz, J. E. 1977. Theory of Local Public Goods. In: M. S. Fieldstein and R. P. Inman, eds. *The Economics of Public Services*. New York: Halsted Press, pp. 274–333.

Stiglitz, J. E. 1982. The Theory of Local Public Goods Twenty-Five Years after Tiebout: A Perspective. *Working Paper No. 954*. Washington, DC: National Bureau of Economic Research

Stiglitz, J. E. 1998. International Financial Institutions and the Provision of International Public Goods. *International Financial Institutions of the 21st Century*. European Investment Bank Papers, 3(2).

Stiglitz, J. E. 1999. Knowledge as a Global Public Good. In: I. Kaul, I. Grunberg, and M. A. Stern, eds. *Global Public Goods. International Cooperation in the 21st Century*. New York: Oxford University Press, pp. 308–25.

Stiglitz, J. E. 2006. Global Public Goods and Global Finance: Does Global Governance Ensure that the Global Public Interest is Served? In: J. P. Touffut, ed. *Advancing Public Goods*. Aldershot, UK: Edward Elgar, pp. 146–64.

Varian, Hal R. 1992. *Microeconomic Analysis*. New York: W. W. Norton & Company.

Notes on contributor

Douglas C. Comer is a principal at Cultural Site Research and Management. He was the Chief of the US National Park Service Applied Archaeology Center for over two decades and is a Fulbright Scholar in Cultural Resource Management. He is Co-President of the ICOMOS International Scientific Committee on Archaeological Heritage Management (ICAHM), serves as ex-officio Trustee for the Society for American Archaeology on the US International Committee on Monuments and Sites (US/ICOMOS), is Senior Editor for the Springer publication series *Multidisciplinary Perspectives on Archaeological Heritage Management*, and Co-Editor of the Conservation and Preservation Section of the *Encyclopedia of Global Archaeology*. He has conducted and overseen planning and research efforts at numerous areas around the world, including US National Parks, World Heritage Sites on five continents, National Monuments, and areas under the stewardship of the US Bureau of Land Management and Department of Defense, and has published widely on cultural resource management and aerial and satellite remote sensing for archaeological research and heritage management.

Correspondence to: Douglas C. Comer, Cultural Site Research and Management, 2113 St Paul Street, Baltimore, MD 21218, USA. Email: dcomer@culturalsite.com

PUBLIC ARCHAEOLOGY, Vol. 13 Nos 1–3, 2014, 135–50

Archaeology and Economic Development: Commitment and Support from the World Bank Group

ARLENE K. FLEMING

Cultural Resource and Development Specialist, USA

The policies and standards of the World Bank and the International Finance Corporation contribute significantly to the identification, excavation, documentation, study, protection, management, and publication of archaeological sites, structures, and material. Following a description of these policies, examples of projects in four regions of the world illustrate how they have been applied, together with national laws and regulations, benefiting archaeology and the archaeological record at local, national, and international levels, while involving affected communities and educating the public at large. The commitment of international financial institutions creates opportunities that archaeologists have yet to fully realize.

KEYWORDS World Bank, International Finance Corporation (IFC), archaeology and infrastructure development, Environmental Impact Assessment, cultural heritage

Introduction

Archaeology in the development context
The World Bank and the International Finance Corporation (IFC) are two of five organizations within the World Bank Group,[1] an international development institution cooperatively owned by 188 member countries including donors and borrowers. These component organizations are:

The World Bank, which consists of the:
- International Bank for Reconstruction and Development (IBRD);
- International Development Association (IDA);

In addition to:
- the International Finance Corporation (IFC);
- the Multilateral Investment Guarantee Agency (MIGA);
- the International Centre for Settlement of Investment Disputes (ICSID).

DOI 10.1179/1465518714Z.00000000061

The World Bank, established following World War II as the IBRD, lends to governments of developing and middle-income countries; the IFC lends to private sector entities investing in these countries. Both the World Bank and the IFC provide loans, credits, guarantees, technical assistance and various other types of support to their clients with the objectives of stimulating social and economic development and reducing poverty.

As financial institutions dedicated to improving economic and social conditions in their client countries, both the World Bank and the IFC invest in archaeology on occasion as a component in lending operations where it is deemed a contributing factor to development, notably for stimulating tourism. More importantly, in a broader context, both institutions include archaeological material in their environmental and social policies and standards applicable to operations involving earth moving or other modifications of the landscape. The World Bank's Operational Policy 4.11 — Physical Cultural Resources and the IFC's Performance Standard 8 — Cultural Heritage, specifically require attention to archaeological sites, structures, and artefacts that may be impacted by a project. Both institutions also require that projects they finance, in whole or in part, comply with laws and regulations of client countries governing archaeological management and discovery of archaeological material during construction.[2]

In the World Bank and the IFC, policies and standards regarding material culture — including archaeology — fall under the rubric of environmental protection and management. This relationship between material culture and environment was first elaborated legally in 1969, in the National Environmental Policy Act (NEPA) of the United States, wherein cultural heritage is included with biophysical and social factors as a component of environment. Since 1969, the basic concepts of NEPA, including the definition of environment to include cultural heritage, and the requirement for environmental assessment prior to development actions, have been disseminated throughout the world. As a part of this process, development institutions including the World Bank have been influential in the establishment of environmental authorities, laws, and regulations in their client countries, including the process of Environmental Impact Assessment (EIA).

The EIA is intended to achieve a balance between the objectives of development and environmental protection for individual projects. In the process, the geographical area likely to be affected by a project is determined; biophysical, social, and cultural heritage features within the area are identified; and the proposed project's impact is assessed. Alternatives to the project design and/or mitigating measures may be proposed to alleviate negative impacts. The EIA involves a variety of specialized disciplines and skills in collecting, organizing, and analysing information on the human and natural aspects of a designated project impact area and generally leads to an Environmental Management Plan (EMP) to be followed during implementation of a project. In principle, the EMP should include provisions for managing any archaeological material identified during the EIA, as well as for 'chance finds' discovered during the course of a project.

Development projects present valuable opportunities for archaeologists. The EIA, required for these projects, is based on a 'spatial' approach and seeks to discover the prehistoric, historic, and contemporary material cultural characteristics of an entire project impact area. Given the fact that a very small portion of the earth's surface has been systematically surveyed for archaeological remains, projects that require EIAs have the potential to considerably augment the archaeological record. Some development projects span large areas allowing archaeologists to use available technologies and methods for efficiently gathering and analysing information. These include geographic positioning systems (GPS), geographic information systems (GIS), and remote sensing (RS), as well as a host of new and evolving technologies and applications. Moreover, many development projects are in areas that are likely sources for archaeological evidence, for example: power and agricultural projects in river valleys, transportation projects along ancient routes, development of coastal areas, and water and sanitation projects in historic urban enclaves. Furthermore, the costs of EIAs and EMPs are borne by the development project proponents. When archaeological sites, structures, or artefacts have been identified during preparation or implementation of a development project, the project proponents often provide support for archaeological documentation, excavation, and management, or attract support from other sources.

In a number of countries, participation of archaeologists in EIA is well established. However, in most developing and transitional countries, where projects financed by World Bank and IFC occur, opportunities are frequently missed for identifying, studying, protecting, and managing archaeological evidence in the context of such projects. The World Bank and IFC make a significant contribution to this end, both through their policies and standards and by requiring client countries to comply with their own laws and regulations. Archaeologists can reinforce these actions by expanding their understanding of development and their participation in the process.

The following sections explore the policies and standards of the World Bank and IFC regarding cultural resources, including archaeology, and describe the management of archaeological sites, structures, and material in projects within four geographical regions: Europe, Latin America, Africa, and East Asia. The examples illustrate attention to the identification, excavation, documentation, protection, analysis, publication, and use of archaeological materials, and the resulting significant benefits to archaeology and the archaeological record at local, national, and international levels, as well as to inhabitants of communities within a development project area and to the public at large.

The World Bank's Operational Policy (OP) 4.11 — Physical Cultural Resources

During Fiscal Year 2012, the World Bank's Board of Executive Directors approved US$35.4 billion in financial assistance to its client countries. Included in this amount were US$20.6 billion from the IBRD to middle-income nations and US$14.8 billion from IDA in credits and grants to the poorest countries of the world (World Bank, 2012). Most loans, credits, and grants provided by the World Bank to its client countries must comply with a suite of eleven policies, as applicable. These policies specify mandatory provisions for safeguarding and managing various environmental, social, and legal aspects of development. They comprise a separate policy for each of the following: environmental assessment (including basic requirements for EIA), natural habitats, physical cultural resources, forests, pest management, involuntary resettlement, indigenous peoples, safety of dams, international waterways, disputed areas, and use of country systems.[3]

OP 4.11 — Physical Cultural Resources, approved by the Board of Executive Directors in 2006 (WBOM, 2006), revised and expanded the Operational Policy Note 11.03 — Management of Cultural Property in Bank-Financed Projects, issued in 1986. Physical cultural resources are defined in OP 4.11 as movable or immovable objects, sites, structures and groups of structures and natural features and landscapes that have archaeological, paleontological, historical, architectural, religious, aesthetic, or other cultural significance. They may be located in urban or rural settings, and they may be above or below ground, or underwater. Their cultural interest may be at the local, provincial, or national level, or within the international community. The policy acknowledges that these resources are important as sources of valuable scientific and historical information, as assets for economic and social development, and as integral parts of a people's cultural identity and practices.

OP 4.11 stipulates that physical cultural resources are to be included in a project's environmental assessment and management. Hence archaeological sites, structures, and artefacts should be considered during the course of the EIA as part of screening, base-line data collection, surveying, consultation with local communities and other stakeholders, consideration of national and other applicable laws and regulations, identification of any necessary mitigation measures, and inclusion in the project's EMP. The policy also calls for public disclosure of the EIA report and the EMP, except where such disclosure would endanger the cultural resources (for example, by specifying the location of unexcavated archaeological sites) or pose a threat to persons with knowledge of the resources. Instructions for managing cultural heritage during project implementation or operation are to be provided in the project EMP. This includes procedures for handling any chance finds of archaeological or other cultural material discovered during construction and other project activities. Procedures are in accordance with the client country's laws and regulations governing such finds.

The World Bank's attention to physical cultural resources in its investment projects is intended to assist borrowing countries to strengthen capacity for resource identification, protection and management. The EIA study and report, and creation of the project EMP are generally provided by EIA consultants engaged by the project proponents in the borrowing country and reviewed by environmental authorities. The World Bank provides oversight, reviewing the terms of reference and the draft report, and approving the final EIA and EMP. Inclusion of physical cultural resources is intended to bring cultural heritage and archaeological authorities into the development planning and implementation process. However, since their participation is often lacking, it generally requires a pro-active stance on the part of cultural authorities and professionals — including archaeologists — as well as technical assistance and other capacity building activities for the host government. OP 4.11 provides for such support, both at the individual project level, and if deemed appropriate by the Bank and a client country, on a broader national scale.

In an effort to stimulate and strengthen concern for cultural resources, the World Bank created two guidance tools to aid in implementation of its policy. The first is the *Physical Cultural Resources Safeguard Policy Guidebook* containing instructions for professionals involved in considering various types of material culture within the EIA process, and examples for applying the policy to several categories of development projects (World Bank, 2009). The Guidebook has been widely disseminated and used in training within the World Bank, its client countries, and elsewhere. It is available in several languages: English, French, Spanish, Arabic, Chinese, and Portuguese. The second tool under development is a compendium of *Physical Cultural Resources Country Profiles*, including one for each client country of the World Bank. The Profile contains an introduction to the cultural heritage of the subject country, including typologies, general locations, and sources of inventories, as well as information on administrative and legal management provisions and institutions, on professional experts and organizations in the component sub-fields of cultural heritage. It also cites environmental laws and regulations, including those for EIA.[4]

The World Bank safeguard policies were formulated with the assumption that most loans and credits are for operations wherein the scope of the project and area of impact are known at the outset. However, in an increasing number of operations, sub-projects are defined and their location determined during the course of the loan or credit period. Hence there is a need to establish at the outset a procedure for completing numerous EIAs and EMPs as sub-projects come online. As client countries have gained experience with EIA over the past decades, the World Bank is increasingly focused on assessing their capability for environmental and social management, and where necessary, on improving standards and performance As a part of this effort, the World Bank supports training and provides guidance to cultural heritage and environmental professionals as well as to project proponents and construction workers in its client countries, to regional development banks, and to EIA consultants through organizations such as the International Association for Impact Assessment (IAIA, 2012).

The International Finance Corporation's Policy on Social and Environmental Sustainability and Performance Standard 8: Cultural Heritage

The IFC has established a 'Sustainability Framework' as a holistic approach to assessing the capacity of its private sector borrowers for environmental and social management. Financing private sector operations in regions and countries with limited access to capital, the IFC provides equity, long-term loans, structured finance, and risk management products, as well as technical assistance and advisory services. During Fiscal Year 2012, the IFC invested US$20.4 billion, including nearly US $5 billion mobilized from other investors to support private sector activities in developing countries (IFC, 2012a).

In 2006, following an extensive review and assessment of its environmental and social safeguarding policies, the IFC adopted a restructured approach consisting of a Policy on Social and Environmental Sustainability and eight performance standards intended to help its borrowers manage their social and environmental performance with a focus on results. Further assessment and refinement led in 2012 to establishment of a three-part IFC Sustainability Framework for development and risk management (IFC, 2012b). Within this Framework, the Policy on Environmental and Social Sustainability describes IFC's commitments, roles, and responsibilities relating to environmental and social sustainability. Eight Performance Standards addressing facets of environmental and social sustainability provide guidance to IFC's private sector clients for identifying, avoiding, mitigating and managing risks and impacts in projects, including engagement of stakeholders. The Performance Standards are: (1) Assessment and Management of Environmental and Social Risks and Impacts; (2) Labor and Working Conditions; (3) Resource Efficiency and Pollution Prevention; (4) Community Health, Safety, and Security; (5) Land Acquisition and Involuntary Resettlement; (6) Biodiversity Conservation and Sustainable Management of Living Natural Resources; (7) Indigenous Peoples; and (8) Cultural Heritage. IFC requires its clients to apply the Performance Standards, as appropriate, and provides a Guidance Note for each standard (IFC, 2012b). The third component of the Framework, the Access to Information Policy, contains IFC's institutional disclosure obligations regarding investment and advisory services.

Performance Standard 1: Assessment and Management of Environmental and Social Risks and Impacts (PS 1) requires the private sector borrower to conduct an environmental and social assessment in coordination with responsible government agencies and third parties, as appropriate, in order to identify a project's impacts, risks, and opportunities (IFC, 2012c). PS 1 applies to all projects in which such risks and impacts are identified, and the client is obligated to manage them through an Environmental and Social Management System (ESMS) as defined and described in the standard, including ensuring effective community engagement and continuing to manage environmental and social performance throughout the life of a project. The ESMS also must comply with relevant national law and international treaty obligations of the country in which a project is undertaken. In the interest of furthering good practice, the IFC encourages its clients to apply the ESMS to all of its project activities, regardless of the financing source.

Performance Standard 8: Cultural Heritage (PS 8) aims to protect cultural heritage from adverse impacts of project activities, to support its preservation, and to promote equitable sharing of benefits from the use of cultural heritage (IFC, 2012d). Applicability of PS 8 is determined during the process of assessing environmental and social risks and impacts of a project, as required by PS 1. Necessary actions are managed through the client's ESMS in accordance with PS 1. Cultural heritage is defined in PS 8 as:

(i)   tangible forms, including moveable or immovable objects, property, sites, structures, or groups of structures, having archaeological (prehistoric), paleontological, historical, cultural, artistic, and religious values;

(ii)   unique natural features or tangible objects that embody cultural values, such as sacred groves, rocks, lakes, and waterfalls; and

(iii)   certain instances of intangible forms of culture that are proposed to be used for commercial purposes, such as cultural knowledge, innovations, and practices of communities embodying traditional lifestyles. (IFC, 2012d)

The requirements of PS 8 apply whether or not the cultural heritage has been legally protected or previously disturbed. PS 8 mandates compliance with applicable national law for protection and management of cultural heritage, and the host country's obligations under international treaties, with special reference to UNESCO's

1972 Convention concerning the Protection of the World Cultural and Natural Heritage (The World Heritage Convention).

In general, the IFC's policy and standards are less prescriptive than the World Bank's safeguard policies. PS 1 requires an environmental and social assessment and an ESMS, but does not specify that the assessment be an EIA, and PS 8 stipulates that, in identifying and protecting cultural heritage, the client is to ensure internationally recognized practices and competent professionals for heritage protection, field-based study, and documentation. PS 8 states that the client is responsible for designing and siting a project to avoid negative impacts on cultural heritage, while ensuring that the ESMS contains provisions for managing any chance finds during project construction or operation. Consultation is required with communities affected by a project — both for identifying cultural heritage and for decision-making regarding the heritage — as is involvement by relevant national or local regulatory agencies entrusted with heritage protection. Clients are responsible for ensuring access to cultural sites by customary users. PS 8 distinguishes three categories of cultural heritage: replicable, non-replicable and critical, providing definitions and requirements for managing each.

The Equator Principles and financial institutions

The influence and impact of IFC's environmental and social sustainability policy and performance standards are considerably expanded through their use by other major financial institutions. In 2002, four private sector international banks reached an agreement with IFC to formulate the Equator Principles (EP) wherein they would voluntarily apply IFC's policies for determining, assessing, and managing environmental and social risks in their project financing. When the IFC created a new policy and eight performance standards for environmental and social sustainability in 2006, the EP institutions followed suit, adopting EPII. The Equator Principles Association, formed in 2010, by 2013 was serving seventy-nine member institutions based in thirty-five countries (Equator Principles, 2013a). A Strategic Review of the EPs resulted in Equator Principles III, which became effective in January 2014 (Equator Principles, 2013b). This revision is congruent with the IFC's Sustainability Framework issued in early 2012. The EPs are applicable to projects with a total capital cost above US$10 million; to project finance advisory activities; to upgrades or expansions of existing projects with significant environmental or social impacts; and to funding administered by an EP Financial Institution. As the EP member institutions vary widely in capacity for implementing the EPs, a need for training regarding the performance standards, including PS 8 for cultural heritage, presents an opportunity for archaeologists.

The mandatory policies of the World Bank and the IFC provide the impetus for their respective government and private sector clients to consider the impact of development projects on known archaeological sites, structures, and material, and to manage any chance finds during construction. These policies also require compliance with laws and regulations of the host country and often serve to highlight and strengthen compliance with them. In some cases, with the encouragement of project proponents and the World Bank or IFC, financial and technical support for archaeology has exceeded policy requirements. Four examples — two pipelines financed in part by IFC, and two hydropower projects including World Bank financing — are illustrative.

Archaeology as a beneficiary of development

Europe: Baku Tbilisi-Ceyhan oil pipeline

The Baku-Tbilisi-Ceyhan (BTC) pipeline transports oil from the Caspian Basin in Azerbaijan, through Georgia and Turkey to the port of Ceyhan on the Mediterranean coast, a distance of 1768 km. The pipeline corridor contains numerous prehistoric and historic sites, as the line traverses territory of ancient trade routes. The region had not been systematically surveyed, and research in Azerbaijan and Georgia had been hindered by decades of isolation that affected the capacity for survey, excavation, and analysis (BP Caspian, 2014; Smithsonian Institution, 2011).

The project, managed by the BTC Consortium (BTC Co.), comprised a coalition of eleven oil companies led by British Petroleum (BP). Following completion and review of an EIA in each of the three countries involved, in 2003, the IFC together with the European Bank for Reconstruction and Development joined several national export credit agencies in financing the project. The pipeline was completed in 2005. Participation by the IFC mandated compliance with its safeguard policies requiring that cultural heritage be covered in an EIA prior to investment approval. Based on findings of an EIA conducted for each country and on relevant national laws and regulations, a Cultural Heritage Management Plan was devised for each of the three countries that included instructions for handling cultural sites and artefacts discovered by chance during construction. Each EIA included a baseline survey for cultural heritage sites. Sites deemed most threatened or valuable were fully investigated after the respective EIAs were finalized. During construction, monitoring and necessary excavation were undertaken and in the post-construction phase, archaeological material was analysed, conserved, and published in two illustrated bilingual books: English/Azeri and English/Georgian (Taylor, et al., 2011).

The preparation, construction, and operational phases of the BTC pipeline project yielded rich results. Financial resources from multiple partners enabled research, conservation, and analysis, while providing technical assistance and strengthening local capacity for managing cultural heritage. Professional relationships between cultural heritage specialists in Azerbaijan, Georgia, Turkey, and colleagues in the West are continuing following completion of the pipeline. Three major benefits — identifying cultural sites, fostering local, national, and regional identity, and building management capacity — are illustrated in a brief summary of activities in Azerbaijan under the AGT (Azerbaijan, Georgia, and Turkey) Pipelines Archaeology Program (Smithsonian Institution, 2011).

The BTC Co.'s investment in archaeology in Azerbaijan began with work in Gobustan, a natural preserve of approximately 6000 acres, west of Baku. Investigation in a corner of this preserve traversed by the pipeline complemented surveys of a larger area, which led to recording hundreds of unexcavated archaeological sites as well as over 6000 panels of rock art. This provided documentation that enabled the Gobustan National Historical-Artistic Preserve to become a UNESCO World Heritage Site in 2007. Contract archaeologists for the BTC Co. and staff of the Azeri

Institute of Archaeology and Ethnography collaborated on pipeline-related investigations; more than sixty new sites were identified, with excavations at nearly 50, dating to the Copper Age, Bronze Age (with remains from 1500 to 700 BCE), Hellenistic Greek and Roman periods, as well as the Middle Ages. Approximately 1500 complete pottery vessels and several bronze daggers were found in 230 graves excavated at two Bronze Age sites (Taylor, et al., 2011).

The combination of technical assistance and financial support, totalling over US$1 million, has assisted the Institute in enhancing its facilities (C. Polglase, pers. comm., 2011). A conservation laboratory was established with materials and equipment and Azeri archaeologists were trained in modern conservation techniques. An additional investment from BTC enabled improved storage, documentation, and management of collections by providing materials and training. Technical assistance and training also facilitated analysis and publication of excavation reports. During the preparation and construction phases of the pipeline, the BTC Co. worked with some eleven non-governmental organization committees to evaluate the impact of the pipeline on communities, considering a variety of topics, including cultural heritage.

FIGURE 1   Archaeological excavation along the Baku-Tbilisi-Ceyhan Pipeline route in Azerbaijan.

Latin America: PERU LNG natural gas export project

In 2008, IFC joined other financial institutions by lending US$300 million for the PERU LNG natural gas export project, which constituted partial financing for the largest foreign direct investment in the country's history. PERU LNG, the project sponsor, is a Peruvian company established in 2003 by a group of international oil and gas companies. IFC's role included advising PERU LNG on optimizing environ-mental standards and ensuring benefit to local communities in some of the country's poorest regions. The project included construction of Peru's first gas liquefaction plant and a marine loading terminal, as well as a new 408 km pipeline extending from the Andean community of Chiquintirca in Ayacucho to Melchorita on the Pacific coast south of Lima, as an extension of an existing pipeline network located east of the Andes mountains. Construction was completed in June 2010 (Lockard, 2010).

The archaeology programme of the PERU LNG Project was conducted in accord-ance with the IFC's PS 8 — Cultural Heritage and Peruvian law and regulations governing management of cultural patrimony under the authority of the Ministry of Culture (Peru, 2001). The law regarding compliance-based archaeology states that investigations must occur prior to any construction activity by private entities and governmental agencies. Regulations define four types of archaeological investigations required prior to development projects, as follows: (1) Survey without Excavations — to identify potential sites in the project impact area; (2) Evaluation with Excavations — to determine archaeological site boundaries; (3) Archaeological Rescue — to excavate all archaeological remains and recover artefacts from within the project area; and (4) Emergency. Following completion of the first three phases, a Certificate of the Inexistence of Archaeological Remains (CIRA) is issued and development project construction activities can begin. Archaeological monitoring plans are required for the construction period, as are 'chance finds' procedures. All archaeological finds are the property of the state.

The PERU LNG Archaeological Project obtained 231 CIRAs and excavated 137 archaeological sites, removing all archaeological remains from the project area so that it could thereafter be certified as containing no archaeological sites. An additional 140 sites were discovered and investigated as chance finds during construction. PERU LNG exceeded legal requirements by conducting thorough analyses of artefacts from the majority of sites excavated, a major contribution to the value of the archaeologi-cal investigations. The work involved more than 200 professional Peruvian archae-ologists and some 2000 local community members who assisted with excavations, site registration, and cleaning artefacts under supervision of the archaeologists. Thus community inhabitants learned about the prehistory of their locality (Lockard, 2010; G. Lockard, pers. comm., 2011).

The Peruvian regulation requiring publication of compliance-based archaeological projects is rarely enforced. However, the PERU LNG Archaeological Project pro-vided a bilingual book for the public presenting the results of the project and basic information on archaeology, including the importance of studying and protecting archaeological sites, and relevant Peruvian laws and regulations. This extensively illustrated, bilingual English/Spanish book was distributed to local communities in the PERU LNG impact area and universities throughout the country (Lockard, 2010). A second book for professional archaeologists is forthcoming. PERU LNG also spon-sored a temporary exhibit at the National Museum of Peru which featured artefacts recovered during the project.

Archaeological sites discovered along the pipeline route date from the Initial Period (c. 1800–1000 BCE) to the Colonial Period (1532–1821 CE), and contain remains of the Paracas culture, the Nazca and associated cultures of the Early Intermediate Period, the Wari Empire, the Chincha culture, and the Inka Empire. Four archaeological complexes containing two or more individual sites were remarkable for their architecture and/or density of artefacts. The PERU LNG pipeline was rerouted to avoid a plaza and terraces of the Corpas Complex located on a steep hillside in the Ayacucho highlands.

Africa: Lesotho Water Sector Improvement Project: Phase 2 — Metolong Dam and water supply programme

The IDA credit provided through the World Bank is a relatively small portion of the financing for this project which aims to support the Government of Lesotho (GoL) in developing a long-term solution for supplying water to the lowlands, including the capital city, Maseru, and to expand the water distribution network in an environmentally sustainable, socially responsible, and economically viable manner. The project includes construction of the Metolong Dam on the South Phuthiatsana River, with a catchment area of 250 sq. km. IDA's involvement requires that the World Bank's safeguard policies, including OP 4.11 — Physical Cultural Resources, be applied for the entire project (World Bank, 2010).

The impact area of the Metolong Dam contains drawings on rock faces and surface indications of unexcavated sites as discovered in surveys during the 1970s and 1980s (Mitchell & Arthur, 2012). The Department of Water Affairs of the GoL specified that the Environmental and Social Impact Assessment (ESIA) should include an archaeological reconnaissance study of the project impact area and a protocol for managing chance finds during construction. In the ESIA report of 2008, the chapter on cultural heritage included: the GoL's statutory requirements; description of archaeological remains identified by era, and of the rock art; a description of living heritage; impacts of the dam, inundation area, transmission, pumping stations, infrastructure, and essential services on the cultural resources; a cost estimate for a cultural heritage management plan during construction; recommendations; references; maps, diagrams, and photographs documenting the nature and location of the cultural heritage (Lesotho, 2008; Mitchell, et al., 2008).

The ESIA identified fourteen cultural sites of varying importance and condition in the dam's reservoir area. A plan for excavation and detailed documentation also included provisions for capacity building in the GoL's Department of Culture and a public extension programme financed by US$1.2 million in the IDA credit for a Cultural Resources Management and Development Plan (CRMDP) within the component for Environmental and Social Management. Following consultation with national and international researchers and UNESCO, the number of affected sites was expanded to twenty-six (Arthur & Mitchell, 2010). Two archaeological sites — Ha Makotoko and Ntloana Tsoana — contain long habitation sequences dating back 12,000 to 8500 years and are considered to be of international significance. The CRMDP provides for inventory, assessment, recording and excavation of the archaeological sites, as well as documentation of living cultural heritage, and includes dissemination of the findings through publication and other means.

The plan calls for collaboration between the African Archaeology Department of the University of Oxford, the GoL Department of Culture, the National University of Lesotho, and the Rock Art Institute at the University of the Witswatersrand in

FIGURE 2   Local community participation in archaeological excavation at the Metolong Dam site.

South Africa. There are provisions for display and interpretation of the cultural materials as well as for public education and participation in the excavations. Proximity of the dam to Maseru, and to several cultural and natural sites, presents an opportunity for developing a cultural tourism route. Successful completion of the CRMDP prior to impoundment of the Metolong Dam is required under the covenants of the financing agreement between the World Bank and the GoL. Periodic reporting on the cultural heritage work has included presentations by the contractors to all stakeholders and donors.

East Asia: Hydropower Project and Nam Theun 2 Social and Environmental Project

As the largest and most complex hydropower project in Laos to date, Nam Theun 2 (NT2) included construction of a large dam on the Nam Theun River, a 450 sq. km reservoir, a powerhouse, a 130 km double circuit 500-kV transmission line to the Thai power grid, and a 70 km single-circuit transmission line to Lao's domestic grid. Financial participation by the World Bank was approved in 2005, requiring that the Bank's safeguard policies be applied and that the project involve poverty reduction and appropriate environmental and social management. The World Bank's commitment also included a US$42 million IDA Partial Risk Guarantee and a US $20 million

IDA Grant for the Nam Theun 2 Social and Environmental Project (NTSEP). NT2, implemented by the Nam Theun 2 Power Company (NTPC) and the Government of Lao PDR, became operational in 2010 (World Bank, 2004).

The project's planning phase included extensive study and risk analysis conducted over nearly a decade. As part of this investigation, a multi-volume Physical Cultural Resource Survey, completed in 2004, covered the Nakai Plateau, designated as the reservoir location, the Downstream Channel area, as well as transmission line impact areas, and other construction sites, including roads. Using the draft World Bank OP 4.11 — Physical Cultural Resources as a guide, Earth Systems Lao, an environmental consulting firm engaged by the NTPC, augmented earlier cultural heritage studies by identifying additional cultural sites through several means, including a literature review, community consultation and knowledge surveys, selected transect surveys involving satellite imagery, and walk-over surveys. The study team included cultural heritage specialists and archaeologists from the consulting firm and the Government of Lao PDR, as well as international experts (ESL, 2004a; 2004b).

The pre-project surveys of the Nakai Plateau and the Downstream Channel Area identified spirit sites, historic structures, Buddhist temples, burial sites, and one pale-ontological site but no ancient archaeological remains. However, the survey report recommended that provisions for chance finds be established in the event that archaeological or other cultural material might be discovered during construction and that workers on the project be instructed regarding the nature and importance and care of cultural sites and artefacts. Although previous surveys had identified karst caves in the region as potentially yielding archaeological or paleontological remains, and the project would involve quarrying karst outcroppings, the quarry sites were not included in the pre-project survey. However, a detailed Physical Cultural Resources Plan for the project implementation phase did mention the Pha Phen Quarry in Bolikhamsay Province which contained a rock cave shelter with a stratified sequence of prehistoric living floors, a few stone tools, beads and pottery shards (NTPC, 2005).

Laotian archaeologists were present at Pha Phen during karst limestone quarrying for the NT2 dam construction when one cave yielded a fully intact flexed male skeleton dated to the Neolithic period by advanced AMS radiocarbon analysis. The skeleton was found amidst cord-marked decorative pottery, shell beads and butchered animal bones, artefacts commonly present in Neolithic burials found in Northern Vietnam and Northern Thailand. Additional archaeological surveys in the area identified other potentially significant cave sites for further investigation, three of which were excavated subsequently by Laotian archaeologists yielding corded pottery, quantities of beads, including two 'Indo-Pacific' type glass beads, stone tools, and butchered animal bones. These are important finds for documenting human habitation during the Neolithic era in Laos as well as in the South East Asia region. The archaeological survey, excavation, and research were funded by the NTPC (Sayavongkhamdy & Souksavatdy, 2011).

Opportunities for archaeologists

The four projects described above produced significant benefits for archaeologists and the archaeological record, benefits that were instigated by the policy requirements of the World Bank and IFC. In each case, inclusion of archaeology in pre-project environmental assessment and in environmental management plans was a condition for project approval. Project financing included the costs of assessment as well as continuing support for all phases of archaeological work from identification through documentation, excavation, analysis, and publication for academic and popular audiences. Adherence to the policies of IFC and the World Bank required project proponents to comply with relevant laws and regulations governing archaeology in the host countries, including provisions for chance finds in project management pipent plans. The projects provided technical assistance for archaeologists and in some cases financed, and garnered additional financing, for facilities and institutional capacity enhancement.

These large, high-profile projects illustrate the possibilities created by the policies of two international financial institutions in the development field. However, the maximum benefit from the policies and commitment of these institutions requires that archaeologists throughout the world assume a knowledgeable and active role in the development process. This requires vigilance, including keeping abreast of development projects in their conception, planning, preparation, implementation and operational phases. It entails a detailed understanding of national laws and regulations pertaining to archaeology, as well as of the policies of a project's financing institutions, and awareness of individual development projects, including their characteristics, location, impact area, and schedule. Archaeologists must develop collaborative working relationships with development project proponents, environmental authorities and impact assessment consultants. There are many opportunities for preparing archaeologists to take a proactive role in development, including adding courses to formal archaeological curricula, as well as facilitating training in informal formats at international, regional, and national professional meetings and through electronic media.

The development process offers an invaluable opportunity to identify, document, excavate, analyse and publish information from archaeological sites located in or near project impact areas. The intensive investigation of a development project's impact area may bring to light many sites that would not attract archaeologists as places for excavation and study. In some instances, a project design may be altered to avoid or mitigate damage to particularly valuable sites. Singly and in aggregate, sites encountered in the development process contribute to our understanding and appreciation of human habitation on earth. Hence, participation by archaeologists constitutes not simply an opportunity, but an imperative.

Acknowledgements

The author thanks Christopher Polglase (Senior Consultant — Cultural Resources, ERM) for information on archaeological work relating to the BTC Pipeline and Gregory Lockard (Archaeology Program Manager, HDR, Inc.) for PERU LNG.

Notes

[1] Information about the World Bank Group is available at: <http://go.worldbank.org/D2ALRSK6O0>.

[2] Non-material culture, including cultural practices and a project-affected population's relationship to the natural environment, is covered under the World Bank's Operational Policy 4.10 — Indigenous Peoples and the IFC's Performance Standard 7 — Indigenous Peoples, as well as in paragraph 16 of Performance Standard 8.

[3] In October 2012, the World Bank began a two-year process to review and update its environmental and social safeguard policies with the objectives of improving coverage of environmental and social risks, improving environmental and social outcomes in projects and programmes, and strengthening capacity for sustainable development in its client countries. Operational Policy 4.00 — Use of Country Systems, is an initial effort to assess the ability of selected countries to meet World Bank safeguarding standards through compliance with their own laws, regulations and procedures.

[4] The Physical Cultural Resources Country Profiles are not public documents at this time.

Bibliography

Arthur, C. & Mitchell, P. 2010. The Archaeology of the Metolong Dam, Lesotho: A Preliminary Assessment. *Antiquity*, 84(325) [online] [accessed 5 November 2013]. Available at: <http://www.antiquity.ac.uk/projgall/mitchell325>.

BP Caspian. 2014. Baku-Tbilisi-Ceyhan Pipeline [accessed 14 January 2014]. Available at: <http://www.bp.com/en/global/corporate/search.html?searchTerm=Baku-Tbilisi-Ceyhan+pipeline&_charset_=utf-8>.

Earth Systems Lao (ESL). 2004a. *Nam Theun 2 Physical Cultural Resource Survey: Draft Report Downstream Channel Area*. Vientiane: Earth Systems Lao.

Earth Systems Lao (ESL). 2004b. *Nam Theun 2 Physical Cultural Resource Survey: Draft Nakai Plateau Report*. Vientiane: Earth Systems Lao.

Equator Principles. 2013a. Environment & Social Risk Management for Project Finance [accessed 14 January 2014]. Available at: <http://www.equator-principles.com>.

Equator Principles. 2013b. Equator Principles III [accessed 14 January 2014]. Available at: <http://www.equator-principles.com/index.php/about-ep/about-ep>.

International Association for Impact Assessment (IAIA). 2012. Home [accessed 26 May 2014]. Available at: <http://www.iaia.org>.

International Finance Corporation (IFC). 2012a. Annual Report 2012 [accessed 5 November 2013]. Available at: <http://www1.ifc.org/wps/wcm/connect/CORP_EXT_Content/IFC_External_Corporate_Site/Annual+Report>.

International Finance Corporation (IFC). 2012b. IFC Sustainability Framework: Policy and Performance Standards on Environmental and Social Sustainability; Access to Information Policy, Effective 1 January 2012 [accessed 14 January 2014] Available at: <https://www.scribd.com/fullscreen/84697434?access_key=key-1d08v46kzf4u4h6nu17e>.

International Finance Corporation (IFC). 2012c. IFC Performance Standard 1: Assessment and Management of Environmental and Social Risks and Impacts [accessed 5 November 2013]. Available at: <http://www.ifc.org/wps/wcm/connect/3be1a68049a78dc8b7e4f7a8c6a8312a/PS1_English_2012.pdf?MOD=AJPERES>.

International Finance Corporation (IFC). 2012d. IFC Performance Standard 8 Cultural Heritage [accessed 5 November 2013]. Available at: <http://www.ifc.org/wps/wcm/connect/dd8d3d0049a791a6b855faa8c6a8312a/PS8_English_2012.pdf?MOD=AJPERES>.

Lesotho, Government of. 2008. Metolong Dam Environmental and Social Impact Assessment (ESIA) Final Report. Vol. 5: Cultural Heritage (Archaeology) Impact Assessment [accessed 5 November 2013]. Available at: <http://www.metolong.org.ls/Metolongdocs/Metolong%20Dam%20Environmental%20and%20Social%20Impact%20Assessment%20Feb%202008.pdf>.

Lockard, G. 2010. *Proyecto Arqueologico/Archaeological Project*. Lima: Melchorita. PERU LNG.

Mitchell, P. & Arthur, C. 2012. The Archaeology of the Metolong Dam, Lesotho. *The Digging Stick*, 29(1).

Mitchell, P., Arthur, C., & Hine, P. 2008. *Metolong Cultural Resource Management Inception Report*. Oxford: University of Oxford, School of Archaeology.

Nam Theun 2 Power Company (NTPC). 2005. Environmental Assessment and Management Plan (EAMP): Annex O: Physical Cultural Resources Plan [accessed 5 November 2013]. Available at: <http://www-wds.worldbank.org/external/default/WDSContentServer/WDSP/IB/2005/09/13/000011823_20050913170228/Rendered/PDF/E385v10rev.EAMP.March2005oAnnexes010.pdf>.

Peru, Government of. 2001. Law No. 27580 Stipulating Protection Measures to be Applied by the National Institute of Culture (INC) for the Execution of Works in Immovable Cultural Property [accessed 14 January 2014]. Available at: <http://www.unesco.org/culture/natlaws/media/pdf/peru/pe_ley27580_spaorof.pdf>.

Sayavongkhamdy, T. & Souksavatdy, V. 2011. Excavations of Cave Sites at Pha Phen, Bolikhamsay Province, Lao PDR. Social Sciences Journal, 4(9): 76–83.

Smithsonian Institution. 2011. AGT — Ancient Heritage in the BTC — SCP Pipelines Corridor: Azerbaijan — Georgia — Turkey [accessed 5 November 2013]. Available at: <http://www.agt.si.edu>.

Taylor, P. M., Polglase, C. R., Museyibli, N., Koller, J. M., & Johnson, T. A. 2011. Past and Future Heritage in the Pipelines Corridor: Azerbaijan, Georgia, Turkey. Washington, DC: Smithsonian Institution Asian Cultural History Program.

World Bank. 2004. Project Information Document (PID) Update: Joint PID for Naum Theun 2 Hydropower Project and Nam Theun 2 Social and Environmental Project. Report No.: 30967 [accessed 14 January 2014]. Available at: <http://www-wds.worldbank.org/external/default/WDSContentServer/WDSP/IB/2004/12/15/000160016_20041215170545/Rendered/PDF/30967oLAoPIDoPo492900NTSEP.pdf>.

World Bank. 2009. World Bank Physical Cultural Resources Safeguard Policy Guidebook [accessed 5 November 2013]. Available at: <http://siteresources.worldbank.org/INTSAFEPOL/Resources/PhysicalCulturalGuidebook.pdf>.

World Bank. 2010. Water Sector Improvement Project (Second Phase). Project Information Document (PID) Appraisal Stage [accessed 14 January 2014]. Available at: <http://www-wds.worldbank.org/external/default/WDSContentServer/WDSP/IB/2010/03/09/000334955_20100309043619/Rendered/PDF/AB43140P1081431aisalPIDMarch052010.pdf>.

World Bank. 2012. Annual Report 2012 [accessed 5 November 2013]. Available at: <http://issuu.com/world.bank.publications/docs/annual_report_2012_en?e=1107022/2001324>.

World Bank Operational Manual (WBOM). 2006. Operational Policy 4.11 — Physical Cultural Resources [accessed 5 November]. Available at: <http://web.worldbank.org/WBSITE/EXTERNAL/PROJECTS/EXTPOLICIES/EXTOPMANUAL/0,,contentMDK:20970737~menuPK:64701637~pagePK:64709096~piPK:64709108~theSitePK:502184,00.html>.

Notes on contributor

Arlene K. Fleming has advanced degrees in archaeology and telecommunications. She is engaged in projects that bring new financial resources, technologies, and approaches to cultural heritage protection and management in the event of armed conflict, natural disasters, climate change, and infrastructure development, especially in developing countries. At the World Bank, Ms Fleming advises and participates in cultural heritage projects and policy formulation for safeguarding physical cultural resources in Bank-financed projects. Ms Fleming is co-chair of the Cultural Heritage Section of the International Association for Impact Assessment (IAIA). She has served as advisor to international organizations including UNESCO, the World Monuments Fund and the Getty Conservation Institute, as well as to the US Department of Defense and the National Park Service.

Correspondence to: Arlene K. Fleming, 9122 Maria Avenue, Great Falls, Virginia, 22066, USA. Email: arlenekfleming@gmail.com

PUBLIC ARCHAEOLOGY, Vol. 13 Nos 1–3, 2014, 151–63

Cultural Heritage Management and Economic Development Programmes: Perspectives from Desert Fringes Where IGOs and NGOs Have No Locus

Gerald Wait

Nexus Heritage, UK

Jeffrey H. Altschul

Nexus Heritage, UK and Statistical Research Inc., USA

The range of organizations involved in some way with cultural heritage management stand in proxy for an equally wide range of concerns and viewpoints. While these viewpoints differ considerably in detail, we suggest that a fundamental objective of all these organizations is to ensure that an appropriate kind and degree of cultural heritage work occurs within development contexts. The last twenty years has witnessed such progress in the underlying principles of economic development (in 'developed' or 'developing' world countries) that the notion of heritage and economic development as equally necessary in order for a sustainable future is shared by all the major participants. We explicitly include the 'developers' as a participant in cultural heritage management. Our experience is that private companies sponsoring development are rarely opposed to undertaking heritage work, although they desperately want clear guidance on what this work is supposed to entail. Both heritage and development organizations have a valuable role to play in promoting sustainable economic development, but our experiences in the very differing desert fringes of Senegal and Mongolia suggests that neither alone, nor the two in concert, are truly effective, and that the role of individuals and organizations acting with professional and ethical responsibility is pivotal in this endeavour.

KEYWORDS heritage management, sustainable economic development, professionalism, professional associations, consultants and national heritage agencies

© Taylor & Francis 2014   DOI 10.1179/1465518714Z.00000000062

Introduction

The range of individuals and organizations represented in this publication stand in proxy for an equally wide range of concerns and viewpoints in the heritage and archaeology sectors at large. While these viewpoints often differ considerably in detail, we might — with some risk of oversimplification — suggest that the fundamental concerns of all the authors in this volume are with ensuring that an appropriate kind and degree of cultural heritage work occurs within development contexts. Furthermore, our observation is that over the last twenty years there has been progress in the underlying principles of economic development (in 'developed' or 'developing' world countries), in that all major participants now understand that both heritage and economic development are equally necessary for a sustainable future. We explicitly include the 'developers' whether it be mineral extraction, infrastructure construction, urbanization companies or non-profits, and so on. Our experience is that these entities are rarely opposed to undertaking heritage work, although they desperately want clear guidance on what this work is supposed to entail.

So why the plethora of organizations on the heritage preservation side of the equation? The International Monetary Fund (IMF) and the 'development banks' (see Fleming, this volume) represent the 'carrot' approach — leading development into ethical compliance by offering financial incentives or practical support. Other organizations (including many of the charitable/voluntary sector advocacy organizations that are perhaps unfairly lumped together as part of the 'green' or ecological movement) are effectively 'sticks' trying to beat mining and other major infrastructure developments (which may be either private companies or indeed state parties) into compliance. Both have a valuable role, but our experiences in the very differing desert fringes of Senegal and Mongolia suggest to us that neither alone, nor the two in concert, are truly effective, and that the role of individuals and organizations acting with professional and ethical responsibility have a pivotal role to play in sustainable economic development.

We begin with what we suggest is a basic universal goal of development, which is a search for a better future. Nothing could be simpler in its motivation or more difficult in its application. For the purposes of this paper a 'better future' is taken to mean many things — less poverty, better education and healthcare, a more sustainable approach to the use of physical resources. It explicitly includes the conservation and management of the elements of the past that survive in the present and may be used to provide a sense of identity, character, origins, direction, and progress to people now and by people in the future. We (the authors) know little about the causes of or solutions to poverty, almost nothing about education, and only a little about healthcare, so our contribution is concerned only with sustainable conservation and management of heritage resources.

With differing emphasis we suspect achieving the proper balance between conservation and management of cultural heritage is something widely shared in our profession, and in our experience of twenty years of international heritage consultation it is as near a universal truth as we know. The differing emphases (some heritage professionals limit their work to archaeology, others to historic buildings, some are cultural anthropologists, and some are more holistic in spanning many of these categories of cultural heritage) give rise to very different ways of looking at and working towards these goals, and in turn this has led to very different types of organizations. Our experience has been that no one type of heritage organization will fit all contexts. If we are all, at a basic level, comfortable with a goal of sustainable conservation and management of heritage resources for the benefit of future generations, then we will want to work wisely with all such organizations that have a useful locus in any set of circumstances. In our experience this has rarely been achieved — sometimes through some very basic misunderstandings — and moreover one of the more versatile organizational approaches has been much under-utilized. This is the role that professional associations, underpinned by codes of conduct and professional standards, can play in supporting the activities of both consultants and of national heritage agencies. In particular it is our experiences on two quite different projects that have given rise to our musings. There are some similarities and some differences: both are equally instructive.

Two projects on desert fringes

Sabodala, Senegal

The first project involved our two organizations, Nexus Heritage[1] and Statistical Research, Inc. (SRI),[2] in the Environmental and Social Impact Assessment (ESIA) process for a new gold mine at Sabodala in the south-eastern Sahelian desert-fringe landscape of Senegal, which started in 2009 (see Figure 1). This project involved a detailed pedestrian survey of several thousand hectares comprising over 90 per cent of the zones of potential impacts of the gold mine, and discovered 251 previously unknown archaeological sites. Of these, seventeen were surveyed in detail and sample

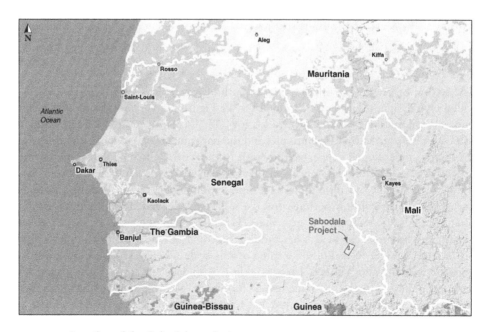

FIGURE 1   Location of the Sabodala project.

excavations were conducted at six sites. The sites were characterized in types including: resource processing sites, fieldhouses, farmsteads, hamlets, villages, polity centres, and sacred sites. In parallel, detailed ethnographic studies and intangible heritage surveys were conducted in the eleven villages within the concession, with especial emphasis upon the roles of blacksmiths, musicians, griots, and of the Kankourang (the music and dance have now been added to the World Heritage List as intangible cultural heritage).

This was something of a landmark project in many ways. It was the first time that a major development in Senegal was expected and required to follow internationally prescribed processes. In addition to our organization, implementation was achieved in partnership with the Institut Fondamental d'Afrique Noire (IFAN)[3] from Senegal. The approach explicitly integrated both tangible archaeological heritage with intangible cultural heritage, involved local expertise from the earliest planning stages, and produced results of such academic importance as to merit a full publication authored by ourselves and our colleague, Dr Ibrahima Thiaw from IFAN (Thiaw, et al., 2014).

One might think that such a project was propelled by strict regulations or that it was a consequence of the mining industry's historical failure to treat cultural heritage in a serious and adequate way. Unfortunately, one would be wrong. Cultural heritage was included in the Terms of Reference of the ESIA because the consultant (representing SRK Consulting UK Ltd) who was commissioned to prepare the ESIA saw a suspicious-looking rock that he thought might have been a prehistoric tool (M. Vendrig, pers. comm., 2009). He did not have to include cultural heritage in his assessment; no one in the government was clamouring for its inclusion, and there were no Non-Governmental Organizations (NGOs) or Inter-Governmental Organizations (IGOs) taking an interest in cultural heritage in the area. That the baseline study of the site was performed to a very high standard was not driven by government or lender oversight. Instead, it was internally driven by SRI corporate standards which require all projects of a certain size to include independent peer review (Altschul, et al., 2010).

Oyu Tolgoi (OT), Mongolia

The second project began in 2011, in the south of Mongolia's Gobi desert at a place called Oyu Tolgoi ('Turquoise Mountain') (see Figure 2). The motivation was again mineral exploitation by Oyu Tolgoi, LLC (or 'OT') (a joint venture between Ivanhoe Mines, later acquired by Rio Tinto plc, and the government of Mongolia), in this case the largest undeveloped copper-gold deposit in the world. The in-country permitting process was completely different from that of Senegal. Yet, even with a specific law, the Mongolian Law of Cultural Heritage, and a rudimentary cultural heritage compliance framework, cultural heritage for the mine still depended on the intervention of individuals. Our champion was the OT/Ivanhoe Mines employee in charge of community relations. He had long-standing personal ties to Mongolian culture and history and wanted to make sure a mine of this scale would have a lasting, positive impact on Mongolian culture. He was able to convince OT to sponsor a cultural heritage plan (CHP — in some cases termed a cultural heritage management programme), not simply for the mine, but for entire South Gobi.

The works were undertaken by a consortium called the Mongolian International Heritage Team which includes SRI and Nexus, partnered with the Mongolian

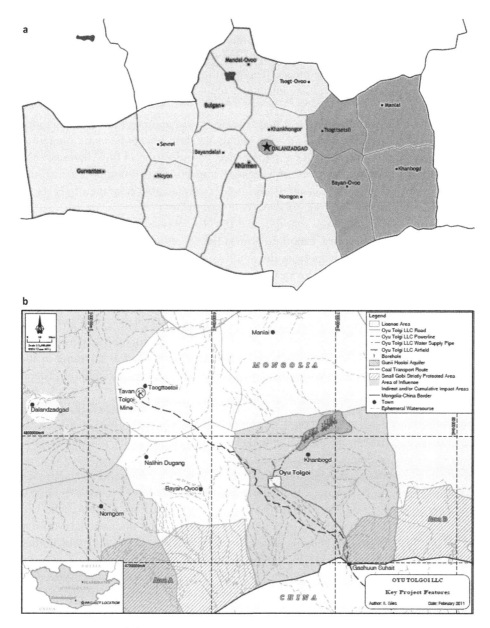

FIGURE 2   Location of the Oyu Tolgoi project.

Academy of Sciences Institute of Archaeology, the University of Arizona, and Sustain-ability East Asia, LLC, along with several other heritage specialists drawn from inside and outside Mongolia — again we emphasize the involvement of a wide range of premier local experts from the outset. These works, as was the case in the Sabodala project, explicitly included and combined archaeology and intangible heritage as well as palaeontology.

The work involved compiling and synthesizing extensive surveys and investigations of hundreds of archaeological sites (spanning the last few millennia), numerous paleontological sites of international importance, consideration of built heritage such as monasteries within the zones of potential impacts of the mining works, and detailed investigations and consultations about the intangible heritage of the Gobi region generally and of the zone of impacts in particular.

NGOs and IGOs have been incorporated into the project as advisors and stake-holders. The CHP Advisory Committee included representatives of NGOs, elders groups, herders, and educators from the South Gobi. ICOMOS Mongolia also has a representative on the CHP Advisory Committee and has been active in the develop-ment of World Heritage nominations for resources of international importance located within a zone of wider impacts.[4] Without exception the cultural heritage NGOs and IGOs supported the CHP. The lone critic of the CHP, OT Watch, is an NGO specifically set up by the IGO Bank Watch, which monitors the activities of the World Bank Group. Their criticism was not specifically directed at anything in the CHP, but more that the development would negatively impact Mongolia in general and the South Gobi in particular (MWM, 2012).

The OT CHP design has been largely successful (Gunchinsuren, et al., 2011) in raising the awareness of, and directing efforts to, the preservation of aspects of cultural heritage adversely affected by the mining proposals. Its implementation, however, is still in doubt. The project champion mentioned above has left OT, and those put in his place have questioned the need for such a comprehensive approach to cultural heritage. Fortunately, the mining giant Rio Tinto has assumed administra-tive control of OT and ownership of the mining concession from Ivanhoe, who had previously been dealing with the local *soum* governments and the national Ministry of Mines. Rio Tinto has been a strong supporter of the OT CHP, which they highlighted in their recent guidelines for integrating the management of cultural heritage issues in mineral exploration, mine development and mine operation (Rio Tinto, 2011). While nothing is assured, we remain hopeful that the CHP plan will be implemented.

Strengths and weaknesses

Some of the strengths and weaknesses of the structures in place in the projects in Mongolia and Senegal are already visible in these thumbnail sketches. Perhaps the most fundamental weakness is the absence of an effective regulatory authority within developing nations' governmental departments. In such contexts, economic development originates from outside, either from institutions such as the Interna-tional Finance Corporation (IFC)/World Bank, the European Bank for Reconstruc-tion and Development (EBRD), the African Development Bank (ADB) — or from non-governmental commercial entities such as mineral exploitation/mining companies. In our opinion, the IFC's Performance Standards are more policy statements than standards *sensu strictu*, and it would impossible for anyone other than a professional specialist to understand whether a recipient of IFC/EBRD monies has actually complied with an IFC Performance Standard in any meaningful, measurable way (cf. Fleming, this volume). What independent audits can do, however, is determine whether milestones have been reached. For example, in the case of OT, the lender compliance audit did not evaluate the quality of the CHP, at least in part because they lacked the expertise. They could, however, determine that the CHP had not been implemented and cite OT for this failure.

We are not suggesting that performance standards — the IFC's in particular — are not valuable — just the opposite, they are immensely valuable as statements of intent, but standing alone they are insufficient. They need supporting practice guidance. Most important of all there need to be people in place in relevant government departments who understand both the spirit of the standards and also have knowledge of the actual works that would be necessary to satisfy a practice guide. Moreover, as the OT case underscores, the IFC/World Bank/EBRD must clarify not only what is expected of a recipient country to meet the standards, but also undertake due diligence reviews to ensure that this in fact has been done.

Ironically, on the other side of the development dialogue are the mineral exploiters, the infrastructure builders, the house-builders — and almost all will have dealt with archaeology and heritage preservation issues before and we believe they will (either happily or with resignation) integrate heritage into their programmes (by working to protect and respect heritage assets whilst still exploiting the mineral resources they are there for) if only they are given clear guidance on what this should include. The problem is that without clear guidance, the developer has to decide how much heritage work (how many investigations, excavations, social programmes, or promoting of intangible heritage practices) is enough to satisfy those organizations who are helping to finance the project. In our experience, not surprisingly, developers tend to sponsor too little heritage work as opposed to too much. So the good news is that, at the end of the first decade of the twenty-first century, we find that we have achieved the position where the 'developer' is no longer trying to ignore heritage (see, for example, Rio Tinto, 2011; also ICCM, 2003: Principle 3). Twenty years ago this statement could simply not have been made, so this is a measure of very important progress and success. But there is still some way to go.

A two-pronged strategy

It seems to us that the problems surrounding issues of archaeology, heritage, and economic development — which we think apply widely in developing countries — are twofold:

- lack of in-country capability in the form of appropriately skilled and trained heritage officers and professional infrastructures.
- lack of adequate professionalism among heritage practitioners — in-country and among international practitioners.

This is unpalatable, certainly. Let us examine each in more detail.

First, the need for far greater capability at national and local levels in developing countries is not a proposition we would expect heritage specialists to disagree with very much. By making the point, we do not mean to be overly critical. The reasons for this situation are well known and probably inevitable. They are closely tied to past poverty, present economic limitations, and fear of the either/or decision and the resulting political unwillingness to prioritize heritage, leading to lack of investment in appropriate training for officials. In effect, developing countries fail to recognize the benefits that heritage can provide by means of tourism for example, and fearing that asking mining or infrastructure developers to undertake heritage work will halt development proposals, those governments in developing countries de-prioritize their own heritage, and may even prevent their own heritage officials and NGOs from being heard. Escaping the conundrum is not straightforward. We propose a two-pronged strategy, one working to build or enhance cultural heritage infrastructure and the other to build expertise and capacity in its performance.

Many heritage IGOs and NGOs are either by definition or by custom focused upon working with 'world class' heritage sites and assets (for example, the World Monuments Fund: see Ackerman, this volume). This is sensible as the heritage assets that are judged most culturally significant by a global audience are also the assets most likely to attract financial support, enabling the organization to act and make a difference 'on the ground'. However, this focus is poor preparation for working with the remaining heritage, which may be valued locally or nationally in different ways. In the UK where the heritage inventory is probably as well developed, and the landscape as intensively surveyed, as anywhere, heritage assets that are either of international importance (i.e. World Heritage Sites) or national importance constitute less than 21 per cent of the known assets. The remaining 79 per cent of known heritage assets are by and large the ones we are concerned with in projects such as ours.

It is worth presenting the basis for this claim, as this illustrates the complexity of the position. These figures are an order-of-magnitude estimate, based on the best figures available for the United Kingdom where historic environment professionals have long engaged in a practice of counting things. In 2003 it was estimated that there are around one and a half million sites listed on Sites and Monuments Records (SMRs) around the country (English Heritage, 2003). This was regarded as a reliable estimate at the time based on 40 per cent sample of the many SMRs.

The management of such heritage assets is — even in the UK — not achieved so much by legislation as through planning and development control, or spatial planning processes. These processes can be labyrinthine in their complexity and are qualitatively very different from such instruments as the World Heritage Convention. IGOs or NGOs are less likely to be routinely involved in management decisions in this context, and if and when they are engaged they come with the baggage of being viewed by parties either favouring or opposing changes in management on the basis of their more common involvement with the world heritage. Thus, in the UK, IGOs and NGOs are viewed as inherently opposed to development by the commercial development side (as, in our experience, this is their usual position vis-à-vis conservation or development at World Heritage Sites). Therefore, IGOs or NGOs are seen as inherent allies of the supporters of heritage, who hope that the presence of an IGO in debates about development will give enhanced importance to any assets affected. This is not necessarily true (and not fair) but, like all such perceptions with a sufficient truthful element, it appears to be widely held.

In response to the need for up-skilling of governmental officers, a group of heritage professionals (including consultants, World Bank officers, academics, and officers in the departments of culture) from some developing countries met in Oxford, England in 2011, and created the International Heritage Group. This group is a global action network that balances 'top-down' global expectations with 'bottom-up' local needs. Regional, national, and sub-national professional bodies will be engaged as pivot points between global and local interests. Transformation will be driven by three core activities — Analysis, Advocacy, and Advice:

> **Analysis** comprises published scholarly research, conferences and conference contributions, and reports and position papers on global trends and questions as well as specific issues in Archaeological Heritage Management (AHM) theory, policy, and practice. IHG will produce an annual Global Situation Analysis of Capacity Building in AHM.

> **Advocacy** entails pro bono interventions concerning general questions as well as specific issues in AHM theory, policy, and practice on behalf of individual professional colleagues, professional bodies, or the field of AHM more broadly.

> **Advice** includes pro bono and paid professional opinion concerning general questions as well as specific issues of AHM theory, policy, and practice. (see IHG, n.d.)

Certainly other organizations are working on the issue: the World Archaeological Congress, Society for American Archaeology, European Archaeology Association, the International Committee on Archaeological Heritage Management (see Comer, this volume), and others. Rather than presuming that any one group will have 'all the answers', it might be more productive to propose that these groups work in a more coordinated fashion. This is a very busy sector and progress will be made by several groups.

Our second prong is case specific, but is illustrated in each of our case studies. Without being too simplistic, nothing is likely to point to a better way forward than small successes, such as the OT CHP and the Sabodala Cultural Heritage Project. Projects such as these give courage to take bigger risks to achieve bigger successes. Here we coupled experts from developed countries with decades of experience in the fields of cultural heritage management — archaeology, palaeontology, anthropology, history, education, heritage tourism, museum studies, and public outreach — with in-country experts in regional and local culture, history, and archaeology. Our goal was to coach our in-country colleagues in the techniques and objectives of Cultural Heritage Management, changing their perspective of heritage from one of academic research to public benefit. Success is not simply measured by a comprehensive and thoughtful study, but by our country hosts taking ownership and control of their country's heritage. Success is less about completing the compliance process, and everything about ensuring the best heritage outcome. The mine will go in, and the culture will survive; our job is to help others make these results improve society more than each left alone.

Internationalizing the profession

There may be a means of generalizing from the specific to the general. The absence of a professional voice representing local, regional, and national publics in terms of heritage matters is felt keenly. Even where professional cultural heritage advisors to development agencies are present (by no means a universal occurrence) and behave in accordance with professional codes of conduct, there can be perceptions of bias. Far more important is the simple fact that a design team for any sort of development, no matter how professional their work, cannot be expected to see all the opportunities or all the advantages or disadvantages to the options.

We have been using words like 'professional' quite freely — but what do we mean by this? Briefly, a profession is an occupation in which 'skilled' practitioners undertake their duties 'impartially', according to a 'code of ethics', and are subject to the 'oversight' of their fellow practitioners by being members of an organization. Characteristics of professional organizations include a code of professional conduct, entry conditions for membership, including subscription to the code and a requirement to demonstrate competence, requiring continuing education to qualified members (publications, conferences, courses, etc.), promoting development of the discipline and representing the profession, and equal concern for practitioners, practice, and clients. Individuals may act professionally, but they may not really be described as professionals unless there exists, and they belong to, a professional organization. These definitions with minor variations are recognized by most governments, including the USA, the UK, and the EU.

It is worthwhile to divert momentarily to elaborate upon professional associations, as we contend that these have an important role to play. Lord Benson's definition (Benson, 1992), which is perhaps the most robust definition, includes:

1. The profession must be controlled by a governing body, which in professional matters directs the behaviour of its members. For their part the members have a responsibility to subordinate their selfish private interests in favour of support for the governing body.
2. The governing body must set adequate standards of education as a condition of entry and thereafter ensure that students obtain an acceptable standard of professional competence. Training and education do not stop at qualification. They must continue throughout the member's professional life.
3. The governing body must set the ethical rules and professional standards that are to be observed by the members. They should be higher than those established by the general law.
4. The rules and standards enforced by the governing body should be designed for the benefit of the public and not for the private advantage of the members.
5. The governing body must take disciplinary action, if necessary expulsion from membership, should the rules and standards it lays down not be observed, or should a member be guilty of bad professional work.
6. Work is often reserved to a profession by statute — not because it was for the advantage of the member, but because of the protection of the public, it should be carried out only by persons with the requisite training, standards, and disciplines.

7. The governing body must satisfy itself that there is fair and open competition in the practice of the profession so that the public are not at risk of being exploited. It follows that members in practice must give information to the public about their experience, competence, capacity to do the work, and the fees payable.

8. The members of the profession, whether in practice or in employment, must be independent in thought and outlook. They must not allow themselves to be put under the control or dominance of any persons or organization that could impair that independence.

9. In its specific field of learning, a profession must give leadership to the public it serves.

Heritage is not trivial and the need for professionals, professional organizations, and for transparently professional action underlies much that we debate in the heritage disciplines. Because authoritative professional voices do not exist within local, regional, and national governments in most developing countries that are able to create effective dialogue, review mechanisms must be shifted outside of government to find a second-best solution. To return to our desert-fringes projects in Senegal and Mongolia, we had to enlist independent experts to serve as reviewers of our work. This eases concerns that might be expressed about the technical quality of our work, and to some extent answers questions that might be asked about the impartiality of our ethical approach to the work by providing the needed peer review of both technical competence and ethical performance.

At present, few of the criteria defining professional associations are present in the international heritage arena. What is missing includes a more transparent extension of existing organizations into international applicability. Codes of ethics are by definition universal, governing a professional's work wherever that work takes place. Standards that elaborate on how codes may be best put into action are nearly as universal but guidance about the detailed implementation of standards are likely to be country-specific as they must be more closely tied to legal structures, planning and control systems and social custom. Thus, the ethical conduct and technical work of a professional as a member of a professional association should be relied upon, or quasi-legal redress sought, no matter where their work was undertaken.

To help to illustrate this we can point out that the Institute for Archaeologists (IfA), based in the UK, explicitly states that it is not a UK institute and tells its members that they must comply with its code of ethics and professional standards wherever they practice. To support this the IfA is proposing and has adopted changes to its Code of Conduct, has prepared a clause to cover this consideration in its draft Standards and Guidance for archaeological consultants, has run a session to guide members working in 'developing' countries at its annual conference as a training event, has created a group to support and help develop the skills of its international consultant members, and is in discussion with other institutes about cooperation (see IfA, 2009).

Conclusion

Our interests in making these points are more than simple altruism. Heritage specialists remain vulnerable to accusations of bias unless their actions are open and transparent to external scrutiny. This represents a risk to the specialist personally, as well as to his/her organization, and to the specialist's client. These risks — even of an unsubstantiated accusation — are simply too serious to be easily accepted. In purely business terms of risk management, the case is equally clear: it simply makes good business sense. The benefits of internationally accepted professional codes and standards, and hence of an international professional association, are thus applicable to the individuals and organizations involved and to the processes of impact assessment and conservation management. Professionalism becomes a means of ensuring an ethical approach to technically competent cultural heritage management work — anywhere. We, our mining clients, and our in-country host colleagues, may all reasonably expect mining and infrastructure development projects to bring not only sustainable economic development but greater knowledge, understanding and appreciation of a host-country's cultural heritage.

Notes

[1] Nexus Heritage is a private limited company offering an integrated range of cultural heritage consultancy services (including archaeology, historic building conservation, and cultural/intangible heritage anthropology) worldwide.

[2] Statistical Research Inc. (SRI) is a private consultancy based in the United States that provides comprehensive cultural resource management services worldwide.

[3] IFAN (the Institut Fondamental d'Afrique Noire) is the archaeological research institute at the University Cheik Anta Diop Dakar, and also serves as advisor to the Department of Culture. IFAN also includes sections of anthropology, botany, and other disciplines.

[4] Such resources included the dinosaur fossil beds of the 'Flaming Cliffs' at Bayan Ovoo and the Mongolian *Urtyn Duu* or 'long song' (the mythological stories of the origins of Mongolia, set to music and sometimes to dance) which is much practised in the Gobi, and was already then being mooted for nomination as world intangible heritage. However, these resources were not considered as part of the South Gobi CHP.

Bibliography

Altschul, J. H., Thiaw, I., & Wait, G. 2010. *Baseline Report on Heritage and Archaeological Studies for the Proposed Oromin Mine, Sabodala, Senegal. Sabadola Cultural Heritage Program.* Technical Report 6. Sabodala Cultural Heritage Program. Tucson: Statistical Research.

Benson, Lord. 1992. Criteria for a group to be considered a profession, as recorded in Hansard (Lords), 8 July, 1206–07.

English Heritage. 2003. *Heritage Counts.* London: English Heritage.

Gunchinsuren, B., Altschul, J. H., & Olsen, J. W. eds. 2011. The Oyu Tolgoi Cultural Heritage Program [accessed 3 April 2014]. Available at: <https://openaccess.leidenuniv.nl/bitstream/handle/1887/19517/Willems2011b.pdf?sequence=2>.

International Council on Mining and Metals (ICCM). Sustainable Development Framework [accessed 9 December 2013]. Available at: <http://www.icmm.com/our-work/sustainable-development-framework>.

International Heritage Group (IHG). (n.d.). Homepage [accessed 18 January 2013]. Available at: <http://www.internationalheritagegroup.net>.

Institute for Archaeologists (IfA). 2009. IfA Codes, Standards and Guidelines [accessed 3 April 2014]. Available at: <http://www.archaeologists.net/codes/ifa>.

Mine Watch Mongolia (MWM). 2012. A Useless Sham — OT ESIA Review [accessed 18 November 2013]. Available at: <http://en.minewatch.mn/wp-content/uploads/2012/12/A-Useless-Sham-OT-ESIA-Review.pdf>.

Rio Tinto. 2011. Why Cultural Heritage Matters: A Resource Guide for Integrating Cultural Heritage Management into Communities Work at Rio Tinto [accessed 3 April 2014]. Available at: <http://www.riotinto.com/documents/reportspublications/rio_tinto_cultural_heritage_guide.pdf>.

Thiaw, I., Wait, G., & Altschul, J. H. 2014. *Sabodala Cultural Heritage Studies.* Walnut Creek, CA: SRI Press and LeftCoast Press.

Notes on contributors

Gerald Wait has thirty years of experience as an archaeologist and heritage resource preservation specialist. He is a director of Nexus Heritage — an organization providing heritage resources management services worldwide. Dr Wait is an expert in conservation and management planning, heritage site management, and interpretation for the general public. He has prepared conservation and/or management plans for over fifty historical period and heritage sites in North America, the UK, Romania, Ireland, Egypt, Lebanon, and China. He is was principal investigator for the intangible cultural heritage component of the Environmental Social Impact Assessment (ESIA) for the proposed Sabodala gold mine in Senegal, and was principal heritage advisor for proposed iron mines in Sierra Leone, a gold mine in Burkino Faso, and on a copper-gold project in Mongolia at Oyu Tolgoi. He is currently on secondment as Cultural Heritage Advisor for SouthStream Transport bv based in the Netherlands.

Correspondence to: Gerry Wait, Nexus Heritage, Hexagon House, Avenue 4 Station Lane, Witney OX28 4BN, UK. Email: Gerry.wait@nexus-heritage.com

Jeffrey H. Altschul has been involved in cultural resource management for thirty-five years. He has served as chairman and founder of Statistical Research, Inc. (SRI) and chairman and co-founder of Nexus Heritage in 1983; consultancies based in the USA and UK, respectively, which together provide cultural heritage services worldwide. He also is president and founder of the SRI Foundation, a not-for-profit organization in the USA that advances historic preservation through research, education, and training. Altschul holds a PhD in anthropology from Brandeis University. He is currently president of the Society for American Archaeology. He is a Principal in SRI and a Principal and Director of Nexus, in which capacities he led the International Mongolian Heritage Team which undertook the innovative and far-reaching work at Oyu Tolgoi.

Correspondence to: Jeffrey Altschul, SRI, 6099 E. Speedway Blvd, PO Box 31865, Tucson, AZ, 85751-1865, USA. Email: jaltschul@sricrm.com

PUBLIC ARCHAEOLOGY, Vol. 13 Nos 1–3, 2014, 164–77

A Tale of Two Villages: Institutional Structure and Sustainable Community Organizations

PETER G. GOULD

University of Pennsylvania Museum of Archaeology and Anthropology, USA

This paper describes the organizational features of community-controlled economic development ventures associated with heritage sites located in two contrasting rural communities, one in Ireland and the other in Belize. The paper demonstrates that sustainable community organizations share institutional governance features that reflect general principles previously identified by scholars of common pool resources and community heritage tourism projects. The paper argues that archaeologists or heritage specialists working with local communities to develop sustainable economic development projects are more likely to succeed if attention is paid to the establishment of appropriate governance institutions for the project that are rooted in local conditions but follow proven governance principles.

KEYWORDS community archaeology, governance institutions, common pool resources, economic development, sustainability

Introduction

As numerous papers in this volume demonstrate, many archaeologists are initiating projects to assist communities to realize economic benefits from nearby archaeological and heritage resources. A search of the literature reveals some examples of development projects relating to archaeology that have survived for many years (Davis, 2011; de Merode, et al., 2003; Gamarra, 2010; Silverman, 2006). However, Díaz-Andreu's (2013: 232–34) recitation of failed projects in Latin America illustrates the conventional wisdom in the field that the globe is littered with failed field museums and community projects that have gone undocumented. The pressing question for archaeologists is: do insights exist into how better to do this work in a manner that can make archaeologists' efforts more successful?

This paper will address one potential response to that question, an answer inspired by literatures in economics, political science, and project evaluation. That literature suggests that archaeologists need to pay closer attention to the nature of the

    DOI 10.1179/1465518714Z.00000000066

community institutions they create as they try to advance economic development. For the purpose of illustrating this issue, this paper will present data derived from my PhD research (Gould, 2014), examining the governance institutions of community-based economic development projects in communities adjacent to archaeological sites. The data presented here are drawn from extensive qualitative and quantitative interviews with community leaders and project members and reviews of internal documents conducted in two such locations between 2010 and 2013.

The two communities described here, one in a small Irish village in County Clare and one in a small Maya village in central Belize, have little in common from the standpoint of history, culture, or community politics. Yet both are home to decades-old community projects rooted in environmental and archaeological heritage. These two village projects exhibit common characteristics that may inform the way archaeologists think about establishing and sustaining community-level development activities. The argument presented here is that commonalities in the nature of the governance institutions in these two community organizations, and the manner in which those institutions relate to local conditions, are important contributors to the sustainability of these organizations across several decades.

One project, the Burren Centre, is located in Kilfenora, a small village midway between Galway and Limerick on Ireland's western coast. Kilfenora is situated in a region known as 'The Burren', a limestone karst landscape that has been home to humans for more than 6000 years (Carthy, 2011). In 1972, a plan was launched in Kilfenora by local leaders and an outside adviser to establish a centre to interpret the unique environmental and archaeological heritage of the Burren for tourists. Today, the Burren Centre is the largest employer in the village and the reason that 25,000 to 30,000 tourists visit each year, helping to sustain the village's unusually collabora-tive culture even in the face of the recent Irish economic crisis (interviews with F. Connole, 8 March 2012; J. Keane, 9 October 2011).

The village of Maya Centre, Belize presents a strong contrast. Situated on the entrance road to the Coxcomb Basin Wildlife Sanctuary, the approximately fifty households in Maya Centre are Mopan Maya families who moved to the area in the 1970s after a dispute in a neighbouring village. Men in the community tend to leave the village during the day for work, generally in agriculture. Family disputes, religious differences, and political divides all contribute to a far less harmonious community than Kilfenora. Nonetheless, since 1987, a cross-section of the women in the community has coalesced around the Maya Centre Women's Group (MCWG), which sells traditional crafts produced by local families. It is a primary source of cash income to this community.

This paper tells the tale of the heritage-related projects in these two villages and the lessons to be gleaned from their success.

Governance institutions, communities, and sustainability

What is a governance institution? By 'institution', scholars of institutional economics mean what Douglass North has called 'the rules of the game' (1990: 4). These may be formal rules, laws, regulations, contracts, patents, or procedures enforced by entities such as the officers of organizations, bureaucracies, or even the courts. Alternatively, they may be informal rules such as traditions, taboos, and community compacts that are enforced through informal social structures such as ostracism, public shame, or other penalties. Institutional economists argue that institutions serve distinct purposes by reducing the 'transaction costs' (such as those to obtain information or to enforce agreements) and the risks of commercial relationships (Acheson, 1994; Williamson, 1998).

The ideas of institutional economists have been extended by scholars studying common pool resources, which are resources owned or controlled in common by a defined group. Examples are grazing lands, forests, fisheries, or irrigation systems managed on a community-wide basis. These scholars have examined the many examples of collaborative ventures that refute what Hardin (1968) famously termed the 'tragedy of the commons' and demonstrated that there are institutional commonalities in the way communities have self-organized to manage common pools (Ostrom, 1990; Poteete, et al., 2010). Thus, governance institutions may be seen as the rules, traditions, and practices created to manage the affairs of a community project. Viewed in this light, community-based governance institutions must promote assurances of good faith, redress grievances, or otherwise enable individuals to engage in relationships requiring some degree of trust. Rules and regulations of community organizations, particularly those that engage in commercial transactions, serve an identical purpose.

'Community' is a critical notion in this conversation. Anderson (2006) has popularized the notion of 'imagined communities' that may be comprised of geographically dispersed groups sharing a common interest or groups coalescing around a notional commonality such as family, nationality, or a community of expertise such as 'heritage professionals' (Smith & Waterton, 2009: 11). From this perspective, every heritage site is inevitably a potential collision-ground for competing 'communities' and every community-based project engages a network of 'communities' with overlapping membership (Haggstrom, 1983; Richards & Hall, 2000; Shackel & Chambers, 2004; Stonich, 2005; Sutton Jr, 1983; see also Leventhal; Morris; Pyburn, this volume). Thus, from the standpoint of practical institution making, the community that matters is the complex and conflicted one that archaeologists find on the ground. Therefore, the word 'community', as used in this paper, simply means all of the residents who live in the vicinity of an archaeologist's project, whether or not they are a culturally homogenous group and whether or not individuals have competing traditional, religious, economic, or political claims on the heritage resources. Indeed, it is precisely the fact of those competing interests that compels a focus on the governance mechanisms through which the intra-community politics in economic development projects are played out at the local level.

Finally, what are 'sustainable' projects and institutions? In an environmental context, sustainability seeks to balance the demand for development from corporate and individual interests with the 'carrying capacity' of a resource. Carrying capacity, a biological concept, may be seen as 'the maximum number of a species that can be supported indefinitely by a particular habitat [...] without degradation of the environment and without diminishing the carrying capacity into the future' (Hardin, 1977: 113). Carrying capacity has been extended to historical and cultural assets by scholars of the tourism industry, who use the concept to describe the conditions necessary to the preservation of the natural environment and the physical features of historic sites such as archaeological ruins (Murphy, 1985). Numerous comprehensive definitions of sustainable development have been offered and even more indicators of sustainability proposed (see Kates, et al., 2005; Marshall & Toffel, 2005). In this paper, however, following Ostrom (1990), the notion of 'sustainability' applied to these projects is simply their institutional survival across long stretches of time.

The Burren Centre

Running from Galway Bay nearly to the County Clare seat of Ennis, the Burren is a unique limestone karst environment where glacial activity millennia ago created an ecosystem in which alpine and Mediterranean plants grow side by side. Tillable soil is scarce but there is plenty of surface fodder for the beef and dairy cattle, sheep, and goats that give life to its economy. While the first clearly attributable archaeological remains in the Burren date from the Mesolithic, herders and farmers asserted a settled presence in this part of western Ireland in the warmer Neolithic period (Carthy, 2011). Within a short span, they began to domesticate the rugged landscape and to construct the oldest artefacts remaining in the Burren, a collection of megalithic dolmen and tombs epitomized by the iconic portal tomb at Poulnabrone (*c.* 3200 BCE). By the sixth century CE, Christian churches appeared in the landscape; cathedrals, such as the one now ruined in Kilfenora, had their founding late in the first millennium, when local clans built stone ring forts and field walls to protect family and livestock (Carthy, 2011). One systematically examined ring fort, Caherconnell, has C-14 dated artefacts to the seventh century CE and assigned structural remains to the late Neolithic or early Bronze Ages (Comber, 2012). As one essayist of the region has noted, 'the Burren is more than just an open-air museum, it is an archaeologically saturated landscape' (Clements, 2011: 25).

Kilfenora is a former market town on the southern edge of the Burren. Residents frequently describe Kilfenora in the late 1960s as 'derelict', citing seventeen or so abandoned houses in a village centre that even today numbers no more than about fifty structures, many newly built. This was also the time when the west of Ireland was at the early stages of an economic revival led by the growing importance to international air travel of nearby Shannon Airport. The Chairman of the Shannon Development Corporation, Brendan O'Reagan, saw development around the airport's free trade zone and tourism in Limerick's hinterland as potential offsets to the decline of rural communities in the region. In 1969, village leaders asked O'Reagan for help and he dispatched a young associate, Brian Mooney, to Kilfenora.

There was a long tradition of community-funded, committee-led efforts to improve Kilfenora when Mooney arrived. When asked today, residents can name more than twenty voluntary organizations in this village of 463 people, each led by a volunteer committee. Mooney began in 1969 by organizing a series of educational lectures in Kilfenora while he met with local figures and slowly assembled a committee to manage a tourism project. Mooney encouraged the creation of an 'interpretive centre' for tourists to learn about the ecology and heritage of the Burren before setting off to discover it for themselves. His process was to engage community leaders, primarily from Kilfenora and pivotally including Kilfenora's parish priest and a 'village elder' (a local farmer), in an extended dialogue that culminated in the establishment of the Burren Centre (interview with B. Mooney, 7 March 2012).

The project was incorporated in 1975 as a for-profit cooperative of residents in three villages in County Clare (Connole, 2006). The idea was to construct the Centre on an abandoned site in the main square in Kilfenora and from there promote tourism throughout the Burren area. The Centre was financed by a grant from Bord Failte, an Irish tourism development authority, and from the proceeds of an offering of shares in the Burren Centre's parent organization to local residents. About 300 individuals, from the vast majority of households in Kilfenora, subscribed at least IR£5 per share (some residents contributed much more, although each shareholder receives only one vote at business meetings). About 80 per cent of the shareholders lived in Kilfenora, while 10 per cent were from each of two neighbouring villages.

The Centre, which opened in 1975, housed a model of the Burren and other exhibits through which visitors were guided by local students. In 1981, two adjacent buildings were acquired and converted into tea-rooms to serve visitors and house a crafts shop. In its first decade, the cooperative launched a number of other projects, seeking to expand its economic development impact. These included ventures to produce fruit jams, peat firebricks, and wooden toys. By the early 1980s all had failed due to poor planning and marketing or inattention to costs, with only the interpretive centre, tea shop, and craft sales businesses enduring commercially (IPC, 1983).

From the early 1990s until 2000, the Centre faced two related crises. First, in 1991, national government officials sought to situate a new interpretive centre adjacent to Mullaghmore Mountain in the heart of undeveloped Burren land, a location less than 15 km from Kilfenora. Burren Centre officials saw this proposal as potentially fatal to the Burren Centre. Fearful of alienating powerful government funders but in an uncertain economic situation itself, the Burren Centre's governing Committee opposed the Mullaghmore project but also sought a contingency funding arrangement. Other shareholders believed more aggressive and public opposition was essential. Ultimately, nearly 50 per cent of the shareholders turned out for a 1991 Extraordinary General Meeting (EGM) to debate the strategy. After robust debate, the Committee's position prevailed by majority vote.

Subsequently, in 1993, local business owners who were fearful that the Centre might founder in the wake of the Mullaghmore controversy sought to eliminate Article 5 of the centre's governing 'constitution', which precludes shareholders who are owners of competing local businesses (such as pubs or retail shops) from sitting on the Centre's governing Committee. Protagonists on each side differ regarding the others' motivations, but in interviews they are unanimous that their mutual concern was to ensure continued life for the Burren Centre itself. At a second EGM, in 1993, Article 5 was retained by majority vote and competitors remain barred to this day from the Committee. The ten-year legal fight over the Mullaghmore centre, which was waged primarily by a group located in the nearby village of Kilnaboy on the road to Mullaghmore, finally ended in 2000 when the Irish Supreme Court quashed the Mullaghmore project. Shortly after, a new Irish government provided almost IR£1 million in funding to the Kilfenora centre to acquire additional land and construct an expanded interpretive centre, which opened in 2001.

Formally, the Burren Centre is the primary activity of the Comhar Conradh na Boirne Teoranta (the 'Comhar'), an enterprise organized under Irish cooperative laws. Technically, the Comhar is a for-profit entity, though it has never declared a dividend. Co-ops are a traditional rural collective structure in Ireland, where a government entity, the Irish Cooperative Organisation Society, Ltd (ICOS), provides governance principles in the form of a model 'constitution'. The Burren Centre adopted the standard form ICOS constitution in 1975, updated it in the 1980s, and follows it to the letter.

Day-to-day operations of the Comhar are delegated to paid professional management under the supervision of a volunteer governing Committee whose members are nominated by other shareholders prior to the Annual General Meeting each year. The Committee, which has the authority to undertake most actions, is headed by a Chairman and includes a Vice Chair, Secretary, Treasurer, and occasional assistant officers, all chosen by the Committee itself. Quorums, voting procedures, eligibility to serve and the mechanisms for removing shareholders or Committee members are all stipulated in the constitution, as are requirements for an annual audit and the frequency of meetings. Additional policies are approved by the Committee. For example, in July 1983 the Committee adopted a cycle for rotating its own membership and established limits for members to two consecutive three-year terms. Questions of interpretation of the constitution are resolved by the Committee or, in a dispute, may be arbitrated by ICOS. Decision-making at the centre is quite formal at Committee and shareholder meetings, with raised-hand voting reportedly common and, in at least one EGM, a secret ballot. The Committee of the Burren Centre has resisted changes to the constitution. Indeed, in the midst of the 2001 construction project, the chairman at the time reached his six-year term limit. Committee members debated altering the rules to enable him to stay, but ultimately chose to abide by the constitution.

Albeit with some government assistance, the Burren Centre has been financially successful. The original display centre was built for IR£26,000 in 1975 with shareholder and government funding and volunteer labour from the village. In 2010, the Comhar reported gross revenue of €287,545 virtually identical to the prior year, of which €87,791 represented a grant from the national government to employ the disadvantaged (interview with F. Connole, 8 March 2012). Most of the centre's income comes from admission fees to the exhibit and from sales in the retail shop and tearooms. On a cash basis (pre-depreciation), the Comhar recorded a small profit in each of the five years ending in 2011. All cash and banking matters are managed by the Comhar's paid manager, although cheques must be signed by two Committee members.

This income supports a permanent staff of five and about thirteen seasonal workers, typically students from Kilfenora and neighbouring villages, making the Centre the village's largest employer. Financially, the Burren Centre is self-sufficient on an operating basis, but reliant on external support for major capital improvements and for some portion of the employment opportunities it offers. The village today has three pubs, two grocers, a youth hostel, a clothing store, and a crafts shop. In 2012, nearly all residential and commercial structures in Kilfenora were occupied. Over the decades, the Burren Centre has directly spawned three other privately run tourist businesses in the region. In interviews, business owners unanimously confirm the importance of the Burren Centre to their businesses, 73.3 per cent of all community members interviewed said they or their family had benefited directly from the Centre, and all respondents agreed that Kilfenora would be 'worse off' were the Burren Centre to close.

The Maya Centre Women's Group

A small section of the region known as the Cockscomb Basin in Belize was declared a National Forest Reserve/Jaguar Preserve on 2 December 1984 — the first protected area devoted to the largest feline species in North America. The reserve was gradually extended until, in 1995, the area — now known as the Cockscomb Basin Wildlife Sanctuary (CBWS) — encompassed 122,000 acres, incorporating a vast range of rivers and valleys bounded by the Maya Mountains (BAS, 2008). Well inside the park lands, inaccessible to most visitors, are the ruins of a three small Maya archaeological sites.

In a pattern characteristic of archaeological and environmental reserves in Belize and elsewhere, the park was created as an exclusionary zone. Eleven Maya families living in a small village called Quam Bank on the CBWS lands were ordered to relocate immediately after 2 December 1984, with several moving to the village of Maya Centre. Furthermore, existing residents of Maya Centre were ordered to abandon slash and burn farms on the park's perimeter and residents were banned from hunting on park grounds. Given those impacts, unless the local community could be motivated to restrain their incursions into the park and support conservation, the fledgling park was threatened by local resistance. This set the stage for the community-based preservation experiment to provide an alternative income source to the residents of Maya Centre, today a village of 400 persons in about fifty households that spans the entrance road to the CBWS (interview with E. Saqui, 27 May 2013).

Virtually from its inception, the CBWS has been subject to a co-management arrangement with an environmental non-governmental organization, the Belize Audubon Society (BAS). The BAS first sought to garner support for the park by employing Maya Centre residents, ultimately retaining Ernesto Saqui, the village's only college graduate, as Park Superintendent with a staff of several wardens drawn from Maya Centre's small population. Coincidentally but importantly, Saqui also was Chairman of the Maya Centre Village Council.

After a false start in mid-1987, when village men walked out of an initial meeting in protest over the idea of a women's group, Saqui obtained agreement from the villagers later that year to create the Maya Centre Women's Group and construct a small building to sell traditional crafts made by MCWG members. Women were given the lead because most men left the village every day to find work, while most women stayed at home. Products included weavings, pottery, and slate carvings incorporating Maya calendars and other traditional motifs. For five years from 1987, Saqui coached the group in accounting, business management, and problem-solving skills, contributing to the governance institutions of the Women's Group, before stepping back to leave the women to run the group (interview with E. Saqui, 9 June 2013).

When an entrance charge to access Cockscomb was established in 1988, the BAS authorized the Women's Group to sell tickets, offering the group 10 per cent of the proceeds. A small thatched-roof building was erected in 1989 to house the group's wares at the intersection of the CBWS access road and the Southern Highway. Although a village dispute led to an arson fire at the cooperative building within a year of its construction, it was quickly rebuilt and within a few years twenty women were involved in the cooperative. In 2002, the thatched roof building was replaced with a larger cement structure that was financed by a BZ$40,000 (BZ$2=US$1) grant from the European Union matched with BZ$15,000 from the Women's Group's funds. In 2009, the facility was expanded again with BZ$30,000 from the Women's Group's funds to add a roadside restaurant building designed to support an eventual second-floor expansion to include a small museum of Maya culture. The restaurant was outfitted through a grant from the European Commission, and the Young Men's and Women's Christian Association of Belize provided training in cooking and hospitality management to Women's Group members. By 2013, however, the restaurant had failed due, according to MCWG members interviewed, to the group's inability to manage the procurement of food and the operation of a restaurant.

The losses incurred by the MCWG related to the restaurant venture caused the group to cease dividend payments for three years and resulted in some loss of membership. In 2009, fifty-four women were members of the Women's Group, representing the large majority of the village's sixty-five households. By 2013 membership had fallen to forty members, the result of the restaurant failure, deaths, members who moved away, and two expulsions of members who started competing businesses. Nonetheless, the MCWG catered to about 9300 visitors to the CBWS in 2012 (interview with D. Lizama, 14 June 2013). In the twelve months ending in June 2013, individual members of the Women's Group's received craft sales proceeds of about BZ$120,000 and the MCWG earned over BZ$29,000 in income in addition.

Tourist-related businesses have been lucrative for Maya Centre beyond the Women's Group. Two other households in the village have opened overnight facilities and small restaurants of modest quality but modest cost. Three retail stores service local and tourist requirements, two corn mills produce flour for the restaurants and local families, and three family-maintained crafts retail stores sell family-made items in competition with the cooperative. At least six village members maintain active businesses guiding CBWS visitors at a typical price of about BZ$100 per visitor. One family of three guides estimated that they conducted 140 tours each year of two or more people, translating into about BZ$14,000 in income for those three families each year (interview with G. Chun, 25 January 2010). According to Saqui, whose own family competes with the cooperative, spin-off businesses were part of his original vision, although the Women's Group resisted the creation of competing businesses when they first appeared.

The Women's Group is a central engine of the village's tourist economy. It is well supported within the village even by those families with competing businesses. It also has become a political force, integrating a village that otherwise is divided along family, religious, and political-party fault lines. The chairwoman is seen as one of the four leading figures of the village, along with the head of the Parent-Teacher Association for the village school, the head of the Water Board, and the Village Chairman. The Women's Group has been the recipient of grants, is the official partner of the BAS in ticketing, assists BAS to book the camp-style lodgings inside the park, and helps build demand for tour guides, taxis, and other services in Maya Centre. There is no food service at CBWS, so overnight campers must eat in Maya Centre or buy their food from local stores. Since a large proportion of the tour groups visiting Maya Centre are led by guides from nearby resorts on the Caribbean beaches, the Women's Group ensures that Maya Centre is not just another village one drives through on the way to a Belizean tourist attraction.

The Maya Centre Women's Group is registered with the Belizean government as a Non-Governmental Organization. As noted above, the group has four sources of operating revenue. First, the Women's Group receives 10 per cent of the price for every ticket to CBWS that is sold at their shop (BZ$10 for foreigners, BZ$2.50 for Belizeans; visitors also can purchase tickets at the sanctuary office). Second, craft sales are substantial and 10 per cent of the revenue is retained by the MCWG. Third and fourth, the MCWG earns revenues from soft drink sales to tourists and corn milling services to local families.

Members must live in Maya Centre, but membership in the MCWG is not an automatic right. Upon reaching eighteen years of age, women may apply for membership, which is decided by majority vote of the members. Successful applicants must pay a BZ$200 'initiation fee' to the group. The group has neither a written constitution nor by-laws, but new members sign a contract accepting the obligations of membership, violation of which can lead to expulsion. Among the most important rules are requirements that members not engage in competitive business activities, and a mandatory obligation to attend meetings, to work a specified number of volunteer shifts selling at the shop while wearing traditional Maya costume, and to participate in regular cleaning shifts at the MCWG building. A fine is levied on members who do not attend meetings or perform other duties.

The Women's Group is led by an unpaid executive committee of seven members. Every two years, ten members are nominated by the members to serve on the committee. Members elect seven individuals to serve on the committee in a raised-hand vote in an election supervised by a representative from the Belizean Women's Department. The individual with the most votes is named Chairlady, the second vote recipient is Vice Chairlady, and so on until all seven offices are filled in order of votes received. This system precludes divisive politicking in this disputatious village, as no individual 'runs' for a particular office; she must agree to serve in any capacity to which the group elects her.

The duties of the officers are substantial. Financial reconciliations are conducted at monthly meetings at which every member of the executive committee must be present to confirm the sales reports and the attribution of sales revenues to members. The Chairman and Treasurer are jointly responsible for the chequebook. Ticket sale proceeds are conveyed by two members of the committee to the bank in Dangriga, thirty minutes away by bus, and as many as four members may accompany when the MCWG's own revenues are deposited. Annual dividends are allocated by the executive committee based on seniority with the group. Major actions, such as grant applications, are overseen by the executive committee.

Members usually meet quarterly in a mandatory general meeting at which sale proceeds are dispersed, membership applications reviewed, and other business of the cooperative conducted. The Chairlady may call other meetings if required. Although no financial statements are prepared, all members are entitled to review and question the sales ledger book and the bank statements of the group at each quarterly meeting before distributions of proceeds are made. The cooperative does not compile regular financial statements, but it is clearly financially successful. In recent years, the cooperative has been able to accumulate BZ$45,000 to invest in their two building-expansion projects, typically pays a 'dividend' to members from its retained profits (although losses from the restaurant precluded payments from 2010 to 2012), has periodically contributed funding to support the cost of a teacher's aide in the village school, has been able to make other charitable contributions to villagers, and always retains at least BZ$7000 in working capital.

Institutional features

The PhD research from which this case study has been drawn (Gould, 2014) examined a broader array of institutional features that are relevant to these two organizations plus a third in Peru in the context of comparing those features to common pool resource theory. However, five of the common features of these two very different projects are highly relevant to archaeologists seeking to pursue economic development objectives at their sites. They are:

1. Each project incorporates collective choice arrangements rooted in local conditions

Both of these projects are democratically managed private enterprises. Shareholders of the Burren Centre elect the management committee and approve major corporate decisions at Annual General Meetings. Twenty per cent of the shareholders have the right to call Extraordinary General Meetings in the event of disputes. The management committee itself operates on majority vote principles. At Maya Centre, the cooperative's members elect officers for two-year terms and participate actively in the quarterly distribution meetings. All major decisions at the MCWG are made by majority vote of the members. The Burren Centre operates similarly to a traditional British corporation in a reasonably harmonious community. The MCWG, by contrast, has adopted a complex officer selection process, majoritarian decision-making, and financial transparency that are designed to minimize political stresses in a less harmonious setting. Both organizations, however disparate, are managed on democratic models.

2. Institutional features of each group facilitate change and conflict resolution

Through democratic procedures, significant changes have occurred in the mission and operations of both the Maya Centre and the Burren Centre co-ops. In each case, the governance rules of the organization encouraged the voicing of differing views while mitigating conflict by resolving differences through majoritarian procedures. Each has survived major internal challenges, the Mullaghmore-related debates in Ireland and the failure of the restaurant in Maya Centre, by relying on existing democratic mechanisms to manage disputes. Furthermore, electoral processes and term limits forestall the accumulation of power in one person or faction that would undermine the cohesion of the organization or inhibit the ability to take risks on new ideas.

3. Each project provides meaningful economic value to the community

The Maya Centre Women's Group directly provides significant cash income to all members through both proceeds from individuals' crafts sales and dividends from the profits of the MCWG itself. Spin-off benefits from the MCWG to the rest of the Maya Centre community are limited, since traffic through the village to the park would continue without the group's presence, but the sizable membership of the MCWG touches a large proportion of the fifty or so households in the village. The Burren Centre's economic impact is both direct and indirect. It is the largest employer in the village, but it also has generated a flow of visitors to the town who generate demand at local pubs, grocery stores, and shops that is fully acknowledged by shop owners. Finally, the Burren Centre stimulates tourist traffic elsewhere in the region. Support for each venture within the community very much reflects the widespread economic impact each has had. The economic benefits that derive from the projects provide important motivation to the participants to invest their time in sustaining the organizations.

4. Each group was started with leadership from influential community members

Even though the idea for the Burren Centre is attributed to an outsider, the initiative to bring him in and the leadership of the venture itself was entirely local. Moreover, a prominent Kilfenora farmer and the local priest are cited in interviews as being pivotal to acceptance by the broader community of the proposal to create the Burren Centre in Kilfenora. The parish priest was the group's first chairman. In Maya Centre, the village chairman initiated the Women's Group, managed local gender and family politics, and coached the members for five years. In this way he not only legitimized the project within the village and negotiated its complex politics, but also provided more sophisticated leadership to start the venture. In both cases, the influential local leaders who launched the projects eventually withdrew from active involvement.

5. Outside funding and advice was provided in a 'light touch' mode

Both of these ventures have benefited significantly from outside funding and operational advice, but neither has experienced efforts by outsiders to direct the activities of the venture. Funding has generally come without operational strings attached, leaving the members to manage their projects through internal processes. Where advice has been offered, it has been in the form of training or recommendations, not directives, and usually has not come from funding entities. Those who have assisted the members and leaders of the co-ops have done so without overruling the democratic and local management of the enterprise itself. Halstead (2003: 15), citing Brian Jones, has labelled this 'light touch adaptive management'.

The common features of these two projects are typical examples of those encountered in community-based common pool management regimes and in community-based sustainable tourism projects. Ostrom (1990; 2009) has described a more comprehensive list of common features of CPRs that includes points one, two, and four. All five points have been identified in various studies of sustainable tourism projects (Halstead, 2003; Jordan & Duval, 2009; Long, 2008; Murphy & Halstead, 2003; Murphy, 1985; Newsham, 2004; Ngo, et al., 2008; Reeves, 2008; Winter, 1998). Moreover, many of these same features arise in the World Bank's extensive review of its own local and community driven development projects over sixty years (Binswanger-Mkhize, et al., 2010). Even analyses supported by the Organization for Economic Cooperation and Development that focused more generally on decentralized, government-led development efforts have identified the necessity for similar structures at the local level if community-governed projects are to succeed (Greffe, 2005).

Building on these previous studies, this review of the Burren Centre and the Maya Centre Women's Group lends support to the argument that, notwithstanding differences in social, cultural, and economic contexts, certain common institutional features can be associated with robust, long-surviving community-managed projects. The features identified in this paper, in particular, may be interpreted as enhancing trust and difference-bridging social capital (Putnam, 2000: 21–24) among project participants, creating economic incentives for participants to invest time and resources to support the projects, and establishing mechanisms to enable change and resolve conflicts in a manner that facilitates risk-taking and mitigates potentially destructive differences among members.

Archaeologists seeking to pursue economic development projects at the local level should pay close attention to governance institutions. By supporting and encouraging, but not supplanting, the community's decision-making processes, by ensuring widespread economic benefits within the community, and by planning with community members to create governance structures that are robust in the face of change and conflict, archaeologists are more likely to create ventures that, like the Burren Centre or Maya Centre's Women's Group, prove sustainable for decades and not just for the few years excavation teams may be in town.

Acknowledgements

The author wishes to acknowledge helpful comments from Richard Hodges on an earlier draft of this paper and from the peer reviewers and editors of *Public Archaeology*.

Bibliography

Acheson, J. M. 1994. Transaction Costs and Business Strategies in a Mexican Indian Pueblo. In: J. M. Acheson, ed. *Anthropology and Institutional Economics*. Lanham, MD and London: University Press of America, pp. 143–65.

Anderson, B. 2006. *Imagined Communities*. London and New York: Verso.

Belize Audubon Society (BAS). 2008. Cockscomb Basin Wildlife Sanctuary [accessed 2 May 2014]. Available at: <http://www.belizeaudubon.org/protected_areas/cockscomb-basin-wildlife-sanctuary.html>.

Binswanger-Mkhize, H. P., de Regt, J. P., & Spector, S. 2010. *Local and Community Driven Development*. Washington, DC: The World Bank.

Carthy, H. 2011. *Burren Archaeology*. Wilton, Ireland: The Collins Press.

Clements, P. 2011. *Burren Country*. Wilton, Ireland: The Collins Press.

Comber, M. 2012. *Caherconnell Archaeological Project Summary of Fieldwork to Date 2012*. Carron, Ireland: Burren Forts, Ltd.

Connole, F. 2006. *Community Services Business Plan for the Burren Display Centre, Ltd*. Kilfenora, Ireland: Comhar Conradh na Boirne Teoranta.

Davis, P. 2011. *Ecomuseums: A Sense of Place*. New York and London: Continuum International Publishing Group.

Díaz-Andreu, M. 2013. Ethics and Archaeological Tourism in Latin America. *International Journal of Historical Archaeology*, 17: 225–44.

Gamarra, R. M. 2010. Huacas de Moche: Arqueología y desarrollo comunitario. In: L. V. Alvarez, ed. *Arqueología y Desarrollo: Experiencias y Posibilidades in el Perú*. Trujillo, Peru: Ediciones SIAN de Luis Valle Alvarez, pp. 169–80.

Gould, P. G. 2014. Putting the Past to Work: Archaeology, Community and Economic Development. Unpublished PhD thesis, University College London. Available at: <http://discovery.ucl.ac.uk>.

Greffe, X. 2005. The Instruments of Good Governance. In: S. Giguère, ed. Local Governance and the Drivers of Growth. Paris: OECD Publications, pp. 39–88.

Haggstrom, W. C. 1983. The Psychological Implications of the Community Development Process. In: L. J. Cary, ed. Community Development as a Process. Columbia, MO: University of Missouri Press, pp. 84–112.

Halstead, L. 2003. Making Community-Based Tourism Work: An Assessment of Factors Contributing to Successful Community-Owned Tourism Development in Caprivi, Namibia. Windhoek: Directorate of Environmental Affairs and Wildlife Integration for Livelihood Diversification.

Hardin, G. 1968. The Tragedy of the Commons. Science, 162(3859): 1243–48.

Hardin, G. 1977. Ethical Implications of Carrying Capacity. In: G. Hardin and J. Baden, eds. Managing the Commons. San Francisco: W. H. Freeman & Co., pp. 112–25.

Irish Productivity Centre (IPC). 1983. Confidential Report to Comhar Conradh na Boirne. Kilfenora, Ireland: Comhar Conradh na Boirne Teoranta.

Jordan, L. A. & Duval, D. T. 2009. Heritage Management and Tourism in the Caribbean. In: D. J. Timothy & G. P. Nyaupane, eds. Cultural Heritage and Tourism in the Developing World: A Regional Perspective. London and New York: Routledge, pp. 186–208.

Kates, R. W., Parris, T. M., & Leiserowitz, A. A. 2005. What is Sustainable Development? Environment, 47(3): 8–21.

Long, C. 2008. Heritage as Pro-Poor Tourism: The Case of Vieng Xay, Laos. In: R. Amoeda, S. Lira, C. Pinheiro, F. Pinheiro, and J. Pinheiro, eds. World Heritage and Sustainable Development. Barcelos, Portugal: Green Lines Institute for Sustainable Development, pp. 227–36.

Marshall, J. D. & Toffel, W. M. 2005. Framing the Elusive Concept of Sustainability: A Sustainability Hierarchy. Environmental Science & Technology, 39(5): 673–82.

de Merode, E., Smeets, R., & Westrik, C. 2003. Linking Universal and Local Values: Managing a Sustainable Future for World Heritage. Paris: UNESCO World Heritage Centre.

Murphy, C. & Halstead, L. 2003. 'The Person with the Idea for the Campsite is a Hero': Institutional Arrangements and Livelihood Change Regarding Community-Owned Tourism Enterprises in Namibia. Windhoek: Directorate of Environmental Affairs.

Murphy, P. E. 1985. Tourism: A Community Approach. New York: Methuen.

Newsham, A. 2004. Who's Involved in What? Participation in Natural Resource Management Institutions and 'Community based Tourism Enterprises' in Two Conservancies in Northwest Namibia. Windhoek: University of Namibia.

Ngo, M. H., Wong, Y. C., & Heng, C. K. 2008. Examining Conservation Possibilities on Urban Heritage Environment — its User Relation in Hanoi, Vietnam. In: R. Amoeda, S. Lira, C. Pinheiro, F. Pinheiro, and J. Pinheiro, eds. World Heritage and Sustainable Development. Barcelos, Portugal: Green Lines Institute for Sustainable Development, pp. 259–70.

North, D. C. 1990. Institutions, Institutional Change, and Economic Performance. Cambridge: Cambridge University Press.

Ostrom, E. 1990. Governing the Commons. Cambridge and New York: Cambridge University Press.

Ostrom, E. 2009. A General Framework for Analyzing Sustainability of Social-Ecological Systems. Science, 325(24): 419–422.

Poteete, A.R., Janssen, M.A. & Ostrom, E. 2010. Working Together: Collective Action, the Commons and Multiple Methods in Practice. Princeton, NJ: Princeton University Press.

Putnam, R. D. 2000. Bowling Alone. New York: Simon & Schuster.

Reeves, K. 2008. Place, Community and Heritage Tourism in Luang Prabang: Conserving and Interpreting the Intangible Heritage and Built Environment of an Historical Cultural Landscape. In: R. Amoeda, S. Lira, C. Pinheiro, F. Pinheiro, and J. Pinheiro, eds. World Heritage and Sustainable Development. Barcelos, Portugal: Green Lines Institute for Sustainable Development, pp. 311–18.

Richards, G. & Hall, D. 2000. The Community: A Sustainable Concept in Tourism Development? In: G. Richards and D. Hall, eds. Tourism and Sustainable Community Development. London: Routledge, pp. 1–14.

Shackel, P. A. & Chambers, E. J. 2004. Places in Mind: Public Archaeology as Applied Anthropology. New York and London: Routledge.

Silverman, H. 2006. *Archaeological Site Museums in Latin America*. Gainesville, FL: University Press of Florida.

Smith, L. & Waterton, E. 2009. *Heritage, Community and Archaeology*. London: Duckworth.

Stonich, S. C. 2005. Enhancing Community-Based Tourism Development and Conservation in the Western Caribbean. In: T. Wallace, ed. *Tourism and Applied Anthropologists: Linking Theory and Practice*. Berkeley, CA: University of California Press, pp. 77–86.

Sutton Jr, W. A. 1983. The Sociological Implications of the Community Development Process. In: L. J. Cary, ed. *Community Development as a Process*. Columbia, MO: University of Missouri Press, pp. 57–83.

Williamson, O. 1998. The Institutions of Governance. *The American Economic Review*, 88(2): 75–79.

Winter, M. 1998. *Decentralized Natural Resource Management in the Sahel: Overview and Analysis*. London: International Institute for Environment and Development.

Notes on contributor

Peter G. Gould received his PhD in 2014 from the Institute of Archaeology, University College London. He is a Consulting Scholar to the Penn Cultural Heritage Center of the University of Pennsylvania's Museum of Archaeology and Anthropology and an adjunct professor of archaeology at the American University of Rome. Previously, he has been chief executive or board chairman of numerous industrial and service companies in the United States and in Europe. In the 1970s, he held the senior staff position at the US President's Council of Economic Advisers and was Deputy Assistant Secretary for Export Development at the US Department of Commerce. He has served on the boards of several non-profit organizations, including the Sustainable Preservation Initiative, and was for six years the chairman of the Zoological Society of Philadelphia.

Correspondence to: Peter Gould, 563 Warwick Road, Haddonfield, New Jersey, 08033, USA. Email: pgould8@gmail.com

PUBLIC ARCHAEOLOGY, Vol. 13 Nos 1–3, 2014, 178–86

Can Rock Art in Africa Reduce Poverty?

Terry Little

Trust for African Rock Art, Kenya

Gloria Borona

Trust for African Rock Art, Kenya

The construction of physical barriers as protection of rock art against the threats of graffiti, vandalism, encroachment, deforestation, quarrying, and other human activity is rarely effective. The best barrier is a community which has an emotional or economic link to the heritage. Engaging local communities in the management, conservation, and valorization of sites and ensuring that they are beneficiaries of the heritage lays the foundations of those protective barriers. One of the ways the Trust for African Rock Art (TARA) has been doing this is through the development of responsible rock art tourism. In 2008, TARA's partnership in a project with the people of Mfangano Island, Kenya, led to the official opening of the Abasuba Community Peace Museum, the gateway to the Island's rock art and other heritage. The project provided a community project model which TARA has subsequently used in Kenya, Malawi, Niger, Tanzania, and Uganda.

KEYWORDS rock art, Africa, community management, valorization, tourism

Introduction

Africa's rock art and tourism

Many consider Africa to have the greatest diversity of rock art of any continent on earth. There are nine UNESCO World Heritage rock art sites in Africa (TARA, 2013). Such listing has benefited African rock art by raising global awareness of this heritage as well as increasing tourism in some cases (Sanz & Keenan, 2011). It is safe to say, however, that most sites have not been prepared to take advantage of or deal with the issues of increased tourism, often due to factors such as undeveloped infrastructures or lack of models of how to involve local communities in management and benefit sharing. Africa's rock art sites — listed or not — face numerous conservation challenges, such as residential or agricultural encroachment, uncontrolled quarrying, and deforestation for charcoal burning, graffiti, and vandalism.

The Trust for African Rock Art (TARA) is a non-governmental organization founded in Nairobi in 1996, whose mission is the conservation and valorization of

   DOI 10.1179/1465518714Z.00000000067

this heritage. It achieves this through a combination of survey and documentation, exhibitions, publications, and, more recently, community projects. Apart from the Sahara Desert, most rock art sites in Africa are found in or around areas inhabited by communities that, despite the possible emotional or cultural links to the paintings or engravings, are often the source of conservation problems. Physical barriers, while useful in keeping some people and animals away from the art, often violate the harmony between the actual site and the larger landscape. Fence materials, gates, and metal barriers often end up as raw materials in local constructions. Based on experience, TARA believes that the most effective way of conserving rock art is through involvement of local communities.

Conservation, communities, and rock art

According to UNESCO, communities involve all forms of non-state actors (2007: 3). This is from the smallest group of citizens, in whichever form they manifest themselves, to groups of indigenous, traditional, and or local peoples. Chirukure and Pwiti (2008) state that a community refers to a group of people with ethnic bonds that are linked into a unit with a common cultural identity, defined by racial origins, religion, nationality or tribal affiliation. TARA considers a community to be the present inhabitants of the territory where rock art sites are located. This is because the people who feel a sense of ownership for the heritage are most likely to assume responsibility for its conservation when they are engaged in its use and management. Some archaeological heritage such as rock shelters, rock art, or stone enclosures (for example, *madzimbabwe*[1]) (see Ndoro, 2006), and their associated landscapes hold cultural and spiritual significance because the communities regard them as part of their cosmological environment, a place they respect because of its ability to connect them with their ancestors and the spirit world, 'a space that communicates and entrenches traditional, cultural and spiritual values espoused by the community' (Van Rensburg & Koltze, quoted in Jopela, 2011: 2).

Rock art has become an area of major tourism interest in some parts of the world, for example the Lascaux caves in France, Kakadu in Australia, Altamira in Spain, and uKhahlamba/Drakensburg in South Africa[2] (Sanz & Keenan, 2011). Rock art tourism could have an important impact in countries like Kenya because it can attract people away from the overcrowded resorts and game parks, and direct them to remote rural areas where income generation resulting from tourism can have a substantial positive impact on local communities.

TARA has partnered with communities and national heritage bodies in the conservation, management, and valorization of rock art sites around Africa, a process which began in Dabous, Niger in the early 2000s. The goal of TARA community projects is to promote responsible rock art tourism that ensures the improvement of local livelihoods by embracing a broad scope of development (social, economic, environmental and cultural). The guiding principles of our projects are:

- management by objectives
- real community involvement
- capacity building and empowerment
- equity and impact assessments.

We believe that target communities more often than not have a clear idea of what their needs are and how they feel these should be addressed; ideas that are taken into account as we develop activities and implement our projects (see Borona & Nyasuna, 2009). In 2008, TARA had the opportunity of working with the Abasuba people on Mfangano Island, Lake Victoria, Kenya to develop and implement a community-based tourism project, focusing on the island's rock art and showcasing our key objectives that are outlined above.

Case study: Mfangano Island, Lake Victoria, Kenya

The context
Lake Victoria is the largest lake in Africa and the source of one of Africa's mightiest rivers, the Nile. Its northern shores are situated just below the Equator and three countries — Kenya, Tanzania, and Uganda — share its waters. Many islands punctuate the vastness of the lake, most of them in Uganda and Tanzania, although a few are on the Kenyan side. Two of these, Mfangano and Rusinga, with their adjacent shores, provide the nucleus of the Suba District. The largest island, Mfangano, rises steeply from the great lake, a hunched-over giant, clothed with green vegetation. Its rocky backbone rises over 300 m above the lake and is exposed as tall red cliffs in some places. The shore is edged by black rocks with overhanging fig trees, beaches with black-and-white volcanic sand and narrow strands of reeds. The people reside in homesteads along the narrow shoreline and on the steep slopes of the mountainous island. They are primarily fishermen and small-scale farmers growing maize, millet, cassava, beans, and fruit, and rearing cattle, goat, sheep, duck, and chicken. Hedges of yellow-flowered *Thevetia peruviana* bushes border many homesteads, and wild morning glories abound in fallow fields. Beautifully painted canoes can be seen lined up on the beaches or at work out on the lake (TARA, 2008).

Engravings and paintings on stone are found throughout Africa and represent an important element of universal cultural heritage. Kenya, being on the confluence of migration routes and cultural traditions, possesses an interesting variety of rock art, some of it believed to be as much as 4000 years old. The Mfangano Island rock art sites are all paintings, while there are a few cupule sites[3] on the mainland. The art is geometric and is believed to have associations with rain-making (TARA, 2008).

While Mfangano Island and the surrounding areas of the Suba District are beautiful, life for many of its inhabitants is difficult. In conversation with local residents we learned that some consider this to be the epicentre of HIV/Aids infection for the region; educational opportunities are limited and unemployment is endemic. Life for many is a hand-to-mouth existence. What could TARA do — if anything — in such circumstances? There is nothing in the organization's stated mission about reducing poverty or improving people's lives. Ours is to document and promote awareness of rock art and ensure its conservation. Would it even make sense to develop tourism products for this area? Until 2005, tourists were largely unable to visit rock art in Kenya, as the sites were unrecorded or unknown. At best, they were inaccessible, lacked interpretive information, and were unprotected from vandalism. Even though a few sites had been opened to visitors with TARA's support, there was not much local experience or expertise in developing this kind of cultural tourism.

The project: Abasuba Community Peace Museum

In February 2007, TARA colleagues Terry Little and Gladys Nyasuna-Wanga travelled to Mfangano Island to see the work done by the founder of the Abasuba Community Peace Museum, Jack Obonyo. Jack inherited the parcel of land where the museum stands from his father when he was marrying, as is custom, but his desire to protect and promote the unique culture of his people led him to donate the land for the construction of a small community museum in 2000. He began to collect artefacts, carried out research on the Abasuba culture, and liaised with local elders and youths to encourage conservation of the nearby rock art sites. Jack learnt about TARA through a newspaper article in one of the Kenyan dailies and visited our exhibition at the Nairobi National Museum in 2005. The Abasuba Community Peace Museum is one of the very few community-managed museums in Kenya. The current museum buildings, constructed in 2008 with the support of TARA and the Kenyan Tourism Trust Fund, replicate local architecture and, in addition to acting as a gateway to the island's rock art heritage, were designed to showcase the heritage of the Abasuba people and to serve as a community cultural centre.

After much reflection and discussion during our visit with Jack in 2007, we believed that promoting tourism — responsibly — could generate jobs and income and that it could help increase local people's pride in their heritage. This would, in fact, be the most effective means of conserving the heritage. People who know, love, and benefit from their heritage would naturally be in the frontline to preserve and protect it. Jack's subsequent visit to the TARA office led to the signing of an agreement between the Abasuba Museum and TARA which was at the foundation of our 2008 tourism project. While the Suba rock art sites had been opened to the public in 2005, we identified a need for more resources to develop a larger museum, directional and interpretive signage, as well as piers and docks in order to enhance visitors' experiences at the sites. The project objectives were: increasing local awareness of the heritage, conservation, promotion of the heritage, development of basic tourism infrastructure, and, above all, improvement of community livelihoods (Borona & Nyasuna, 2009).

At the time, the Kenyan Government was making efforts to develop the Western Circuit around Lake Victoria for tourism. TARA saw this as an opportunity and subsequently submitted a proposal to the Tourism Trust Fund (TTF) for a community project with the five interrelated objectives noted above. The TTF was funded by the European Union with support from the Kenyan Government. The news of approval of a 14.5 million Kenya shilling (US$250,000, at the time) grant by the TTF was received with great excitement at TARA and within the Suba community. Finally the treasures of Suba District would be made available and marketed for tourism! Anticipation and expectation were high among the community members as TARA prepared to implement, together with the Abasuba Community Peace Museum, its biggest community project ever.

Ultimately, the project experience was a rich one — full of highs and lows, aggravations and frustrations, as well as immensely satisfying achievements. For TARA it constituted a worthwhile case study in the field of cultural heritage which we have built upon and modified for undertaking similar projects in East Africa. A description of the project, and discussion of its successes and challenges are laid out below.

The project activities that were implemented related to each of the objectives. To create awareness of the existence and importance of the rock art heritage in the district we held community engagers' workshops and produced publicity materials. These workshops deviated from the standard training approach. They constituted a forum for community members to share, learn, and compare notes which led to the development of a common conservation message. To achieve the conservation objective we developed a conservation and management plan, carried out an environmental impact assessment and trained guides. Marketing and promotion activities included: creation of a brand, production of a video, booklets, a website, and promotional giveaways like stickers, hats, and t-shirts, and the organization of events like concerts and exhibitions. Infrastructural developments in this project were quite substantial. There was signage development to highlight the storylines which were created to accompany visitors on the hikes to the rock art sites. Two boats were purchased, one a locally crafted wooden boat and one a motor boat. Piers were constructed at the museum and at two of the rock art sites to improve accessibility.

The largest component of the project was the construction of the new museum and community centre. The idea of putting up two distinct structures came after the initial grant came when we realized that these structures would be critical in creating different revenue streams. The idea was that a community centre with a restaurant, kitchen, and meeting rooms might be able to generate income to manage activities at the museum/learning centre. We were able to convince the TTF of the value of this idea and they increased their contribution to make up the cost difference. Together, these buildings would constitute the gateway to the island's cultural heritage, including the rock art.

Building infrastructure was a major challenge on the island. Mfangano is only accessible by a sporadic — sometimes dangerous — boat service. The expensive alternatives are to charter a boat or a private plane, both of which we had to do during the course of the project. There were no roads or electricity at the time of the project. Delays of disbursements from the donor, an inflexible implementation timeframe, and the political instability and uncertainty following the contested elections of December 2007 created significant obstacles to the project's implementation. The new museum was officially opened in October 2008, nine months after ground breaking in a ceremony attended by government officials, the diplomatic community, the funders, and hundreds of community members.

Some results, some challenges, some failures

In order to create revenue streams for the local population, almost all of the materials (stones, sand, thatching grass, etc.) were locally sourced and the construction workers were all from the district. We had many first-hand accounts of how these funds were used: school fees were paid, hospital bills were cleared, goats and cattle were bought, and more than a few bottles of spirits were consumed.

Easy landing
The piers/landing bays constructed during the project are used by community members as well as tourists. Before their construction, community members had to wade through the muddy lake waters from the boat drop-off point — or pay a small fee to

be carried on the back of a hefty human. There are local 'beach committees' in charge of maintaining the piers through the collection of modest fees from the boat trade, but this has not worked out well and the piers have been badly deteriorating.

Where does the money go?

There are two main rock art sites to visit. Mawanga is the more accessible site — an easy thirty-minute walk from the boat dock. Kwitone is a demanding two-hour walk, but with dramatic views of the island and lake and better conserved paintings. The museum manages these sites in collaboration with site committees who are selected by the clans in whose jurisdiction the sites are found. Visitors pay an entry fee and a guide fee. These fees are divided amongst the guide, the museum, and the site committees, which fund projects in their constituencies.

A rock art kindergarten

One encouraging example of community intervention is at Mawanga: the Mawanga Rock Art Kindergarten. The site management committee decided to use the collected funds for a school because the nearest school was too far for the youngest children. They have now expanded and there are sixty children and two teachers in two classrooms.

Hello telephony

Another community benefit which is a direct result of the project is the provision of telephony to the area of the Mawanga site, which did not have a mobile phone network up until 2010. This absence of a way to communicate and organize visits between the guests, guides, and the museum resulted in many misunderstanding and unhappy visitors. TARA approached Safaricom, Kenya's largest mobile service provider, which subsequently put up a telecommunications mast at that end of the island. While this is a huge benefit for the site, it also benefits the local people who had been cut off from mobile phone communication. In addition, Safaricom pays annual fees to the school where the mast is situated and a part of these funds is shared with the kindergarten.

Funding limits

Funding for culture is limited around the world, but even more so in Africa where issues like health and education are prioritized. This has been a motivation for TARA to conceive projects which use heritage to leverage economic development. In this case, the EU-funded TTF was keen to develop new tourism products in Western Kenya, a region where up until that time there had been little investment in the tourism infrastructure and promotion. And while we managed to successfully undertake an important project which reflects our organizational missions, the administrative demands from the EU were a huge burden for our small organization that took a long time to overcome (cf. Wait & Altschul, this volume). Another short-coming of this funding — and most project funding, in fact — is the timeframe. In this case we were given a timeframe of less than a year which means that there was very limited time to build and ensure the long-term institutional and administrative stability of our partners on the ground. The result is that, three years after closing the project, the Abasuba Museum is still rather dependent on TARA in terms of programming and administrative support.

Accessibility

A serious problem, particular to this type of alternative tourism, is that most rock art sites are found in places that are off the usual tourism circuits. That means poor transportation service and bad (or no) infrastructure. As an NGO we have very little influence on major capital investments in infrastructure. On the other hand, the inaccessibility of the sites can make them 'exclusive', and we have been looking at the high-end range of tourism. The Trust has been putting together some exclusive rock art tourism packages with helicopter pilots, tour guides, and stakeholders involved in this kind of tourism, but there are no results to report as yet.

Government policies

Despite efforts to engage the responsible tourism bodies, in our experience the governments of the countries where we have worked (Kenya, Malawi, Tanzania, Uganda) are yet to recognize rock art as a potential tourism product that can contribute to tourism earnings. The main focus for tourism in these countries tends to be natural heritage, especially wildlife and beaches. To date, there has not been much willingness to invest in other types of tourism.

Sustainability

For a small museum without any government support and without the capacity to mobilize substantial funding, the museum has had to think of innovative ways of sustaining their operations without sacrificing its missions (but often with some compromises). From very humble beginnings this museum has been a willing partner in trying out innovative approaches to generating money. These include providing modest camping facilities, restaurant and bar service, satellite television (football and soap operas seem to be the biggest draws), mobile phone charging, money transfer services, and boat hire. If a museum provides services and products that are in sync with the public they serve, then there is a lot of potential for growth.

Conclusion

In endorsing TARA's work, former UN Secretary-General Kofi Annan said:

> Africa's rock art heritage is the common heritage of all Africans and all people. It is a cultural gift from our ancestors [. . .] we must save this cultural heritage before it is too late. Two initiatives are especially critical: educating our children and engaging local communities. (Kofi Annan and Africa's Rock Art, 2005)

According to the UNESCO (1972) Convention on Protection of the World Cultural and Natural Heritage, 'Heritage without community involvement and commitment is an invitation to failure and that heritage protection, should, wherever possible, reconcile the needs of human communities, as humanity needs to be at the heart of conservation'. Using a few ancient rock art paintings as a starting point, TARA and the Abasuba Community Peace Museum have revived the life and soul of a beautiful, yet remote, island community where the young people share the same aspirations as those in similar circumstances around the world: to move out and go to the capital, or at least the closest city. The Abasuba Community Peace Museum is an example of a new kind of museum that is involved in the lives of its community. The museum is in itself a valuable resource: a gateway, a meeting room and facilities, a gathering place, a destination for travellers, a place that offers programmes for both the youth and elders. The project was achievable because there was goodwill from many sides, modest funding support to get it off the ground, a highly motivated initiator, and local, national, and international institutional support. Has rock art on Mfangano Island reduced poverty? We have seen many positive changes on the island in terms of infrastructural, cultural, and social outputs. We want to believe the answer is yes, but we will need now to collect and review the economic data to see whether we can talk about a real economic impact.

Notes

[1] The word 'zimbabwe' (plural 'madzimbabwe') is derived from the Shona words 'dzimba dza mabwe' and means 'houses of stone'. Archaeologists and historians believe that from the thirteenth to fifteenth centuries Great Zimbabwe was the capital for a large area in southern Africa. Throughout this region there are smaller but similar 'madzimbabwe'.

[2] In 2013 the uKhahlamba/Drakensburg World Heritage site was extended to include a national park in Lesotho. It is now known as Maloti-Drakensburg.

[3] Cupules, small cups or depressions ground into the rock, are found on every continent on earth. They are very common in Africa and occur in different sizes/forms. The most common are literally the size of a cup. The fact that cupules of all sizes, including the largest, are frequently found in association with rock art sites and also with rock gongs might suggest a spiritual motivation/origin.

Bibliography

Borona, G. & Nyasuna, W. 2009. *Managing Community Projects: TARA and the Abasuba Community Peace Museum*. Nairobi: TARA.

Chirukure, S. & Pwiti, G. 2008. Community Involvement in Archaeology and Cultural Heritage Management: An Assessment from Case Studies in Southern Africa and Elsewhere. *Current Anthropology*, 49(3): 467–83.

Jopela, A. 2011. Traditional Custodianship: A Useful Framework for Heritage Management in Southern Africa? *Conservation and Management of Archaeological Sites*, 13(2–3): 103–22.

Kofi Annan and Africa's Rock Art. 2005. Directed by V. Waldock, T. Hill & D. Coulson. New York.

Ndoro, W. 2006. Building the Capacity to Protect Rock Art Heritage in Rural Communities. In: N. Agnew and J. Bridgland, eds. *Of the Past to the Future: Integrating Archaeology and Conservation. Proceedings of the Conservation Theme of the 5th World Archaeological Congress Washington D.C., 22–26 June 2003*. Los Angeles: The Getty Conservation Institute, pp. 336–39.

Sanz, N. & Keenan, P. eds. 2011. *Human Evolution: Adaptations, Dispersals and Social Developments*. Paris: UNESCO World Heritage Centre, pp. 100–05.

Trust for African Rock Art (TARA). 2008. *The Attractions of Suba District*. Nairobi: TARA.

Trust for African Rock Art (TARA). 2013. Rock Art in Africa [accessed 3 April 2014]. Available at: <http://africanrockart.org/?option=com_content&view=article&id=86&Itemid=103>.

United Nations Educational Scientific and Cultural Organization (UNESCO). 1972. Convention Concerning the Protection of the World Cultural and Natural Heritage [accessed 3 April 2014]. Available at: <http://whc.unesco.org/en/conventiontext/>.

United Nations Educational Scientific and Cultural Organization (UNESCO). 2007. Convention on Protection of the World Cultural and Natural Heritage: 31st Session. Christchurch, New Zealand [accessed 3 April 2014]. Available at: <http://whc.unesco.org/archive/2007/whc07-31com-24e.pdf>.

Notes on contributors

Terry Little is the Chief Operations Officer at TARA where he has led the development of outreach and community rock art programs in Kenya, Malawi, Niger, Tanzania, and Uganda. Previously he has been a lecturer in communications and marketing of cultural heritage at the University of Cassino and at the Venaria Reale/University of Torino, Italy, as well as a programme officer in the collections department at ICCROM for twelve years.

Correspondence to: Terry Little, PO Box 24122 Karen, Nairobi 00502, Kenya. Email: terry@africanrockart.org

Gloria K. Borona is a conservationist who has a keen interest in ensuring that communities be constructively engaged in the management of their resources as primary stakeholders. She has worked on concept development, fundraising, and implementation of community rock art conservation projects in Kakapel, western Kenya with the Iteso people, Lokori, northern Kenya with the Turkana people, in Mfangano Island, Lake Victoria Kenya with the Abasuba people, in Uganda with the Iteso people, Malawi with the Chewa people, and in Tanzania with the Rangi people. In 2009, she co-authored a publication 'Managing Community Projects: A Case of TARA and the Abasuba Community Peace Museum' to document this particular project and share experiences as well as challenges. She holds an MBA (Strategic Management) from the University of Nairobi and a Bachelor of Environmental Studies (Community Development) from Kenyatta University. Gloria is currently undertaking a PhD programme in forest resources management at the University of British Columbia.

PUBLIC ARCHAEOLOGY, Vol. 13 Nos 1–3, 2014, 187–99

Wildebeest Kuil Rock Art Centre, South Africa: Controversy and Renown, Successes, and Shortcomings

DAVID MORRIS

McGregor Museum, Kimberley, South Africa

This paper reviews the development of the Wildebeest Kuil Rock Art Centre, in South Africa, open for just over a decade. The run-up to the project's launch was not without difficulties, caused by both community and official mandates. Yet despite achieving a measure of critical acclaim the site has only niche market appeal. Sustainability was possible only after securing operational subsidization. As that support begins to be scaled down, Wildebeest Kuil, as a case study, compels an assessment of its specific successes and shortcomings relative to issues of a more general nature that enhance or impede the role of South African archaeological sites in economic development.

KEYWORDS South Africa, Wildebeest Kuil, rock art, community archaeology, heritage tourism

Introduction

In 2001 Wildebeest Kuil, a rock art site and visitor centre outside Kimberley, in South Africa, was opened to the public. In the twelve-month run-up to its launch, the project faced contestation by different community constituencies and wavering government support. It subsequently achieved a measure of critical acclaim, but visitor numbers have fallen far short of initial estimates. A subvention by the McGregor Museum in Kimberley in terms of staffing and funding enabled the site to remain open. Recently, capital enhancement of the facility through tourism sector funding, intended to boost visitor numbers and, ultimately, revenues for the community, has generated more difficulties than benefits. Questionnaire results have indicated that some of the assumptions about likely tourist interest were wide of the mark. The site has continued to be viable only through support from the McGregor Museum. At a time when that support has begun to be scaled down, the case of Wildebeest Kuil forces a hard look at issues particular to this site and its context, and those of a more general nature relative to the role of South African archaeological sites in economic development.

© Taylor & Francis 2014   DOI 10.1179/1465518714Z.00000000068

The author has been involved as part of the project team of Wildebeest Kuil from its inception.

Background

The Wildebeest Kuil Rock Art Centre has as its principal feature a low hill over which are spread a few hundred Later Stone Age rock engravings. The site entered the colonial archive in the 1870s by way of rock art copies and discussion by geologist George Stow (1905) who ventured there after establishment of the diamond-mining town of Kimberley. Engravings from Wildebeest Kuil were subsequently sent to the Colonial and Indian Exhibition of 1886 in London, and two ended up in the collection of the British Museum (Fock, 1965). In later years, the site's proximity to Kimberley made it a regular place of interest for prehistorians passing through town — amongst them, Miles Burkitt (1928), the Abbé Breuil, and Desmond Clark (1959).

Once legislation provided for declaration of heritage sites in South Africa from 1936, a small number of archaeological features in the Kimberley area were granted national monument status. But Wildebeest Kuil was not one of them. Local museum director and rock art specialist Maria Wilman (1933: 5) considered the site 'not of great importance' (albeit, for important visitors, usefully near to Kimberley). Official listing of significant South African sites prior to the 1990s was notoriously colonialist in emphasis (Deacon, 1993), some pre-colonial sites, like the Nooitgedacht glacial pavements (with rock engravings), passing muster more for their geological than their archaeological attributes.

The idea of an 'archaeological route' was developed by the McGregor Museum in the 1980s to address this neglect of pre-colonial heritage. Its value for tourism was promoted as much as its potential as an educational resource for schools and communities (Morris, 1989; 2003). Archaeological findings, then eschewed in school history curricula, could broaden perspectives on Africa's past, while from a conservation viewpoint it was hoped that a better-informed public would appreciate and support efforts to protect — and to research — the traces of the past (cf. Mazel, 2008). Further, it was explicitly suggested that the diversion of tourists off the major Johannesburg to Cape Town route, to sites in Kimberley's rural hinterland, might channel economic benefits to smaller towns through fuel, food, and accommodation sales and patronage of small enterprises that might spring up around the heritage sites on the 'archaeological route'.

Open-air displays had been created previously on a small scale at the Earlier Stone Age sites of Canteen Kopje (1940s) and Doornlaagte (1960s), and the model of putting up information boards was repeated at Nooitgedacht (1980s) (Morris, 1989). In the early 1990s, a site museum, representing a somewhat larger investment, partly by local government, was built at Wonderwerk Cave, and in 2000 new displays were put up at Canteen Kopje and the nearby Barkly West Museum, financed by grants from foreign embassies (Turkington, 2000). These projects anticipated, at least in principle, some of the aspirations of the *Ukhamba* programme — South African archaeology's later initiative to transform the way the discipline is taught, practised and communicated to the public (ATAC, 2009) — as well as some of the objectives more recently proposed in the *Strategy for the Palaeosciences* (STD, 2011). Both these programmes give emphasis to schools outreach, the promotion of public archaeology, increasing the visibility of archaeology in the media, and creating opportunities for non-university-trained workers.

More immediately, though, late 1990s political discourse in South Africa was affording greater emphasis to cultural heritage. President Thabo Mbeki propagated the concept of an 'African Renaissance'. The placement of a rock painting image at the centre of the nation's new coat of arms was a key instance of rock art being drawn upon in the quest for new and unifying national symbols (Smith, et al., 2001). The trend continues, with rock art motifs flanking an image of Nelson Mandela in new bank notes launched in 2012. All of this seemed — and seems — auspicious for a wider awareness of pre-colonial history and of rock art in particular. Cultural tourism was re-branded as a sector able to redress past imbalances and benefit communities previously disadvantaged (Duval & Smith, 2012; Mahony & van Zyl, 2002).

The Wildebeest Kuil rock art project was to have been a modest addition to the existing 'archaeological route' (Morris, 2003). In the event, resources for a much more ambitious 'Rock Art Centre' were made available from the Poverty Relief Fund of South Africa's national Department of Environmental Affairs and Tourism, channelled via the Rock Art Research Institute at the University of the Witwatersrand (Laue, et al., 2001). With rock art tourism at its core, this was intended to be a self-sustaining poverty-alleviation project, generating jobs for guides and promoting community crafts.

Remarkably, the project ran to schedule (funding was awarded for completion within just twelve months) and, in December 2001, the Centre was opened jointly by the Premier of the Northern Cape, Manne Dipico, and the head of SA Tourism, Cheryl Carolus. Wildebeest Kuil soon achieved a measure of success but, over a decade on, successes have been tempered by shortcomings and low visitor numbers, with one calamity having left a permanent scar on the hill. These issues are explored in detail below. Aspects of the project's evolving dynamics are specific to its particular history, and those of the parties involved in its development and operation. The site was developed in tandem with the Game Pass project in the Ukhahlamba/Drakensberg Park (Laue, et al., 2001) — one of South Africa's World Heritage Sites — where the achievement of sustainability for rock art tourism has also been a challenge. The recent analysis by Duval and Smith (2012) provides a useful comparison.

Rocky ride to opening

Several attributes favoured the choice of Wildebeest Kuil for cultural tourism development in 2000–2001: its location near to Kimberley, its ease of access off a major road, and its situation along the 'archaeological route' with other existing or potential public archaeology sites. Additionally, in fulfilment of the requirements of the Poverty Relief grant from central government, there was a readily defined 'community' who would serve as beneficiaries. From 1996, Wildebeest Kuil has been situated on land owned by the !Xun and Khwe San[1] (linguistically distinct indigenous minority groups with a common recent history, discussed below), and managed by a Communal Property Association.

As previous experience had shown (for example, in the case of Canteen Kopje and Barkly West Museum), the negotiation of a project of this scale, with multiple stakeholders, could be enormously testing and time-consuming (Turkington, 2000). Having a highly circumscribed community as primary stakeholder and beneficiary, this aspect of the Wildebeest Kuil project could be (and, to meet the twelve-month deadline, needed to be) fast-tracked. But there was a feeling from the outset that consultation and negotiation needed to go wider.

The !Xun and Khwe were refugees with an awkward history of involvement in the Namibian war, having come originally from different areas of Angola some 2000 km north of Kimberley (Sharp & Douglas, 1996). With the advent of independence in Namibia in 1990, they were evacuated to South Africa as a community of soldiers and their dependants attached to the South African Defence Force. Housed temporarily in separate !Xun and Khwe army-style tent towns at Schmidtsdrift near Kimberley, their move, after 1996, to the adjacent farms Platfontein and Wildebeest Kuil, nearer still to town, followed, for most of the community, a process of closure on this military episode in their history. Naturalized as South Africans, the !Xun and Khwe, now resident in the Platfontein township, have leveraged a distinct cultural identity, amongst the subcontinent's indigenous minorities. They are today, indeed, some the few remaining people still speaking Khoe-San languages. In this indigenous mode they associate themselves readily with Southern African San heritage in general, and with the engravings of Wildebeest Kuil in particular. Lindsay Weiss (2005) has shown how the site itself, situated by chance on land purchased for resettlement, became part of the strategic positioning of !Xun and Khwe citizenship.

The links, implicit at first, are given much more explicit expression in the notion of a !Xun and Khwe 'return' to this area, defended by reference to the engravings and a supposed earlier retreat by 'Bushmen' to the Kalahari following the arrival of Europeans at the Cape (Morris, 2012). The argument draws on an old myth propagated, inter alia, in South African school history texts of the twentieth century (e.g. van Jaarsveld, 1969). But while there is no archaeological or historical evidence for any kind of original link between the !Xun and Khwe and the engravings of Wildebeest Kuil, such links may well exist for descendants of Khoisan[2] people of this area. The latter are members of a much less coherent community of Afrikaans-speaking 'Coloured' people, who are relatively less able to show Khoisan 'authenticity' or descent. Their colonial-era ancestors — survivors of the genocide of the eighteenth and nineteenth centuries (De Prada-Samper, 2012) — suffered language loss and cultural transformation, with incorporation into a generalized 'Coloured' underclass in colonial society by the beginning of the twentieth century. Their links with the engravings, albeit likely, would be impossible to substantiate.

Therefore, the chosen beneficiaries for poverty relief in the Wildebeest Kuil project were, in a sense, the 'wrong' community — or only one of the relevant ones. Controversy erupted in the local press following public announcement of the project, when people claiming Khoisan descent in the local 'Coloured' community protested their exclusion. The issue had been anticipated and, with a representative of this constituency serving on the project Steering Committee, the matter was resolved without any major negative impact at that stage. Grievances over exclusion may well have continued to fester or flare up had the project gone on to become a major commercial success, but in the event it has not and, on the contrary, it has been the !Xun and Khwe who have been dissatisfied about projected returns on their involvement.

A more serious difficulty revolved around participation of the provincial govern-ment department responsible for heritage. A senior member, invited to serve on the Steering Committee, attended none but the inaugural meeting. As the project progressed, one of his staff took umbrage at perceived usurpation of government's mandate to preserve heritage and issued a call for provincial and district stakeholders to withdraw support and involvement. Fortunately, the principal government partner at that stage was not provincial but national and, at the opening, the Premier of the Northern Cape officiated alongside the CEO of the national tourism authority, SA Tourism. The political head of Sport, Arts and Culture in the province — whose portfolio included museums and heritage — was absent. Subsequently the various departments concerned have softened their stance and some have become actively supportive.

Wildebeest Kuil experience

The experience designed for visitors to the site is scripted as a metaphoric pilgrimage (Blundell, 1996), starting and ending at a visitor centre built at the foot of the hill. An 800 m trail takes visitors to the engravings. A display and film introduce the archaeology, history, and rock art, and the recent history of the !Xun and Khwe people. The narrative is not straightforward. As already intimated, the link between the site and the !Xun and Khwe people is coincidental — or all-important — depend-ing on which version is to the fore. This had a bearing on the blending or juxtaposing of accounts of site and people in the display, film, and trail.

The site itself contains more traces from the past than pertain solely to rock engravings (Morris, 2003; 2012). There is Stone Age material long predating the art, while traces of events much later than the engravings include stone kraals, and ruins from a late nineteenth-century hotel midway between the Vaal River diamond dig-gings and the mines of early Kimberley (Weiss, 2009). A scattering of rusted food tins in one area is of Anglo-Boer War vintage, reflecting troop movements after the Siege of Kimberley. Twentieth-century remains include a derelict farm-worker house and associated ash heap (excavations here — the archaeology of farm-worker life — reveal recent rural pasts not well documented in more conventional sources). In sum, the site is a nexus of jostling histories and possible interpretations which seldom entirely cohere. Provocatively, there is the hint of a synthesis linking the engravings with the twentieth-century ash heap (given the incorporation of surviving indigenous people here into colonial society mainly as farm labour), over the more intuitive cultural narrative that most visitors and some stakeholders would expect (associating the rock art more directly with the !Xun and Khwe). Recognizing 'the necessary social complexities of archaeological, pre-colonial and colonial histories' (Meskell & Scheermeyer, 2008: 154), there is a multi-vocality at play which has been worked into the displays, the film, and the trail.

The trail itself consists of a progressive peeling away of layers — or, rather, a revelation of histories 'enfolded' within, as Ingold (1993) would insist, rather than 'inscribed' or 'layered' upon the landscape. At the hilltop, appreciation of the engrav-ings is facilitated through ethnography, historical references, and the ways researchers have construed the evidence. Towards the end of their walk, visitors are brought face to face with the conflict of the colonial era, and the closure of the frontier that followed swiftly on the discovery of diamonds around 1870. The story is told of Kousop, a rare instance of a named individual from the end of the Stone Age in South Africa, who was leader of the last independent Khoisan occupants of the Wildebeest Kuil hill (Péringuey, 1909). He and 130 of his followers were killed near here in 1858 after they mobilized attacks on encroaching colonial farmers (Schoeman, 1995). The 150th anniversary of this event was marked at Wildebeest Kuil in July 2008.

A vital dimension to the experience is the interaction between visitors and guides, the latter inevitably providing a mix of learned insights on rock engravings and views from their own personal histories and contexts. A comment by Megan Biesele (1993: 202), made with reference to Kalahari folklore, is apposite: the stories that are told are 'full of the past' but in ways 'very complexly related to the present'.

Acclaim — yet visitor numbers are low

As an experience, the Wildebeest Kuil Rock Art Centre has achieved a measure of critical acclaim (e.g. Martin, 2008; Weiss, 2007; 2012). Remarks in the visitors' book are almost universally positive. Flagged in the major tourist guidebooks and with a digital media presence (e.g. Wildebeest Kuil, 2013), the site has featured in magazines, books, and television documentaries. And yet, as a commercial venture, it draws relatively few visitors, far short of the initial estimates on which sustainability was based — often much less than a hundred monthly compared with a budgeted 1000 adult visitors per month (Turkington, 2001).

It is doubtless significant that, relative to the major themes in Kimberley's tourism marketing, pre-eminently the history of diamonds and mining, and the legendary names of diamond miners Rhodes and Barnato (Roberts, 1976; TBH, 2013), rock art occupies only a supplementary slot. Accuracy of tourism information is also an issue: one prominent Kimberley brochure placed the site on the wrong road out of town, while lack of knowledge amongst tourism front-desk personnel is notorious, not just with respect to Wildebeest Kuil. A similarly, somewhat secondary focus for rock art relative to other attractions is noted by Duval and Smith (2012) in their analysis of rock art tourism in the Ukhahlamba Drakensberg Park, where, in that instance, mountain scenery and natural heritage consistently trump culture. In both cases, an older master narrative still prevails, whether centred on precipitous peaks or mining magnates, and transforming it would appear to require more a shift in the tourist mindset than merely 'improved marketing'.

Better marketing may well help to a degree, but when a consultant to government promised that a (costly) marketing make-over for Wildebeest Kuil would increase visitorship from less than 1 per cent of the Northern Cape's tourist market to around 10 per cent (CKLM Consultancy, 2007), it became critical to understand exactly who was currently visiting Wildebeest Kuil and why (Morris, et al., 2009). If, as some of us suspected, the site has only niche market appeal, how valid were the assumptions on which sweeping projections were being made by a well-meaning tourism sector? How relevant were the analogues on which initial estimates of sustainability had been based? And what might be the consequences for relations between project and community, when !Xun and Khwe leaders were led to anticipate material spin-offs from vastly inflated tourist numbers?

Sobering survey results based on a 2007–08 on-site questionnaire have only confirmed what was suspected, that the site has markedly niche appeal. With about a third of visitors being international, the remainder come from across the spectrum of South African society. But educational profiles and preferences suggest an unusually discerning and intellectually engaged subset of tourists. About 66 per cent are university graduates, half of them having post-graduate degrees. They tend not to pursue eco-tourism opportunities, but take in a range of other cultural or heritage sites while in the area, usually self-driven rather than on organized tours (Morris, et al., 2009). A small but significant number actively follow an academic interest in the site itself or in relation to the !Xun and Khwe (occasionally the centre has been a venue for seminars); while others are writers, journalists, photographers, and artists who add to the intellectual outcomes that accrete around the development (Morris, 2012: 242).

These indices underscore the warnings of 'Pro-Poor Tourism' literature on the dangers of inflating community expectations concerning income levels, let alone basic sustainability, in projects such as this. In an Australian context, where Aboriginal communities face high levels of unemployment (comparable !Xun and Khwe joblessness rises above 70 per cent), Ryan and Huyton (2000: 54) go so far as to suggest that 'the promotion of Aboriginal tourism without a better understanding of the true nature of tourist demand is irresponsible, socially dangerous and obscene'.

Some broadening of the market appeal at Wildebeest Kuil might be achieved, questionnaire results implied, by 'value-adding' an eco-tourism aspect to the site, laying on organized tours from the city, and strengthening the 'archaeological route' with other sites in the region (Morris, et al., 2009). Encouraging more regular use by schools and the education department — current use is occasional — would not only boost gate-takings, but also afford substance to changed school curricula which now include pre-colonial history.

Support from the McGregor Museum, Kimberley

Given the low visitor numbers, prospects of achieving sustainable jobs at Wildebeest Kuil, with community benefits, had looked bleak. Funds left over from the original development of the site, meant to cushion initial outlays until sustainability was achieved, proved insufficient when the project failed to bottom out and grow. Guide and manager salaries, and the costs of lights and water, security, and insurance, exceeded income in gate-takings. Salaries themselves were low and, after training, several guides were lost to better-paid jobs (some moved to a community radio service, *XKfm*, and, as journalists, have proven useful allies for the site and for heritage).

Run at first by a dedicated Trust, Wildebeest Kuil may have been closed in less than five years had an annual subvention in terms of staff and funds not been secured from a provincial museum budget, channelled through the McGregor Museum, Kimberley. The museum deployed a permanent staff position at Wildebeest Kuil and created a further contract post on a much-improved salary scale. It further committed to training community members employed by the South African San Institute (SASI) at the Wildebeest Kuil craft shop (but given high SASI staff turn-over — up to seven individuals in nine months — no effective training could take place; the craft shop eventually closed before this intention could be fulfilled).

With museum support from the end of 2004, the Wildebeest Kuil Rock Art Centre reached a platform of subsidized sustainability. With staff in place, the maintenance and insurance safety-net proved essential (theft of the water pump and some 30,000 South African Rand worth of electrical cables in 2008 would have crippled the site without this support). Managing community expectations continued to be crucial. !Xun and Khwe interests became, if anything, more strongly represented, the Platfontein community being more widely consulted, in the planning of project enhancements after 2007. In light of this experience, at least under the circumstances prevailing in the region, it was questioned to what extent niche market heritage sites could or should be considered as sustainable job creation opportunities in the first instance (Jacobson, 2012; Morris, et al., 2009). At best, it seemed, the prospects would be marginal, although greatly improved where projects could be linked with and subsidized by existing organizations such as museums.

For as long as start-up funding lasted, a small staff complement from the !Xun and Khwe community was employed. In the longer term this could not be sustained, and revenues accruing to community members from the sale of craftwork at the site, because of low visitor numbers, have been limited. From the outset, running costs have exceeded gate-takings and other sources of income. If the Wildebeest Kuil Rock Art Centre has benefited the host community, it has done so not so much in tangible returns as in various intangible outcomes (discussed further below).

'Annus Horribilis'

As 2010 drew to a close, there should have been cause for satisfaction. Wildebeest Kuil was featuring more and more in various media including Johnny Clegg's art and landscape documentary, *A Country Imagined* (Curious Pictures, 2010); in an interactive educational book and DVD *Pathways Through the Interior* (AMA, 2011); and it was one of seven South African palaeoscience sites selected by the national Department of Science and Technology for multimedia treatment in a focused educational and tourism series that would include national newspaper coverage and a web blog (Inglis & Vilakazi, 2010). Posted on *Youtube* were stories about the site in the !Xun and Khwe languages (Khwe Elders, 2009; !Xun Elders, 2009). Wildebeest Kuil was also the venue for an international workshop on recording rock engravings, part of a Franco-South African collaboration on rock art, drawing students from several African countries, Europe and North America (Maina, 2010).

Further, in the hope of enhancing the tourism potential of the site, funding was secured for a number of capital interventions. Initiated by the provincial Department of Economic Development and Tourism, this included a project to upgrade and landscape the entrance area, providing improved parking, as well as a barbecue facility that might help to attract returning local visitors seeking weekend recreation outside the city. A planned extension of the building was to make extra display space available to tell more of the specific twentieth-century history of the !Xun and Khwe communities. A cycle route around the base of the hill was envisaged that would highlight the ecology of the site and thereby broaden its tourist appeal.

As the year ended, however, a devastating fire raged up the hill and destroyed the boardwalk that afforded visitors access to the engravings on the hilltop. Fortunately, the boardwalk had weaved between, rather than over, the engravings: the intense heat of the fire left a swathe of shattered rock in its path. The fire, fanned by wind, was started by youngsters from the community who hunted water-birds at the nearby dam, then cooked them on open fires alongside. Increasingly, the immediate environs of the rock art site have been a resource for a community under acute economic stress. Water was accessed here when the municipal supply to the township failed in 2010. In winter, trees on and around the hill are cut down for fuel. Anything made of metal that can be loosened or moved — including much of the fence around the site, electrical cabling and pumps, even old rusted heritage traces — are removed to exchange for cash at the scrap merchants.

Awareness of a worsening socio-economic context was already informing discussion about the site. An earlier McGregor Museum annual report (McGregor Museum, 2008) referred to Talia Soskolne's 2007 study which 'presented a stark reminder of the real context of poverty and need in the Platfontein setting', which was 'seemingly replicated a thousand times over across our largely rural province'. The report asked pertinently, 'whose interests are served by our archaeological work; who are these heritage sites we develop really for? Certainly not just tourists'. It warned against 'hyping the stereotypes and romanticising, as aspects of "culture", what in reality is rural poverty'. Projects should not be 'driven by short-term agendas and the imperatives of international/commercial tourism, at the longer-term expense of the local poor and needy'. The report asserted a commitment to 'seek in whatever ways we can to increase visitor numbers and gate-takings', while not compromising 'on the real issues and the integrity of the site and those involved in it' (McGregor Museum, 2008: 6).

Since 2010, the global economic downturn has impacted local tourism as a whole, reducing visitor numbers at Wildebeest Kuil still further. Far more critically, this has coincided with shrinking provincial government commitment to sustaining museums and heritage sites. A number of vacant posts in the museums unit in the Northern Cape were unfunded in early 2012, reducing the staff complement to below 60 per cent. Redeployment of one of the staff members from Wildebeest Kuil to a key position elsewhere became 'unavoidable', leading to closure of the Rock Art Centre over weekends from August 2012, until further notice. With opening hours then hinging on the availability of one staff member, the site is inevitably closed more often (when leave is owed to the guide, or when illness prevents him from being at his post). A year later, museum staff had fallen to below 50 per cent of posts filled.

Conclusions

The discussion above highlights the challenges to the sustainability and successes specific to Wildebeest Kuil, which are contingent on its unfolding dynamics. Some key issues emerge.

At the outset, conceptions of 'community' in the eyes of different players had a role in shaping the project. Expectations of more or less well-defined communities connected with particular segments of space and/or slices of the past prevailed as much amongst tourism planners as in the views of indigenous groups who are often more than willing to resort to a matching 'strategic essentialism' (Robins, 2001). A landscape of themed heritage spaces, much like a jigsaw puzzle, makes for neat tourism marketing in nodes and routes. But the sites themselves — Wildebeest Kuil being a prime example — seldom reflect this tidiness: if they are like jigsaw pieces, there are components from different puzzles layered up and dispersed across the landscape. Nor are the communities quite so coherent, with crosscutting interest groups (Jensen, 2004). Multiple stories and meanings in places represent convergences of dynamic social processes involving a diversity of people and groups through time. Perhaps one of the successes at Wildebeest Kuil has been the way complexity was negotiated and reflected — even if at times this threatened to derail the project.

Poverty issues have become increasingly significant in the decade since opening the site, with evidently burgeoning exploitation and theft of resources and property. Few of the !Xun and Khwe identify with a project which fails to deliver the material benefits it initially promised. Less easy to demonstrate than hard income are the intangible benefits such as open community access to the Centre as a venue for meetings and training workshops, and for hosting occasional government or United Nations visits — where the Wildebeest Kuil film projects community history to the outside world. On such occasions Wildebeest Kuil Rock Art Centre stands for community pride and self-esteem. Understandably clutching at any development opportunity, the leadership seriously entertains a current proposal for building a solar energy plant on land near to the site. Questions from Wildebeest Kuil about the plant's possible incompatibility with conservation and tourism have been described as tantamount to 'scientific elitism' opposing development. 'The engravings do not last', said one of the elders alluding to recent fire damage, 'but the sun lasts for ever'.

Operational constraints clearly constitute the single greatest threat to sustaining the Wildebeest Kuil Rock Art Centre. The department responsible for tourism in the Northern Cape — recently having invested in expansion and upgrades at the Centre (see above), and projecting itself as being well-positioned for promoting cultural and heritage tourism — indeed seeks to bolster and market the attraction. But ironically, just as it does so, the department managing museums and heritage has withdrawn the means for keeping the doors open over weekends and public holidays. The McGregor Museum, with reduced staffing, points also to increased operational costs consequent on capital upgrades, resulting in higher monthly outlays it can no longer afford. There must clearly be meaningful interaction and formal inter-departmental commitment around the development of heritage and tourism in order to pre-empt these kinds of problems. A comparable 'key problem factor' holding back sustainable rock art tourism in the Ukhahlamba Drakensberg Park, Duval and Smith (2012) have found, is, again, the division of responsibilities between separate management authorities — in that instance with respect to natural and cultural heritage — at a more proximate level within the park.

There remains much room for understanding the dynamics of heritage tourism, particularly archaeological and rock art tourism, in Southern Africa, so that we might better appreciate how sites could generate the hoped-for economic benefits (see Little & Borona: this volume). A pattern that emerges from work in the Ukhahlamba Drakensberg Park and in the current study at Wildebeest Kuil is that dominant tourism narratives about mountains and nature and the diamond mining story of Kimberley, respectively, displace rock art to a subsidiary position as local attractions. Another site in the region, Twyfelfontein in Namibia, by contrast, is a remote site without significant local competition, while situated along a major tourist route to the Etosha Pan: it gets some 60,000 visitors per annum (Duval & Smith, 2012: 148) more than the several Drakensberg sites and Wildebeest Kuil put together. It is clear that different configurations of sites relative to tourist behaviours, local marketing mantras, and operational support, give rise to varied outcomes.

The one setback that ought to have been preventable at Wildebeest Kuil was the removal of staff and consequent weekend closures. Jacobson (2012) would see this as symptomatic of a widespread crisis he refers to in South African museums today, in which provincial museum services, local museums and museum posts are being shut down or lost through lack of funding and political interest. The crisis unfolding at Wildebeest Kuil is being repeated, moreover, at the internationally significant Wonderwerk Cave, also in the Northern Cape. 'Large, grandiose politically-inspired projects flourish', adds Jacobson; but too often, in local rural settings, 'neglecting or closing down small community museums is nothing less than closing down their history' (2012: 149). Jacobson argues that the relevance of these local efforts should be measured not just in visitor numbers, but in terms of intangible benefits. Effectively, at Wildebeest Kuil, it is Khoisan history that, through the limiting of public access, for now over weekends, is being marginalized yet again. It is to be hoped that the implications of closing down this history would provoke a rethink and the restoration of the means for Wildebeest Kuil and other sites like it, many of them archaeological, to operate. Perhaps eventually they will shift perceptions to give pre-colonial history a more central place in the South African narrative.

Notes

[1] San refers to an indigenous minority, some of whom self-identify as Bushmen, erstwhile hunter-gatherers of Southern Africa.

[2] Khoisan is an anthropological term, coined by Schultze and popularized by Schapera (Barnard, 1992), referring to speakers of click languages in Southern Africa, historically known as 'Bushmen' and 'Hottentots'. Where possible or appropriate specific groups names such as !Xun or Khwe are used.

Bibliography

Africa meets Africa (AMA). 2011. The Africa meets Africa Project [accessed 1 May 2014]. Available at: <http://www.africameetsafrica.co.za/pathways.html>.

Association of Southern African Professional Archaeologists Transformation Action Committee (ATAC). 2009. ASAPA Transformation Action Committee: Unpublished Draft Proposed Strategic Plan for Implementing the Transformation Charter for South African Archaeology.

Barnard, A. 1992. *Hunters and Herders of Southern Africa: A Comparative Ethnography of the Khoisan Peoples.* Cambridge: Cambridge University Press.

Biesele, M. 1993. *Women Like Meat: The Folklore and Foraging Ideology of the Kalahari Ju/'hoan.* Johannesburg: Witwatersrand University Press.

Blundell, G. 1996. The Politics of Public Rock Art: A Comparative Critique of Rock Art Sites Open to the Public in South Africa and the United States of America. Unpublished Masters dissertation, University of the Witwatersrand, Johannesburg.

Burkitt, M. C. 1928. *South Africa's Past in Stone and Paint.* Cambridge: Cambridge University Press.

CKLM Consultancy. 2007. Wildebeest Kuil Rock Art Centre: Phases 3 & 4 Development Concept and Financial Model Report. Unpublished report.

Clark, J. D. 1959. *The Prehistory of Southern Africa.* Harmondsworth, UK: Penguin Books.

Curious Pictures. 2010. *A Country Imagined, with Johnny Clegg*. 13-part television documentary series, premiered on SABC2, 25 April 2010.

Deacon, J. 1993. Archaeological Sites as National Monuments in South Africa: A Review of Sites Declared Since 1936. *South African Historical Journal*, 29: 118–31.

De Prada-Samper, J. M. 2012. The Forgotten Killing Fields: 'San' Genocide and Louis Anthing's Mission to Bushmanland, 1862–1863. *Historia*, 57: 172–87.

Duval, M. & Smith, B. W. 2012. Rock Art Tourism in the uKhahlamba/Drakensberg World Heritage Site: Obstacles to the Development of Sustainable Tourism. *Journal of Sustainable Tourism*, 21: 134–53.

Fock, G. J. 1965. Two Rock Engravings from South Africa in the British Museum. *Man*, 65: 194–95.

Inglis, R. & Vilakazi, N. 2010. The Sans of Time. *Sunday Times*, 18 October 2010 [accessed 17 April 2014]. Available at: <http://www.timeslive.co.za/lifestyle/travel/2010/10/18/the-sans-of-time>.

Ingold, T. 1993. The Temporality of the Landscape. *World Archaeology*, 25: 152–74.

Jacobson, L. 2012. Review of Holo & Alvarez, 2009, eds. Beyond the Turnstile: Making the Case for Museums and Sustainable Values. *South African Archaeological Bulletin*, 67: 148–49.

Jensen, S. 2004. Claiming Community: Local Politics on the Cape Flats, South Africa. *Critique of Anthropology*, 24: 179–207.

Khwe Elders. 2009. Wildebeest Kuil — Khwe [accessed 17 April 2014]. Available at: <https://www.youtube.com/watch?v=WqoiqEWtA6U&noredirect=1>.

Laue, G., Turkington, T., & Smith, B. 2001. Presenting South African Rock Art to the World: Two Major New Rock Art Site Developments for 2002. *The Digging Stick*, 18(3): 5–7.

Mahony, K. & van Zyl, J. 2002. The Impacts of Tourism Investment on Rural Communities: Three Case Studies in South Africa. *Development South Africa*, 19: 83–103.

Maina, E. 2010. Kimberley Rock Engravings Workshop. *TARA Newsletter*, 12 (December 2010) [accessed 17 April 2014]. Available at: <http://africanrockart.org/wp-content/uploads/2013/10/TARA-Newsletter-No.-12.pdf>.

Martin, J. P. 2008. *A Millimetre of Dust: Visiting Ancestral Sites*. Cape Town, SA: Kwela Books.

Mazel, A. D. 2008. Presenting the San Hunter-Gatherer Past to the Public: A View from the uKhahlamba-Drakensberg Park, South Africa. *Conservation and Management of Archaeological Sites*, 10: 41–51.

McGregor Museum. 2008. Annual Report 2007/8 [accessed 17 April 2014]. Available at: <http://www.museumsnc.co.za/aboutus/AnnualReports/Annual%20Report%202007-8.pdf>.

Meskell, L. & Scheermeyer, C. 2008. Heritage as Therapy: Set Pieces from the New South Africa. *Journal of Material Culture*, 13: 153–73.

Morris, D. 1989. Archaeology for Tomorrow: The Site Museum as Classroom at Nooitgedacht. *Southern African Museums Association Bulletin (SAMAB)*, 18(8): 291–94.

Morris, D. 2003. Rock Art as Source and Resource: Research and Responsibility Towards Education, Heritage and Tourism. *South African Historical Journal*, 49: 193–206.

Morris, D. 2012. The Importance of Wildebeest Kuil: 'a hill with a future, a hill with a past'. In: B. Smith, K. Helskog, and D. Morris, eds. *Working with Rock Art: Recording, Presenting and Understanding Rock Art Using Indigenous Knowledge*. Johannesburg, SA: Wits University Press.

Morris, D., Ndebele, B., & Wilson, P. 2009. Who is Interested in the Wildebeest Kuil Rock Art Centre? Preliminary Results from a Visitor Questionnaire. *The Digging Stick*, 26(2): 17–18, 23.

Péringuey, L. 1909. On Rock Engravings of Animals and the Human Figure Found in South Africa. *Transactions of the South African Philosophical Society of South Africa*, 18: 401–20.

Roberts, B. 1976. *Kimberley, Turbulent City*. Cape Town, SA: David Phillip.

Robins, S. 2001. NGOs, 'Bushmen' and Double Vision: The Khomani San Land Claim and the Cultural Politics of 'community' and 'development' in the Kalahari. *Journal of Southern African Studies*, 27: 833–53.

Ryan, C. & Huyton, J. 2000. Who is Interested in Aboriginal Tourism in the Northern Territory, Australia? A Cluster Analysis. *Journal of Sustainable Tourism*, 8(1): 53–88.

Schoeman, K. 1995. Kausob. In: E. J. Verwey, E. W. Verwey, and N. E. Sonderling, eds. *New Dictionary of South African Biography*, 1: 110–12. Pretoria, SA: HSRC Publishers.

Science & Technology Department (STD). 2011. The South African Strategy for the Palaeosciences, 23 August. Unpublished draft for discussion.

Sharp, J. & Douglas, S. 1996. Prisoners of their Reputation? The Veterans of the 'Bushman' Battalions in South Africa. In: P. Skotnes, ed. *Miscast: Negotiating the Presence of the Bushmen*. Cape Town, SA: University of Cape Town Press, pp. 323–29.

Smith, B. W., Lewis-Williams, J. D., Blundell, G., & Chippindale, C. 2001. Archaeology and Symbolism in the New South African Coat of Arms. *Antiquity*, 74: 467–68.

Soskolne, T. 2007. 'Being San' in Platfontein: Poverty, Landscape, Development and Cultural Heritage. Unpublished Masters thesis, University of Cape Town.

Stow, G. W. 1905. *The Native Races of South Africa*. London: Swan, Sonnenschein.

The Big Hole (TBH). 2013. Homepage [accessed 17 April 2014]. Available at: <http://www.thebighole.co.za/>.

Turkington, T. 2000. Realising a Dream: Canteen Kopje and the New Barkly West Museum. *The Digging Stick*, 17(3): 1–3.

Turkington, T. 2001. Northern Cape Rock Art Tourism Project: Co-Ordinator's Report, May 2001. Unpublished report to Steering Committee, Kimberley, 3–4 May 2001.

Van Jaarsveld, F. A. 1969. *New Illustrated History, Standard VI*. Johannesburg, SA: Voortrekkerpers.

Weiss, L. M. 2005. The Social Life of Rock Art: Materiality, Consumption, and Power in South African Heritage. In: L. Meskell, ed. *Archaeologies of Materiality*. London: Blackwell, pp. 46–70.

Weiss, L. M. 2007. Heritage-making and Political Identity. *Journal of Social Archaeology*, 7: 413–31.

Weiss, L. M. 2009. Fictive Capital and Economies of Desire: A Case Study of Illegal Diamond Buying and Apartheid Landscapes in 19th Century Southern Africa. Unpublished PhD dissertation, Columbia University.

Weiss, L. M. 2012. Rock Art at Present in the Past. In: B. Smith, K. Helskog, and D. Morris, eds. *Working with Rock Art: Recording, Presenting and Understanding Rock Art Using Indigenous Knowledge*. Johannesburg: Wits University Press, pp. 217–27.

Wildebeest Kuil. 2013. About [accessed 17 April 2014]. Available at: <http://www.wildebeestkuil.itgo.com/>.

Wilman, M. 1933. *The Rock Engravings of Griqualand West and Bechuanaland, South Africa*. Cambridge, UK: Deighton Bell.

!Xun Elders. 2009. Wildebeest Kuil Story, told in !Xun [accessed 17 April 2014]. Available at: <https://www.youtube.com/watch?v=CQVHs9yPFZs>.

Notes on contributor

David Morris, a graduate of the Universities of Cape Town and the Western Cape, heads archaeology at the McGregor Museum, Kimberley, in South Africa. His principal interest and doctoral research focused on rock art in South Africa's Northern Cape Province. He has an involvement in developing public archaeology projects in the area, including Wildebeest Kuil. His publications include the co-authored *Karoo Rock Engravings* (with John Parkington and Neil Rusch, 2008) and co-editorship of *Working with Rock Art* (with Ben Smith and Knut Helskog, 2012).

Correspondence to: David Morris, McGregor Museum, PO Box 316, Kimberley, 8300, South Africa. Email: dmorriskby@gmail.com

PUBLIC ARCHAEOLOGY, Vol. 13 Nos 1–3, 2014, 200–12

Heritage and Development: Lessons from Cambodia

Dougald J. W. O'Reilly

The Australian National University, Australia

The destruction of cultural heritage is motivated by many factors, but most often in the developing world the motivation is extreme poverty. Local people living in areas rich in cultural heritage assets are often either mute bystanders to theft or active participants, encouraged by middlemen to excavate illicitly or chip ornamentation from temples. Heritage Watch, an international heritage preservation organization, launched an initiative at the Koh Ker temple complex in Cambodia that stressed the sustainable use of heritage and education for the benefit of preservation. The lessons learned during this project have been applied in the organization's new initiative at Banteay Chhmar, Cambodia.

KEYWORDS heritage, development, Cambodia, lessons, looting

Introduction

In December 2008, the Australian Government announced an AUD$1.13 million grant to assist the Cambodian Government to better protect the archaeological site of Angkor, a World Heritage site (McMullan, 2008). This grant is just the latest in a series of efforts that integrate heritage and socio-economic development in Cambodia, one of the poorest countries in Asia.

After decades of conflict beginning in the 1970s, including the war between Lon Nol and the communist insurgence, the arduous period of Khmer Rouge rule and the later invasion of Cambodia by Vietnam, Cambodia's infrastructure was in poor condition. Cambodia's fortunes began to change with the signing of the 1991 Paris Peace Accords. Since the late 1990s Cambodia has become more politically stable and the country's economy saw incredible growth in the mid-2000s and has averaged over 6 per cent per annum since (CIA, 2012). This growth is attributable to favourable agreements with the United States Government in the manufacture of clothing in addition to the development of tourism (Guimbert, 2011).

Steps have been made in rebuilding civil society and government institutions, including the interior police and taxation office and the institution of democratic elections. These improvements have been heavily supported by the international

   DOI 10.1179/1465518714Z.00000000071

community and many non-governmental organizations (NGOs). Problems, however, still exist. The majority of Cambodians do not work in either the clothing or tourism sectors, but are engaged in agricultural activities, a sector which has seen little improvement. This situation has resulted in a widening gulf between rich and poor in Cambodia. It also has a negative effect on heritage as rural poverty has been linked to the destruction of archaeological sites in efforts to generate income. Aid agencies continually highlight a lack of government investment in the rural sector, high child mortality rates, poor secondary education (particularly for girls), poor access to affordable energy, and unsustainable natural resource exploitation as well as endemic corruption (AusAID, 2003; NZAid, 2006).

Angkor is a sprawling temple site which was inscribed as a World Heritage site in 1992 (UNESCO, 2013). It is receiving increasing numbers of visitors, topping two million people annually in past years. Clearly such visitors have the potential to have a significant socio-cultural impact on the communities around the World Heritage site in terms of poverty reduction. However, such numbers may simultaneously negatively impact the archaeological site and the monuments that populate the landscape.

Heritage and development projects

The reason for the Australian government aid noted above (the cultural value of the site notwithstanding) was the role of Angkor as an income generator for Cambodia. The Australian Parliamentary Secretary for International Development Assistance, Bob McMullan, noted 'Angkor is Cambodia's most valuable tourism and heritage asset. This initiative will help local communities boost their incomes by participating in the tourism industry, drawing on their unique culture and history' (Garrett, 2008). These comments were echoed by Australian Ambassador to Cambodia, Margaret Adamson who noted, 'The [. . .] project will assist in conserving the universal heritage values of Angkor while improving governance and helping to reduce rural poverty' (quoted in Anon., 2009).

The Australian government funding supports a project called the Angkor Heritage Management Framework (AHMF), which is designed to strengthen the technical expertise and governance of the Authority for Protection and Management of Angkor and the Region of Siem Reap (APSARA), the government agency responsible for managing the Angkor Heritage Park. The hope is that 'the benefits of tourism and development at Angkor can be shared fairly, as well as to ensure environmental protection' (Anon., 2009: 10). APSARA clearly has a considerable challenge in managing the vast and varied site of Angkor, which includes a sprawling temple complex, the town of Siem Reap, and a huge area of agricultural land and associated villages.

The AHMF project builds on research by Sydney University's 'Living with Heritage Project' (LWH) which aimed 'to connect conservation policy to the dynamic interaction between cultural heritage, society and the natural environment' (LWH, 2008: 10). This pilot project assessed whether it was possible to establish a framework to manage heritage faced with a number of challenges including increasing tourist numbers and hotel development, land clearance for new farms and homes as people moved to the region to find work, and the attendant potential damage to monuments and the ecology this movement of people may have sparked. The stated aim of the LWH project was to create a monitoring system that would track, visualize, and compare change over time to create a tool for World Heritage site managers to use in implementing policies to achieve sustainable development of a site while being mindful of community needs. The outcome was to be a focus on heritage values and clarity in management objectives that relate both to local community development and to on-the-ground implementation of site management (Fletcher, et al., 2007). A monitoring system using Geographical Information Systems (GIS), remote sensing, and diachronic visualization is hoped to be used to better implement Cambodia's national heritage policies.

The HMF project is not the only initiative that attempted to integrate heritage in efforts to reduce rural poverty to be implemented at Angkor. The New Zealand government invested NZ$5 million in 2010/11 in Cambodia, NZ$1.5 million of which went to a project that was aimed at a providing support to APSARA. In a strikingly similar effort to the Australian grant project above, the New Zealand Aid Programme is assisting with the implementation of the 'Angkor Participatory Natural Resource Management and Livelihoods project' (see NZAid, n.d.) with the goal of assisting park communities to increase their livelihood opportunities from natural resources and tourism in a sustainable manner. It appears as if there are competing and overlapping goals in the Australian and New Zealand strategies at Angkor. The New Zealand plan was to implement 'A well-integrated and sustainable park management plan that introduces the practical principles of co-management between the government and the local communities in and around the park' (Someth & De Silva, 2006: 123). It was proposed that the project would also spur social and economic empowerment for the 'poor local communities' through community development and environmental initiatives. To support these initiatives in an ongoing manner, it was also proposed that legislation and a regulatory framework be implemented.

Heritage Watch

Other, more modest efforts at poverty reduction have been made. Heritage Watch[1] is a non-profit organization, which has been working since 2003 to protect Cambodia's archaeological resources. The organization was formed as a reaction to the dramatic increase in heritage destruction in Cambodia since 2001, a trend spurred largely by poverty. Villagers around Cambodia began to illegally excavate archaeological sites and sell the artefacts they found at local markets or to middlemen. Prior to the implementation of the poverty reduction and heritage project discussed in this paper, Heritage Watch had implemented a number of projects including researching the trade of illicit Cambodian antiquities and documenting at-risk sites across the country, increasing the likelihood that looted objects will be recovered. Since the antiquities trade survives largely on ignorance of both those who loot and buy antiquities, education is a vital effort. With generous funding from the US Department of State, Heritage Watch launched a national public awareness campaign in 2004, using informative radio and television commercials, educational comic and storybooks, and community workshops for villagers in heavily looted areas (Heritage Watch, 2014a). Tourists were also informed about the negative consequences of buying looted antiquities through public exhibits, a tourism magazine, and a business certification campaign called 'Heritage Friendly Tourism' (Heritage Watch, 2014b).

Another long-term goal of Heritage Watch is to address the main cause of looting, which is primarily poverty. Cambodia's temples are one of the country's most important economic resources, as they are the impetus behind the country's growing tourism industry. If properly developed, this industry will be a sustainable means of bettering the lives of the Cambodian people and protecting their heritage. Heritage Watch is therefore interested in informing local people about the heritage resources they live with and encouraging the development of a tourist industry that is sound yet profitable.

The following section will discuss two case studies, demonstrating Heritage Watch's efforts at mitigating heritage loss through community development projects.

Koh Ker project

Background

With the above goals in mind, Heritage Watch implemented a project at Koh Ker, a former capital of Cambodia, located in a remote part of the country's Preah Vihear Province. The city, 60 km north of Angkor, was built in the tenth century with architecture of a scale that is impressive even in comparison with the temples of Angkor. It was not, however, built practically, as its location lacked a reliable water supply. The capital returned to Angkor within the century (Coe, 2005).

Due to Koh Ker's former inaccessibility — it was in Khmer Rouge territory until 1998, and efforts to remove landmines leftover from the civil war are only recent — it was an ideal target for looters. Looting reached a height in the 1990s, but continues today, largely driven by poverty. The people of Koh Ker are very poor, and many are widows and amputees. Based on interviews with local villagers, it seems the poverty has been further exacerbated by heavy logging, largely illegal, which has drastically reduced the community's already scant natural resources. Koh Ker has the potential to become one of Cambodia's main tourist destinations, since it can now be visited as a day-trip from Siem Reap (the town closest to Angkor, the country's principal tourist attraction). But tourism will only benefit the site — and the local community — if developed in a sustainable manner.

From June 2007 through December 2008, Heritage Watch implemented a project aimed at reducing poverty at Koh Ker and surrounding villages. The first stage in the project was an assessment of training needs and the level of local poverty in the target area. A number of significant issues were identified in the communities around the temple site of Koh Ker. The majority of the population survives through subsistence farming and hunting, with 85 per cent living on less than one US dollar a day. Ninety-five per cent of the villagers were found to be illiterate (Heritage Watch, 2009). While most of Cambodia has enjoyed peace and physical security since the 1990s, the Koh Ker village chief stated that the process of reconciliation and reintegration did not occur in the Koh Ker area until 2000 (Heritage Watch, 2009). Many of the local community are former Khmer Rouge combatants and had become conditioned to an isolationist mentality. Working in the area, Heritage Watch staff found many people to be very shy or even afraid of outsiders. As the project progressed, it became apparent that there were also serious alcohol abuse and family violence problems at Koh Ker.

Other less serious issues also impact the community and consequently any effort to implement a sustainable development and capacity-building project. Such development projects typically rely on community participation and group decision-making. At Koh Ker there is a lack of public participation in the local decision-making process, although this centralized top-down system is largely characteristic of Cambodian society as a whole. Community meetings are usually held solely for the purpose of providing information to the locals and organized under the authority of the village or commune chief. There is no 'up-flow' of information in these communities.

Clearly, these issues present serious impediments to establishing a successful business model based around heritage tourism at the village level. The above issues are further compounded by the distinct lack of awareness about heritage issues, especially regarding local responsibility for heritage preservation and protection. Looting is an issue that, according to most respondents from the village of Koh Ker, is 'up to the authorities'. It should, however, be acknowledged that, in our experience, it is not locals who engage in looting but outsiders who are often protected (even to the point of being armed) by high-ranking groups or individuals. There remains a lack of trust between the villagers at Koh Ker and authorities, the result being that the former are often too intimidated to report cases of looting at the site.

The villagers around Koh Ker have limited exposure to tourism and local communities do not gain considerable benefits from this or related activities. This can be attributed to a lack of basic education or experience in small business activities and poor access to resources in general. On major Cambodian public holidays, when considerable numbers of visitors come to Koh Ker, non-local people arrive at the site to set up short-term businesses selling souvenirs and food while the locals continue to engage in subsistence activities.

Implementing the project

The challenges faced by Heritage Watch in implementing the project were substantial, including trying to inculcate an awareness of tourism marketing, basic language skills (in Khmer as well as English), establishing small and medium-sized enterprises, and teaching technical knowledge of the temples. All are exceptionally difficult challenges for the majority of local people. Engagement with NGOs in a sustained manner was also a new phenomenon for many of the villagers. There are very few NGOs operating in the area, although some visit on a bi/tri-monthly basis to provide awareness or treatment for malaria prevention, child health, or basic service provision.

To promote the protection of the Koh Ker temple complex while providing a sustainable development strategy that ensured the people in the region would directly benefit, a number of strategies were implemented for the project. Heritage Watch committed itself to providing education to the local community on the value of heritage conservation by conducting Community Heritage Awareness Meetings and helping to protect the temples by forming the Community Heritage Patrols (ChiPs). Heritage Watch was committed to improving the livelihoods of the local community at Koh Ker through tourism by providing training in both Khmer and English literacy, tourist guiding, small business management, ox-cart tours, product development, and merchandising training, beekeeping, and ceramic production. Heritage Watch also established a Day Care Centre for pre-primary education.

The Community Heritage Awareness Meetings targeted 156 beneficiaries over six separate meetings, plus two further meetings with visiting tourists and one with a local travel agency. The training focused on the importance of heritage protection and the services and work being undertaken in the area by Heritage Watch. It again became clear as a result of this training that villagers themselves were not involved in the looting and were strongly opposed to it. This fact made the integration of the CHiPs a simpler matter. Eleven villagers in Koh Ker commune were selected for participation in the CHiPs project with the aim of assisting in the reporting of heritage theft to the local authorities, including the Ministry of Interior's Heritage Police and the APSARA authority. Each of the participants received a bicycle, facilitating ease of movement while patrolling the extensive temple complex and increased speed for reporting problems. The bicycles also assisted individual patrol members in their daily income generation activities, such as collecting and transporting water, food, firewood, and so on. To encourage pride, dignity, and recognition while patrolling the temple complex, each patrol member was supplied with a khaki uniform and 25 kg of rice per month (worth about USD$10) which provided basic assistance to patrol member's families in an area where it is estimated that food security is assured for only four to six months per year (Heritage Watch, 2009).

Several training initiatives were attempted to improve relevant skills in the villages. During the first three months of project implementation, twenty-five local adults attended daily literacy classes for three and a half hours per day. After the construction of a field office/training centre, fifty-six local teenagers were selected and divided into three classes that came to study English two and a half hours every day for the first three months of the project. Local teenagers and adults received two hours of training per week on the history of Koh Ker temple and the optimum ways to safely explore the complex. The training also included lessons on morality in relation to heritage protection.

Eleven Koh Ker villagers were encouraged to identify basic small business concepts to help them create tourism-based revenue streams through hourly workshops held three times a week during the project period. To encourage the establishment of sustainable heritage-based business activities, the target community was provided with two oxen and an adapted traditional cart. The aim was that the cart would be used to take tourists around the site in a traditional manner. The target group was also provided with necessary training and materials to produce palm-sugar candies in moulds that replicated traditional Cambodian themes (i.e. temple shapes and Apsara dancers[2]). The production of these innovative treats was sustainable as there are many sugar-palm trees in the area and the villagers already extract palm juice from this resource. The aim was to sell these candies at the site, as well as establishing an ongoing contract with some of the larger hotels in Siem Reap for retail possibilities as well as use in 'on-pillow gifts' for guests.

In a similar vein, training in honey extraction was organized for the local community. Honey is a commodity that is in great demand by Siem Reap's high-end hotels and there is a plentiful supply in the forests surrounding Koh Ker. This component of the training was out-sourced to apiary experts who encouraged the villagers to collect wild honey and establish hives on their own properties. Additionally, Heritage Watch was approached by an NGO with an interest in re-invigorating traditional ceramic production techniques as part of the larger Heritage Watch project at Koh Ker. The aim was to have a ceramic product that could be locally produced and sold.

All of the above activities were demanding on the participants and required a significant reorganization of their use of time. To assist participants in the project and to provide basic education and communication skills to children prior to beginning primary school, Heritage Watch established a day care centre with a local woman as its facilitator. The centre, which was established through generous assistance of the NGO, Protect the Earth, Protect Yourself (PEPY), provided training to children aged three to five years old in basic skills, such as polite greetings, basic literacy, and mathematics.

I will return later in the paper to review the outcomes of the Koh Ker project, but now will address the latest Heritage Watch initiative.

Banteay Chhmar

In January 2008, the Global Heritage Fund, a US-based non-profit organization, launched an architectural conservation project at Banteay Chhmar. One of the project goals was to develop local tourism capacity and Heritage Watch was invited to participate in building the capacity of local people around the temple site. In 2009, the Archaeological Institute of America awarded Heritage Watch a Site Preservation Grant to support Heritage Watch's proposed Banteay Chhmar Heritage Protection Project (Heritage Watch, 2014c). The aim of the project is to ensure that the local community near the Angkorian-period temple of Banteay Chhmar is prepared and properly trained to manage and implement sustainable heritage tourism practices to ensure the long-term preservation of the site.

Banteay Chhmar is a temple that was constructed during the reign of King Jayavarman VII at the end of twelfth century CE (Coe, 2005) and has great potential to attract tourists to a remote part of Cambodia. The temple, with its enigmatic 'face-towers', is similar to Jayavarman's state temple called the Bayon at Angkor. Regrettably, the temple has faced several depredations, including the theft of a 12 m section of wall decorated with Buddha images. Fortunately, the wall was intercepted on its way to Thailand and is now displayed at the National Museum (Mydans, 1999). The area around Banteay Chhmar is also notable for the proliferation of Prehistoric sites, many of which have, regrettably, been looted. Given all these factors, the area is an excellent location for Heritage Watch activities.

One of the Heritage Watch project goals is to ensure the benefits of tourism development are filtered back into the local community and distributed appropriately amongst community stakeholders as part of the Community Based Tourism (CBT) group, which was organized in 2007. The goal is to increase local interest in the preservation of Banteay Chhmar, ensuring the site is protected and development is sustainable. Through English language training, guide training, and Heritage Protection Workshops, the members of the local CBT group will become the stewards and protectors of the site of Banteay Chhmar. As tourism at Banteay Chhmar increases, the CBT members will be trained in English and as professional guides, enabling them to directly benefit financially from tourists and visitors to the Banteay Chhmar area.

Through 'Heritage Protection Workshops', Heritage Watch is implementing outreach programmes to educate the general public and local communities of the importance of protecting the cultural heritage of Banteay Chhmar and Cambodia as a whole. The Heritage Protection Workshops have focused on educating local communities about the importance of cultural heritage, its protection, and the long-term benefits, both cultural and economic, of preserving and protecting their local and national cultural heritage. These programmes are being undertaken in close cooperation with the Cambodian Ministry of Culture and Fine Arts.

The first workshop focused on the issue of looting of archaeological sites and its impacts. Heritage Watch provided a comic book and children's book in Khmer focusing on looting and its impacts in Cambodia, as well as other printed information in both Khmer and English languages. For the second workshop, the target audience of eighty-two people was the wider community of Banteay Meanchey Province as well as relevant government and non-government organizations. The event was also covered by local and national media, providing wider reach for the messages being communicated by Heritage Watch.

One of the most important aspects of the project, if the CBT are to be able to adequately host and guide visitors to the site, is English language training. To this end, Heritage Watch recruited an English language teacher to work with the students at Banteay Chhmar, liaising with the relevant CBT members. After an English language assessment of the CBT members, fourteen individuals were selected for the programme and the group was separated into two levels of English classes, beginner and intermediate. Students attending classes receive a stipend to support their families while they are unable to work because of their studies.

Heritage Watch will also launch a Guide Training Programme (GTP) and will produce a guide manual for the training of current and future guides. The CBT members who successfully complete the English language training programme will participate in the GTP. Upon completion of the GTP, the aim is to have the CBT members receive certification from the Department of Tourism in Banteay Meanchey. In the first year of the project Heritage Watch has secured support from the Ministry of Culture and Fine Arts, the Department of Tourism in Banteay Meanchey, the District Governor, the Head of Provincial Department of Culture, the Head of Heritage Police Unit in Banteay Chhmar, the Chief of Commune, and the Chief of the Village. It has also implemented an English language program at Banteay Chhmar and maintained an 80 per cent attendance rate of students for the year. Further, two Heritage Protection Workshops have been conducted, one for all CBT members and the second for the wider community.

Discussion

The efforts at Banteay Chhmar are less ambitious in many ways that those at Koh Ker and the two communities differ in many ways. At Banteay Chhmar, a CBT group already existed. The level of interest and organizational capacity of those involved in this initiative clearly exceeded that of the participants at Koh Ker. The Koh Ker project has provided a number of lessons for Heritage Watch with regard to implementing a traditional sustainable development-style project in relation to a heritage resource. Some components of the project were more successful than others, and the particular challenges of working in a remote rural area added to the difficulty in implementing the project.

The Community Heritage awareness training and patrols were embraced by all stakeholders and the target groups participated fully and were very motivated with regard to these activities. This component of the project was bolstered with additional media such as Heritage Watch sponsored national TV spots and the posting of Heritage Watch awareness/anti-looting posters and pamphlets in the target area. Since Heritage Watch's arrival in the target area, only two minor heritage-related incidents were reported — an act of vandalism and an attempted theft. The success of this component of the project notwithstanding, there were some apparent political barriers that impeded efforts at raising local heritage awareness at Koh Ker. In the concluding months of the project the APSARA Authority requested that Heritage Watch terminate the heritage patrol component of the project for unspecified reasons. Heritage Watch complied with the request following Heritage Watch's policy of engaging with and respecting all levels of local authority.

The skills-training initiatives had mixed success. In general, the participants enjoyed the literacy training and improvements were observed. Most fared better on basic calculations than reading or writing. By the end of the project, only eleven local adults continued attending the classes, but their ability to read and write Khmer script had greatly improved. After the initial three months of the English language training, numbers decreased due to access issues and agricultural commitments during the monsoon season. By the end of the project, only twelve people continued to actively attend class. Although their English had improved, it was still not to the level required for holding conversations with international visitors to the temples. A similar result was observed in Banteay Chhmar. Based on feedback from the English language teacher and test results from the students, it became clear that the students did not, after the first year, possess the required level of English language skills to participate in the Guide Training Programme. As a result, Heritage Watch will carry out a second year of English language training and push the start date for the guide training back by several months.

The weekly training on the history of Koh Ker greatly improved the target group's knowledge, and, more importantly, their confidence when talking to visitors about the Koh Ker complex. The low levels of basic education in the target group made formal understanding of small business concepts a challenge for the Heritage Watch trainers, but some of the participants were experienced market/subsistence agricultural traders, and these individuals made progress in the formal understanding of concepts such as market pricing, stock, and sales.

Though there were limited results in terms of the local Koh Ker population immediately being able to engage in revenue raising activities, considerable advances were made. Importantly, the local target community became aware of tourism as a sustainable source of income that is predicated on the preservation of the Koh Ker temple complex. Equally significant was the reversal of the insular attitude of the target community. The majority of the stakeholders are now far more confident and welcoming of visitors to the area. Given the turbulent recent history of the area, this is a considerable advance. The greatest success of the training components has been recognition of the villagers' efforts by the APSARA Authority and the better relations that have been fostered between the parties. At the start of the project, only twenty villagers were employed with APSARA as cleaners and patrol members. It was learned there were considerable misunderstandings between these stakeholders and the Heritage Watch Team worked hard to resolve them. By project's end, fifty villagers were employed by APSARA and they had improved their daily income generation, thus contributing to reducing poverty. APSARA are pleased with an increased awareness of what is required by employees (e.g. not leaving their post without permission).

In general, progress on support for small business activities was slow but steady. The major challenges were a combination of participants' poor levels of education and a reluctance to try new approaches. Persuading the target group to rely less on agriculture (which is insufficiently productive to provide food) and forest foraging to create tourist-based revenue streams requires a long-term programme of support, monitoring, and trust-building. A one-year project timeframe was inadequate to achieve these goals and funding to extend the project was sought but not acquired. The ox-cart tours, while appealing, were not very successful because the majority of visitors to Koh Ker, coming by bus, do not have enough time to travel in this way, preferring to explore the temples on foot. The creation of palm-sugar candies was also a challenge for Heritage Watch, as it was exceptionally difficult to persuade villagers to shift from using palm juice to make alcoholic wine (a highly popular local beverage) to producing the candy to sell to visitors.

Due to continued production problems relating to this reticence, the commercial connections with Siem Reap hotels was never established. The honey collection and home production of honey also was beset by problems. The local community are exceptionally adept and experienced at utilizing bees in the forest. However, their collection methods are unsustainable because they harvest entire hives, reducing the likelihood of a continued bee population in the area. Participants were encouraged to harvest just a part of the hive and to establish hives on their own properties and harvest honey sustainably and conveniently, but it was difficult to persuade the majority of participants to abandon their traditional practices. With the ongoing depletion of natural forest, the current system is not sustainable, and the four families that were convinced to try the new method have continued to produce honey on their own land and will, in the long term, enjoy the benefits.

The ceramic production training was the most challenging part of the project and as a result there was a five- to six-month extension required on the initial project timeframe. The target beneficiaries expressed greater interest in this component than any other, but there were problems because the external expert was inconsistent in offering the training.

The Koh Ker community continues to suffer from extreme poverty, poor education, a lack of social services, and decreasing access to dwindling natural forest resources on which they have relied for decades. Domestic violence continues to be a serious problem in Koh Ker (as with many other deeply impoverished and remote Cambodian communities) — 85 per cent of women surveyed reported that their husbands are abusive towards their wives or children when they are drunk or unhappy (Heritage Watch, 2009).

Yet, even considering the difficulties and challenges faced in the implementation of the Heritage Watch Sustainable Development and Heritage Preservation Project at Koh Ker, there were many positive outcomes. Based on post-project surveys, most participating villagers reported feeling more committed to heritage preservation and understanding more about the benefits of the temples for all stakeholders. Many of those involved in the project overcame their shyness and social isolation, and are now welcoming and talkative to visitors to the temples. Business activity in Koh Ker village has expanded beyond the one grocery shop in existence at the project's start. More importantly, there is a better, though still very basic, awareness of market forces relating to tourism. Social participation at Koh Ker improved at the project's conclusion with monthly meetings between local stakeholders organized by the chiefs of the villages. Local micro-credit agencies were also becoming established in the area assisting families to organize weddings, build houses, invest in agricultural equipment, and so on. It also appears that Heritage Watch's efforts were instrumental in encouraging education in Koh Ker. More children attended school than before the project was implemented, and many local children utilized the day care centre library, now sadly destroyed by a fire.

The Heritage Watch Koh Ker project has gained considerable public attention at the local, national, and international levels (Shelton & Amrak, 2007; *The Guardian*, 2009). As a result, the issues of the preservation of the Koh Ker temple complex, the importance of wider heritage protection, the positive impact of heritage tourism and the sustainability of involving local stakeholders have been widely accepted. The Heritage Watch Koh Ker project has been recognized as a sustainable model by the APSARA Authority and UNESCO, the latter of which used the project as a basis for the Creative Industries Support Programme and requested Heritage Watch to be involved in the drafting of the successful funding proposal for that programme.

In 2009, the Archaeological Institute of America awarded Heritage Watch the prestigious 'Preservation Award' for its efforts at Koh Ker (AIA, 2009). Heritage Watch acknowledges that the greatest challenge facing the Koh Ker temple complex is tourist numbers increasing faster than the potential capacity of local stakeholders to exponentially benefit from them. There have also been further efforts to integrate the local community at Koh Ker in development of the site as a tourist destination by the Hungarian Jaya Koh Ker Project (JKKP). The Hungarian team has reported similar challenges in working with the villagers of Koh Ker to those experienced by Heritage Watch (RAF, 2009). Heritage Watch is incorporating the lessons learned at Koh Ker to its current development project at Banteay Chhmar temple, and it is hoped that this initiative will provide the building blocks for an independent community-based tourism industry that will not only serve to enrich the local population but encourage the preservation of the temples and surrounding archaeological sites.

Conclusion

Archaeologists and heritage professionals are concerned about the preservation of heritage around the world, but it is rare that heritage can be separated from a local community, and this fact means there will always be pressure on the heritage resources if that community is not economically secure. It is for this reason that UNESCO's World Heritage Committee has strict guidelines regarding the management of such sites. Pressure on heritage sites can be especially intense in the developing world and, as such, Cambodia is a good case study for the intersection of heritage preservation and local social development needs. As we have seen in the review above, a broad spectrum of projects have been implemented in Cambodia that seek to integrate heritage and development.

It is clear that there are significant challenges to be overcome by the agencies charged with managing heritage sites and dealing with the various impacts on local communities and the demands of those communities. In some cases communities that live in proximity to heritage sites have yet to benefit from their situation. There is tremendous potential for implementing sustainable tourism and development projects at such heritage sites, but it is crucial that the process be carefully planned and implemented. Local communities need to be provided with the tools required to successfully transition from a subsistence agricultural existence to one based on revenue from tourism. Legislation also needs to be used to protect the local population's right to benefit from a heritage site so that others with better skills and education do not appropriate the heritage resource for their own benefit at the expense of extant communities.

In preparing local communities to benefit from their local heritage resources and to actively protect it, it is important to be cognizant of local conditions (i.e. education levels, social problems, political relationships, general capability and the attitude of participants). Heritage NGOs should collaborate closely with experienced development NGOs to avoid duplication of mistakes. For example, it is important to work with the middle range of society in terms of poverty, not the most impoverished, as their capacity may be less or these individuals less inclined to participate or take up the necessary skills.

The view of heritage in the development world seems to be changing and this is a positive shift. Heritage is now coming to be viewed as a resource that might aid sustainable development efforts in certain areas. Development organizations and NGOs are beginning to recognize the income generation potential of heritage sites. This shift in policy may have the side effect of protecting and preserving these assets for future generations, but for it to be successful and sustainable there is a need to incorporate heritage experts in the implementation of projects that are based at or near heritage resources to ensure proper management.

Notes

[1] Further information about Heritage Watch can be found on the organization's website: <http://www.heritagewatchinternational.org>.

[2] The Apsara dancers are celestial beings and bear no relationship to the APSARA acronym referred to earlier.

Bibliography

Anon. 2009. Helping Cambodia to PROTECT its World Heritage icon. *Living Heritage*, 1(4): 10.

Archaeological Institute of America (AIA). 2009. Archaeological Institute of America Awards Site Preservation Grant to Heritage Watch [accessed 4 February 2014]. Available at: <http://archaeological.org/news/currentprojects/78>.

Authority for Protection and Management of Angkor and the Region of Siem Reap (APSARA). 2005. Strategy [accessed 22 May 2011]. Available at: <http://www.autoriteapsara.org/en/apsara/urban_development/strategy.html>.

Australian Agency for International Development (AusAID). 2003. *Australia–Cambodia Development Cooperation Strategy 2003–2006*. Canberra: Department of Foreign Affairs and Trade.

Central Intelligence Agency (CIA). 2012. World Factbook [accessed 10 February 2013]. Available at: <https://www.cia.gov/library/publications/the-world-factbook/geos/cb.html>.

Coe, M. 2005. *Angkor and the Khmer Civilization*. London: Thames and Hudson.

Fletcher, R., Johnson, I., Bruce, E., & Khun-Neay, K. 2007. Living with Heritage: Site Monitoring and Heritage Values in Greater Angkor and the Angkor World Heritage Site, Cambodia. *World Archaeology*, 39(3): 385–405.

Guimbert, S. 2011. Cambodia 1998–2008: An Episode of Rapid Growth. In: A. Lall, ed. *Facets of Competitiveness: Narratives from ASEAN*. Singapore: World Scientific Publishing, pp. 151–83.

Garrett, P. 2008. Australia Helping Cambodia Protect World Heritage Icon. Australian Government media release [accessed 21 May 2014]. Available at: <http://www.environment.gov.au/minister/archive/env/2008/mr20081201a.html>.

Heritage Watch. 2009. Sustainable Development and Tourism Project — Final Report. Unpublished Report submitted to the Archaeological Institute of America.

Heritage Watch. 2014a. Heritage Watch Projects [accessed 4 February 2014]. Available at: <http://www.heritagewatchinternational.org/heritage-watch-projects.html>.

Heritage Watch. 2014b. Heritage Friendly Tourism Campaign [accessed 4 February 2014]. Available at: <http://www.heritagewatchinternational.org/heritage-friendly-tourism-campaign.html>.

Heritage Watch. 2014c. Heritage Watch at Banteay Chhmar [accessed 4 February 2014]. Available at: <http://www.heritagewatchinternational.org/heritage-watch-at-banteay-chhmar.html>.

Living with Heritage (LWH). 2008. Living with Heritage [accessed 22 May 2011]. Available at: <http://acl.arts.usyd.edu.au/angkor/lwh>.

McMullan, B. 2008. Australia Helps Cambodia Protect World Heritage Icon [accessed 23 May 2011]. Available at: <http://www.environment.gov.au/minister/archive/env/2008/mr20081201a.html>.

Mydans, S. 1999. Raiders of Lost Art Loot Temple in Cambodia. *The New York Times* [accessed 4 February 2014]. Available at: <http://www.nytimes.com/1999/04/01/world/raiders-of-lost-art-loot-temples-in-cambodia.html>.

NZAid. 2006. NZAid Cambodia Strategy, 2005–2010. [accessed 21 May 2014]. Available at: <http://www.scribd.com/doc/45405015/Nzaid-Cambodia-Strategy>.

NZAid. n.d. Cambodia: New Zealand Aid Programme [accessed 4 February 2014]. Available at: <http://www.aid.govt.nz/where-we-work/asia/asean-regional/cambodia>.

Royal Angkor Foundation (RAF). 2009. *Jaya Koh Ker Project Annual Report*. Budapest: Royal Angkor Foundation and Hungarian IndoChina Corporation Ltd.

Shelton, T. & Amrak, K. C. 2007. Koh Ker Gears Up for Tourism. *The Phnom Penh Post* [accessed 4 February 2014]. Available at: <http://www.phnompenhpost.com/national/koh-ker-gears-tourism>.

Someth, U. & De Silva, L. 2006. APSARA-NZAID Cooperation Project. *International Coordinating Committee for the Safeguarding and Development of the Historic Site of Angkor Fifteenth Technical Committee*. Siem Reap: UNESCO, pp. 123–14.

The Guardian. 2009. Preserving Cambodia's Heritage. *The Guardian* [accessed 4 February 2014]. Available at: <http://www.theguardian.com/world/2009/feb/23/cambodia-heritage>.

United Nations Educational Scientific and Cultural Organization (UNESCO). 2013. Angkor [accessed 4 February 2014]. Available at: <http://whc.unesco.org/en/list/668>.

Notes on contributor

Dougald O'Reilly is currently employed at the Australian National University in the School of Archaeology and Anthropology. He is the founder of Heritage Watch and served as the organization's Director until 2013 when he joined the Board of Heritage Watch. He is currently undertaking archaeological research in Cambodia near Angkor.

Correspondence to: Dougald O'Reilly, School of Archaeology and Anthropology, The Australian National University, Canberra, ACT, Australia. Email: dougald.oreilly@anu.au

PUBLIC ARCHAEOLOGY, Vol. 13 Nos 1–3, 2014, 213–25

The Community Heritage Project in Tihosuco, Quintana Roo, Mexico

Richard M. Leventhal

Penn Cultural Heritage Center, University of Pennsylvania, USA

Carlos Chan Espinosa

El Museo de la Guerra de Castas, Mexico

Eladio Moo Pat

La Comunidad de Tihosuco, Mexico

Demetrio Poot Cahun

La Comunidad de Tihosuco, Mexico

Maya culture is usually identified through spectacular ruins of a once great civilization lost in the jungles of Central America. Although the Maya people today see some continuities and connections to this ancient culture, they see an even stronger and more direct connection to their recent history and heritage. The Caste War rebellion in the Yucatan of the mid-nineteenth century is a critical historical moment for the modern Maya of the region and is reflected in the more recent Zapatista movement of Chiapas. These continuities and changes in the representation of the Maya past are the focal point for this paper. The Tihosuco Community Heritage Project, described in this paper, highlights a Maya view of history and the past. This type of community project focuses upon issues of contested heritage and provides a model for the identification and preservation of heritage in the future.

KEYWORDS community, development, archaeology, Maya, rebellion

Introduction

This paper has a number of co-authors. All of us are part of the central committee of the Tihosuco Community Heritage Project and have been working together for the past three to four years. The ideas in this paper are connected to all of us and are the result of a series of conversations and discussions among ourselves and with many of

DOI 10.1179/1465518714Z.00000000069

the people of Tihosuco, Mexico. The details of this paper, however, are mine (Leventhal) as it is written in English for an English-language publication. My co-authors are all Spanish speakers and the project is conducted fully in Spanish.

Archaeology within the Maya area has clearly had an economic impact within the region. One cannot look at sites such as Chichen Itza in Mexico with over 2 million visitors each year (UnionYucatan, 2014), Tikal in Guatemala with over 200,000 visitors per year (PrensaLibre, 2011), or even Xunantunich in Belize with over 50,000 visitors per year (Institute of Archaeology, Belmopan, Belize, pers. comm., 2014) without understanding the incredible power of archaeological or heritage tourism. I believe that large-scale site development tied to tourism is an ongoing and active model of site preservation and economic development at the national level throughout the world.

In addition, the initial archaeological and conservation work at all of these sites has clearly been important for the economic growth and development of the surrounding regions. Hundreds of thousands, if not millions of dollars have been spent by archaeological projects. Such projects have principally focused on the excavation and eventual consolidation of the ancient pyramids and other ancient buildings, although oftentimes local infrastructure has been developed by these archaeological projects. 'Community archaeology' has become a central part of archaeological projects around the world (Marshall, 2002). The same can be said about the current development and growth of new programmes related to heritage. The word 'community' is constantly used almost to justify or create an acceptable model for how to proceed with heritage preservation. It is almost impossible today to go onto a heritage preservation website without the concept of community being invoked. But before we celebrate this concept, we have to analyse what this 'community archaeology' really is.

I think the reason for this increased use of the word 'community' is the desire to buy into the widely held concept that heritage, preservation, and communities go together as an obvious grouping. As I move forward with this paper, I want to analyse the nature of the connection of communities to heritage preservation and then to discuss a slightly more complex relationship before discussing a new project in Mexico that I hope encompasses all of the ideas I am discussing here.

Community and communities

What are communities and why do they seem to be so important as we study heritage, the past, and even economic development? The word 'community' has been actively used in anthropology and is often overused to the point where anthropologists begin to avoid it as an all-encompassing concept with no meaning. But the word and the ideas behind the word are important, for 'community' continues to appear in the literature and in our study of human societies.

A 'community' is perhaps best described as a self-identified group of people who are connected to one another and acknowledge that connection. This does not mean that the identification is constant and even similar throughout societies. Rather we see individuals participating in an entire range of communities at any one time and the inclusion within one group does not mean that all are part of overlapping communities (Amit, 2002; Cohen, 2002; Joseph, 2002).

I would like to turn to Michael Herzfeld's concept of cultural intimacy as we try to define communities. Herzfeld (1997) discusses both the intimate expressions of community institutions within cultures while at the same time he acknowledges the importance of actors within societies who use solidarity and intimacy of expressions to indicate community connections. The people who are part of communities have an emotional, embodied, and sensual connection with that community — however it might be defined by the people of that community. Communities are people, and the connections are real and emotional rather than cold and calculated.

Communities, therefore, are real expressions of the connections between people. Although the specific nature of a community can be difficult, if not impossible to define, the concept of community remains an important one for anthropology, archaeology, and heritage studies.

Community, archaeology, and conservation

Why are both archaeology and conservation studies tightly tied to the concept of communities and their importance for the preservation of heritage? In the past, and even in today's world, both archaeology and conservation/heritage studies have been tied more to sites and artefacts than to living people. Archaeology was traditionally perceived as a discipline studying the dead and the nature of past societies. It was not associated with the modern world other than through *National Geographic* magazine, documentaries, and movies like *The Mummy* or *Indiana Jones*.

However, as archaeology and anthropology moved into the second half of the twentieth century, there was an intellectual shift within the post-modern and post-processual worlds. This movement connected archaeology and the results of its work to people living today (Preucel, 1991). In the United States, this movement possibly began with the realization that living Native American communities were not only the descendants of the people who had built the ancient and historic sites under study, but also were directly interested in the preservation and control of these sites today. What archaeologists and conservation programmes accomplished on the landscape was not purely an intellectual or touristic exercise, but rather one that had a direct cultural and economic impact upon living people (Ardren, 2002).

In the United States this resulted in the passage of the Native American Graves Protection and Repatriation Act in 1990 and the development of a National Museum of the American Indian (opened in 2004). In addition, internationally, there was a growing awareness of the importance of archaeological and conservation work for living people (Fine-Dare, 2002; Trope & Echo-Hawk, 2000; Watkins, 2005; Yellow-horn, 1996). Tourism and economic development were one favourable outcome of such research and preservation programmes. In addition, local museums along with national museums in many small and developing countries became the locus for the storage and display of materials from the past.

All of this connects archaeology and conservation to both a past and dead population and a present, living group of peoples. This is the point during which archaeologists have begun to acknowledge their work with communities. And, as I have articulated above, these communities are real — I will not spend time here arguing about the nature and reality of these communities (cf. Meskell & Van Damme, 2008).

The next question, therefore, must focus on the relationship between the archaeo-logical and preservation communities and local communities. There has always been a relationship between these groups. Even in the nineteenth century or early part of the twentieth century, archaeologists (along with preservation scholars) would begin the exploration for and excavation of ancient sites by setting up a base camp either within or provisioned through a local community. This relationship was a straight-forward economic one whereby the community provided a service that was paid-for by the archaeologist and team. This was not a relationship that considered the herit-age of the local community or gave them a research or cultural stake in the work. In modern terminology, this was a hierarchical relationship with the research team and archaeologist at the top with the power and money, and the local community on the bottom providing the services.

I would argue that this hierarchical relationship continues today — even as archae-ologists and other researchers talk about communities and how to bring communities into their research. The relationship is still one-sided and is based upon the archaeologist and preservation team as the people who initiate a project and then usually tell the local community how important they are for the project and for this relationship.

Rather than point fingers at others in this field, let me recount some of my experiences related to communities and archaeologists working particularly in Mesoamerica. As an archaeologist working in Belize, Mexico, Honduras, and other Mesoamerican countries, projects would usually start with a series of meetings with the permitting agencies of the national government — a conversation that focused on where I wanted to work and the type of work that might be done. This was followed up by meetings with local communities near the archaeological sites to be examined or located within or nearby the exploration region. Issues of land to be utilized or explored, pay structure, living arrangements, labourers, and so on were all part of this conversation. Perhaps there was even a conversation about long-term develop-ment of the archaeological site and the possibility of local tourism that might benefit this local community.

But this relationship remained hierarchical with the positions of power occupied rather firmly by the archaeologists and/or by the people focused on the long-term preservation and conservation of the site. The last twenty-five to thirty years have clearly brought about a change from purely the research-focused archaeology of the past where local communities and even the long-term preservation of the site were not part of the conversation. They were not even part of the educational process for archaeologists, historic preservation scholars, or anthropologists. The most recent approach in these disciplines has put the following words and concepts in the fore-front of work: 'heritage', 'community engagement', and 'development'. But, as we have said, the structural relationship between the outside researcher and the local community remains broadly the same. That outside researcher identifies the work, identifies the site, identifies the nature of the heritage asset to be conserved, and iden-tifies the aspects for development. What has changed? In terms of a relationship and connection — not much.

The goal of this special issue of *Public Archaeology* is to connect and analyse the nature of and relationship between archaeology, heritage, and economic development. Hidden within these words is another concept — the need to shift the relationship between the outside researcher and the community. If it is a long-term sustainable development that we are talking about, then we must think about the nature of community and identify the community as the primary place for decisions and structural power.

It is the community that must identify the heritage to save and use for development. And it is the community that must make a series of decisions about the nature of that heritage, its prospective use for development, and their willingness to participate in these projects. Such decisions might not always be made along the lines of culture or beliefs, and might be made along economic and pragmatic issues. But the power shift is essential for long-term development. My co-authors and I believe that not only must communities be the focus for long-term heritage preservation, but they must also be the focus and driving force of development programmes associated with this preservation and with heritage.

One final introductory point is critical: with the shift in this power relationship we must also consider the identification of heritage both for preservation and development. It is easy for an archaeologist or heritage specialist to identify heritage; it is more difficult to stand on the side lines and let others make those decisions. But that is what must be done — providing advice, ideas, schemes, programmes, and information. In the modern world, as heritage is a constantly evolving concept and with all cultures and societies constantly preserving and destroying heritage, it is local communities who can best think about and identify their heritage, decide what heritage can be preserved (and in what form), and what can be used for development. It is not only working with communities — it is letting them make decisions and perhaps giving them the information and tools to help make those decisions.

Case study: the Tihuosuco Community Heritage Project

My interest in the Maya rebellion of the nineteenth century started in the 1990s and resulted in a small programme of exploration and excavation at abandoned refugee villages in Belize. But around 2005, my continued interest in the Caste War of Yucatan (1847–1901) was coupled with a growing dissatisfaction about the nature of the relationship between archaeological projects and local communities. Around this time, I began to wander through the region of the Yucatan in Mexico, the centre of the Caste War rebellion. As I arrived in many of these small towns in eastern Quintana Roo, I did not find the typical tourist representation of the ancient Maya (mural or sculpture) within each town's plaza. Rather, I found statues of Maya Caste War leaders and remains of military equipment of the time. This war was clearly the focus of the Maya conception of heritage within this region.

The small town of Tihosuco located in the state of Quintana Roo, in roughly the geographic centre of the Yucatan peninsula, was even more focused on the rebellion. It has a town museum devoted to the Caste War (the Museo de la Guerra de Castas) and a large but only partially renovated church. During my first of several trips into Tihosuco, I met many people (including my co-authors) and discussed my interest in studying the Caste War through the archaeology of abandoned towns and sites in the surrounding jungle landscape. During these conversations, there seemed to be great interest among the people of Tihosuco to show me ancient sites and to even let me excavate (loot) them, buy the artefacts, and return with the material to the United States. But when the discussion turned to Caste War sites on Tihosuco lands, I was clearly and firmly told that there were none.

Today I do not recall why I continued to return to Tihosuco about every two to four months to sit and talk with the people of the town — I certainly enjoyed these conversations and made many friends. But I was clearly not progressing with my attempt to find Caste War sites and start a heritage project. After about two to three years of visits to the region and to Tihosuco, things changed. I can remember the morning because I was in a larger neighbouring town and got a call from Carlos Chan Espinosa (Director of the Caste War Museum and one of the co-authors of this paper). He had to come to this town to get some parts for his car and we agreed to meet and get some coffee. As we were sitting, he asked, 'Are you serious about finding Caste War sites? Do you really want to start a project?'.

After clearly restating my interest, Carlos simply said, 'Let's go'.

I was surprised, and asked what he meant. Carlos said that there were indeed a series of Caste War sites on Tihosuco land including the remains of the hacienda, or estate, of one of the rebellion leaders. He told me they had been protecting these sites for many years and did not allow many people to visit — certainly, very few outsiders. I asked about why he was now taking me to these sites. He indicated that, although I was an outsider and they did not know me or trust me, after my two to three years of visits, they were willing slowly to start to show me these sites and begin a conversation about the development of a project.

What brought about this change within the community? This is a difficult question to answer with any sense of certainty. Clearly, I had returned enough times to the region and to Tihosuco to begin to develop a series of friendships with numerous people. However, I also think that there has been a growing perception within Tihosuco and throughout the region that the social and economic future was not seen in a positive light. Many of the young adults of Tihosuco cannot find work within the town or the region and move to Cancun and the Maya Riviera to gain employment. Most of this work is either in construction or low-paying hotel work and is oftentimes seasonal. And there is also an awareness that many of these young adults gradually do not return to Tihosuco. The opening of the door to me of the previously protected Caste War heritage may have been the result of numerous circumstances and internal community conversations that intersected at the time of my arrival and repeated visits to Tihosuco and the region.

The Caste War (1847–1901)

The Caste War, which began in the dry limestone flats of the Yucatan Peninsula in 1847, was one of the most successful indigenous uprisings in the history of the Americas and led to the existence of an independent Maya state that remained semi-autonomous for over fifty years. Yet, the Caste War was also a war of factions, Maya against Mexican, Maya against British, Mexican against British, and Maya against Maya. Inhabited by the Maya for well over three thousand years, the Yucatan had become a political and economic focus for the Spanish colonial powers centred in Merida. By the early 1800s, traditional Maya extended-family networks were breaking down as village political identities and local economic interests increasingly guided the administrative organization of the Maya villages and towns spread across the Yucatan Peninsula (Dumond, 1997; Reed, 2001).

Following a series of events in the summer of 1847, 'the conflagration swept over the eastern three-quarters of the peninsula [. . .] as the rebels drew to their cause possibly a fourth of the entire peninsula population' (Dumond, 1997: 3). The demands of the Maya included the abolition of all taxes and the guaranteed right to sufficient land. Despite their success, the Maya forces were never truly united, but multiple Maya factions worked in concert to push their way to the outskirts of Merida. By mid-1848, the Yucatan elite population had been driven to Merida where preparations were being made to flee the peninsula, leaving it entirely in Maya hands. Likely connected to the need to plant their fields, the rebel forces did not complete their advance upon Merida, thus turning the tide of the war. Instead, the rebels retreated and a large number of Maya returned to their villages. In late 1848, the remaining Maya forces were driven eastward by a renewed Yucatecan military advance, beginning a fifty-year period of isolated fighting and ongoing resistance by the rebels. By the end of that year, it is estimated that over 200,000 people had been killed or dislocated by the war.

In late 1850, a small group of Maya witnessed a divine visitation in the form of a talking cross. Though little is known about the establishment of the 'cult' of the cross, a new town, Chan Santa Cruz, was founded in the eastern Yucatan as the home of this divine miracle. Giving the rebels new hope, the cross reportedly spoke the words of God directly to the Maya, calling for Maya independence and religious autonomy. With newly identified Maya priests, the Talking Cross united a beleaguered population with a resurgence of religious hope and rebel spirit. These Maya established control over eastern Yucatan and, through friendly trading networks with the British, managed to maintain political autonomy for almost fifty years (Dumond, 1997; Reed, 2001).

Contemporary heritage values

The Caste War is a critical period in the creation of the modern Maya as an independent and identifiable cultural group in Central America. My research and work within Tihosuco have led me to understand that the modern Maya tie their cultural identity and ongoing resistance in the Yucatan, in Chiapas (the Zapatista revolution), and in Guatemala back to the Caste War.

The 'Guerra de Castas' (the Caste War), also called the 'Guerra Social Maya' (Maya social war), is one of the most important heritage events of the Yucatan region while, at the same time, being one of the most difficult events to define. The causes of the war have been debated both within academic circles and within communities throughout Yucatan and Quintana Roo. Economic, social and ideological factors, along with dramatic inequalities of power, have all been discussed as possible causes (Dumond, 1997; Reed, 2001; Rugeley, 1996).

Another concept relates to the difficulty in creating a temporal definition of the war — did it end after the first five years? After fifty-four years in 1901 with a treaty? Or, in fact, does the 'Guerra de Castas' continue today? Again, this is debated and discussed in many places — particularly in the Maya communities of the region. However, it is clear that the Guerra de Castas defines the identity and the stories of the region, along with its communities, landscape, and even the nature of the region's most basic building block — the household. Identity in this central and eastern part of the Yucatan is tied to people, places, and things — all associated with the Guerra de Castas.

At a macro-level, the ancient Maya as defined by archaeologists and the large number of ancient sites are all part of the Maya past. But this connection of ancient to modern, although clearly 'real', tends not to be a primary point of heritage identity within this region. The Guerra de Castas stands out as the defining heritage event of the region. Statues of Guerra de Castas heroes adorn the local parks and the surrounding landscape is defined by abandoned towns, churches, haciendas, and ranchos rather than by ancient sites and tourist attractions.

The Tihosuco Community Heritage Project

The Tihosuco Community Heritage Project was formally initiated in 2011. Primary partners in this project are the communidad de Tihosuco, the ejido[1] de Tihosuco, el Museo de la Guerra de Castas, and the Penn Cultural Heritage Center of the University of Pennsylvania. This project developed after numerous meetings, discussions, visits, and work between members of the Tihosuco community and people from the Penn CHC. This project is a combined community heritage preservation project, a community economic development project, and a community archaeological-preservation project for Guerra de Castas sites in the region.

During a short five-week period in June and July of 2011, the project started with a focus within three primary areas:

1. The Caste War Sites of Culumpich, Tela, the Fort, and abandoned local haciendas
2. Caste War Museum
3. General activities within the Tihosuco Community.

Caste War sites

Near Tihosuco, there are two important Caste War sites that have been preserved and protected by the community. These abandoned sites are Culumpich, the hacienda of Jacinto Pat, one of the first Maya leaders of the war, and the nearby town of Tela or La'al Kaj (La'al Kaj is a modern name and the nineteenth-century name for this town appears to be 'Tela'). A third site was located in 2011 and appears to be a fort from the Caste War time period located to the east-south-east of Tela. All three of these sites are abandoned but appear to be in a relatively good state of preservation.

With the assistance of the community and ejido of Tihosuco, a small crew was established for the work at these Caste War sites. Preliminary work at all of these sites consisted primarily of clearing, mapping, and attempting to understand the nature and overall layout of the sites.

Culumpich

At Culumpich, the main hacienda house of Jacinto Pat was identified along with two primary outbuildings with extensive stone architecture and one building defined by a single course of stone. In addition, Culumpich has an extensive water system and wall system.

All of the buildings at Culumpich, including the hacienda house, are elliptical in shape (parallel front and back walls with rounded end walls forming the other two sides). This form of building is associated with Maya people and culture and is typical of houses within the Yucatan. It is interesting to note that Jacinto Pat, as a relatively wealthy landowner, was able to build a hacienda and secondary buildings in a more typical Mexican or Yucatecan style with squared corners and elaborate facades. These elliptical buildings at Culumpich clearly indicate Jacinto Pat's interest in identifying himself and his community as being ethnically Maya to the core.

The main hacienda building is set up on a raised, elliptical shaped terrace with constructed retaining walls. This is reminiscent of ancient Maya buildings (in fact, this raised terrace might be ancient in initial construction). Off to one side of this hacienda building are a series of squared rooms at ground level. These rooms were probably the focus for ancillary activities associated with the main house such as storage, cooking, and so on. Finally, on the interior of one of the well-constructed outbuildings, we found what was probably a maize or grain storage unit. It is constructed like a well with a defined, circular wall — but the interior only extends down about 3 ft to ground level. Similar features have been found at Tela.

The wall system is extensive and defines a series of enclosures — probably for cattle or other animals. The wall system includes well-constructed and plastered walls ranging in height from 4 ft to 8 ft. The main entrance to the hacienda is part of this wall system. One entered through a large iconic arch that today seems to define Culumpich in photographs and in writing. Entrance to the hacienda started by passing under the stone arch and then included climbing up a monumental staircase over a water feature and another wall into the internal area of the Pat hacienda.

The water system is a complex one that moves water into cattle troughs scattered throughout the central area of the hacienda. This system is centred on a raised platform with a central well, a large holding pool for the water, a ramp to reach the top of the platform, and a grotto under the ramp with a scratched drawing of a siren and cross on the wall of the grotto.

Tela (aka La'al Kaj)

La'al Kaj is the modern name (Place of Thistles) for an abandoned town located about 8.5 km to the south/south-east of Tihosuco. It was apparently abandoned at the beginning of the Caste War — within the 1847–48 time period (although the details will have to be confirmed in the near future). With the assistance of Julio Hoil Gutierrez, we are just beginning to define this town as 'Tela'.

Tela is defined by a large two-level central plaza. The lower section of the plaza is located to the north. The southern and eastern sides are marked by what appears to be a natural rise creating an upper plaza area. The edges of the plaza are marked by low dry-laid stone walls that also serve as house compound walls. The church and surrounding compound are located near the south-east corner of the plaza. The central cenote is located just to the north of the plaza. Within compounds ringing the plaza are a series of stone buildings. There is one 'Spanish' or 'casa colonial' building located on the western edge of the plaza. Both the church and casa colonial are located on the edges of the upper plaza. All of the other stone buildings (preliminary count of four or five) are elliptical in form with a perishable roof (Martos López, 2006).

Major roads extend from the plaza in all directions. Generally the site is laid out with a longer axis along the north–south line and a shorter east–west line. From the plaza, major roads extend about 1.25–1.50 km to both the north and south. In contrast, the east and west roads run only about 0.75–1.0 km.

The area of the site is not actively used for milpa — it has been set aside as a biological reserve. This reserve has preserved not only the rainforest but also all of the walls and nineteenth century features. A brecha or cut-line has been established around the preserve/site and is opened every year by the men of Tihosuco. However, we found in mapping along the brecha that there was clear evidence that walls, roads, and nineteenth-century features extended beyond the cut-line. These outlying areas will have to be explored at some point in the future.

The fort

Approximately 1.5 km to the east-south-east of La'al Kaj is another feature that has been identified by the community of Tihosuco. This appears to be a nineteenth-century fort with an open central area surrounded by a wall. Most of the wall is dry-laid stone preserved to about 0.75–1.0 m in height. However, at several points along the wall, well-preserved sections mark different size openings that are defined by walls constructed of stones, mortar, and plaster. These seem to mark possible guard and gun placements on the interior of the fort. The fort was only briefly explored and more work will be necessary to clear it, map it, and define the date and function of the architecture.

Museo de la Guerra de Castas

One central part of this community heritage project is the Caste War Museum in Tihosuco. For many reasons, this museum is one of the central points in the heritage of the town and the region. The museum is one of the few public institutions in Tihosuco that is focused upon bringing people together for community activities. Youth, children, women, and elders are all active groups in the community centred upon the museum. Several programmes were initiated this past summer focused upon raising the visibility of the museum both locally and internationally.

We worked to identify ways to connect the museum to the Internet through improved access and the creation of a well-designed and clear web page. The website was specifically requested by the personnel of the Caste War Museum as an attempt to attract more visitors — both international and Mexican. During June and July of 2011, detailed information about the museum was gathered. This included material related to mission, exhibits, programmes, activities, classes for children, and so on. In addition, photographs were taken of the museum, the exhibits, the people of the museum, and the activities of the museum. With this background information, the museum's own website was initiated at the end of 2012 (see CWM, 2013).

One of the specific needs identified by the Director of the Museum was the creation of a guide to be used by English-speaking visitors. Photographs of all text panels were taken and an initial translation has been completed. The length of the text seems to make it difficult to produce a brochure for English-speaking tourists. Therefore, a shorter brochure that summarizes the museum sections was created. In addition, a

Spanish version of this guide was produced and has had much more of an impact within Tihosuco and the region than originally expected. Many residents of Tihosuco have read the new brochure and expressed their interest in both the Caste War story and their connection to this recent history.

Finally, the Penn Cultural Heritage Center supported a variety of programmes within the Museum with resources and funds. For example, a camera was donated to the museum to allow better documentation of activities and developments.

The Tihosuco community

The Penn Cultural Heritage Center directly provided the resources for the ejido to purchase a new sound system to be used at their meetings.

In addition, an ongoing series of conversations were initiated in 2011 within the community of Tihosuco. This included numerous informal discussions as well as formal weekly meetings that brought project and community members together to discuss important issues of the present and future.

Some of the issues discussed related to trash and recycling, the nature of heritage, the preservation of heritage and the past, the Internet, the recording of colonial architecture in Tihosuco, and tourism — including both the good parts and more difficult sides of tourism. One of the major issues related specifically to community and economic development within Tihosuco. How could the community use its past and its heritage to create a controlled and sustainable future for Tihosuco? We did not reach final conclusions but understood that these questions needed more discussion and exploration.

Conclusion

Within Tihosuco and the surrounding areas, the Guerra de Castas defines the past, the present, and the ongoing discussions about the future. In the past, this is most evident with the relationship of the two towns of Tihosuco and Tela. In the nineteenth century there seems to have been some sort of connection between the two communities. Tihosuco was apparently the centre for the Español or Yucateco occupation of the region, as evidenced by both the stories of local residents and the existence of a large number of colonial houses in the pueblo. It is said that Maya people were not allowed into the main Tihosuco church but used a small side chapel. In contrast, the evidence we have gathered from the neighbouring town of Tela is that it was a more Maya-focused community with mostly elliptical buildings (other than the church and one casa colonial).

In the present, the reoccupation of the region following the Guerra de Castas has been focused within Tihosuco with occasional and minimal occupation at Tela. Within Tihosuco, people are living in the midst of nineteenth-century casa colonials and the apparent splendour of that time period. And there are deep memories of people and place — even by the Maya people from the north who re-inhabited the region at the end of the nineteenth century and beginning of the twentieth century. Culumpich is a sacred place of reverence and great importance. Tela has been preserved by the ejido — outsiders are not allowed in without community consent.

And, finally, the feast day of Saint Michael the Archangel, the patron saint of Tela, and its church, is a major Tihosuco festival each year at the site.

Heritage tied to continuity and memory of place continues with very specific connections to Culumpich and Jacinto Pat and more generally with the Guerra de Castas town of Tela.

Discussions about the future have tended to focus on attempts to create a more viable economic future for Tihosuco. Ejido lands are fully used and committed to older residents, meaning young people are moving away to Cancun or to other beach developments to find work. Tourism is a word often used even if the concepts are not well understood or complete. But the desire to preserve the memory of the past is clashing directly with the need to think about an economic future about and for the Guerra de Castas within the region.

Note

[1]   Ejidos are cooperative land tenure organizations common in Mexico.

Bibliography

Amit, V. 2002. Reconceptualizing Community. In: V. Amit, ed. *Realizing Community, Concepts, Social Relationships and Sentiments*. London and New York: Routledge, pp. 1–20.

Ardren, T. 2002. Conversations about the Production of Archaeological Knowledge and Community Museums at Chunchucmil and Kochol, Yucatán, México. *World Archaeology*, 34(2): 379–400.

Caste War Museum (CWM). 2013. Home [accessed 15 April 2014]. Available at: <http://www.museogc.com/Museo/E-home.html>.

Cohen, A. 2002. Epilogue. In: V. Amit, ed. *Realizing Community, Concepts, Social Relationships and Sentiments*. London and New York: Routledge, pp. 165–70.

Dumond, D. 1997. *The Machete and the Cross*. Lincoln, NE: University of Nebraska Press.

Fine-Dare, K. 2002. *Grave Injustice: The American Indian Repatriation Movement and NAGPRA*. Lincoln, NE: University of Nebraska: Lincoln Press.

Herzfeld, M. 1997. *Cultural Intimacy: Social Poetics in the Nation-State*. London and New York: Routledge.

Joseph, M. 2002. *Against the Romance of Community*. Minneapolis, MN: University of Minnesota Press.

Marshall, Y. 2002. What is Community Archaeology? *World Archaeology*, 34(2): 211–19.

Martos López, L. A. 2006. Lalcah, un pueblo olvidado en la selva de Quintna Roo. *Boletín de Monumentos Históricos*, 7: 2–20.

Meskell, L. & Van Damme, L. 2008. Heritage Ethics and Descendent Communities. In: C. Colwell-Chanthaphonh and T. J. Ferguson, eds. *Collaboration in Archaeological Practice*. Walnut Creek, CA: Altamira Press, pp. 131–50.

PrensaLibre. 2011. Disminuye ingreso de turistas a parque Tikal [accessed 14 April 2014]. Available at: <http://www.prensalibre.com/noticias/Disminuye-ingreso-turistas-parque-Tikal_0_433156710.html>.

Preucel, R. W. 1991. The Philosophy of Archaeology. In: R. W. Preucel, ed. *Processual and Postprocessual Archaeologies, Multiple Ways of Knowing the Past*. Center for Archaeological Investigations, Southern Illinois University at Carbondale, Occasional Paper 10: 17–29.

Reed, N. A. 2001. *The Caste War of Yucatán*, revised ed. Stanford, CA: Stanford University Press.

Rugeley, T. 1996. *Yucatán's Maya Peasantry & the Origins of the Caste War*. Austin, TX: University of Texas Press.

Trope, J. F. & Echo-Hawk, W. R. 2000. The Native American Graves Protection and Repatriation Act: Background and Legislative History. In: D. Mihesuah, ed. *Repatriation Reader: Who Owns American Indian Remains*. Lincoln, NE: University of Nebraska press, pp. 123–68.

UnionYucatan. 2014. Chichén Itzá crece 47% en número de visitantes [accessed 14 April 2014]. Available at: <http://www.unionyucatan.mx/articulo/2014/02/13/cultura/chichen-itza/chichen-itza-crece-47-en-numero-de-visitantes>.

Watkins, J. 2005. Through Wary Eyes: Indigenous Perspectives on Archaeology. *Annual Review of Anthropology*, 34: 429–49.

Yellowhorn, E. 1996. Indians, Archaeology and the Changing World. *Native Studies Review*, 11(2): 23–50.

Notes on contributors

Richard M. Leventhal is the Executive Director of the Penn Cultural Heritage Center, Professor in the University of Pennsylvania Department of Anthropology, and Curator in the American Section of the Penn Museum. He is the former Williams Director of the University of Pennsylvania Museum of Archaeology and Anthropology, the former President and CEO of the School of American Research in Santa Fe, NM, and the former Director of the Cotsen Institute of Archaeology at UCLA. He received his BA and PhD in Anthropology from Harvard. He has done extensive archaeological field research in Belize, Mexico, and other parts of Central America for over thirty years. Dr Leventhal lectures and writes on the preservation of cultural heritage and cultural sites, on the need to prevent the looting of global heritage resources, on the acquisition policies of museums, and the relationship within communities between heritage and economic development. He has worked extensively with law enforcement agencies both in the United States and internationally to stop the illegal movement of antiquities.

Correspondence to: Richard Leventhal, Penn Museum, 3260 South Street, Philadelphia, PA 19104, USA. Email: rml@sas.upenn.edu

Carlos Chan Espinosa is a life-long resident of Tihosuco, Quintana Roo, Mexico. He has been the Director of the Caste War Museum in Tihosuco for the past twenty years. Email: chancarlos26@hotmail.com

Eladio Moo Pat is a lifelong resident of Tihosuco, Quintana Roo, Mexico. For the past three years he has worked for the Felipe Carillo Puerto Municipal Transit Police.

Demetrio Poot Cahun is a lifelong resident of Tihosuco, Quintana Roo, Mexico. He was the head of the Tihosuco Ejido (Comisariado Ejidal) for three years from 2011–13.

PUBLIC ARCHAEOLOGY, Vol. 13 Nos 1–3, 2014, 226–39

Preservation as 'Disaster Capitalism': The Downside of Site Rescue and the Complexity of Community Engagement

K. Anne Pyburn

Indiana University, USA

As ethics have increasingly become a topic of interest for archaeologists, 'heritage preservation' has become harder to define. What was once thought to be a very simple and benign idea is now seen clearly as a colonial construction. There are no reliable rules to guide decisions about how heritage should be preserved, even if it is possible to determine which heritage should be preserved. However, most archaeologists and preservationists accept that the final say belongs with the people whose heritage or community is the focus of a preservation programme. In this paper I consider how imposed preservation schemes, buttressed by hyped-up public concern about the 'loss' of archaeological sites, can alienate people from their resources, making them vulnerable to predatory organizations. I bring in contrasting case studies from my own work in Belize and Kyrgyzstan to exemplify the complex ramifications of promoting preservation.

KEYWORDS preservation, disaster capitalism, Kyrgyzstan, Belize, community-based archaeology

Introduction

Received wisdom in the literature on economic development is that top-down strategies do not work and that long-term relationships are necessary to develop local infrastructure and community commitment to sustainable programmes. Sustainability results from grassroots engagement that develops locally appropriate strategies and addresses local needs. Archaeology has become linked with economic development as a potential boost for tourism and community assistance. In addition to revealing attractive tourist destinations, archaeology offers seasonal short-term employment that can develop technical skills in local communities that are translatable into jobs. It is also claimed that an interest in local heritage preservation can be empowering for economically disadvantaged groups whose heritage has been ignored, disrespected, or even erased.

   DOI 10.1179/1465518714Z.00000000070

In fact, there is no inherent relationship between archaeological research on past societies and the improvement of a local economy. Archaeology is an outgrowth of colonial interest in other cultures and does not comfortably translate into grassroots issues such as poverty and political oppression within those subject cultures. Traditional archaeological research focuses on cultural factors of little interest to living communities, such as the early development of agriculture or cities, monumental art and architecture, and literacy, which have a greater appeal for national governments; or environmental degradation, warfare, and political collapse, that often reflect badly on descendant communities. Site preservation and development for tourism may receive grassroots support, but only insofar as local communities are willing to improve their economies by shaping their heritage identity for a non-local audience, which often requires exoticism and stultifying displays of staged 'authenticity'. There simply is no way for archaeology to become a grassroots initiative without changing the practice of and attitudes to archaeology itself.

In this paper I document some of my own changing attitudes with a comparison of case studies from my community development and heritage preservation attempts in Belize and Kyrgyzstan.

The irony of the 'non-renewable resource'

Almost every popular article or television show about archaeology mentions that it is a 'non-renewable resource' (Cameron, 1994; see also Comer, this volume). This has become the standard refrain, just as environmental destruction and the threat of extinction are the standard conclusion of any nature programme. But archaeology is renewable; it is being renewed every second of every day; we are renewing it right now. According to archaeology's processualist ancestors, who were interested in cultural processes, human behaviour, and generalizable knowledge to be derived from material culture, people continue to perform activities that leave traces in the world. Historical archaeology of a colonial plantation and the garbology of Mexico City are as likely to identify generalizable knowledge about human behaviour as digging up the Maya site of Tikal, in Guatemala.

If, on the other hand, the goal is to understand history, although there is no shortage of documentation, scholars cannot claim to understand the recent past much more clearly than the distant past; we have *more* information but not even complete agreement about what happened during the battles of Trafalgar or Antietam or the Bulge. And there is even less agreement about why. It is ironic that archaeologists write definitive articles about ancient economies when they clearly cannot understand the one in which they live.

What is really lost when an archaeological site, however defined, is destroyed? The artefacts of human actions and the contexts that give them archaeological meaning are lost; some of the lost artefacts were probably unique so we will never know about them. Some that survive out of context lose much of their interpretability. But even *in situ*, we cannot know what they meant to the people who left them behind; we hypothesize, analogize, and estimate based on what we already know.

Archaeologists usually wax poetic about the *longue durée* — about how only archaeologists can see the shape of change in human patterns over time. A similar argument, but not quite the same, is that to have any idea of what the world was like before the modern world system, and therefore have an idea about the range of possibilities for human organizations, we need archaeological data, since everything recorded as western history was from the perspective of a precursor, or a participant, or a promoter of the world system (Pyburn, 2004).

Unfortunately, this is exactly where archaeologists tend to fall short, because almost every study that has been done in the last hundred years has tended to show that 'everything we know is true'. Despite the claims of post-processualism to add nuance and uncertainty to archaeological interpretation, very little that gets published runs counter to a traditional Western colonial view of the past, and what there is rarely makes it beyond the pages of scholarly journals. If you peruse the latest issue of *Archaeology Magazine* you will discover that ancient women were dominated, inhabited private space, cooked food, and raised children; ancient people were violent, especially the men, and sometimes did unspeakable things to each other; subsistence strategies have not always been able to keep up with population growth, climate change, and greed; and humans everywhere throughout time have lived in nuclear patriarchal families. There are a few others, and of course there are innumerable variations on these themes, but in reality these 'discoveries' are nothing of the kind. Is another example of people doing exactly what we see ourselves doing right now a good use of scarce resources? I say this because in an anthropological sense these studies do not add to knowledge, but also because they reify the status quo in the present by constructing a primordial pedigree for it. And if the nuance and uncertainty never reach outside the academy is archaeology's contribution to the world what archaeologists claim it is?

The scientific value of the objects and patterns that occur in archaeological contexts is a factor of the context of the discovery as much as the nature of the discovery itself. Often the discoveries reported in the London *Times* or *National Geographic* find-of-the-week column were actually 'discovered' long before they became news. The point is that what archaeologists discover is a result of the questions that they ask and the implementation of a research design, but also what is media-friendly. Twenty-five years ago Richard Wilk (1985) showed that archaeological interpretations are susceptible to the politics of their era, and few archaeologists still think science exists outside culture. But when people are concerned about climate change, evidence of drought in the ninth-century Maya Lowlands becomes a discovery.

So if archaeologists are not really digging up 'truth' but have some control over their discoveries by choosing the questions to be asked, and the information purveyed, and the interpretations pitched to *USA Today*, it is fair to ask if the academic research of archaeologists is really worthwhile. That question cannot be answered in a definitive way, but it merits serious consideration. My own answer is 'occasionally'. But those occasions are often overshadowed by findings that are not worthwhile and are even damaging to living people and have the potential to be used for political purposes in the present. Archaeological data are just not robust enough to justify being presented as incontrovertible truth. One of my most esteemed colleagues, who shall remain nameless, once said to me in an email: 'I have the right to say that the Maya were warlike, because my data prove that it was true'. It is not possible to prove that something is true. You can only substantiate scientific propositions by failing to prove that they are false. But as Cojti Ren (2006: 10) points out, 'the history of our people has also been colonised'.

The reason for posing this uncomfortable question about the value of archaeological research is that there is another reason for the constant media harangue about the loss of 'the' archaeological record. In reality the multinational corporations, national governments, and preservation-oriented Non Governmental Organizations that complain about site destruction are not always primarily concerned about archaeological sites or scientific knowledge. And as scientists, archaeologists are concerned about preservation of data but not really about the preservation of monuments which once reconstructed and trodden upon by a million tourists lose much of their scientific value (Willems, 2012). By throwing in our lot with the tourist industry and the preservation industry and the projects of nation states, we get attention and respect and the chance to keep digging. But archaeologists do not really share the goals of these organizations.

As scientists, archaeologists are not really glamorous. We do heavy, dirty, physical labour, tedious analyses of discarded junk, bone fragments, and chemical residues, complicated statistical manipulations, high-tech mapping, university lecturing, and struggle with the overbearing bureaucracies of universities, governments, and funding agencies. Of course, it is nice to find something pretty or golden, but most scientifically valuable data are neither. More often, the archaeologist is stuck trying to figure out how to make a silk purse out of a dreary phytolith or an abandonment layer so that non-specialists will see some value in their work. To please the public we accept the pretence that archaeology is a glamorous treasure hunt for things and occasionally facts that are old and beautiful, unique and original, weird and creepy, and therefore valuable not just as data but as titillation, as treasure, and of course as 'lessons from the past'. Along with this image of our goals as scientists (which are apparently not very scientific) is the image that if we are 'real' archaeologists — successful archaeologists — we embody the Indiana Jones sense of adventure and scornful attitude toward spiders, snakes, and Indigenous People.

But the political and global business impetus to empathize with our fear of loss and support site preservation is not motivated by a desire for tenure or a feature headline in the *Washington Post*. The multinationals that support the agenda of UNESCO and ICOMOS, along with the national governments that are eager for world heritage recognition reap another kind of benefit. That is, they promote the idea that looting and site destruction are rampant and creating an impending crisis in order to justify moving into local areas to promote preservation of resources by taking control of them. This is clear if you look carefully at who really profits most significantly from the granting of world heritage status (Labadi & Long, 2010).

This is the reverse of the usual complaint about site destruction resulting from the greed of multinationals and the land grabs of governments which refuse to recognize and protect the cultural heritage sites that support Indigenous land claims or curb economic development. Certainly, such claims are demonstrably accurate. But site protection and rescue, just like environmental preservation, can be used to promote the interests of the wealthy at the expense of the poor, and to impinge on human rights under the guise of the 'world heritage'.

Disaster capitalism

In a recent article Rebecca Zarger (in prep.) notes that, in the wake of Hurricane Iris, which devastated many farms and homes in southern Belize in 2001, local resistance to construction of a hydroelectric dam was weakened to the extent that the dam got built, going into service amid resurging protests. Resistance — and regret — rose back to pre-Iris levels, but it was too late. Her study provides 'insight into how apertures created by disasters accelerate shifts in access to critical resources and claims on space and place'. In the case of the hurricane, Zarger believes that people experienced uncertainty, since their livelihoods were disrupted, and displacement, since many people migrated to find work to mitigate the effects of the hurricane damage on their family economies. This displacement was exacerbated by development agencies that came on the scene to help by providing alternative sources of support for damaged farms, support that may inadvertently put those farms out of business.

The link between disaster, development, and displacement is well documented in the development literature and these three threats have been tagged as one of the prime movers of globalization (Klein, 2008). Zarger's most interesting contribution is her argument that Iris created an 'aperture' — a context in which 'the state, foreign investors, and transnational corporations step into a post-disaster space and quickly remake the damaged or threatened landscape to suit their purposes and desires'. Although she is careful not to cast Belizean farmers merely as victims, insisting that throughout the process they maintained some degree of agency, Zarger nevertheless identifies this scenario as a form of 'disaster capitalism'.

There are some important parallels to be drawn between the aperture created by natural disasters, wars, or economic upheavals, and the aperture that is often created by the crusade to preserve archaeological sites. The concept of 'disaster capitalism' explains the problem of allowing or even encouraging the state, foreign investors, and transnational corporations to help 'preserve' archaeological sites. The scenario begins with publicity about the impending loss of material heritage, cast as a disaster of enormous proportions — a loss to all humankind and certainly a loss to the local communities who are about to become the victims of their own ignorance, either because they are the victims of disaster or because they are not practising site preservation. In stage two some benevolent government bureau or civic-minded multi-national corporation or development agency, often in collaboration with a well-meaning archaeologist, is shown to be mitigating the 'disaster' by 'educating' the locals about the true value of local archaeological resources. Locals must learn not to damage 'world heritage' in order to develop pride in their identity, and get new jobs, usually first as labour underwriting research and then through tourism promoted as a 'sustainable industry' (there is the displacement). Stage three is not usually reported in the news, except as glowing praise for the benefactors' contribution to national economic wellbeing and global heritage, or occasionally as complaints about the locals' failure to commit time and energy to the project they have so generously been given.

The most elegant of these scenarios are those that are actually created by the transnational corporations and government agents that step in to mitigate them. So, for example, Rio Tinto — the global mining conglomerate — is saving various sorts of heritage that are at risk, risk that is most significantly posed by Rio Tinto. And in the course of the mitigation of disaster through development and displacement, the mine gets dug and control of local resources shifts or solidifies (see Wait & Altschul, this volume). Citing LauraJane Smith (2006) multinational corporations now side with locals to argue against the imposition of 'authorized heritage' by outsiders. While Baird (2009) argues that this scenario allows for a new degree of autonomy for Indigenous Peoples in some circumstances, it is hard to see how the multinationals working directly with small villages and impoverished communities can be trusted to help people make the most informed decisions.

Despite my introduction, this paper is not an argument against capitalism or an attack on corporations. Blaming multinationals for capitalist practices is a waste of time. But it is imperative that we look honestly at the political ecology of capitalism so that, in cases where scholars and scientists have some influence over economic agendas, we attempt to mitigate the effects of the greed, ignorance, and arrogance of the 'haves' over the 'have-nots', and try not to promote and enhance greed, ignorance, and arrogance arising as a defence at the local level. At least we need to be as clear as we can about whether our efforts to do good in the world are not actually making things worse for those people and things we hope to save. Sometimes it may even be possible to make things better, but to do this we need more than good intentions and money. There will have to be some sacrifice.

What 'grass-roots' means

In this section I want to compare two of the projects I have been responsible for over the course of my career, both of which have a development component. One, in Belize, was not a community-based programme but has been what I would call community-centred. The second, in Kyrgyzstan, is a community-based programme but not what I would call community-centred. I am pleased (sort of) with the outcomes of the Belize project and the progress of the project — now several projects — in Kyrgyzstan, but they are completely different in approach, goals, resources, and cultural context. The relevance of these two programmes for a discussion of archaeology and development is that in both cases my ethnographic mission was to identify the right things to do about friendship, equity, education, scientific research, heritage preservation, economic development, the archaeological record(s), ethno-archaeology, and political manoeuvring and then how to do the right things. The contrasting results of these two projects suggest something interesting about archaeology and development.

Belize

In 1989, I documented the ancient city of Chau Hiix in the jungle in northern Belize, because of the interest in the site in the nearby village of Crooked Tree. The (then) 500 Creole residents handle the lands and resources around their homes as a common pool where they graze their cattle, hunt, fish, and bring tourists to see the more glamorous wildlife which remains plentiful because it is relatively inedible. To keep outsiders from netting all the fish, and trapping all the game, and bringing tourists in to hunt the monkeys and jaguars, the village collaborated with the Massachusetts Audubon Society — a New England conservation organization — to create the

Crooked Tree Wildlife Sanctuary. As stewards of this sanctuary, the residents can continue to use their resources as they have for 300 years, but keep outsiders from doing unsustainable commercial extraction (see CTWS, n.d.).

I was brought in to 'discover' Chau Hiix because villagers who graze their cattle and hunt near Spanish Creek found non-locals looting the ancient ruins. When outsiders showed enough initiative to get into that inaccessible place and dig a very deep laborious hole, it became clear to the local community that archaeological sites can also be part of a common resource pool that could benefit the village through tourism just like the wildlife sanctuary. The village chairman saw that selling artefacts, like selling jaguar pelts and monkey parts, would not provide a sustainable livelihood and would likely only benefit a few people, but tourists to the wildlife sanctuary could be sold an infinite number of side trips to visit the ruins. So the village went looking for an archaeologist, contacted me through a family connection, and invited me to come see their site. The rest is history.

Before I began excavating, I negotiated with the Belizean commissioner of archaeology, Harriott Topsey, to promise the village (and me) government investment in its development as a tourist destination. Harriott and I walked over the site and he and I outlined a scenario of preservation that seemed like an intelligent compromise between preservation of the natural resources of the wildlife sanctuary and the cultural resources of the site. We decided which trees should be cut, which ones left, and how buildings should be consolidated. It was probably a hare-brained scheme, since the logistics of getting to Chau Hiix are prohibitive, but I thought they could be overcome and from the start I described my project as effecting a compromise among the preservation needs of the archaeology (the government mandate), the needs of the village (economic development), and the needs of the wildlife to persist in a relatively pristine and protected environment that had been used sustainably by humans for a very long time. At the instigation of Crooked Tree Village, I negotiated with representatives of the Massachusetts Audubon Society and various government ministries to get the site included in the protected zone of the Crooked Tree Wildlife Sanctuary. Harriott Topsey died in 1995, but it was a few years before I accepted the fact that our hare-brained scheme had died with him.

Over the course of twelve field seasons spread out over the eighteen years between 1989 and 2007, I brought about $500,000 in wages into the village of Crooked Tree. Most seasons I paid the highest wages of any archaeologist in Belize (according to the Belize Department of Archaeology), because I wanted to pay a living wage, not a minimum wage. Several people worked with me for the entire time and I promoted them and raised their salaries every year that I could. By the final season in 2007, all the teaching of excavation techniques for my American field school students was done by Belizeans. Lots of village houses were built, lots of vehicles and phones and household appliances were bought, lots of trips to the US were made, and lots of kids were educated. But there were also lots of bets on horse races and cricket games, and lots of fast living and drug habits fuelled by my project salaries.

During this time I spoke in the local school about fifteen times, I spoke formally to the village council ten times and informally constantly. I accumulated and shipped a library of books to the village school twice, donated two desktop computers and three laptops, and arranged six site tours for the whole village at which all artefacts and field notes were on display. In 2003, I borrowed back from the government the artefacts we had dug up over the years and arranged a show for the village in the village. I sponsored school trips to the national museum and ten visitors to the US. I got a loan from the Interamerica Foundation for the village to hire its first site guard.

Having vicariously experienced the result of leaving excavated artefacts unprotected between seasons, I stored anything that might be worth stealing in the national repository in Belize's capital city, Belmopan, at the end of each season. Additionally, I spent a sizeable amount of money on a cinder block storage building with a cement floor, tin roof, and burglar bars on the doors, which was presided over by the watchman I paid out of grants and out of my own pocket continuously for eighteen years. Human remains, which could not be protected in the storage bodega and which could not be housed in Belmopan, I was permitted to borrow so I could take them to the US for curation and study.

I brought in professional potters four different times to hold village workshops to see if residents might want to make pottery for tourists to buy. I advertised the site as a tourist destination in *Archaeology Magazine*; I brought in four television crews to promote tourism. I gave tours and trained tour guides and paid for signs to orient visitors. I gave rides, food, equipment, vehicles, advice, and friendship. I do not know how many presentations I made at the Belize national archaeology meetings, but I am sure my students' presentations raise this number to over thirty. My project produced seven dissertations, four Masters' theses, and data used in over 200 publications and presentations at meetings all over the world.

Kyrgyzstan

In 2004, I accidentally went to Kyrgyzstan. My trip resulted from a polite invitation from the American University of Central Asia and my own curiosity. I knew nothing about Kyrgyz archaeology or heritage politics. I found myself in a place where there was no cultural resource management at the government level and where many citizens do not believe that Kyrgyzstan even has archaeological resources.

In reality Kyrgyzstan is an archaeological paradise; it has every sort of material remains imaginable from Paleolithic rock art to Medieval cities that flourished along the silk roads to the Bronze and Iron Age burial mounds of armoured warriors (cf. Kohl, 2011). Turkic writing on rocks scattered across the Tien Shan Mountains identifies the grazing territories of ancient clans. But tour operators, guides, college students, and even the Deputy Minister of Tourism patiently explained to me that Kyrgyzstan has no archaeology because the true Kyrgyz have always been nomads and nomads do not leave anything behind.

It became apparent to me that although people in the northern urban part of Kyrgyzstan were vaguely aware that there were the remains of ancient Buddhist temples and giant Medieval cities that they did not consider these 'Kyrgyz'. The disconnection between the common perception among educated people in the capital city that Kyrgyzstan has no archaeology and the use of Medieval urban sites as emblematic of regions in the south where a larger percentage of the population speaks Uzbek seemed scary to me. My worst fears were realized in 2010 when ethnic violence between Kyrgyz and Uzbek speakers caused the deaths of at least twelve people in and around the city of Osh. This was not the first of such clashes.

Archaeology notoriously gets its funding from patriotically motivated governments with political and economic interests in producing particular constructions of the past. The way this sort of nationalism co-opts UNESCO's world heritage agenda has recently been discussed (Askew, 2010) and the further twisting of these preservation programmes into scenarios of 'disaster capitalism' has already been mentioned. My concern was that, as has happened often in the past, a programme of nationally supported and internationally funded archaeology was about to be deployed to essentialize the Kyrgyz people as 'nomadic' in the service of stigmatizing, ousting, and generally mistreating Kyrgyz citizens who were going to be excluded from this 'authentic' nomadic heritage, in particular people who speak Uzbek. In one of his last speeches before he was thrown out of office, President Bakiev stated that the history of Kyrgyz nomads had been underappreciated and announced that his regime would support a new era of scholarly research as well as the production of movies and popular works focused on the achievements of nomads.

I decided that the hieroglyphs were on the wall for Kyrgyz nationalism and that it was reasonable to ask people outside the major northern cities about their ideas about heritage, ethnic identity, and archaeology. My thinking was that, since archaeological research often functions to provide a foundation for essentialist rhetoric that justifies exclusion and oppression and even interethnic violence, maybe it could also work the other way. That is, what if people got their ideas about heritage from each other rather than their government or USAID or UNESCO or Rio Tinto? What if people were shown more than one trajectory from the archaeological past, and introduced to a more complex heritage before the campaigns to promote ethnic pride (aka ethnic sovereignty) and (selected strategic) site preservation got underway?

I started out just asking people that I met questions about their ideas about heritage and got such an enthusiastic response I was emboldened to keep going. Although I found the answers to my questions riveting, it was what Kyrgyz people said to each other that was most powerful. My Kyrgyz colleagues had spent years trying to explain to students, the public, and foreign scholars that the burial mounds that cover the countryside were actually built by the ancestors of modern Kyrgyz people. The urban Kyrgyz I met believe that the mound builders left before the Kyrgyz came. A Kyrgyz colleague was with me when I asked the deputy of a tiny northern village (also a professional sheep herder) whom did he think built the mounds we could see in every direction from his farmstead. Without hesitation, he replied, 'My ancestors'. The Kyrgyz archaeologist was as pleased as I was.

I got a grant from the US State Department to hold four workshops, including one that allowed me to bring twelve Kyrgyz people to the US to investigate approaches to heritage management. I took them to see community museums to meet with various heritage specialists, including Mac Chapin who did some of the first Indigenous maps projects (Chapin, et al., 2005), public archaeologists, park service archaeologists, and specialists in archaeology and education and in museum studies. The Ziibiwing Center of Anishinabe Culture & Lifeways agreed to host us and we spent three days at the Center in Mt Pleasant, Michigan, since Indigenous Americans have specialized knowledge about ethnicity and nationalism and oppression. At the end of the trip the Kyrgyz visitors designed the final workshop for themselves and invited me to participate in *their* project. On the last day of the workshop the group proposed thirteen small-scale grassroots heritage projects. In the years since this workshop, while I have sought a new source of support and wasted time being a college professor, my Kyrgyz colleagues have proceeded without me. Their new Sacred Heritage Association has been incorporated with full recognition of the government and an education programme has arisen in the south aimed at land use planners and schoolchildren. They now have funding from The Intellectual Property Issues in Cultural Heritage (IPinCH) project to support phase two of the Kyrgz proposals, several of which have a significant economic development component (Pyburn, 2013; in press).

Discussion

Crooked Tree bought into focus the preservation ethic promoted by the Belize government and various local and international interest groups. The commitment to preservation is sincere, but it is clearly mitigated by factors beyond local and national pride. Believing that site preservation would inevitably follow from community interest and site significance, I promoted a series of discoveries at the site that occasionally made local news, but none that elevated preservation of the site above the expense of surmounting the logistics of its development. My emphasis on the fact that the site was continuously occupied through the Maya 'collapse' and discovery of a huge hydrological system that created sustainable agricultural production never made the *New York Times*.

The Crooked Tree community tried to bring archaeological preservation within their existing system of land use. On occasions when the government came close to funding a watchman or establishing a road, the village recognized this would take control of the site out of village hands and give it to the government. Since this would clearly interfere with the village's ability to profit from the site, I saw this as likely to contribute to site destruction, so I resisted it right alongside the village, though it probably was never really close to happening. Lack of elite-focused discoveries and resistance to government control surely played a part in the trajectory of the Chau Hiix Project.

As with any impoverished community, whether in a developing nation or not and whether the residents feel they are descended from the ancient residents or not (Crooked Tree residents identify themselves as Creole, not Maya), site preservation for its own sake or for 'the future' is considered a frivolous and even ridiculous waste of energy and time. This is not because they are not 'educated'. It is because they need medical care, clean water, a source of income, and security against hunger, which are all much more important and none of which can be taken for granted.

I believe I helped the residents of Crooked Tree by providing information about the world that would otherwise have come only from television, tourists, and residents returning from stints working in the US. I made a great effort to encourage critical thinking about all sorts of research and development programmes. Probably more importantly I provided enough income to allow a few people some degree of security and choice, but not enough to effect displacement. What I failed to do was align my own interests as a scholar and an archaeologist closely enough with theirs, so that Crooked Tree people were able to help me. Of course, they educated me and supported my research with their goodwill and hard work, but the longer-term goal of preservation and development that was the foundation of the plan I made with Harriott Topsey was not met.

In contrast, over a much shorter period of time, with much less money and no localized cultural skills — I speak no relevant language — Kyrgyz project members have moved ahead and implemented a series of preservation initiatives that are so exciting I continue to be astounded. The formal incorporation and acknowledgement by the Kyrgyz government of the Kyrgyz Sacred Heritage Association was an effort that required many hours of work and resulted in a book-sized document of the articles of incorporation. The Osh project members have begun an educational out-reach campaign funded through UNESCO to produce posters for schools showing what archaeological sites look like. When pictures of archaeological sites located around Osh were first presented to a meeting of government land use planners, they recognized the places in the pictures, but no one had realized they were archaeological sites. The planners were so excited about this new information, they were shouting out ways to begin to educate the public to preserve their sites.

According to the 'experts', the government of Kyrgyzstan is the first true parlia-mentary democracy in Central Asia, a failed or (my favourite term) 'confused' state. I think at least some of the misunderstanding about what is going on in Kyrgyzstan's rapidly developing post-colonial political economy is that people who live there do not fit into a colonial stereotype. They are not slowly becoming more civilized, as the Chinese had thought, or more urbanized as the Russians tried to institute, nor even are these the people whose labour and complementary subsistence patterns made the rise of settled populations into cities possible. To a certain extent all these scenarios are correct, but as Scott (2010) points out, refusal to become or to be dominated by a settled centralized state is a closer approximation of history than nascent stateness, failed stateness, or political 'confusion'.

In fact, maintenance of a nearly ungovernable tribally organized system (my Kyrgyz colleagues and friends characterize themselves as tribal) is what appears to be a democracy to some pundits, a failure to others, and a confusing situation to most. It also might have helped Kyrgyzstan remain relatively free of post-Soviet despotism and made two coups and one actual election possible in the past ten years, with not much bloodshed by Central Asian, much less South-West Asian standards. Yes there has been ugliness, violence, and some horrible human rights violations, and there is every possibility for there to be more, but, so far, no mass slaughter.

Site preservation through 'disaster capitalism' will not work for Kyrgyzstan both because the friable and infinitely complex tribal alliances that cross cut the country — ethnicity, history, political convictions, and subsistence strategies — and because many people do not know they have anything to preserve. Lack of centralized author-ity makes government-multinational-preservation crusaders less of a threat, though outsiders often do not understand this and go right ahead with schemes that go nowhere. For example, with funding from Japan, UNESCO mounted a large-scale preservation project for the site of Krasnaya Rechka, 35 km outside the capital. According to my Kyrgyz colleagues several million dollars were spent on consultation and the construction of a roof over a small portion of the site of an ancient monastery complex. A few years later the roof is damaged and is funnelling water into the mud brick structure rather than away from it, and locals have 'repurposed' the attractive tiles that had been used for site consolidation. National heritage is not a local responsibility here.

A grass roots project means that the people who stand to benefit or lose define their own problems. If we go in to solve a problem that people do not have — such as the crisis of site destruction — we are creating a disaster that promotes the sort of capitalism and development that the locals do not control and that does not solve their actual problems. It also leaves them in a completely different condition the result of which is unknown and unpredictable. But I went in with a different attitude. I was not trying to preserve something; I was trying to see what Kyrgyz people wanted to preserve and what they thought about different types of preservation and how, or if, I had any skills that they could use to solve problems. I asked people I met whether they saw the issues I know something about as related to their problems as a nation, as individuals, as members of various groups, including tour guides and archaeologists and sheep herders.

Conclusion

I have worked in Belize over the course of twenty-five years. Belizeans speak English and so do I. I have been to Kyrgyzstan five times, totalling less than one year. Kyrgyz people speak Russian, Kyrgyz, and Uzbek, and I do not. The result of my work in Belize is vague and unquantifiable. The result of my work in Kyrgyzstan is dramatic and measurable. In Belize I developed what I call the rules of engagement for community-based research (Pyburn, 2003); in Kyrgyzstan I violated most of them in favour of letting Kyrgyz people design the research and make the rules.

The differences between these two places are vast but the similarities are salient. Both are recently postcolonial, rapidly globalizing nation states in political turmoil attempting to reckon with a complex history and a multi-ethnic population. It will be years before I develop a satisfactory explanation for the contrast in my experiences in the heritage business in these two countries. I am pretty sure that I have been more successful in Belize and less successful in Kyrgyzstan than it appears by superficial measures. But I do have a couple of tentative conclusions.

First, the practice of ethnography is important, but not a panacea and it is imperative that archaeologists like me do not get overconfident about the accuracy and utility of our ethnographic knowledge. Rather than doing ethnography to convince people to share colonial devotion to preservation, it is more realistic and I now believe more ethical to do ethnography with a goal of educating yourself so you can make your goals intelligible to the people whose heritage and neighbourhoods you invade. You need their permission, their informed consent; they do not need yours.

The information the locals need from academic researchers is what programmes of economic development have worked and not worked in comparable situations and ideas based on your experience in their community and respect for their values about how to adapt these ideas to solve the problems that they identify. An archaeologist is not going to be able to offer much but a minimal responsibility is to make the intentions, resources, and limitations of any given research transparent, so that people can decide whether archaeology and heritage management pose a danger and whether any of the skills or international connections research might offer could be useful for them. More local knowledge improves the outsiders' chances of discovering something to offer and becoming welcome and figuring out how to go beyond not harming anyone to actually doing some good.

Second, my work in Belize has been personal and on a human scale. I did not try to bring heritage to the locals or preservation to the disenfranchised. I brought myself: my goodwill, my resources, my knowledge, and my friendship, no more and no less. I got the same in return. My efforts in Kyrgyzstan are also on a modest scale, but there I did not have my own project, I did not have an agenda of research on material culture to take up my attention. I just worked to share as much information as possible, and to figure out what people could use and how I could help them get it. I am far from finished.

But the products of my Kyrgyz work will be projects that grow and develop and have an impact far beyond my small idea that started the project. With just a little boost from me, there now really is a Kyrgyz Sacred Heritage Association whose members all kept close tabs on each other throughout the recent interethnic violence. The main product of my Belize work, in addition to some very promising archaeological data, is really just me. I think I did ok by the residents of Crooked Tree. But what they taught me made it possible for me to take my first step toward community engaged archaeology in Kyrgyzstan.

Bibliography

Askew, M. 2010. The Magic List of Global Status: UNESCO, World Heritage, and the Agendas of States. In: S. Labadi and C. Long, eds. *Heritage and Globalization (Key Issues in Cultural Heritage)*. London and New York: Routledge, pp. 45–66.

Baird, M. 2009. The Politics of Place: Heritage, Identity, and the Epistemologies of Cultural Landscapes. Unpublished PhD thesis, University of Oregon [accessed 26 March 2014]. Available at: <http://gradworks.umi.com/33/95/3395204.html>.

Cameron, C. 1994. The Destruction of the Past: Nonrenewable Cultural Resources. *Journal of Non-renewable Resources*, 3(1): 6–24.

Chapin, M., Lamb, Z,. & Threlkeld, B. 2005. Mapping Indigenous Lands. *Annual Review of Anthropology*, 34: 619–38.

Cojti Ren, A. 2006. Maya Archaeology and the Political and Cultural Identity of Contemporary Maya in Guatemala. *Archaeologies; Journal of the World Archaeological Congress*, 2(1): 8–19.

Crooked Tree Wildlife Sanctuary (CTWS). n.d. Crooked Tree Wildlife Sanctuary [accessed 19 February 2014]. Available at: <http://ambergriscaye.com/pages/town/parkcrookedtree.html>.

Klein, N. 2008. *The Shock Doctrine: The Rise of Disaster Capitalism*. New York: Picador Press.

Kohl, P. 2011. *The Making of Bronze Age Eurasia*. London: Cambridge University Press.

Labadi, S. & Long, C. eds. 2010. *Heritage and Globalization (Key Issues in Cultural Heritage)*. London and New York: Routledge.

Pyburn, K. A. 2003. Archaeology for a New Millennium: The Rules of Engagement. In: L. Derry and M. Malloy, eds. *Archaeologists and Local Communities*. Washington, DC: Society for American Archaeology, pp. 167–84.

Pyburn, K. A. 2004. *Ungendering Civilization: Rethinking the Archaeological Record*. London: Routledge.

Pyburn, K. A. 2013. Notes from the Field: Progress Towards Cultural Heritage Protection in Kyrgyzstan [accessed 19 February 2014] Available at: <http://www.sfu.ca/ipinch/outputs/blog/notes-field-progress-towards-cultural-heritage-protection-kyrgyzstan>.

Pyburn, K. A. (in press). Activating the Past: Using Archaeological Research Findings to Challenge the Present. In: S. Atalay, L. Rains Clauss, R. H. McGuire, and J. R. Welch, eds. *Transforming Archaeology: Activist Practices and Prospects*. Palo Alto, CA: LeftCoast Press.

Scott, J. C. 2010. *The Art of Not Being Governed: An Anarchist History of Upland Southeast Asia*. New Haven: Yale University Press.

Smith, L. J. 2006. *Uses of Heritage*. London: Routledge.

Wilk, R. 1985. The Ancient Maya in the Political Present. *Journal of Anthropological Research*, 41(3): 307–26.

Willems, W. 2012. Problems with Preservation in Situ. *Analecta Praehistoria Leidensia*, 43/44: 1–8.

Zarger, R. K. (in prep.). Displacement at Home: The Reorganization of Space, Resource Access, and Mobility after Hurricane Iris in Southern Belize.

Notes on contributor

K. Anne Pyburn is Provost's Professor of Anthropology and Director of the Center for Archaeology in the Public Interest at Indiana University. She is Vice President of the World Archaeological Congress, directs 'Community Cultural Resource Management for the Silk Road' funded by Intellectual Property Issues in Cultural Heritage (IPinCH) initiative, is senior editor of the One World Archaeology Series, and former co-editor of *Archaeologies: The Journal of the World Archaeological Congress*. Pyburn was PI on the Chau Hiix Project investigating the political economy of an ancient Maya community; her research was been invited and facilitated by the residents of Crooked Tree Village and the Institute of Archeology of Belize. Pyburn was also the co-author and director of the MATRIX Project (Making Archaeology Teaching Relevant in the XXI Century). She writes about the archaeology of gender, settlement patterns, cities, and the ancient Maya; and about ethics, community involvement, and public education in archaeological research.

Correspondence to: K. Anne Pyburn, Department of Anthropology, SB130, 701 East Kirkwood Avenue, Indiana University, Bloomington IN, 47405-7100, USA. Email: apyburn@indiana.edu

PUBLIC ARCHAEOLOGY, Vol. 13 Nos 1–3, 2014, 240–49

Heritage and Economy: Perspectives from Recent Heritage Lottery Fund Research

Robert Bewley

Heritage Lottery Fund, UK

Gareth Maeer

Heritage Lottery Fund, UK

There is clear and irrefutable evidence that archaeological and historical sites have the potential to be the catalysts for economic, social, and political change. The issue facing us is how might we understand the conditions which turn the potential into reality. For that to happen we need research into the contribution that heritage makes to social and economic life. This paper provides an overview of this recent research undertaken by the Heritage Lottery Fund. It demonstrates the importance of having good evidence on which to base decisions and develop future policies, but argues that a reliance on the economic case alone is not sufficient. It concludes by suggesting that, in the current economic climate, it will be important for heritage organizations to use the argument for the economic benefits of the heritage within the cultural value context, and with as wide an array of potential supporters as possible and not just national and local governments.

KEYWORDS heritage, economy, lottery, tourism, employment

Introduction

For many years there was a commonly held belief that the source of most of the problems in the 'heritage world' (for want of a better term) was one of resources — and especially money. However, when trying to understand why the heritage sector does not play a more central and important role in societies today, the biggest hurdles, in our view, are not financial but political and intellectual. Only when these barriers have been overcome can the use of resources (money, people, time, equipment, transport, and technology) be harnessed. There is a political nature in everything we

   DOI 10.1179/1465518714Z.00000000063

do — even weather forecasts have political dimensions (as they reinforce national boundaries).

One of the barriers — when viewed from outside the sector — is the heritage itself; because of the need to preserve and protect the heritage this 'extra cost' is seen as a barrier to development. The intellectual barrier exists when there is too narrow a definition of the heritage.[1] In the grain of every place, every building, or location (urban and rural) there is 'heritage of value', be it explicit, implicit, tangible or intangible, hidden or blaringly obvious, but if this is not recognized or understood it will not be valued, and thus can be lost rather than enjoyed and cared for.

In the United Kingdom, we are in the very privileged position of having a Heritage Lottery Fund (HLF), which derives its income from the sales of lottery tickets. For every £1 worth of lottery tickets sold, 'good causes' receive 28p, of which 20 per cent (or 5.6p) goes the Heritage Lottery Fund. For the financial year 2013–14 this will provide an income for grant giving of over £400m for HLF to distribute in grants to heritage projects, ranging from £3000 to over £5m (HLF, 2013).

This is an uncommon, but successful model. The only other one we know about in Europe which uses a proportion of its income for good causes is the Loterie Romande (based in Lausanne, Switzerland, founded in 1937 by the six French-speaking cantons) which helped to restore the wonderfully evocative Chateau Chillon. But there is nothing on the scale of the UK's HLF anywhere else in the world. The significance of HLF (for this paper) is not that it has contributed c. £5bn to the heritage sector since 1994 (HLF, 2013), but that it exists at all.

In 1994, the Prime Minister of the UK, John Major, created a National Lottery. This event has proved to be transformational for the heritage, arts, and sport (especially in 2012 with the London Olympics and Paralympics). Through the Lottery, the UK has managed to breach a major political and intellectual barrier. Namely that funding for the arts, sport, heritage, and charities and communities would no longer have to compete with taxpayer income for the big government departments — health, defence, education, and welfare. The decades of underfunding for the heritage, understandable when in competition with hospitals and schools, appeared over.

It could be argued that we are gambling with our heritage (or that John Major was), but since 1994 there have been 30,000 projects funded and the income has been maintained (HLF, 2013) — in fact increased since the recession and the financial crisis, which began in 2008. The relevance of lottery funding is not just the extra resources it has provided, but the understanding it has conferred that the 'good causes' are important in their own right. If heritage (considered an expensive luxury by so many, or a barrier to growth by others) had to forever compete with the essentials of running a country — economic prosperity, defence, education, health, and welfare — it would continue to be a low funding priority and therefore the benefits the heritage brings to society, at all levels, would be diminished.

A vision realized?

So, how can we show what this vision of a better-funded heritage has delivered in reality?

The first reaction to this question, within the heritage and cultural sector more widely, has often been to reach into the evaluator's toolbox and pull out an economic impact model. Economic impacts are a convenient tool, because of the quantified results they produce, because (amongst economists at least) there is broad agreement on the underpinning logic of the models and consistency in how they should be used; and because economic impacts relate to one of those main government 'essentials' — economic growth — thus making heritage appear relevant to decision and policy makers.

The ubiquity of economic impact results has been experienced first-hand by HLF since the organization published, in 2010, the first comprehensive assessment of the economic contribution of heritage-based tourism to the UK economy. This report, *Investing in Success* (HLF, 2010), was based on two sources of analysis. The first was research undertaken by Oxford Economics to look at the extent that tourist visits in the UK — undertaken by both inbound tourists and UK residents — are motivated by an interest in heritage. The highlighted figure from this research was that heritage-based tourism is a £12bn a year industry which supports 195,000 full-time equivalent jobs (Oxford Economics, 2009: 25). The Gross Value Added (GVA) produced by the sector — its contribution to the UK's overall measure of economic output — is £7.4bn a year, making it a bigger industry than electricity, advertising and motor manufacturing, and only just below publishing and agriculture (see HLF, 2010: 8–9).

These results are the consequence of the very high proportion of inbound visitors who, in national tourism surveys, consistently cite heritage as a major motivation for their trip to the UK. Overall, 30 per cent give reasons to do with the country's heritage as the single most important factor in determining their visit. Indeed, heritage is the single most important motivating factor that people cite for their trip to the UK, more important than others such as 'visiting friends and family', 'contemporary culture', 'shopping', or even 'business' (HLF, 2010: 10–11).

However, the research also showed that this impact of overseas visitors is actually rather smaller than that from domestic tourism — simply because of the sheer number of single day and holiday trips made by UK residents within their own country. This is despite the long-term trend towards more holidays abroad. UK residents are responsible for almost 60 per cent of the £12.4bn in total revenue generated through heritage tourism (HLF, 2010: 9).

The second part of the *Investing in Success* publication was based on an extensive evaluation carried out by HLF into the impacts of projects that it had supported. Over five years, more than sixty economic impact assessments were carried out, of completed projects at heritage sites that operate as visitor attractions. The aggregated results from these showed the scale of impact achieved — visitor numbers typically rose by 50 per cent after the HLF-funded project was complete. The extra contribution to the economy made by these visitors was split between on-site spend and — importantly — ancillary spend within the local economy, at a proportion of roughly 30:70; for every £1 spent on a visit, 32p went to the heritage attraction itself and 68p to other businesses in the local economy such as restaurants, cafes, hotels, shops, travel operators. Put these two factors together and the research shows that the amount spent by heritage visitors in a local economy doubles after an HLF-funded project. Further quantified impacts came in the form of jobs created — an average of fifty-three new jobs per project. Extrapolating from the sample to all completed projects at visitor attractions, it was estimated that 32,000 jobs had been sustained, by HLF funding, in the national tourism sector since 1994. Finally, the analysis is capped off by comparing these economic outcomes to the input cost of HLF funding — demonstrating a 'return on investment' of more than 1:4. For every £1m of HLF funding there is an increase in tourism revenues of £4.2m over the subsequent ten years (HLF, 2010: 18–23).

An example of this at a city scale is in Liverpool. The museums in Liverpool are known collectively as the National Museums Liverpool (NML), comprising seven museums (Museum of Liverpool, World Museum, Walker Art Gallery, Merseyside Maritime Museum, International Slavery Museum, Lady Lever Art Gallery, and Sudley House). In 2010–11, there were 2.63m visits to NML sites; 45 per cent were locals, but visitors and tourists (138,400) ensured 75,000 rooms sold in hotels because of gallery and museum visits in the single year. It is estimated that visitors to NML directly generated £34.2m of spend in the local economy in 2011–12; indirectly this produced a further £14m, supporting a further 212 jobs/posts (see Travers, et al., 2005). This analysis was based on those who said that their sole reason for visiting Liverpool was the heritage, demonstrating an under-estimate of the entire impact of the museums as a magnet for visitors to the city. This in one of the most deprived cities in the UK.

At the other end of the country, in the South-East, is Chatham Historic Dockyard. Its economic impact study in 2011–12 claimed that 500 jobs had been created by investment in the dockyard, with an additional £16m per year being spent in the local economy by visitors as a result. The dockyard is increasingly recognized as a hub for creative businesses in the Medway area, thus becoming a source of growth in other types of economic activity besides tourism (DC Research, 2012).

Other studies have looked at the scale of the contribution of the historic built environment in Wales (Ecorys, 2010), Scotland (Ecorys, 2008), and Northern Ireland (Eftec, 2012) — all finding impacts measured in the millions of pounds and thousands of jobs. All of these reports used a similar approach, modelling the impacts associated with tourism and combining it with estimates of the expenditure and employment associated with the maintenance of historic buildings and with heritage-based tourism.

Limits to the economic case

The *Investing in Success* results were widely welcomed by the heritage sector, and have been seized on again and again by organizations, journalists, and politicians wanting to 'make the case' for heritage. The report has probably been the most successful advocacy document produced by HLF, and quite possibly by the heritage sector as a whole in the UK. But does it make the 'case' for heritage? Questions do remain.

Firstly, even the final extension of the analysis to the 'return on investment' comparison only becomes effective as a persuasive tool influencing the allocation of government resources if it compares favourably with alternative types of investment. Or, alternatively, of not investing at all and leaving the money in people's pockets for them to spend as they wish. HLF's evaluation has shown that some projects have produced economic returns comparable to other types of government spending, by achieving 'grant-per-job created' ratios of between £15,000 and £50,000 per job. But these are in a minority, with the average closer to £90,000 per job (GHK, 2009).

Secondly, the results we get from modelling the economic impacts of specific investments are geographically specific. They have significance at the level of the local or regional economy, but a different — much lower one — at the level of the national economy. At the level of the national economy, new investments predominantly redistribute spending, income, and employment, rather than being net additional. In the case of the national economy net additionality is limited to the increase in visits by tourists from overseas or to the extent that it leads to a form of 'import substitution' by encouraging UK residents to holiday within the country rather than going to destinations abroad. If domestic residents have simply substituted one consumer activity for another, no 'extra' income has been generated within the national economy. In that case a more sophisticated economic argument needs to be made, based on a dynamic rather than static analysis. Through this argument public investment can be said to be helpful in supporting the trends in changing consumer preferences that are a constant feature of dynamic market economies. This, though, takes us into the territory of determining the type of economy — the mix of goods and services that is produced within an economy — which we will expand upon below.

Thirdly, the research does not immediately lead to new ideas for policy prescriptions, beyond the request for extra money to achieve extra return. That request is circumscribed not only by the two points made above, but also by perceptions of the overall government budgetary position. So the extent that these arguments have been successful in the UK over the last three years is limited to the extent to which they have helped in minimizing the scale of government cuts, rather than obtaining new resources, given the government's over-riding imperative to reduce its budget deficit.

These circumscriptions can create the sense of evidence fatigue — that whatever compelling economic case is made by the heritage sector is never quite good enough. Sometimes this extends to a cynicism about evidence-based policy-making — the weary recognition of the political reality that policy is made in response to the powers of competing interests across the corporate and public spheres.

So, although the Government's Tourism Policy (DCMS, 2011), published in March 2011, recognized the importance of heritage tourism for economic growth, and looked at ways of reducing regulations and helping to market Britain abroad, the industry did not receive the type of direct support as given to the more politically high-profile car industry (BBC, 2009). This despite the fact that — as the *Investing in Success* report had shown — heritage tourism (never mind tourism as a whole) is a bigger industry and employer.

Beyond economics — cultural value

How should the heritage sector respond to this?

In our view, part of the answer lies not in giving up on the economic argument, but on having a more nuanced understanding of the relationship between heritage and the economy and between economy and social progress. HLF has attempted to deal with this by linking the concept of what the heritage sector produces (heritage 'goods and services') to a vision of the overall trajectory of the UK economy. This work, carried out in partnership with the UK think-tank the Work Foundation,[2] has proved a useful platform for thinking about how the heritage sector may develop in the future, based on ideas about where 'demand' for its goods and services will come from (Work Foundation, 2010).

In particular it allowed HLF to expand beyond the conventional focus on citizens/ consumers as a source of demand (for recreation, leisure, tourism, but also education, learning, and active participation) to a more expansive view that places heritage within a series of sector 'supply chains', and so incorporates demand from business or industry customers as well. One obvious example is the creative and cultural sector where heritage forms part of the 'supporting infrastructure' used by design companies, advertisers, filmmakers, and brand marketers. Another example is the set of scientific/technological businesses that could increasingly look for access to the collections held and managed by many heritage institutions, or that are looking for inspiration to the knowledge residing in heritage organizations, in order to develop new low-carbon products and services. There are some examples of existing practice here, such as the Natural History Museum's science consulting service (NHM, 2014), but more could be developed as the UK economy becomes increasingly knowledge-based.

This way of thinking about heritage and economy takes our advocacy away from the 'positive' to the 'normative', away from a passive demonstration of current economic 'contribution' to a more active engagement with future economic potential — the economy we would 'like' as well as the economy that is 'likely'. The importance of this work was to demonstrate the different ways that heritage can play an important role in economic recovery — suggesting new rationales for both public sector investment in core assets, and also new potential streams of earned income from business and consumer demand. It allows the heritage sector to enter the conversation about what sort of economy we want in the future, rather than mechanistically calculating its contribution to the one we have today.

The importance for the sector to engage in public debate on these terms has been well summed up by the economist John Kay (2010), who pointed out that the cultural sector in general makes the mistake of speaking of 'the economy' as if it were 'a monster outside the door that needs to be fed and propitiated'. But, as Kay points out, the only intelligible meaning of 'benefit to the economy' is the contribution that an activity makes to the welfare of people: it is the welfare derived from the goods and services that are produced in an economy that is really important, not the input costs of jobs and capital.

Others have taken these ideas further. Understanding that the economy is a means to an end, rather than an end in itself, is the core idea behind the interest in 'wellbeing economics', by now a decade-long movement for social progress to be re-conceptualized around the objective of promoting individual and social wellbeing, ending the over-emphasis on Gross Domestic Product growth (NEF, 2011). Although strong arguments can be advanced to support the claim that increasing GDP (hence, in theory, average income) is positively linked to increasing wellbeing, a growing body of evidence has shown this relationship breaking down. This may be due to a breakdown in the distribution of the proceeds of growth and/or because of saturation, for some parts of the population at least, with the satisfaction that comes from materialism and consumerism. For example, Jackson (2009) argues that the primacy of growth in government policy is explained by the necessity of maintaining overall levels of employment, given that improved labour productivity from technological development tends to reduce labour demand over time. This growth, Jackson argues, is dependent on the continuous replenishment of consumer demand, fed by consumers' need for 'novelty', in the form of new and more exciting products. This idea of 'novelty' was identified as the source of economic growth as early as in the work of Joseph Schumpeter, and built into his theory of 'creative destruction' as the motivating force behind capitalist economies. But Jackson combines this idea with the work of psychologist Shalom Schwartz, to propose the idea of a society in balance when the tension between two distinct but opposing values in our psychological make-up are not excessively skewed. One of these two is the tension between, on the one hand, 'openness to change (or novelty)' and, on the other, conservation — 'in other words between novelty and the maintenance of tradition' (Jackson, 2009: 163). But, if economic growth is dependent on the skewing of this balance towards novelty, how far can it be compatible with the conservation of heritage?

Jackson's way out of this conundrum — with much relevance for the heritage sector — is to ask questions about what sort of economic structure will be conducive to the creation of 'flourishing' lives that are not heavily linked to satisfying a thirst for novelty. His answer is an economy with a greater focus on cultural activity, on volunteering, on experience, curiosity, learning, on local, democratic involvement, and on environmental improvement (Jackson, 2009: 193). All conditions of flourishing lives that HLF research has demonstrated are frequently the outcomes of heritage projects (BOP Consulting, 2011).

It is this wider range of benefits that HLF has tried to research thorough our programme evaluation work, rather than solely concentrating on the narrow and more simply quantified one of economic impact. In turn, our understanding of why these benefits are delivered can be traced back to work on 'cultural value' which HLF did around the middle of the last decade with John Holden and Robert Hewison at the UK think-tank Demos[3] (Demos, 2004). In the UK this was a time of some disillusion in the arts and cultural sector with what is often termed 'instrumentalism'. That is, the idea that the value of the arts, culture, heritage can only be made in terms of quite narrowly defined benefits — especially around economic impact, skills, some types of social or community impacts (see, for example, Gibson, 2008). The 'cultural value' work was an attempt to counter a perceived omission by putting culture — in HLF's case, heritage — back into the debate. This was done by making a distinction between three sets of value.

One was indeed the 'instrumental' set of social and economic benefits, which was acknowledged to be important. But it was paired with a second set, termed the 'intrinsic' values of heritage. In doing this, the Demos/HLF work did not intend to mean that heritage has a single, definable intrinsic value, but that it is valued by people. A third set of values — institutional values — was also included in the framework, relating to the way that cultural organizations go about their work, and on what they base their 'legitimacy', defined as the public endorsement or support that exists for the work of the organization (Demos, 2004).

The importance of intrinsic values in the framework is that it creates a space for the inclusion of things not often talked about in narrow cost-benefit studies, with their emphasis on instrumental socio-economic outcomes, as recommended in government guidance such as the HM Treasury Green Book (see Gov.uk, 2013). Intrinsic values are what lie behind people's love for heritage; they are about aesthetics and beauty, about a sense of the spiritual, the numinous even. But they are about the intellectual as well — about understanding connections to place, time, and events. They are, too, about tradition and symbolic meaning. These are values deeply felt by individuals, and which are important in how people think about themselves, and about their own identity. But they are also, frequently, values that are shared with others. And they are, of course, highly contested. They are personal and varied: 'whose values?' is as relevant a question here as 'what values?'.

But the important point about this framework was the explicit acknowledgement that it is only *because* heritage has value for people that it is able to provide benefits for people and communities. An over-emphasis on the achievement of social and economic benefits, without an understanding of the heritage assets that provide the foundation for those benefits (including who those assets are valued by and why) cannot hope to realize the full potential of heritage. But not to understand how heritage can be managed to achieve real benefits for people is to leave it under-utilized. Both are needed. The Demos/HLF model has since proven valuable to HLF in operational terms — it forms the basis of the application and assessment process and has been used to structure the Fund's evaluation of its programmes and to assess the impact of its funding.

Conclusion

In our view the 'cultural value' framework remains the best basis on which the heritage sector should make its case for public support. The asset/flow model that it employs is a common conception in economic literature and should be readily understood by policy-makers.

However, in the current economic environment in the UK, these arguments will have to be used within the context of limited central government resources. Given this reality, the health of the heritage sector will depend as much, if not more, on the co-opting of resources and support from networks of public and private institutions, alongside much more loosely affiliated groups and communities, operating at different spatial levels from the national, to the city-region to the local neighbourhood. All are potential supporters inclined to receive the well-being and cultural value arguments with a more enthusiastic response than it has received at the Treasury.

Success in this future depends on those responsible for managing heritage assets developing an understanding of the motivations of social investors, philanthropists and individual donors as well as those of national and local governments.

Notes

[1] HLF uses a very broad definition of heritage, encompassing the so-called natural environment, landscapes, townscapes, buildings, archaeology, oral histories, intangible heritage, and has no limit on how old the heritage has to be (but usually it is more than ten years old).

[2] For further information on the Work Foundation, please see: <www.theworkfoundation.org.uk>.

[3] For further information on Demos, please see: <www.demos.co.uk>.

Bibliography

BOP Consulting. 2011. Assessment of the Social Impact of Volunteering in HLF-Funded Projects: Year 3 [accessed 14 February 2014]. Available at: <http://www.hlf.org.uk/social-benefits-involvement-heritage-projects>.

British Broadcasting Corporation (BBC). 2009. Car Firms get £2.3bn Loan Package [accessed 14 February 2014]. Available at: <http://news.bbc.co.uk/1/hi/uk_politics/7853149.stm>.

DC Research. 2012. Economic Impact of the Historic Dockyard Chatham [accessed 25 January 2014]. Available at: <http://www.thedockyard.co.uk/The_Trust/Economic_Impact_of_The_Dockyard_/Economic_Impact_of_The_Dockyard_.html>.

Demos. 2004. *Challenge and Change: HLF and Cultural Value*. London: Demos.

Department for Culture, Media, and Sport (DCMS). 2011. Government Tourism Policy [accessed 25 January 2014]. Available at: <https://www.gov.uk/government/uploads/system/uploads/attachment_data/file/78416/Government2_Tourism_Policy_2011.pdf>.

Ecorys. 2008. *Economic Impact of the Historic Environment in Scotland*. Edinburgh: Historic Environment Advisory Council for Scotland.

Ecorys. 2010. *Valuing the Welsh Historic Environment*. Cardiff: Cadw.

Eftec. 2012. Study of the Economic Value of Northern Ireland's Historic Environment [accessed 25 January 2014]. Available at: <http://www.doeni.gov.uk/niea/built-home/information/study_of_the_economic_value_of_ni_historic_environment.htm>.

GHK. 2009. *The Economic Impacts of the Heritage Lottery Fund*. London: Heritage Lottery Fund.

Gibson, L. 2008. In Defence of Instrumentality. *Cultural Trends*, 17(4): 247–57.

Gov.uk. 2013. The Green Book: Appraisal and Evaluation in Central Government [accessed 25 January 2014]. Available at: <https://www.gov.uk/government/publications/the-green-book-appraisal-and-evaluation-in-central-governent>.

Heritage Lottery Fund (HLF). 2010. *Investing in Success*. London: Heritage Lottery Fund.

Heritage Lottery Fund (HLF). 2013. Heritage Lottery Fund Annual Report 2012/13 [accessed 25 January 2014]. Available at: <http://www.hlf.org.uk/hlf-annual-report-2012-2013>.

Jackson, T. 2009. *Prosperity without Growth: Economics for a Finite Planet*. London: Earthscan.

Kay, J. 2010. A Good Economist Knows the True Value of the Arts. *Financial Times* [online] 10 August [accessed 25 January 2014]. Available at: <http://www.ft.com/cms/s/0/2cbf4e04-a4b4-11df-8c9f-00144feabdc0.html?siteedition=uk#axzz2kcbxLo8T>.

Natural History Museum (NHM). 2014. Science Consulting [accessed 17 February 2014]. Available at: <http://www.nhm.ac.uk/business-centre/consulting/index.html>.

New Economics Foundation (NEF). 2011. *Measuring Our Progress*. London. New Economics Foundation.

Oxford Economics. 2009. *Economic Impact of the UK Heritage Tourism Economy*. London: Heritage Lottery Fund.

Travers, T., Wakefield, J., & Glaister, S. 2005. *National Museums Liverpool: Its Impact on the Liverpool and the North West*. Report by London School of Economics for National Museums Liverpool. Available at: <http://www.liverpoolmuseums.org.uk/about/corporate/documents/EconomicImpactAug05.rtf>.

Work Foundation. 2010. *Heritage in the 2020 Knowledge Economy*. London: Heritage Lottery Fund.

Notes on contributors

Robert Bewley is the Director of Operations at the Heritage Lottery Fund. He has previously held positions at English Heritage as Regional Director for South-West England and, prior to this, Head of Survey, and Head of Aerial Survey. Dr Bewley still practices aerial archaeology in Britain and Jordan and regularly writes and lectures on prehistoric archaeology, aerial survey and the heritage sector at large. His publications include *Prehistoric Settlements*, *Aerial Archaeology: Developing Future Practice* (as co-editor with Włodzimierz Rączkowski), and *Ancient Jordan from the Air* (with David Kennedy).

Correspondence to: Robert Bewley, HLF, 7 Holbein Place, London sw1w 8nR, UK. Email: bobb@hlf.org.uk

Gareth Maeer is Head of Research at the Heritage Lottery Fund, where he oversees all the Fund's programme evaluation work, as well as the research it undertakes to develop new plans and initiatives. He has been with HLF since 2004, and has carried out extensive research looking at the social and economic impacts of heritage, including work on the links between volunteering and wellbeing, on heritage-based tourism and on the economic role of listed buildings in city development. He has published research for general audiences, such as the HLF publications *Investing in Success* and *New Ideas need Old Buildings*, as well as in academic journals including *Cultural Trends*, the *Journal of Urban Regeneration and Renewal*, and *Municipal Engineer*.

Correspondence to: Gareth Maeer, HLF, 7 Holbein Place, London sw1w 8nR, UK. Email: garethm@hlf.org.uk

PUBLIC ARCHAEOLOGY, Vol. 13 Nos 1–3, 2014, 250–61

Towards a Cultural Economy: Lessons from the American South-West

DEBORAH GANGLOFF

Crow Canyon Archaeological Center, Colorado, USA

The United States has an enviable diversity of public lands that are held in trust for all Americans. However, there is a war raging in the US between exploitative and protectionist ideals. The war's main victim is America's public lands. Some believe that public lands — open landscapes preserved for their scenic beauty, ecological assets (especially clean air and water), and cultural and natural resources — are best used for mining these resources, specifically their energy (oil, gas, and coal) reserves. It is the responsibility of archaeologists to contribute their perspective on this national and international public policy debate and help to build a cultural economy perspective. In addition to highlighting heritage tourism economies built on travel, meals, souvenir, and lodging expenditures, archaeologists must help convey the value of preserving historic sites.

KEYWORDS cultural economy, archaeological preservation, heritage protection, cultural heritage tourism, cultural resources

Introduction

Advocacy: making the economic case for cultural resources

The United States of America has an enviable volume and diversity of public lands; lands held in trust for all Americans. However, there is a war raging in the US between exploitative and protectionists ideals. The war's main victim is America's public lands. Those who believe public lands bring greatest economic opportunity through energy use stand opposed to those who believe that the economic potential of open space lies more in its ability to attract tourism revenue and the value of its ecological benefits. Some believe that such public lands — open landscapes preserved for their scenic beauty, ecological assets (especially clean air and water), and cultural and natural resources — are best used for mining these resources, specifically their energy (oil, gas, and coal) reserves. Protectionists believe that these lands must remain undeveloped to preserve their ecological functions and prevent damage to non-renewable cultural resources. The current recession rocking the economy of America

DOI 10.1179/1465518714Z.00000000064

has only served to heighten this divide between protectionism and exploitation, with jobs and local economies hanging in the balance.

It is the responsibility of archaeologists to contribute their perspective on this national public policy debate. Cultural resources are non-renewable (see Comer, this volume) and can be easily damaged or destroyed by the types of extractive development proposed for public lands. In addition to highlighting heritage tourism economies built on travel, meals, souvenir, and lodging expenditures — a $759 billion business in America per annum (NTHP, 2012a) — how can archaeologists help to place a value on the preservation of historic sites? We know the price of destroying our own history, but do we know its cost?

For public lands in America to receive due consideration of all their values by decision-makers, those of us who advocate for their continued protection must be able to measure and quantify the economic values of these lands — including the economies of their cultural and ecological values. Advances have been made in establishing monetary values for natural resources and their ecological benefits, such as clean air and water; often called ecosystem services (see, for example, Costanza, et al., 1997; MEA, 2005). Similarly, values can be put on cultural resources in terms of heritage tourism (NTHP, 2012a; Stynes, 2012). Those who wish to protect America's public lands must be conversant in the language of economics in order to prevail over those who see them as places for exploitation and development. I will explore this in the next section that presents several case studies.

Crow Canyon Archaeological Center

Crow Canyon Archaeological Center, located in Cortez, Colorado, was founded by Dr Stuart Struever in 1983, professor of archaeology at Northwestern University. He envisioned Crow Canyon as an independent, non-profit organization able to support long-term multidisciplinary research with assets generated from its organizational resources. At that time, archaeology as a science had developed to recognize that the study of the remains of cultures could only be understood when combined with the knowledge of the environmental and biological elements that together make up all of human history. And it was only through the study of the interaction between these factors that important advances could be made in our understanding of culture and cultural change. Dr Struever believed that only a non-profit organization (versus a governmental agency, academic institution, or cultural resources management firm) could set its own research agenda by using private funds donated by interested persons. This autonomy from the funding sources that would dictate research agendas, such as government or foundation grants, or work required by governmental policies, makes the non-profit sector the optimal choice for an independent, autonomous research institution.

Since its founding, Crow Canyon has become a premier institution for archaeological research in the south-western United States. This research is grounded in a series of excavation projects at ancestral Pueblo sites. These excavations, and the subsequent laboratory analyses, have been conducted with the help of nearly 100,000 students and adults in collaboration with American Indians who are the descendants of ancestral Pueblo people. Crow Canyon's invitation to the public to learn about and join in its research is a strategy to build an informed constituency in support of archaeology, cultural resources, and the interests of American Indians. Crow Canyon's reputation has grown as each successive project builds on the results of previous work. During the past thirty years, Crow Canyon has excavated over thirty archaeological sites, providing one of the largest and richest databases in the world for understanding the human past[1] (CCAC, 2012). Through its Governmental Affairs Committee, Crow Canyon has advocated for the protection of cultural resources and insisted on access to these resources for archaeological study. More recently, Crow Canyon has joined with other like-minded organizations (e.g. the National Trust for Historic Preservation, History Colorado, etc.) to make the economic case for cultural resource research and protection. As a non-profit organization, funded with private support, Crow Canyon has the right, but more importantly the responsibility, to advocate for improvements in local, state, regional, and national public policies. By inviting the public to join in its research, Crow Canyon contributes significantly to bringing visitors and interested people to the American South-west as both tourists and participants in its research and education programmes.

Cultural heritage tourism industry

Cultural heritage tourism is an activity in which people travel to experience the places and activities that represent the local history of a particular area. It is a big business, annually contributing $759 billion to the US economy. In the US, travel and tourism is one of America's largest employers, employing over 7.4 million people directly, with a payroll of $188 billion, and providing $118 billion in tax revenues for federal, state, and local governments (NTHP, 2012a).

In 2009, 78 per cent of all US leisure travellers (over 118 million people) participated in cultural and/or heritage activities while travelling. Those who engaged in cultural/heritage related tourist activities spent, on average, $994 per trip versus $661 per trip spent by all US travellers (NTHP, 2012a). Heritage travellers also stay longer on trips, according to the Travel Industry Association of America; 5.2 nights per trip versus 3.4 nights by non-heritage tourists (CHF, 2005). The biggest benefit of cultural heritage tourism is that it helps communities diversify their local economies and to fund preservation of community history, as the money spent at historic sites is reinvested back into the preservation activities necessary to maintain the sites.

While cultural heritage tourism is 'clean', that is, it is not polluting or dangerous, one challenge is to ensure that tourism does not destroy the heritage that attracts visitors. And it does put demands on infrastructure, such as roads, airports, water supply, and public services. It is essential, according to the National Trust for Historic Preservation (2012a), that, in order to make cultural heritage tourism work, a community needs to collaborate with partners, find the fit between community and tourism, make sites and programmes come alive, focus on quality and authenticity, and preserve and protect resources.

Mesa Verde National Park, one of America's premier heritage attractions and a driver for cultural heritage tourism in south-western Colorado, had 559,712 visitors in 2010, who spent $41.3 million in local communities, supporting more than 575 jobs in the local area (MVNP, 2012). Agency-wide, 281 million visitors to America's national parks spent $12 billion in 394 national park communities, according to a study by Dr Daniel Stynes of Michigan State University for the National Park Service. In 2010, National Park tourism supported more than 258,000 jobs nationwide, with payrolls of almost $10 billion and an additional $16.6 billion in indirect value from that payroll (Stynes, 2012).

Attracting business: another economic benefit

A study of Colorado and the Western United States released by Headwaters Economics (2011b) shows that the state's federally protected parks, wilderness areas and monuments are drivers for economic growth. In Colorado, non-metropolitan counties with 30 per cent federal lands or more showed a 345 per cent increase in jobs since 1970, while non-metropolitan counties with no protected lands saw only an 83 per cent job growth (Blevins, 2012). This research goes a long way to dispel the idea that land protection hinders economic development. High-wage industries such as healthcare, finance, real estate, and professional service jobs have led Colorado's job growth. It is, in fact, the access to outdoor recreation, open spaces, and a healthy lifestyle that attracts a diversity of employers to the state.

In November 2011 over 100 economists and related academics sent a letter to President Obama that stated, in part, that they

> believe that federal protected public lands are essential to the West's economic future. These public lands, including national parks, wilderness areas and national monuments, attract innovative companies and workers, and are an essential component of the region's competitive advantage.

They go on to say that

> Today, one of the competitive strengths of the West is the unique combination of wide-open spaces, scenic vistas and recreational opportunities alongside vibrant, growing communities that are connected to larger markets via the Internet, highways and commercial air service. Increasingly, entrepreneurs are basing their business location decisions on the quality of life in an area. Businesses are recruiting talented employees by promoting access to beautiful, nearby public lands. This is happening in western cities and rural areas alike. Together with investment in education and access to markets, studies have repeatedly shown that protected public lands are significant contributors to economic growth. (Headwaters Economics, 2011a)

The economic impact of Crow Canyon and the cultural resources industry on Montezuma County, Colorado

In 2012, Crow Canyon contacted the Southwest Colorado Small Business Center at Fort Lewis College in Durango, Colorado, to request an analysis of the organization's economic impact on Montezuma County, south-west Colorado. The county has 25,000 residents, on roughly 2000 square miles of land (about twelve people per square mile). It is the twentieth most populated county of Colorado's sixty-four counties. The county has been settled since AD 600, although it is estimated that many more people lived there in prehistoric times (estimates vary up to about 100,000 in the twelfth century just before the massive depopulation of the area). The county is made up of about one-third federal lands (US Forest Service, Bureau of Land Management, National Park Service), one-third tribal lands (the Ute Mountain Ute Reservation), and one-third private, state, or county land. Mesa Verde National Park, home to 600 cliff dwellings created and then abandoned in the thirteenth century by the ancient Pueblo, brings many people to Montezuma County, and the town of Cortez, home of Crow Canyon Archaeological Center. There are three incorporated municipalities in Montezuma County: Cortez, Dolores, and Mancos, and a large number of unincorporated communities, including Towaoc, Lewis, Arriola, Mesa Verde, Lebanon, Stoner, Weber, and Battle Rock (see Montezuma County, 2013).

Montezuma County is arguably the most important county for archaeological resources in the United States. It contains the highest density of archaeological sites anywhere in the United States, has the country's premier archaeological national park (Mesa Verde National Park), two national monuments (Canyons of the Ancients and Hovenweep), a major interpretive centre (the Anasazi Heritage Center), many sites and districts listed on the National Register of Historic Places, and Crow Canyon, the South-west's premier archaeological non-profit that promotes research, education, and American Indian partnerships. Montezuma County also has several businesses relating to archaeology and residential subdivisions that are devoted to the preservation of archaeological sites. As such, Montezuma County can be a national model for helping to quantify the impact of archaeology on local economies. The preservation, research, education, and public interpretation of archaeological sites are critical to the long-term economic health of Montezuma County.

To conduct the economic impact analysis of the Crow Canyon Archaeological Center on Montezuma County, payroll and expenditure data were collected directly from Crow Canyon. This information was supplemented by data provided by the Colorado State Demographers office regarding sector employment and labour income. The IMPLAN modelling system[2] was used to provide estimates of direct and indirect economic impacts, which were based on employment numbers drawn from 2010 and calculated in 2012 dollars (Graves, 2012). Created by the Minnesota IMPLAN Group, the IMPLAN software system helps analysts address two common questions about economic study and analysis: how does my local economy function, and what would the economic consequences of a project or action be? IMPLAN creates a localized model to investigate the consequences of projected economic transactions in any geographic region in the United States. Used by over 2000 public and private institutions, IMPLAN is the most widely employed and accepted regional economic analysis software for predicting economic impacts. Some scenarios that can be examined with IMPLAN include:

- What effects would a new industry/technology in my study area generate?
- How many jobs will this project create?
- What is the significance of this company/organization to the local study area economy?

This analysis showed that the total economic impact of the Crow Canyon Archaeological Center on Montezuma County is $5.9 million annually. IMPLAN estimates that the 50 full-time equivalents (FTEs) at Crow Canyon support an additional 23 community jobs and provide $780,000 in addition to the $2.6 million payroll. This creates a 'ripple effect' as these earnings then recirculate through the local economy.

Other impacts leading to the estimated output of $5.9 million are the results of rounds of purchases by businesses and consumers (Graves, 2012). The aggregated Cultural Resource Industry, which includes businesses, non-profit organizations, and government agencies involved in cultural resources, in Montezuma County in 2010, including Crow Canyon, provided an estimated 385 jobs, $13.1 million in wages, and $29.7 million in total output (production). Crow Canyon attracts 2000 students and 300 adults annually to its campus near Cortez. Spending by visitors, not including tuition or programme costs paid to the organization, is estimated conservatively at $257,000, based on information provided by Crow Canyon and extrapolated from a recent visitor expenditure survey in Pagosa Springs, Colorado, a nearby community (BBC, 2012: 10).

There are also many other benefits that are harder to measure but still significant. For example, the Cultural Resource Industry is relatively 'clean' (as opposed to extractive industries), in that it does not use up natural resources nor create polluting by-products. It is also sustainable because the focus is on preserving the resources that people come to see (BBC, 2012). One way to strengthen protection on public lands is to seek National Monument status for those lands, discussed below.

The benefits of National Monuments designation

A National Monument is a designation of public land that provides additional legislative protection and federal funding. In this way it is similar to a National Park, but a national monument can be quickly and easily designated by a President under the American Antiquities Act of 1906 (see below). A national monument can be managed by one of several land managing agencies in the United States; the National Park Service, the Bureau of Land Management, or the US Fish and Wildlife Service (all within the US Department of the Interior), or the US Forest Service (under the US Department of Agriculture).

The American Antiquities Act of 1906 resulted from concerns about protecting mostly prehistoric Native American ruins and artefacts (collectively termed 'antiquities') on federal lands in the West. The Act authorized permits for legitimate archaeological investigations and penalties for persons taking or destroying antiquities without permission. The Act also grants the president of the United States the authority to designate, by executive order, 'Historic landmarks, historic and prehistoric structures, and other objects of historic or scientific interest as national monuments, ensuring their protection' (NTHP, 2012b).

This landmark US legislation has been used by many presidents to protect areas of national significance even when the local authorities did not appreciate their value. Theodore Roosevelt, the first President to issue a proclamation establishing a National Monument in 1906, protected more than one million acres by establishing eighteen monuments in nine states, including Devil's Tower in Wyoming and Petrified Forest in Arizona. President Carter, on 1 December 1978, declared 56 million acres spread over fourteen areas in Alaska as National Monuments. More than 25 per cent of the presidentially created monuments exceed 50,000 acres, including many that ultimately became National Parks, such as Grand Canyon, Glacier Bay, Bryce Canyon, Death Valley, Olympic, and Joshua Tree. Between 1906 and April 2012, fifteen presidents used the Antiquities Act to establish 130 National Monuments.

Most recently, President Obama designated Fort Monroe National Monument in Virginia and Fort Ord National Monument in California (NTHP, 2012b).

The United States Congress also has the power to declare National Monuments and has done so in forty cases (NTHP, 2012b) (Congress also has the power to abolish monuments, but has exercised this option only on rare occasions and usually to provide some alternative form of protection.). Congress has acted to enlarge the monuments, adjust their boundaries, or change their status from National Monuments to National Parks or national historic sites.

Although fifteen of the past nineteen US presidents have used the 1906 Antiquities Act to protect dozens of remarkable historic, cultural, and natural national treasures, implementation of the Act often stirs controversy and has been the focus of numerous attacks. At the time of writing, in the last three sessions of Congress, bills were introduced to limit the presidential authority vested in the Antiquities Act. All of them failed. There have also been numerous legal challenges to monument designations, some of which reached the federal appeals courts; however, these challenges have also failed (NTHP, 2012b).

National Monuments case study: Canyons of the Ancients

The Canyons of the Ancients is a national monument along the western edge of Montezuma County, Colorado, designated in 2000 by President Clinton. Managed by the US Bureau of Land Management (BLM), Canyons of the Ancients covers 178,000 acres that contains more than 6000 identified archaeological sites, of both historical and cultural remains that span thousands of years. It is estimated there are somewhere between 10,000 and 20,000 archaeological sites on the Canyons of the Ancients. The monument maintains relationships with twenty-five Native American tribes, including eighteen Pueblos plus the Utes, Navajo, and Jicarilla Apache. The monument preserves existing rights of way, grazing, and hunting and fishing rights (CotA, 2010).

A recent Resource Management Plan was completed that included negotiations regarding the mining of CO_2 on the monument. Eighty per cent of the lands of the monument are leased, with 190 wells working and another 120 planned during the next twenty years. For each pair of wells, there is one pad which equals a 5-acre area. CO_2 is a finite resource, like many in the energy sector, and it is predicted that the supply at Canyons of the Ancients National Monument will last for another twenty years. It is significant to note that the energy industry contributes 51 per cent of the Montezuma County budget (CotA, 2012).

The Canyons of the Ancients National Monument Resource Management Plan reflects the Bureau of Land Management's mandate to manage its lands for multiple use; including mineral extraction, grazing, timber, and special forest products (e.g. fire wood, Christmas trees), maintaining water and air quality, wildlife management, and preserving scenic beauty. Due to the nature of the monument, cultural resource protection is given priority in decisions of land disturbance. Surface disturbance activities must avoid direct, indirect and cumulative impacts to historic properties or cultural resources, keep to the smallest footprint on the ground as possible, prevent landscape fragmentation, and maintain visual quality. Any disturbance, even in areas where no cultural resources have been found must be monitored by an agency archaeologist. In addition, consultation with Native Americans ensures their involvement in land-use decisions (CotA, 2010).

While many believe that public lands designations work against economic development, this has not been shown to be the case at Canyons of the Ancients or other recently designated National Monuments in the Western United States (Headwaters Economics, 2011b). Between 2000 (the date of designation of the Canyons of the Ancients National Monument), and 2008, the county experienced a 5 per cent increase in population, a 10 per cent increase in service jobs, a 28 per cent increase in non-labour income (investments, entitlements, interest, and rent, etc.), and real per capita income grew 15 per cent. In addition, there was an increase in recreational opportunities and associated businesses — tours, hiking, biking, Recreational Vehicling (RVing), camping, fishing, hunting, skiing, and so on (Headwaters Economics, 2011). The Resource Management Plan for Canyons of the Ancients is a model for how energy exploration and extraction can be balanced with the protection of cultural and natural resource protection.

National Monuments case study: Chimney Rock

Chimney Rock is located west of Pagosa Springs in the San Juan National Forest in Archuleta County in south-western Colorado. It is managed for protection and public interpretation and is the only administratively designated US Forest Service Archaeological Area. Management duties are shared by the US Forest Service and the Chimney Rock Interpretive Association (CRIA). CRIA is a non-profit that operates tours and the Chimney Rock Visitors Center Cabin, as well as raises funds and works to raise awareness of the site's offerings. Chimney Rock attracts scientists, historians and heritage tourists. The site lies on 4700 acres of the San Juan National Forest. Between AD 900 and 1150 it was home to an outlying community of New Mexico's Chaco Canyon, and its residents were the ancestors of today's Pueblo Indians. The community at Chaco Canyon was the centre of the pueblo world during this time. The people at Chimney Rock built over 200 homes and ceremonial buildings high above the valley floor. The Great House Pueblo lies in the shadow of the twin spires that give Chimney Rock its name. It is believed to be an archaeoastronomy observatory for the Lunar Standstill, which occurs every 18.6 years. At this time, from the Great House Pueblo, the moon rises directly between the spires before it begins its journey back south in the sky. The main access trail traverses a high sandstone ridge that reaches 7600 ft (1000 ft from the valley floor) to sixteen individual archaeological sites. These include the excavated sites of the Great Kiva, Pit House, Ridge House, and the Great House Pueblo. The other sites remain unexcavated and represent the potential for further archaeological research at Chimney Rock (Chimney Rock, 2012).

Chimney Rock currently attracts about 12,000 visitors per year. They are a combination of local people, non-local day visitors, lodgers, and campers in the area. The 9720 non-local visitors provide $848,000 in direct economic impact, which includes lodging, dining, retail purchases, and so on. Another $396,900 in secondary economic impact of these visitors is estimated from the recirculation of their expenditures through the community as the businesses that receive the visitors' funds purchase goods and services from other community businesses (BBC, 2012: 9).

Chimney Rock non-local visitors support over 13 FTE of direct employment as well as another 3 FTE indirectly (BBC, 2012: 16). A study by BBC Consulting shows that national monument status could double the economic impact of Chimney Rock on the local economy. By examining several recently designated national monuments similar to Chimney Rock, BBC determined that Chimney Rock is likely to experience extensive tourism growth bringing an additional $1.2 million to the area for a total of $2,433,762 annually (PSCCNR, 2012).

In addition to the economic impact this visitation provides, the people who tour Chimney Rock have the opportunity to learn about the ancient Pueblo Indians and their present-day descendants. Many appreciate for the very first time the impressively sophisticated building and cultural knowledge of these ancient peoples, and gain a greater appreciation for the culture and lifestyle of present-day American Indians.

In 2009, US Congressman Ken Salazar of Colorado introduced legislation into the US House of Representatives to designate Chimney Rock a National Monument. National Monument status would give the site additional visibility and federal resources in the agency's budget, and also provide a clear cultural resource preservation mandate for the US Forest Service. The National Trust for Historic Preservation proposed that the designation maintain Forest Service management guided by a master plan crafted with community involvement (BBC, 2012). This legislation did not pass the US House and died when Representative Salazar lost his seat in the 2010 elections.

Similar legislation was introduced into the US Senate by Senator Michael Bennet of Colorado in 2010, co-sponsored by Senator Mark Udall of Colorado. Encouraged by much advocacy and communication efforts, the newly elected Congressman in the district, Scott Tipton, introduced similar legislation in the US House in 2011. Representative Tipton was convinced of the need for national monument status for Chimney Rock by the economic data presented by Crow Canyon and other groups in a coalition formed to advance this designation (including the National Trust for Historic Preservation, the Western Conservation Foundation, the Conservation Lands Foundation, the Wilderness Society, the San Juan Citizens Alliance, and others). Representative Tipton's bill passed the US House in 2012, but the Senate bill stalled in that congressional body.

The coalition then decided to make the case for a Chimney Rock National Monument directly to the White House. With coalition support, Senators Bennet and Udall asked Congressman Tipton to join them in a bi-partisan effort to ask President Obama to engage in a discussion with the local community to determine whether Chimney Rock warranted a national monument designation under the Antiquities Act of 1906. In a letter, the politicians asked the President to explore all options to give Chimney Rock the recognition and protection it deserves by making it a national monument (Trujillo, 2012). A public meeting was held in Pagosa Springs, Colorado, in May 2012, attended by Harris Sherman, Undersecretary of the United States Department of Agriculture (the federal department over the US Forest Service agency) and nearly 200 local residents, including representatives of the All Indian Pueblo Council, which represents all nineteen pueblos in New Mexico, and the Southern Ute. Response to a Chimney Rock National Monument was overwhelmingly supportive.

President Obama designated Chimney Rock a National Monument on 21 September 2012.

Advocating for improved public policy: lessons learned

The experience of Crow Canyon in advocating for improved public policy and from the examples of the case studies above, a few lessons learned are appropriate to share here. These practices can be used to showcase the unique economic benefits of cultural resources preservation in order to better advocate for improved public policies:

- **Showcase the economics** — Conduct or commission a study on the economic impact of the archaeological sites and cultural resources industry in your area. These studies should include the direct impacts, such as payroll and other expenditures, and indirect impacts, cultural heritage tourism expenditures, direct and indirect, and note the longer-term influence these sites can have on visitors.
- **Build partnerships** — In times of thin resources, support can go further when like-minded organizations partner to share those resources. Others in the community (museums, shops, restaurants, hotels, etc.) may also share the need for economic data, and be helpful in discovering the ways to communicate all the economics of a cultural economy.
- **Engage indigenous or local communities** — It is essential to work in collaboration with indigenous people to ensure that their perspective on cultural resource protection is heard in the policy arena. In addition, archaeological research can benefit immeasurably from the input of indigenous knowledge.
- **Collaborate with government** — Land-managing agencies have challenges and needs that organizations can help fill. They can also bring significant resources to bear on collaborative projects. Government agencies need partners to help them make the case to the public for the value of their work. Partners can leverage limited government funds with private support to make those dollars go much further.
- **Be relevant** — Cultural resource institutions must strive for relevance, and advocacy can be the public face of how relevant an institution can be. Whether your funding comes from private grants or donors, you must make your work relevant to today's issues.
- **Share research with decision-makers** — Policy-makers need data on which to base their decisions. Providing them with objective, independent research to make the economic case for cultural resources and historic preservation can make the difference between good and bad public policy. Policies made by decision-makers are only good when they reflect the real needs of local communities.

Conclusion

There is a growing trend towards the collection and communication of the economics of cultural resources, focusing initially on cultural heritage tourism. As evidenced above, the numbers are impressive. If we can augment that data with ways to calculate and communicate the additional values, such as educational values or future research values, we can make an even more compelling case for cultural resources protection. Site preservation and protection has tremendous educational value. Learning about ancient people and their present-day descendants creates an understanding and fosters an appreciation of diversity and tolerance among people. The economic value of tolerance cannot be overestimated.

The research value of archaeological sites is also extremely high. We have a great deal still to learn about the human experience. Preserving and conserving sites for future research, with new technologies and methods to be developed, is invaluable. We must learn to express this value while we make the case for archaeological site protection.

And finally, advocacy is not just a right but also a responsibility. Advocacy can provide the way in which cultural resources institutions can stay relevant to a constituency. Archaeological organizations must stand for the protection and conservation of archaeological treasures, and have an obligation to educate decision-makers on the value of these precious non-renewable resources. Making the case for cultural resources with an economic argument is the best strategy for success, especially in the current difficult economic climate.

Notes

[1] For further information on the activities of Crow Canyon Archaeological Center, please see <http://www.crowcanyon.org>.

[2] For further information on IMPLAN, please see <http://implan.com>.

Bibliography

BBC Research and Consulting (BBC). 2012. *Economic Impacts of National Monument Designation, Chimney Rock, Colorado*. Denver: National Trust for Historic Preservation.

Blevins, J. 2012. Protected Federal Lands are Fueling Colorado's Economic Vitality. *The Denver Post*, 31 May, p. 11A.

Canyons of the Ancients (CotA). 2010. Record of Decision and Resource Management Plan, June 2010. Colorado: US Department of the Interior, Bureau of Land Management, Colorado State Office.

Canyons of the Ancients (CotA). 2012. [Online] [accessed 24 September 2012]. Available at: <http://www.blm.gov/co/st/en/nm/canm.html>.

Chimney Rock, 2012. [Online] [accessed 24 September 2012.] Available at: <http://www.chimneyrockco.org/index.htm>.

Costanza, R., d'Arge, R., de Groot., R, Farberk, S., Grasso, M., Hannon, B., Limburg, K. I., Naeem, S., O'Neill, R. V., Paruelo, J., Raskin, R. G, Suttonkk, P., & van den Belt, M. 1997. The Value of the World's Ecosystem Services and Natural Capital. *Nature*, 387: 253–60.

Colorado Historical Foundation (CHF). 2005. *The Economic Benefits of Historic Preservation in Colorado — 2005 Update*. Denver, CO: Clarion Association.

Crow Canyon Archaeological Center (CCAC). 2012. [Online] [accessed 24 September 2012]. Available at: <http://www.crowcanyon.org/index.php/about-us>.

Graves, D. K. 2012. *The Economic Impacts of the Crow Canyon Archaeological Center and the Cultural Resources Industry on Montezuma County, Colorado*. Durango, CO: Information Services.

Headwaters Economics. 2011a. Economists Urge President Obama to Protect Federal Lands [online] [accessed 25 March 2014]. Available at: <http://headwaterseconomics.org/land/economists-president-public-lands>.

Headwaters Economics. 2011b. Canyons of the Ancients National Monument: A Summary of Economic Performance in the Surrounding Communities [online] [accessed 24 September 2012]. Available at: <http://headwaterseconomics.org/wphw/wp-content/uploads/ancients.pdf>.

Mesa Verde National Park. (MVNP). 2012. Press release. 'Mesa Verde National Park = visitors, money and jobs for local economy'. Mesa Verde, CO.

Millennium Ecosystem Assessment (MEA). 2005. Washington, DC: Island Press.

Montezuma County. 2013. [Online] [accessed 17 December 2013]. Available at: <http://en.wikipedia.org/wiki/Montezuma_County,_Colorado>.

National Trust for Historic Preservation (NTHP). 2012a. Cultural Heritage Tourism: 2011 Fact Sheet [online]. Washington, DC: National Trust for Historic Preservation [accessed 24 September 2012]. Available at: <http://culturalheritagetourism.org/documents/2011CHTFactSheet6-11.pdf>.

National Trust for Historic Preservation (NTHP). 2012b. The Antiquities Act of 1905: 2012 Fact Sheet (unpublished). Washington, DC: National Trust for Historic Preservation.

Pagosa Springs Chamber of Commerce News Release (PSCCNR). 2012. 'Chimney Rock National Monument Designation is Expected to Double Economic Impact' [online] [accessed 11 July 2012]. Available at: <http://web.pagosachamber.com/news>.

Stynes, D. 2012. Economic Benefits to Local Communities from National Park Visitation and Payroll 2010 [online]. [accessed 24 September 2012]. Available at: <http://www.nature.nps.gov/socialscience/docs/NPSSystem Estimates2010.pdf>.

Trujillo, T. 2012. Udall, Bennet, Tipton Ask President to Consider National Monument Designation for Chimney Rock. Press Release [online] 23 April [accessed 23 April 2012]. Available at: <http://www.markudall.senate.gov/?p+press_release&id=2183>.

Notes on contributor

Deborah J. Gangloff is President & CEO of Crow Canyon Archaeological Center. She holds a PhD in anthropology from Rutgers University. Gangloff has three decades of experience in non-profit management and public policy advocacy at the national level. Prior to Crow Canyon, Gangloff led the Washington DC-based *American Forests* conservation organization (1996–2010), and earlier served as Vice President of Programs. She chaired the US Secretary of Agriculture's National Urban and Community Forestry Advisory Council for five years (1999–2004). Her Board of Directors service includes President of the La Cruz Habitat Protection Project, Vice President of the local public radio station, and a member of the Board of the Friends of Chaco. She also serves on Colorado's Southwest Resource Advisory Council for the USDI Bureau of Land Management. She has been recognized by the US Forest Service, the Natural Resources Council of America, the International Society of Arboriculture, the Sustainable Forestry Initiative, and the Home Depot Foundation for her exemplary work.

Correspondence to: Deborah J. Gangloff, Crow Canyon Archaeological Center, 23390 Road K, Cortez, Colorado, 91321, USA. Email: dgangloff@crowcanyon.org

PUBLIC ARCHAEOLOGY, Vol. 13 Nos 1–3, 2014, 262–77

Do Good, Do Research: The Impact of Archaeological Field Schools on Local Economies

RAN BOYTNER

Institute for Field Research, USA

The economic development of archaeological sites usually refers to tourism. The economic role of actual research is frequently ignored. This paper critically examines the benefits that field research yields, especially at the community level and particularly in the developing world. Its focus is on the economic impact of archaeology field school programmes populated by US-based students. Although most funding for field research is directed towards projects in developed countries, a significant portion is available — and directly supports — projects in developing countries. This paper presents data on archaeological field schools collected in the past five years from four different data sources — the Archaeological Institute of America, the Institute for Field Research, University of California Los Angeles Field Programs, and the Institute of International Education — and summarizes trends at the global scale.

KEYWORDS archaeology field schools, economic impact, international development, education, philanthropy

Introduction

Economic development related to archaeology frequently focuses on the role of tourism and the revenue streams it can generate (for a sample of the diverse writing on the subject, see Bernbeck & Pollock, 2004; Killbrew, 2010; Kohl, 2004; Lopes Bastos & Funari, 2008; Pollock, 2010; Rowan & Baram, 2004; Schnapp, 1996; Silverman, 2002; 2011). A number of specialized organizations — for example, the Global Heritage Fund (GHF), the Sustainable Preservation Initiative (SPI), the World Heritage Fund (WHF), and the World Bank — focus on archaeological sites as leverage for broader economic development and are equally focused on tourism and its potential benefits. Governments are also keen on using the past in general, and archaeology in particular, as a foundation for economic and nationalistic developments (Hamilakis, 2003; Killbrew, 2010; Scham, 2004; Silverman, 2002; Wendrich, 2010; Yahya, 2002).

　　　　DOI 10.1179/1465518714Z.00000000065

Nevertheless, despite great promise and substantial investment worldwide, sustainable returns from development of archaeological sites as tourist destinations are rare.

When archaeological sites are developed for tourism, initial investments in infrastructure, presentation, and training of locals as guides, frequently fail to generate significant or lasting returns. While success stories like Machu Picchu (Peru), the Acropolis (Greece), Chichen Itza (Mexico), Stonehenge (UK), or the Terracotta Army at X'ian (China) are inspiring, these are iconic sites; most investments in archaeological sites as engines for economic growth do not produce the desired outcomes. This paper is not a critical examination of such development, nor does it try to propose remedies or suggest alternatives to this type of investment. Instead, its focus is on the frequently ignored economic benefits and significant impact of research conducted specifically at archaeological sites — limited in terms of total financial investment but long-lasting in impact at the level of local communities. In particular, this paper will present and discuss the impact of archaeology field schools on communities across the world, providing hard data about financial impacts and the regions of the world where they are most felt.

Generally speaking, regardless of scale, time period, or geographic location, research activities at archaeological sites are usually appreciated as purely academic activities. They are considered a prelude to the development of sites but not as a pivotal component in the economic benefits that archaeological sites may yield. Increasingly, archaeologists are asked to set aside funds from their general budgets to be used for the development of sites for general public visitation. The financial, political, social, and cultural returns that research activities per se actually generate are neglected and poorly understood.

Tourists usually visit sites for a brief period of time and spend limited amounts of money locally. Archaeological expeditions, however, stay substantially longer at communities near archaeological sites and make a local impact that is economically broader, deeper, and longer lasting. Archaeological expeditions spend a significant part of their budgets on local housing and food, paying for local labour, purchasing equipment and supplies at local businesses, and use a range of local services (laundry, Internet cafes, etc.). But their impact goes beyond direct financial contribution to local economies. Locals who wish for returned business may protect sites so expeditions will come back for continued research. Archaeologists excavate sites, revealing their history and producing tangible and attractive evidence of the past — objects and features. The comprehensive narratives created through archaeology provide the fundamental information and symbolic iconography that trigger interest and create the genesis for economic development if a site is selected for further development for tourism or as regional or national symbol.

Reproduction of archaeological artefacts using traditional designs and/or methods can produce lucrative micro-economic niches. Whether artisans are instructed by archaeologists or are simply inspired by archaeological finds, the production of replicas can become an engine of development as interest at the local, regional, or international markets in such products increases. The SPI business model at San Jose de Morro in northern Peru is based on ceramic production of Moche pottery and has proven quite successful (see Coben, this volume). This model repeats itself in many others parts of Peru (e.g. Nasca, Cusco, Trujillo) with a broad range of artefacts that include ceramics, textiles, and gourds. It is also quite successful elsewhere in the world (for example, Stanish, 2006).

Finally, archaeological expeditions are packed with young and often idealistic individuals, and long-term relationships between outsiders and locals may develop. Whether through development work, the creation of service-learning projects, or through the (rare) cases of marriage, migration, and remittance, these relationships yield lasting and profound impact on local communities (for example, Moche Inc., 2013).

It has been difficult to measure the economic impact of any of these activities as, thus far, no reliable data have been publically available and no research specifically conducted on the topic. This paper is not an attempt to measure the entire economic impact of archaeology as an industry. Instead, it is a first attempt to quantify and critically examine the impact of archaeology field research on local communities. As a first, this paper is imperfect. Its analysis is based on a number of conjectures and existing datasets that are neither exhaustive nor comprehensive. Yet, this attempt can be used as a baseline that will allow scholars to build on and improve our understanding and quantification of the financial scale and economic impact that field schools have on local communities across the world.

Archaeology field schools

Archaeology field schools have been around for over 100 years, operating as training grounds for students seeking careers in academic archaeology and serving as an arena of 'natural selection' designed to weed out those unsuitable for the profession (Boytner, 2012b; Clarke & Phillipsus, 2011; Gifford & Morris, 1985; Judd, 1968; Mytum, 2011; Perry, 2006; Pyburn, 2003; Springer, 1913; Walker & Saitta, 2002). In recent decades, archaeology field schools have become an important source for the funding and operation of many archaeological projects — especially field schools populated by US-based students (Boytner, 2012a). A significant portion of student tuition is directed to fund archaeological research at the field, and student labour is used as an alternative to hiring local workers. As demonstrated below, the number of field schools offered to students in recent years is large and the economic impact of the method attracts scholars both within and outside US universities.

Most field schools recruiting in North America are populated by students based in US universities (see Table 1). These field schools are principally funded through

TABLE 1

STUDENT NATIONALITY DISTRIBUTION AT THE UNIVERSITY OF CALIFORNIA LOS ANGELES (UCLA) AND INSTITUTE FOR FIELD RESEARCH (IFR) FIELD SCHOOL PROGRAMMES

Nationality	Organization	
	UCLA (2007–10)	IFR (2012)
US	96.3%	87.4%
Canada	2.8%	5.8%
Non US	0.9%	6.8%
Total no.	644	103

programme fees, charged directly to students in addition to and separate from any tuition paid to universities for regular, on-campus academic activities. Since the cost of education in the US is high, field school programme fees are high as well, reflecting real costs on the ground. Significant portions of these programme fees are directed towards supporting research activities. As a consequence, scholars running archaeology field schools secure substantial funding and (usually) an enthusiastic and committed workforce. Students, in turn, are frequently awarded a significant number of academic credit units and engage in often life-changing, meaningful cultural experiences (see Baxter, 2009; Boytner, 2012a; 2012b; Morrison, 2012; Mytum, 2011; Perry, 2004; 2006; Piscitelli & Duwe, 2007).

Archaeology field schools provide incentives that generate significant feedback loops promoting excellence. The better the field school, the more students the field school director can attract. The more students, the more funding, and thus potentially better access to technology and techniques that improve research. As more applications are submitted to any field school, its director can become increasingly selective, choosing only the best students — more committed students who will work faster and produce more and better research results — and further enhancing the quality of the field school. Although the use of students in field schools forces project directors to slow down the pace of research, its considerable financial and pedagogical benefits and the increasing scarcity of other funding sources make field schools an attractive alternative to fund archaeological projects, whether partially or, increasingly, in full.

How much funding do field schools actually generate annually and what is their global economic impact? Thus far, there has been no attempt — at least not one resulting in publication — to measure the financial scale or impact of field schools. Because no agency or independent entity collects consistent or reliable data about archaeology field schools, a number of conjectures must be used to measure impact from the partial data that are available (see below). This study, therefore, should be seen as the beginning of a discussion, and not as the definitive work that establishes the size and scale of the field school industry.

Datasets

This analysis is based on the study of archaeology field schools populated primarily by US students. Many field schools around the world are run by institutions teaching archaeology that seek to train their students in the art of field archaeology, and are thus established as part of the teaching curriculum at archaeology departments (see Mytum, 2011). These field schools are funded as a matter of course by governments or as part of students' general tuition. Data about their costs are not public and difficult to obtain, as it is part of the departments' running budgets. Further, such field training programmes are almost exclusively aimed at matriculating students at individual universities and costs are not publicized as part of marketing campaigns aimed at recruiting outside students.

In contrast, many field schools in the US are actively recruiting students from across the nation. Many websites, social media outlets, Twitter feeds, and other marketing tools are used to reach students who seek meaningful cultural experiences during the summer months and are accustomed and ready to pay for such experiences. It is not

TABLE 2

COUNTRY OF HOME INSTITUTION OF FIELD SCHOOL DIRECTORS FOR PROGRAMMES TARGETING US
STUDENTS (AIA DATASET — SEE BELOW)

Year	Director affiliation	
	US	Non-US
2009 (N=208)	61%	39%
2010 (N=174)	57%	43%
2011 (N=120)	61%	39%
2012 (N=127)	55%	45%

the goal of this paper to critically examine the ethics of this system or to express opinions on its merits and shortcomings. But it is clear that the system is highly attractive to archaeologists from outside the US and that entrepreneurial scholars are attempting to harness some of its economic potential to support their own research activities in projects across the world (see Table 2).

No single comprehensive database for archaeology field schools aimed at US students exists. There are neither government regulations nor licensing requirements that create centralized databases, at neither the federal nor at the state level. Instead, a number of websites aggregate data for students, either through 'bots' (programmes that index websites across the internet) or through direct uploads that scholars insert into pre-set fields. Of the first type of aggregate websites, About.com dominates the segment; its 'bots' comb the Internet and produce short entries and links to archaeology field schools in a highly searchable format. Based on Google Analytics data for the Institute for Field Research (collected 1 September 2012), 30 per cent of all referral traffic came from About.com. It is likely that this pattern is similar for other field schools sites.

Aggregate websites that require field school directors to enter data into pre-set fields are more comprehensive, richer in data, and are better organized for users to obtain information about archaeology field schools. That segment is dominated by two websites — Shovelbums (n.d.) and the Archaeological Institute of America (AIA) (AIA, 2014) — although field schools are but a part of the overall online presence of both entities. Of the two, the AIA website is better organized and easier to navigate, in part because the AIA is a large and prestigious archaeological organization that has the resources to build and maintain a more professional website. It is also more attractive to scholars, as listing with the AIA can be used as seal of approval, although in reality the AIA provides an uncritical conduit for publication of field school existence only. No website provides information on actual enrolment at field schools or any additional follow-up data. Yet, they are still an important source of information and the study of their entries can provide significant information about field school trends.

Research methodology

This study is based on the analysis of four distinct datasets (see Table 3). The first — and largest — is unpublished data generously provided to the author by the AIA. It

TABLE 3

ORIGIN, TEMPORAL COVERAGE, AND SIZE OF DATASETS USED FOR THIS STUDY

Source	Time & Quantity	
	Period	No.
Archaeological Institute of America (AIA)	2008–12	635
UCLA Archaeology Field Program	2007–10	61
Institute for Field Research (IFR)	2011–12	13
(IIE) Open Doors Report	2001–10	N/A

consists of field school entries to its website between 2008 and 2012. Only five field schools were recorded on this database for 2008, so that year is largely statistically irrelevant for this analysis. Data from 2009 through 2012 are much richer and more varied. Although the AIA database offers scholars consistent and easy-to-follow fields to complete, not all field schools entered data to all fields and there is a broad variability in the consistency of data entry.

The second dataset is drawn from the UCLA Cotsen Institute of Archaeology Field School Program, covering the duration of that programme from 2007 to 2010, when the programme was cancelled (Boytner, 2012b). The third is data from the Institute for Field Research (IFR), an independent academic organization that runs archaeology field schools throughout the world (Boytner, 2012a: 31). Data for both the UCLA and IFR programmes are available at significantly higher resolution and level of detail and the conjectures used for the analysis of the larger AIA dataset are based on patterns seen at these two refined datasets.[1]

The final dataset is based on the Open Doors Report published annually by the Institute of International Education (IIE) (IIE, 2011). The IIE documents both inflows of international students to the US and outflows of US students that study in international destinations. While the IIE does not track data on individual disciplines, its overall dataset provides important context for understanding trends in international education of US students. Because the largest dataset used in this study — the AIA database — is incomplete, five different conjectures were used to normalize its analysis so it may reasonably represent genuine trends (see Table 4). Considerable effort was made to maintain a conservative reading of the data and all numbers presented here denote the lower end of the potential range. The result is that the economic impact of field school is likely greater — perhaps considerably — than the numbers illustrated here.

TABLE 4

THE FIVE CONJECTURES USED FOR ANALYSING THE AIA DATASET

Average no. of students per field school	10.8
'Go' rate of field schools	70%
Overhead rate for FS offering credit	40%
Weighted factor for non-published FS	50%
In-State vs. Out-of-State attendance ratio	1:1

The first conjecture addresses the number of US students attending — and paying for — archaeology field schools each year. The AIA database does not follow or record the actual number of students enrolled in any of the programmes published on its website. However, detailed data from the 61 UCLA field schools indicate that the average was 10.8 students per programme (Boytner, 2012b: 91). That same number was applied to the AIA database.

Not all field schools generate enough interest and enrolment. Data from both the UCLA Field Program and at the Institute for Field Research show that some field schools fail to reach minimum enrolment and are cancelled. In addition, not all available spots at field schools are filled. Many programmes go to the field with less than full capacity. Myriad reasons may account for the inability of field schools to recruit the sufficient or maximum number of students, including the geographic location of the project, the reputation of the field school director, the costs associated, or a lack of adequate publicity. Data from UCLA show that 'Go' rate — defined as the percentage of spots filled compared with maximum spots available for each year — was 80 per cent. Given that many of the field schools presented on the AIA dataset were of institutions with less well-known 'brand names' than that associated with UCLA, the 'Go' rate used for this study was lowered to the 70 per cent level.

The third conjecture addresses the issue of reliably calculating the sum of funds available to directors of the field schools. The AIA data indicated that 40 per cent of field schools do not provide any academic credit for students, and thus it is assumed that programme fees are going in their entirety to field school directors to be used in the field. But the remaining 60 per cent of field schools awarded participating students between four and twelve academic units from accredited universities. These credits units do not come free. The accrediting institutions charge fees for these credits, as well as additional overhead costs to manage the collection and oversight of funds for the field school director. Many US universities are rapidly increasing their overhead fees from revenue generating programmes (see data presented in Boytner, 2012b: comments in Boytner, 2012a: 30, and see table 6.2). No data is available about the rate universities charge for overhead and/or credit fees and in the US, there are no standards or set fees. Each university charges a different fee that may change from year to year. Data from UCLA suggest that the fee is around 30 per cent, but that rate increased annually and UCLA is a public university where tuition is comparatively low. Private universities charge significantly higher fees (and tuition). To reflect these differences and create an estimated baseline standard, overhead fee for this study was calculated at 40 per cent of total tuition.

The fourth conjecture addresses the total number of field schools available each year to US-based students. There are two issues of relevance here. First, not all field schools posted on the AIA website list their costs (see Table 5). On average, only 70 per cent of all these field schools provided cost data. The second issue is the incomplete nature of the AIA database. Many field schools are subsidized by universities — either through direct financial support, teaching relief or other indirect support — and such programmes strongly focus on recruiting students matriculating at the home institution of the field school director. Such field schools rarely post on the AIA website (or any other field school aggregator websites) and usually focus their recruitment efforts on students exclusively within their own institution.

TABLE 5

PORTION OF FIELD SCHOOLS POSTING THEIR COSTS ON THE AIA WEBSITE (UNPUBLISHED DATA)

Year	Costs Reported	
	Yes	No
2009 (N=208)	73%	27%
2010 (N=175)	69%	31%
2011 (N=120)	56%	44%
2012 (N=127)	80%	20%

It is difficult to properly compensate for the incomplete listing of all field schools. Based on discussions I had with a broad range of archaeologists from many US universities, I estimate that at least 20 per cent of all field schools do not market their existence using websites outside those of their own university. Adding this number to the 30 per cent of field schools with incomplete cost data produces a 50 per cent weighted factor. This number is added in most cost calculations presented in this work, but it is always presented as such, in addition to the 'hard', unweighted data that are positively present within the AIA database.

The final conjecture addresses cost differences of field schools run by public universities. Such universities charge differential rates between in-state and out-of-state students. This number is important for calculations of overhead costs, since the higher costs of out-of-state tuition are fully absorbed by the university issuing the credits and do not add to funding available to field school directors. Both the UCLA and IFR programmes had more out-of-state students attending their programmes than in-state students (see Table 6). However, many field schools that offer public university credits have significant price differences between in- and out-of-state tuition costs (both the UCLA and IFR had relatively small price differences — $150 to $450 — between the two types of enrolment). It is likely that programmes with large cost differentiation between the two payment types attract more in-state students. For the purpose of this work, therefore, a 1:1 ratio between the two payment types was used in all calculations involving public universities.

TABLE 6

STUDENT RESIDENCE STATUS FOR ENROLMENT PURPOSES

Dataset	Status	
	In State	Out of State
UCLA (N=661)	46%	54%
IFR (N=103)	16%	84%

Economic impact

The data suggest that the economic impact of archaeology field schools is both significant and lasting (see Table 7). The amount of funding generated annually reflects

TABLE 7

FIELD SCHOOL FUNDS AND THEIR REGIONAL DISTRIBUTION

Area	Year			
	2009	2010	2011	2012
No. of FS	*208*	*175*	*120*	*127*
North Am.	27%	20%	18%	10%
Latin Am.	13%	15%	9%	13%
Europe	39%	40%	41%	65%
Asia	3%	8%	4%	1%
Africa	3%	6%	0%	0%
Middle East	14%	10%	24%	10%
Oceania	1%	1%	4%	1%
$ reported	$3,717,801	$3,046,516	$1,683,309	$3,761,482
$ weighted	$5,576,701	$4,569,773	$2,524,963	$5,642,222

the general economic realities within the US, with dramatic declines in revenue in 2010 and 2011, when the full impact of the economic crisis hit student pockets. At the same time, the data illustrate a strong recovery in 2012 and a return to 2009 funding levels — albeit with 39 per cent fewer field schools to generate similar revenue. This increase is consistent with trends seen in general student enrolment in study abroad programmes, were the numbers of students seeking studies outside the US and during the summer months is significantly increasing (IIE, 2011: Duration of Study Abroad).

Field schools generated — on average — over $3 million reported/$4.5 million weighted annually for direct support of field activities. Some of these funds are spent on sponsor institution overhead, equipment, airfare for faculty to travel to site, and sample testing. But a significant portion is spent locally, paying for room and board, transportation, and local labour. Field schools, therefore, have a strong impact on local economies.

Field school funds were not equally distributed across the world (see Tables 7 and 8). Between 2009 and 2012, over $5.8 million was directed towards projects in Europe (Spain, Italy, Greece, Ireland, and the UK captured 47 per cent of these funds) and $2.3 million towards North American field schools. But $1.6 million reported/$2.4 million weighted was spent in the Middle East and over $1.5 reported/$2.2 million weighted in Latin American. These are no small sums, particularly when considering they were directly spent at the local community levels.

Of the top twenty countries in which field schools funds were spent, eleven were outside developed economies (it may be reasonable to exclude Greece and Portugal in such future lists, but this proposition is fraught with political dangers). Combined, over $1.7 million were spent in these countries, delivering significant financial impact at the local community level.

TABLE 8

FIELD SCHOOLS FUNDS GENERATED FOR THE TOP 20 COUNTRIES IN 2009–12
(SUMS ARE NOT WEIGHTED)

Country	Funding Generated		
	Rank	$	% of Revenue
US	No. 01	$1,402,932	17.5%
Spain	No. 02	$1,294,584	16.2%
Italy	No. 03	$1,114,119	13.9%
Israel	No. 04	$682,183	8.5%
Greece	No. 05	$654,084	8.2%
UK	No. 06	$351,351	4.4%
Ireland	No. 07	$312,463	3.9%
Peru	No. 08	$300,744	3.8%
Egypt	No. 09	$256,134	3.2%
Belize	No. 10	$250,413	3.1%
Portugal	No. 11	$232,731	2.9%
Bulgaria	No. 12	$222,642	2.8%
Romania	No. 13	$132,287	1.7%
Macedonia	No. 14	$112,960	1.4%
Mongolia	No. 15	$106,218	1.3%
Australia	No. 16	$97,870	1.2%
Bolivia	No. 17	$95,256	1.2%
Turkey	No. 18	$95,209	1.2%
Jordan	No. 19	$88,757	1.1%
Chile	No. 20	$87,318	1.1%

If we build them, will they come?

Any serious discussion of economic impact must include historical data, but should also attempt to measure and evaluate future trends. Because field schools utilizing US-based students generate revenues through tuition, it is crucial to critically examine whether it is possible to attract greater numbers of students to such programmes. Is the student pool large enough and will students agree to pay field school costs? It is also essential to examine the capacity of archaeology to generate more field schools and produce qualified scholars that can effectively lead such programmes.

The latter is easier to address. The employment rate for qualified archaeologists in the US and across the world is quite profoundly low (Fagan, 2006a; 2006b). In this highly competitive environment, one of the central elements for obtaining an academic position and moving forward in the tenure process is an active field project.

While governmental and private funding for archaeological research is generally declining, the overall costs of field research are increasing (Boytner, 2012a: 29). Scholars must find alternative revenue sources to support their fieldwork. Field schools offer a number of advantages.

First, field schools can generate significant revenue to be used towards funding research if scholars work with entities that direct most of student tuition back to support research. Some universities, as well as new organizations such as the IFR, are strongly committed to such outcomes and direct a significant portion of tuition costs to support field research. The IFR alone generated almost $250,000 — or an average of $20,000 per field school — to directly fund field research in 2012 (for more information, see IFR, n.d.).

Second, field schools offer a long-term and stable source of research funds, as long as the field school director can generate continued interest in her/his programme. Dedication to teaching and careful attention to student learning is not only a prudent economic strategy, it is also an ethical obligation of archaeologists — it is a central pillar of making archaeology a public good. Good field schools can attract increasing numbers of students, which in turn will increase funding. But good field schools can also become attractive to better students, ultimately increasing the quality and efficiency of research.

Third, generating sufficient funds from field schools releases scholars from time required to write grants and allows them to direct more energy towards publication and public archaeology. Both activities can contribute to making sites and their narratives better known to the public, thereby increasing the potential of the sites as tourist destinations. All of the above create strong incentives to attract greater numbers of archaeologists, and particularly young scholars who need funds to establish a research record as they go through the post-doctoral ranks, towards running field schools and tenured academic positions.

But if we develop them, will more students come and attend archaeology field schools? A key dataset to critically examine this question are the data published annually on trends in US study abroad programmes. The IIE annual Open doors Report (IIE, 2011) provides important insights about that industry.

Between academic years 2000/01 and 2009/10 (the latest year for which data are available), the number of US students studying abroad almost doubled, from a little over 150,000 to over 270,000 (IIE, 2011: Host Regions[2]). Perhaps more importantly, the data clearly illustrate that growth took place each year, despite the recent economic crisis and the rapidly rising costs of higher education in the US (IIE 2011: Fast Facts Chart I).

But the increase in numbers is not uniform and the economic changes reflect shifts in student choice. The number of students seeking a long-term study abroad experience — defined as one or more quarters — has been declining, from 51 per cent in academic year 2000/01 to 43 per cent in academic year 2009/10. At the same time, the number of students seeking summer term studying abroad had been consistently increasing, from 34 per cent in academic year 2000/01 to 38 per cent in academic year 2009/10. In absolute terms, the number of students seeking summer terms abroad doubled in the past decade, from 51,955 students in summer 2000 to 102,288 students in summer 2010 (IIE, 2011: Duration; see Figure 1).

Very few of these students participated in archaeology field schools (see Table 9). In summer 2012, only 2.3 per cent of US students attending summer study abroad sessions participated in archaeology field schools. But this is not because the typical US study abroad student does not fit the typical archaeology field school student profile. In fact, over 40 per cent of study abroad students each year major in either

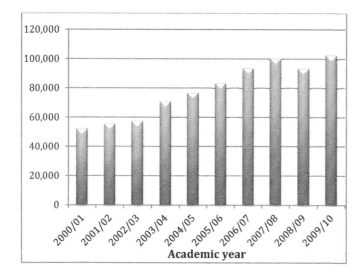

FIGURE 1   Summer abroad attendance of US students (adopted from IIE, 2011: Duration).

TABLE 9

NUMBER OF US STUDENTS ATTENDING ARCHAEOLOGY FIELD SCHOOLS ANNUALLY

Year	# of Students	
	Reported	Weighted
2009	2056	3084
2010	1739	2608
2011	1179	1769
2012	1588	2381

the social sciences, humanities, or the arts (IIE, 2011: Field of Study), the fields of study that usually attract students to archaeology field schools (Boytner, 2012b: 86).

These general trends are expected to increase in ways that may be favourable to raising participation in archaeology field schools. The Senator Paul Simon Study Abroad Act was approved by the US Congress in 2010, but is still waiting to be ratified by the Senate. Although the law enjoys a strong bi-partisan support, the economic crisis of 2008 and the aftermath of political disagreements on budget issues in the legislative branch of the US Government hinders the passage of the law as it requires federal funding. In brief, the Simon Act is seeking to quadruple the number of US students studying abroad to 1 million annually by 2020. It also seeks to redirect students to study in non-traditional locations — defined as any destination outside western Europe[3] (for further discussion, see Boytner, 2012a: 30).

The Simon Act has yet to receive any substantial funding from the US congress. Yet, it strongly signals to universities and students that study abroad is something considered highly valuable and worthy of investment — financial, personal, educational, and temporal. It also signals that destinations in the developing world are valued more highly than the 'traditional' European destinations.

Together, these data suggest that growth in both the number and size of field schools is possible and likely. Archaeology field schools are certainly not for everyone, but the exceptionally high satisfaction rate of participating students — hovering over the 90 per cent point (see Boytner, 2012b: 86, table 6.1) — suggest that they are an attractive option to students who seek meaningful and fulfilling academic experiences during the summer months.

Conclusion

The five conjectures used for the data analysis here produced conservative results. It is likely that actual funding and therefore spending in and impact on local communities, is higher. It is not unreasonable, therefore, to conclude that archaeology field schools can and do make an important economic impact in the locations where they operate. Such impact is both long-term and broad, and includes a wide range of direct and indirect contributions that improve economic conditions for local communities. Making such impacts, of course, does not universally occur and some field schools have only negligible impact, especially if they are a single season project. But many field schools are part of projects that return to the same site and region over numerous years and their impact is significant and important.

Not less important is that the potential growth of field school contributions to local economies, especially at the micro-level, is great. As economic conditions in the US improve and as the US government makes progress in its implementation of the Simon Act, many more archaeology field schools in developing countries can and should be established. They can do good — and a significant amount of it — by doing archaeological research.

There are many opportunities for established institutions to undermine such growth, and the concern is that they will be tempted to do just that. The new economic realities in the West make revenue-generating programmes attractive and lucrative targets for university administrators. Imposing ever-increasing overhead fees on such programmes and trying to capture increasingly more revenue from them may kill the goose that lays the golden eggs, as happened at UCLA (see Boytner, 2012b: 98–99; Parkinson-Morgan, 2011).

Alternatives to such interference are emerging and some are quite innovative. To avoid the meddling of institutional administrators and to maximize funds for research, increasing numbers of archaeologists are turning to models and organizations that allow them to maximize their ability to capture their share of students fees and at the same time keep costs to students reasonable. Field schools that can keep student cost at or slightly above the $5000 mark and award participating students with at least six transferable credit units are increasingly attractive.

The Institute for Field Research is offering just such opportunities. Partnering with Connecticut College, this academically independent organization offered sixteen field schools across the world in 2012, with average fees of $4800 and eight semester-based credit units (valued as twelve quarter-based units). Two other organizations have large offerings of field schools within a single specific region. The Ecomuseum at the Cape of Cavalleria in Spain offered forty three-week field school sessions at four different locations on the Island of Menorca in 2012 alone.[4] Its field school cost is only $2000, although it offered no academic credit units. Balkan Heritage offered five different field schools in Bulgaria in summer 2012 with average cost of $2500 in fees and six credits units (albeit from a Bulgarian institution from which universities in the US will not likely accept the credits). Balkan Heritage field schools vary in length from one to three weeks.[5]

A number of US universities are actively trying to grow their own field school offerings. Summer Program departments are paying increasing attention to archaeology field schools, as these programmes tend to be attractive on two fronts: 1) they attract students to the programmes themselves and 2) they provide imagery and narratives that entice students to visit Summer Program websites and eventually enrol in programmes other than just archaeology. The marketing power of archaeology field schools on a Summer Program department's overall success is not missed by the more sophisticated Summer Program directors.

Innovators are breaking through and those that develop and maintain a reputation for academic and pedagogic excellence will thrive. Whatever the origin of innovations and growth, the combined market and educational forces described here provide strong incentives to breed a greater number of archaeology field school offerings and simultaneously improve their quality. Thus, the future of archaeology field schools seem to be quite bright and their increasing contributions to the economic developments of local communities will dramatically rise in the near- and middle-term future. That is (almost) guaranteed.

Acknowledgements

Many helped with the acquisition and preparation of the databases used for this work. I would like to acknowledge the Archaeological Institute of America, and in particular Mr Kevin Mullen, for providing access to its digital 2008–12 field school entry archive. Ruchika Tanna (USC) worked hard at normalizing the data. Charles Stanish's (UCLA) unwavering support for archaeology field schools is inspiring. The IFR Board of Directors — particularly Mr Yuval Bar Zemer — provides the broad support that such a young organization needs if it is to thrive.

Notes

[1] The author was the Director of the UCLA Program and presently he is the Director of the IFA. The data analysed for this work is unpublished.

[2] The information from this report can also be accessed more readily on the Fast Facts section of the IIE website, available at: <http://www.iie.org/Research-and-Publications/Open-Doors>.

[3] The European 'Grand Tour' seems to be very much alive and well among US students. The Open Doors report indicate that 55 per cent of all US Study Abroad students went to Europe (see <http://www.iie.org/Research-and-Publications/Open-Doors>).

[4] For more information on the Ecomuseum field school, see <www.ecomuseodecavalleria.com>.

[5] For more information on the Balkan field school, see <www.bhfieldschool.org>.

Bibliography

Archaeological Institute of America (AIA). 2014. Archaeological Fieldwork Opportunities Bulletin [accessed 6 April 2014]. Available at: <http://www.archaeological.org/fieldwork/afob>.

Baxter, J. 2009. *Archaeological Field Schools: A Guide for Teaching in the Field*. Walnut Creek, CA: Left Coast Press.

Bernbeck, R. & Pollock, S. 2004. The Political Economy of Archaeological Practice and the Production of Heritage in the Middle East. In: L. Meskell and R. W. Preucel, eds. *A Companion to Social Archaeology*. Malden: Blackwell, pp. 335–52.

Boytner, R. 2012a. The Changing Nature of Archaeological Field Schools. *The SAA Archaeological Record*, 12(1): 29–32.

Boytner, R. 2012b. The UCLA Archaeology Field Schools Program: Global Reach, Local Focus. In: H. Mytum, ed. *Archaeological Field Schools: Constructing Knowledge and Experience*. New York: Springer, pp. 83–100.

Clarke, A. & Phillipsus, T. 2011. Archaeology for All? Inclusive Policies for Field Schools. In: H. Mytum, ed. *Archaeological Field Schools: Constructing Knowledge and Experience*. New York: Springer, pp. 41–60.

Fagan, B. 2006a. Archaeology: The Next 50 Years. *Archaeology Magazine*, 59(5): 18–23.

Fagan, B. 2006b. So You Want to be an Archaeologist? *Archaeology Magazine*, 59(3): 59–64.

Gifford, A. & Morris, E. 1985. Digging for Credit: Early Archaeological Field Schools in the American Southwest. *American Antiquity*, 50(2): 395–411.

Hamilakis, Y. 2003. Lives in Ruins: Antiquities and National Imagination in Modern Greece. In: S. Kane, ed. *The Politics of Archaeology and Identity in a Global Context*. Boston, MA: Archaeological Institute of America, pp. 51–78.

Institute for Field Research (IFR). (n.d.). About IFR [accessed 6 April 2014]. Available at: <http://www.ifrglobal. org/home/about-ifr/16-about/12-about-history>.

Institute of International Education (IIE). 2011. Open Doors Report on International Educational Exchange: Institute of International Education [accessed 1 September 2011]. Available at: <http://www.iie.org/Research-and-Publications/Open-Doors>.

Judd, N. 1968. *Men Met Along the Trail: Adventures in Archaeology*. Norman, OK: University of Oklahoma Press.

Killbrew, A. 2010. Who Owns the Past? The Role of Nationalism, Politics and Profits in Presenting Israel's Archaeological Sites to the Public. In: R. Boytner, L. Dodd, and B. J. Parker, eds. *Controlling the Past, Owning the Future: The Political Uses of Archaeology in the Middle East*. Tucson, AZ: University of Arizona Press, pp. 123–41.

Kohl, L. 2004. Making the Past Profitable in an Age of Globalization and National Ownership: Contradictions and Considerations. In: Y. M. Rowan and U. Baram, eds. *Marketing Heritage: Archaeology and the Consumption of the Past*. Lenham, MD: AltaMira Press, pp. 295–302.

Lopes Bastos, R. & Funari, P. 2008. Public Archaeology and Management of the Brazilian Archaeological-Cultural Heritage. In: H. Silverman and W. H. Isbell, eds. *Handbook of South American Archaeology*. New York: Springer, pp. 1127–35.

Moche, Inc. 2013. Saving the Past by Investing in the Future [accessed 6 April 2014]. Available at: <www. savethemoche.org>.

Morrison, A. B. 2012. More Than Digging Square Holes: The New Role of Archaeological Field Schools. *The SAA Archaeological Record*, 12(1): 23–24.

Mytum, H. ed. 2011. *Archaeological Field Schools: Constructing Knowledge and Experience*. New York: Springer.

Parkinson-Morgan, K. 2011. Archaeology Field Schools Run by the UCLA Cotsen Institute Have Been Temporarily Cut Because of Funding Problems [accessed 1 September 2011]. Available at: <http://www.dailybruin.com/ index.php/article/2011/02/archaeology_field_schools_run_by_the_ucla_cotsen_institute_have_been_temporarily_ cut_because_of_fund>.

Perry, E. J. 2004. Authentic Learning in Field Schools: Preparing Future Members of the Archaeological Community. *World Archaeology*, 36(2): 236–60.

Perry, E. J. 2006. From Students to Professionals: Archaeological Field Schools as Authentic Research Communities. *The SAA Archaeological Record*, 6(1): 25–29.

Piscitelli, M. & Duwe, S. 2007. Choosing an Archaeological Field School. *The SAA Archaeological Record*, 7(1): 9–11.

Pollock, S. 2010. Decolonizing Archaeology: Political Economy and Archaeological Practice in the Middle East. In: R. Boytner, L. Dodd, and B. J. Parker, eds. *Controlling the Past, Owning the Future: The Political Uses of Archaeology in the Middle East*. Tucson: University of Arizona Press, pp. 196–216.

Pyburn, K. A. 2003. What Are We Really Teaching in Archaeological Field Schools? In: L. J. Zimmerman, K. D. Vitelli, and J. Hollowell-Zimmer, eds. *Ethical Issues in Archaeology*. Walnut Creek, CA: Alta Mira Press, pp. 213–23.

Rowan, Y. M. & Baram, U. eds. 2004. *Marketing Heritage: Archaeology and the Consumption of the Past.* Lenham, MD: Alta Mira Press.

Scham, A. S. 2004. Hollywood Holy Land: Can Anyone Ever Know the Facts About the Death of Jesus? *Archaeology,* 57(2): 62–66.

Schnapp, A. 1996. *The Discovery of the Past.* Trans I. Kinnes and G. Varndell. New York: Harry N. Abrams, Inc.

Shovelbums. (n.d.). Shovelbums Comprehensive Archaeology and Anthropology Field School Directory [accessed 6 April]. Available at: <http://www.shovelbums.org>.

Silverman, H. 2002. Touring Ancient Times: The Present and Presented Past in Contemporary Peru. *American Anthropologist,* 104(3): 881–902.

Silverman, H. ed. 2011. *Contested Cultural Heritage: Religion, Nationalism, Erasure, and Exclusion in a Global World.* New York: Springer.

Springer, F. 1913. The Summer School. *El Palacio,* 1(1): 4.

Stanish, C. 2006. Forging Ahead, or, How I Learned to Stop Worrying and Love eBay. *Archaeology,* 62: 58–60.

Walker, M. & Saitta, D. 2002. Teaching the Craft of Archaeology: Theory, Practice and the Field School. *International Journal of Historical Archaeology,* 6(3): 199–207.

Wendrich, W. 2010. From Practical Knowledge to Empowered Communication: Field Schools of the Supreme Council of Antiquities in Egypt. In: R. Boytner, L. Dodd, and B. J. Parker, eds. *Controlling the Past, Owning the Future: The Political Uses of Archaeology in the Middle East.* Tucson, AZ: University of Arizona Press, pp. 178–95.

Yahya, A. 2002. A Palestinian Organization Works to Preserve Sites in the West Bank in the Midst of War. *Near Eastern Archaeology,* 65(4): 279–81.

Notes on contributor

Ran Boytner is the Founding Director of the Institute for Field Research. He specializes in Andean archaeology, with emphasis on social evolution and the relationships between material culture and changes in political, ideological and economic structures. His more recent research is focused on archaeology field schools and their impact on archaeology and the students who participate in them.

Correspondence to: Ran Boytner, Institute for Field Research, 1855 Industrial St #106, Los Angeles, CA 90021, USA. Email: rboytner@ifrglobal.org

PUBLIC ARCHAEOLOGY, Vol. 13 Nos 1–3, 2014, 278–87

Sustainable Preservation: Creating Entrepreneurs, Opportunities, and Measurable Results

Lawrence S. Coben

Sustainable Preservation Initiative, USA

In recent years terms such as 'community', 'local', 'economic development', and 'sustainability' have featured prominently in the discourse of preservation. Yet we have seen little evidence of the successful application of these concepts as most organizations have published broad, vague missives about economic potential and community benefit rather than providing meaningful measures of their results and avoiding discussion of their failures. What are the measures of successful preservation and economic development, and what are the 'returns' both tangible and intangible, of these types of projects? In this paper, I discuss the nature of the prevailing discourse and some potential metrics for measuring success, and then apply these metrics to projects of the Sustainable Preservation Initiative.

KEYWORDS archaeology, economic development, sustainability, community, metrics

Introduction

In recent years, terms such as 'community-based', 'local', 'economic development', and 'sustainability' have featured prominently in the discourse of cultural heritage preservation. Numerous organizations claim to be initiating and implementing projects utilizing these concepts, providing vague anecdotal evidence and unsupported claims of the successful application of these notions. Most organizations, to the extent that they have disclosed any information at all, have published broad, vague missives about economic potential and community benefit rather than providing meaningful measures of their results or discussing failures. Indeed, many of these projects, whatever their merits, appear not to be 'community-based' and 'sustainable', nor do they constitute 'economic development'.

In this paper, I will discuss briefly what constitutes community-based sustainable economic development, and discuss its application in existing preservation paradigms and programmes. I will then discuss potential metrics of project success, both

DOI 10.1179/1465518714Z.00000000072

economically and from a preservation perspective. Lastly, I will apply these metrics to evaluate projects of the Sustainable Preservation Initiative (SPI). I will avoid the debate between the relative merits of top-down versus community-based approaches to economic development (for a discussion of these alternatives, see Ostrom, 1990; 2009). While I am a strong proponent of the latter, I will not address this issue here, but rather demonstrate the efficacy of a community-based approach through a case study of SPI's San Jose de Moro project in Peru.

Discussion of key terms

Community

While there are numerous and expansive definitions of community (see, for example, Anderson, 1991; Gumperz, 2009), for the purposes of this paper community refers to those people residing in the vicinity of a cultural heritage asset who have the potential to be affected by economic development activity at or near that asset. These residents frequently, though not always, are members of a similar political subdivision, such as a village or town. They may, though need not, be culturally homogenous or have ethnic or economic ties.

For economic development to be community-based, a portion of the economic benefits of such development must accrue to the local community. For example, an archaeological site where tourists are bussed in from another town, visit a site and leave, and are guided by someone not living in the community may constitute economic activity, but, since no money or jobs are being created in the immediate locality of the site, it would not constitute community-based development.

Ideally, community-based development will include a strong element of local control as to the nature and scale of economic development. Much recent research by scholars such as Nobel Prize winner Elinor Ostrom (1990; 2009) demonstrates that bottom-up, locally formulated solutions to resource exploitation issues are optimal and more efficacious than those imposed from outside the community. I shall return to this point later in this paper.

Economic development

According to the World Bank, local economic development 'is a process by which public, business and nongovernmental sector partners work collectively to create better conditions for economic growth and employment generation'. Its purpose is 'to build up the economic capacity of a local area to improve its economic future and the quality of life for all' (World Bank, 2011; see also Fleming, this volume).

In addition to these broad goals, at least two others must be added with respect to cultural heritage preservation. First, such development must not destroy or materially diminish cultural heritage, and ideally will provide economic and social incentives to preserve it. In other words, economic development will contribute to the sustainability of cultural heritage, where sustainability is defined as balancing the current exploitation of such heritage while preserving its availability and potential for use by future generations. Second, given the dearth of funding available for cultural heritage preservation, such development must ultimately result in businesses and other economic activity that is self-sustaining and not perpetually dependent upon grants or other funding from governmental or non-governmental sources — that is, economically sustainable.

Sustainability

The term 'sustainability' has multiple meanings and uses in relation to cultural heritage (Coben, 2014). Most frequently, the term is employed in conjunction with or as part of such concepts as sustainable preservation, sustainable development, or sustainable tourism, though these concepts in practice overlap and are closely intertwined. These concepts of sustainability derive from and grow out of the World Commission on Environment and Development (also known as the Brundtland Commission's 1987 report, 'Our Common Future'). That report defined sustainable development as 'development which meets the needs of the present without compromising the ability of future generations to meet their own needs' (Brundtland, 1987: 54). This definition, while vague, called attention to the problem of over-exploitation and damage of natural resources in the pursuit of economic development, and implicitly called for the practice of forms of economic development that better utilize and leave adequate natural resources for future generations. Sustainable development thus merges perpetual economic growth with the maintenance and enhancement of environmental values, thereby providing sufficient resources for both current and future economic development (Throsby, 2002). Sustainability seeks to balance the demand for development from private and governmental actors with the maintenance of conditions necessary for the preservation of the natural environment, or in the cultural heritage context, the physical and landscape features of archaeological and historic sites (Murphy, 1985).

The Brundtland Commission's discussion of sustainability also included social and economic responsibility as important components of sustainable development, though in many discussions these components played a secondary role to the environmental one. Some projects do incorporate these notions with respect to cultural heritage management, strongly considering and incorporating the rights and interests of indigenous and local people (Richards & Hall, 2000).

Sustainable development in cultural heritage

In the latter part of the twentieth and early part of the twenty-first century, scholars and governments began to consider and apply a modified concept of sustainable development to cultural heritage (see, for example, Endresen, 1999; MacDonald, 2004). At times referred to as sustainable preservation, this discussion of sustainability has followed two distinct though related paths: first, the environmental and energy conservation benefits of the preservation and reuse of historic structures, and second, the potential economic and social benefits of the development of cultural heritage sites as touristic attractions or other drivers of economic development (Coben, 2014).

Recognizing the potential to create jobs and revenues through tourism and preservation (and in a few cases the increasing destruction of heritage sites from other forms of economic development), governments, non-governmental organizations (NGOs), and heritage practitioners have begun to consider the potential of cultural heritage as a driver of economic activity and poverty alleviation. The World Bank has described its evolving approach toward cultural heritage as one that begins with 'do not harm', avoiding damaging cultural heritage while implementing other projects (1970–80), to 'specific intervention', investing in particular sites to develop tourism (1980–2000), to the current 'integrated approach' that integrates cultural heritage in local economic development with a focus on historic cities rehabilitation and sustainable tourism (Sierra, 2009: 7). The InterAmerican Development Bank's approach has followed a similar arc (Endresen, 1999).

This evolving method expands the focus of development projects from a particular site to include the community that surrounds it. Most of the World Bank's and similar earlier projects fall under the rubric of preservation projects designed primarily to conserve, protect, and regulate access to and use of a site. The later 'integrated approach' places these sites in a broader context of community-based economic development, with an important if not primary purpose of the use of a site to benefit surrounding communities, with preservation necessary in order to permit continued economic exploitation. Many of these World Bank and similar sustainable economic development projects state that one of their goals is sustaining or conserving cultural heritage assets, allowing their use while preserving them for future generations. In addition to the environmental and cultural benefits from preservation and potential reuse of historical structures, other potential benefits include the creation of jobs, increased retail and handicraft sales and ancillary revenues, serving as a catalyst for local and regional development, the rejuvenation of declining towns and neighbourhoods, gender inclusiveness, and a greater sense of cultural identity for local communities.

The current preservation paradigm

Current preservation paradigms that focus on the conservation of an archaeological site alone, while laudable, are not community-based sustainable economic development. Conservation projects generally produce economic activity that is limited temporally to the duration of the actual work (e.g. wages for workers, local accommodation, meals, etc.) and wholly dependent upon the continued provision of external funding sources. These projects require the employment of significant numbers of experts who do not reside within the community, and any local jobs are temporary in nature. Even if local conservators are trained, these trainees will work only as long as outside funding is present, and will not be able to employ their newly acquired skill in the absence of continued grants or support. Similarly, projects that focus on site protection through such methods such as legal property demarcation, fencing, and hiring of security guards, while helpful, do not constitute sustainable economic development. While conservation and protection may be an element of a plan of community-based economic development, there is no evidence that on their own they inspire or catalyse such activity, in spite of the claims of their proponents to the contrary.

Moreover, the control of almost all of the projects employing such current preservation paradigms lies either with governmental entities or funding NGOs, leaving local communities dependent on their continued support and without the means to manage and preserve their sites themselves. These current paradigms also fail to provide an economic incentive for local communities to continue preserving sites after the departure of archaeologists and conservators. The greatest threats to cultural heritage and archaeological sites are alternative economic uses that are destructive, including looting, agricultural development, grazing, and residential and commercial uses. In the absence of some form of local economic activity, all of these uses are economically superior uses of the archaeological site to that of maintaining and conserving them. And the issue is not solely an economic one: how can we tell an underprivileged person not to economically exploit a site to feed their family, even if that exploitation is destroying the site, without providing a viable economic alternative? Can we provide an opportunity that provides income to that person while simultaneously preserving cultural heritage?

The Sustainable Preservation Initiative (SPI) paradigm

SPI seeks to create a new paradigm to answer these questions. SPI preserves cultural heritage by providing sustainable economic opportunities to poor communities where endangered archaeological sites are located. SPI believes the best way to preserve cultural heritage is creating or supporting locally owned businesses whose success is tied to that preservation, and the Initiative's grants provide a two for the price of one benefit: they create transformative economic opportunities for the local residents while saving archaeological sites for future generations to study and enjoy.

SPI exploits the rapid expansion of extreme tourism and globalization, which has created an enormous potential for locally based tourism and artisan businesses. Even small local economic benefits from these sources can compete successfully against looting and destructive alternative uses of sites. In addition, the creation of local businesses with a vested interest in the preservation and maintenance of a site provides an ongoing and long-term source of incentive and funding for site preservation, as well as all of the benefits normally associated with economic development in poor communities.

SPI works with community and government leaders, local business people, archaeologists, and preservationists. SPI helps create plans for projects and businesses that will be locally owned and that maximize the spending of money in the communities surrounding archaeological sites. Through microlenders, charitable organizations, and other sources of funding, SPI provides small grants to existing or start-up businesses such as tourism, tour-guides, restaurants, hostels, transportation, artisans, site museums, and other rapidly implementable projects. Through this combination of local involvement, decision-making, and ownership, sustainable economic benefits and value will be related to and conditioned upon continued site preservation. These businesses will also provide an ongoing revenue stream to meet preservation and other local needs. This paradigm provides a double benefit: every dollar spent on economic development and the improvement of local people's lives will also contribute to preserving a portion of the world's cultural heritage.

SPI's investment paradigm differs dramatically from most other organizations dealing with preservation. SPI places greater focus on sustainable economic and social investment as opposed to a conservation-only focus. SPI invests in and advises on locally owned and controlled businesses whose success is tied to the continued preservation and sustainable management of local archaeological sites. These businesses will all have an excellent chance of economic success, thereby creating a local constituent group whose economic interest is aligned with site preservation. SPI favours investments that create or stimulate a cluster of businesses, increasing the multiplier effect of its dollars, the economic benefits to the community, and the attraction of additional investors and funding (see SPI, 2014, for a full list of the Initiative's current projects).

The archaeological research associated with a project will generally be taking place locally, so that an 'embedded archaeologist' with strong knowledge of local community power structures is available to advise SPI with respect to the selection of entrepreneurs and ownership structures. These projects must have strong community support — SPI must be wanted (!) — and a contribution of local funding, resources, or in-kind labour and services is expected. Consistent with its focus on 'people not stones', SPI will not fund conservation, except as incident to enhancing the businesses described above. For example, SPI might fund a small amount of conservation in order to enhance a site's touristic experience. In no event will SPI fund a project where more than 20 per cent of the requested proceeds will be utilized for conservation.

Metrics

Measurement of the economic impact of sustainable development has been described as 'nebulous' due to the difficulties of data collection (Rypkema & Chong, 2011: 754) and data has been described as 'hard to come by' (Silberman, 2011: 48). All projects receiving funding from SPI must collect quantitative and qualitative data regarding both business and preservation results. Every SPI project must have discernible methods of evaluation in both of these areas. Economic metrics include:

- jobs created
- revenue generated
- profitability
- additional economic activity generated
- tourist visits stimulated.

Preservation metrics will include:

- site deterioration
- absence or reduction of destructive activities at a site (e.g. agricultural activities, grazing, and looting)
- encroachments (if any) on a site's boundaries
- preservation measures taken by the local community in order to preserve their 'asset'.

SPI utilizes this data to measure the success of ongoing projects as well as to modify and improve its investment paradigm and criteria for future investments. SPI also publishes its data so that others can learn from and comment upon its successes and failures (see SPI, 2014).

Case study: San Jose de Moro, Peru

Located near the northern coast of Peru, San Jose de Moro's archaeological excavations have yielded a treasure trove of archaeological artefacts and information. The site is one of the most important ceremonial centres of the Mochica culture and subsequent cultures. The San José de Moro Archaeological Program (SJMAP) began in 1991 and is directed by Luis Jaime Castillo, professor at Pontificia Universidad Católica del Peru (PUCP) in Lima. SJMAP's excavations at the Moro site have revealed one of the largest and most complex cemeteries and ceremonial centres used consecutively by hundreds of civilizations such as the Moche, Lambayeque, and Chimú. Hundreds of burials, some of them quite complex, have been excavated at the site since 1991, showing that Moro was for a long period of time one of the most important ritual centres for the north coast civilizations. Some of the most significant finds have been seven chamber burials containing the remains of elite Moche Priestesses, and, associated with them, a large assemblage of ceramics, including several remarkable late Moche fineline ceramics (see SJMAP, 2009). However, while the cultural heritage of San Jose de Moro is rich, the local community is a poor one. The average daily wage, even when work is available, is just US$9.50 per day.

The role of SPI

Dr Castillo and his team had attempted to implement community development programmes alongside their excavations. They tried all of the classical non-sustainable paradigms to preserve the site and help the local community such as conservation, education, and small modular museums. Yet by his own admission none of these were effective, either in preserving the site or benefiting the community in a sustainable way. According to Dr Castillo, 'For years we were doing little contributions to the towns, schools, and to some pressing need, but we could never focus on a long term and sustainable effort that was both different from and integrated with the values and goals of the project' (L. J. Castillo, pers. comm., 2012). He realized a sustainable economic-based paradigm was required, and applied for a grant to SPI.

In March 2010, SPI awarded a US$40,000 grant for artisanal and touristic development around the site of San José de Moro. The development plan featured a visitor centre, incorporating a crafts workshop and training centre for young local craftspersons, a store, and an exhibition area. Tourists are able to witness artisans producing their wares as well as purchase the finished artisanal products. The workshop includes training for additional local artisans and provides tourists with the unprecedented opportunity to participate in the ceramic-making process. Adjacent to the exhibition centre are a picnic and rest area, small snack bar, and toilet facilities, also constructed with the SPI grant. A new entrance to the site, replete with Moche motifs and colours, was created and painted. Peruvian archaeologists and residents of San Jose de Moro prepared a guidebook and brochure for the site, with the former being available for sale and the latter being given free to visitors. Peruvian archaeologists also trained local guides.

Julio Ibarrola, a ceramicist renowned for his replicas of late Moche fineline ceramics like those excavated at the Moro site, and Eloy Uriarte, a blacksmith specializing in archaeological tools and implements, direct the workshop and train new artisans. Both men are lifelong residents of San Jose de Moro, and the project has enabled them to utilize their artisan skills and entrepreneurial talents.

Outcomes of the SPI paradigm

Initial job creation

This project has created to date twelve direct permanent jobs for local artisans that provide sustainable income to the community, and an additional twenty temporary jobs that were created for the six-month construction period of the workshop and tourist centre. Felix Salmon, a financial columnist for Reuters, took note of this efficient level of job creation, calling it 'impressive'. According to Salmon (2010), as with SPI projects, 'if you want to create the maximum number of jobs for the smallest amount of money, the best way of doing so is to provide catalytic capital which helps to give a small business the step-up it needs to sustain new jobs on a permanent basis'.

New tourist visits

Prior to the SPI project, almost all of the visitors to San Jose de Moro were local Peruvians, school children, and the occasional foreign tourist who was well read in archaeology. The new centre and project has attracted visitors and buses from several international and foreign tour companies, many of which are now incorporating San Jose de Moro into their regular itineraries. The exact increase is unknown, as inadequate data on visitation is captured at the site, as there is no charge for admission, and no data was collected before the project began. However, these tourists spend significantly, as described below.

Revenues

Prior to the SPI projects, sales for local artisans amounted to roughly US$295 in 2010. Sales at the visitors' centre in 2011 reached US$5100, while US$2000 in sales occurred on a single day in July 2011 to an affluent fifty-person tour group. Unfortunately, this sales volume, unexpected by the local artisans, depleted their inventory, leaving little for subsequent tour groups and resulting in missed sales opportunities. The artisans have learned from this experience and it is unlikely to be repeated in the future. Ceramic replicas by Moro artisans have recently begun to be sold at the Museum of Art (Museo del Arte) in Lima and online through NOVICA — a website specializing in community artisan crafts — creating additional revenue opportunities. In 2012, revenues for SPI-supported entrepreneurs have more than doubled, totalling more than US$11,000 through November of that year. Each artisan retains 80 per cent of the sale proceeds of his or her work, while the remaining 20 per cent is placed into a common fund for materials, maintaining the workshop, and other costs. The artisans themselves determine the level of retention.

Additional economic benefits of the project

SPI's initial investment has inspired additional economic activity to serve tourists visiting the site:

- A non-SPI sponsored ceramic replica stand in competition with ours was established just outside the site's borders.
- Seven local women are now serving traditional lunches in their homes for tourists and other visitors. These women reported to SPI that these activities generated US$2530 in 2012.

- Three local women artisans are selling textiles in the visitor's centre.
- Two new small snack bars (for a total of three in the town) have opened to serve tourists.

Preservation

Local residents now view the site as a valuable economic asset, and the key to sustainable community income, a sea change from its prior attitudes ranging from diffidence to hostility (L. J. Castillo, pers. comm., 2012). Destructive practices, such as looting and encroachment from economic development, have come to a halt. Local officials are recognizing the economic potential not just of San Jose de Moro, but the entire cultural heritage in the area. The municipality of Chepen (where San Jose de Moro is located) is paying for and installing a new entrance and signage on the Pan-American Highway as well as for the publication of additional Moro guidebooks for use by their newly reconstituted tourism board and in their schools. Further, the Mayor of Chepen recently visited the nearby site of Cerro Chepen with police to denounce incursions and eject interlopers trying to grow crops on that site, an unprecedented act by a municipal official that acknowledges the vast potential economic value of the region's cultural heritage.

Conclusion

This paper demonstrates the potential benefits of true community-based, sustainable economic development. For many cultural heritage sites, this approach represents the best way to both improve the lives of impoverished people as well to preserve those sites for future generations. This paper also sets forth key metrics to evaluate these types of projects, and demonstrates that it is possible to collect the data necessary to judge both the economic and other results of a particular grant or investment. All archaeological preservation projects should be similarly evaluated.

Bibliography

Anderson, B. 1991. *Imagined Communities: Reflections on the Origin and Spread of Nationalism*. New York: Verso.

Brundtland, G. (Chairman). 1987. Our Common Future. In: Report of the World Commission on Environment and Development [accessed 10 January 2014]. Available at: <http://www.un-documents.net/our-common-future.pdf>.

Coben, L. 2014. Sustainability and Cultural Heritage. In: C. Smith. ed. *Encylopedia of Global Archaeology*. New York: Springer.

Endresen, K. 1999. Sustainable Tourism and Cultural Heritage: A Review of Development Assistance and Its Potential to Promote Sustainability [accessed 9 May 2014]. Available at: <http://www.nwhf.no/files/File/culture_fulltext.pdf>.

Gumperz, J. 2009. The Speech Community. In: A. Duranti. ed. *Linguistic Anthropology: A Reader*. Malden, UK: Blackwell, pp. 66–73.

MacDonald, S. 2004. Heritage and Sustainability, A Discussion Paper [accessed 9 May 2014]. Available at: <http://www.environment.nsw.gov.au/resources/heritagebranch/heritage/research/sustainability.pdf>.

Murphy, P. 1985. *Tourism: A Community Approach*. New York: Methuen.

Ostrom, E. 1990. *Governing the Commons*. Cambridge and New York: Cambridge University Press.

Ostrom, E. 2009. A General Framework for Analyzing Sustainability of Social-Ecological Systems. *Science*, 325(24): 419–22.

Richards, G. & Hall, D. 2000. The Community: A Sustainable Concept in Tourism Development? In: G. Richards and D. Hall, eds. *Tourism & Sustainable Community Development*. London: Routledge.

Rypkema, D. & Cheong, C. 2011. Measurements and Indicators of Heritage as Development. In: ICOMOS. *Heritage, a Driver of Development, Proceedings of the 17th ICOMOS General Assembly Symposium* [accessed 9 May 2014]. Available at: <http://www.icomos.org/en/component/content/article?catid=157&id=477>.

Salmon, F. 2010. Job Creation Datapoints of the Day. Reuters [online] [accessed 8 March 2010]. Available at: <http://blogs.reuters.com/felix-salmon/2010/03/08/job-creation-datapoints-of-the-day>.

San Jose de Moro Archaeological Program (SJMAP). 2009. Excavations [accessed 4 April 2014]. Available at: <http://sanjosedemoro.pucp.edu.pe/02english/01excavaciones.html>.

Sierra, K. 2009. Leveraging Cultural Heritage Assets for Local Economic Development [accessed 9 May 2014]. Available at: <http://siteresources.worldbank.org/INTCHD/Resources/430063-1250192845352/LeveragingCHAssetsforLED_KSAnnualMeetOct12009.pdf>.

Silberman, N. 2011. Heritage as a Driver of Development? Some Questions of Cause and Effect. In: ICOMOS. *Heritage, a Driver of Development, Proceedings of the 17th ICOMOS General Assembly Symposium* [accessed 9 May 2014]. Available at: <http://www.icomos.org/en/component/content/article?catid=157&id=477>.

Sustainable Preservation Initiative (SPI). 2014. Projects [accessed 6 April 2014]. Available at: <http://sustainablepreservation.org/project>.

Throsby, D. 2002. Cultural Capital and Sustainability Concepts in the Economics of Cultural Heritage. In: M. de la Torre, ed. *Assessing the Values of Cultural Heritage*. Los Angeles: Getty Conservation Institute, pp. 101–17.

World Bank. 2011. What is Local Economic Development (LED)? [accessed 4 April 2014]. Available at: <http://go.worldbank.org/EA784ZB3F0>.

Notes on contributor

Lawrence Coben is the founder and Executive Director of the Sustainable Preservation Initiative (SPI). Coben is also an archaeologist and Consulting Scholar at the University of Pennsylvania Museum of Archaeology and Anthropology. He co-authored the seminal volume *Archaeology of Performance: Theater, Power and Community*, a study of the importance and use of theatrical performance at public events, rituals, and spectacles in ancient societies. He has written numerous articles on the Inca, empires, and cultural heritage, among other subjects. He has directed or participated in projects in Bolivia, Peru, Guatemala, Ecuador, and Jordan (Petra). Coben has started and run numerous energy companies, and still serves on the board of publicly traded companies in the energy sector. He serves on the US Department of Homeland Security's Sustainability and Efficiency Task Force. Coben writes an energy and cultural heritage blog for the *Huffington Post*. He co-wrote the national energy policy for the Lieberman 2004 Presidential Campaign. Coben has a BA in Economics from Yale, a JD from Harvard Law School, and a PhD in Anthropology (Archaeology) from the University of Pennsylvania.

Correspondence to: Lawrence Coben, Sustainable Preservation Initiative, 40 W. 22nd St. Suite 11, New York, NY 10010, USA. Email: larrycoben@sustainablepreservation.org

For Product Safety Concerns and Information please contact our EU
representative GPSR@taylorandfrancis.com Taylor & Francis Verlag GmbH,
Kaufingerstraße 24, 80331 München, Germany

Printed and bound by CPI Group (UK) Ltd, Croydon, CR0 4YY
08/05/2025
01864449-0001